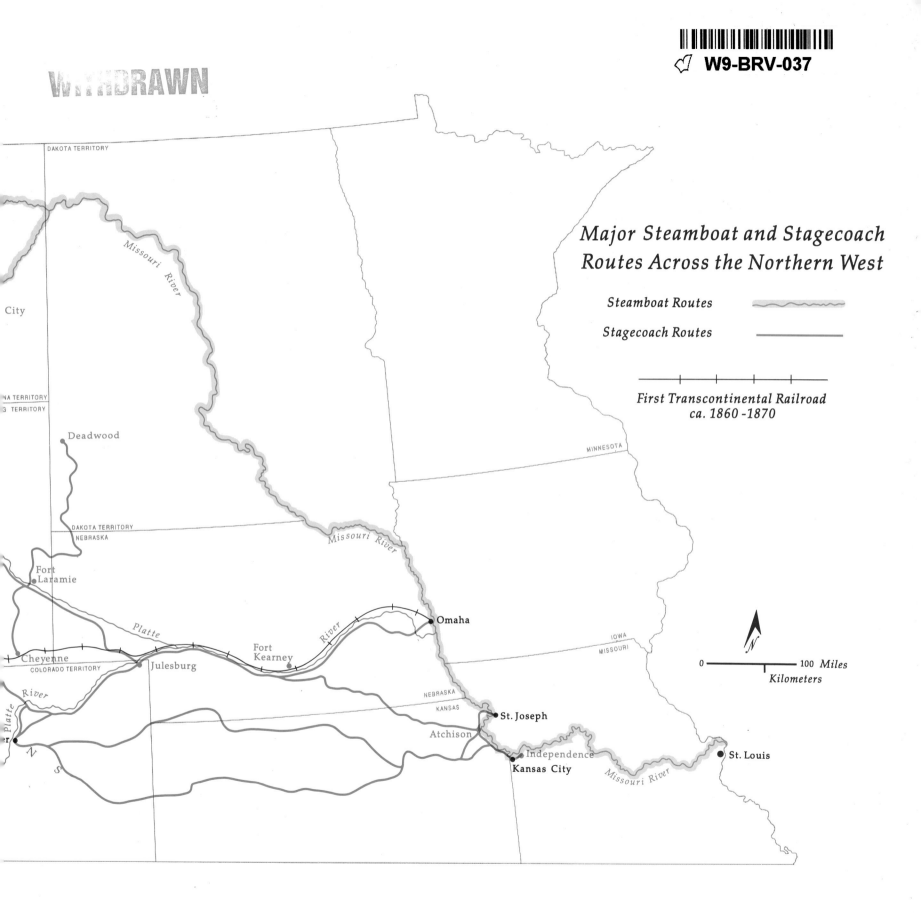

Major Steamboat and Stagecoach
Routes Across the Northern West

Steamboat Routes

Stagecoach Routes

First Transcontinental Railroad
ca. 1860-1870

DAKOTA TERRITORY

Missouri River

City

NA TERRITORY
G TERRITORY

Deadwood

DAKOTA TERRITORY
NEBRASKA

MINNESOTA

Fort
Laramie

Platte

River

Omaha

IOWA
MISSOURI

Cheyenne
COLORADO TERRITORY

Julesburg

Fort
Kearney

Missouri River

NEBRASKA

N

0   100 Miles
          Kilometers

River

r Platte

N

S

KANSAS

St. Joseph

Atchison

Independence

Kansas City

St. Louis

Missouri River

*T*he frontispiece in John Mullan's 1863 Report shows Fort Benton as portrayed by Gustav Sohon.
The head of steamboat navigation on the Missouri River was located on benchland at the foot of
high bluffs where freight could be transferred to wagons or packtrains for the trip farther inland
and steamboats could easily turn around in a natural basin for the return trip to Saint Louis and
other down-river points. Courtesy Day-Northwest Collection, University of Idaho Library.

CALIFORNIA & OREGON STAGE COMPANY.

BRADLEY BARLOW.
J. L. SANDERSON
JAMES W. PARKER.
CHA⁵ C. HUNTLEY.

E. F. HOOKER
SUPERINTENDENT.

CARRIES **WELLS, FARGO & CO**⁵ EXPRESS AND **THE U.S. MAIL.**

VIEW OF **MOUNT SHASTA** 14.442 F⁵ ABOVE THE SEA - ON C. & O. STAGE ROUTE.

A romantic depiction of the California and Oregon Stage Company, a line pioneered by the California Stage Company in 1860. Theodor Kirchhoff wrote of early-day travel in northern California: "Hollow-eyed and groggy we tottered to the stage and continued our painful trek south. At daybreak we reached the Siskiyou Mountains. Passengers trudged to the top, to spare the horses. Here, for the first time, I beheld giant, snowcapped Shasta Butte." Louis McLane, general manager and later president of Wells Fargo, wrote to his wife in 1865 about artistic depictions of travel by coach: "I thought staging looked very well to the lithographer, but was the devil in reality." Courtesy Wells Fargo Bank.

LONG DAY'S JOURNEY

The Steamboat & Stagecoach Era in the Northern West

CARLOS ARNALDO SCHWANTES

UNIVERSITY OF WASHINGTON PRESS   SEATTLE & LONDON

*This book has been published with the assistance
of a generous grant from Wells Fargo & Company.*

Copyright © 1999 by the University of Washington Press
Designed by Audrey Meyer and Veronica Seyd
Endpaper map by Allan Jokisaari
Printed in Hong Kong

Library of Congress Cataloging-in-Publication Data
Schwantes, Carlos A., 1945–

    Long day's journey : the steamboat & stagecoach era in the
northern West / Carlos Arnaldo Schwantes.

       p.   cm.

    Includes bibliographical references (p.   ) and index.

    ISBN 0-295-97691-8 (alk. paper)

    1. Northwestern States—History—19th century. 2. Overland
journeys to the Pacific. 3. Coaching—Northwestern States—
History—19th century. 4. Steamboats—Northwestern States—
History—19th century. 5. Frontier and pioneer life—
Northwestern States. I. Title.

    F593.S339 1999   99-29316
    979.5'041—dc21   CIP

*T*he front cover of a brochure prepared
by the Oregon-Washington Railroad
and Navigation Company celebrated
Tacoma's working waterfront in 1911.
Author's collection.

Puget Sound and Mount Rainier as seen from Whidbey Island. Images from the Pacific Railroad Survey conducted during the 1850s beautifully portray the landscape of the northern West in the early years of the steamboat and stage-coach era, a time for which few photographs are available. Courtesy Day-Northwest Collection, University of Idaho

Stanley Del.

Sarony Major & Knapp, Lith. 449 Broadway NY

*C*ape Disappointment, from the north side of the mouth of the Columbia River, seems peaceable enough as depicted by
Henry James Warre in his Sketches in North America and the Oregon Territory (1848). Most travelers viewed the area as a
malevolent landscape: "Foaming waves divide at random, unpredictably, here. Smack in the center of the mouth, Sand Island
asserts low shores and sporadic growths of reeds and brush. The discerning eye traces the long, white line of surf that opposes
a ship's course, and observes remnants of a wreck. Soon all aboard were happy; the ugly bar was behind; the pilot had steered
safely through those perilous waters despite their dangers. We steamed up a broad, majestic Columbia, here more like a bay
than a river," wrote Theodor Kirchhoff. Courtesy Oregon Historical Society, 85904.

Contents

LAST DAY OF THE SEASON.

West Shore *recorded the popular T. J. Potter and the last day of the season for vacationers to the Oregon Coast in the 1880s. Excursion travel was popular on the waters of the Pacific Northwest from the 1880s through the 1920s and helped to sustain steamboating during the early decades of the railway age, but on the upper Missouri River, tourism never amounted to much. Courtesy Oregon Historical Society.*

*T*he new grain elevator at Albina illustrates part of the 1880s industrial landscape along the Willamette River in the Portland area. Courtesy Oregon Historical Society.

*W*hen Henry James Warre portrayed the Willamette River outpost Oregon City in 1845, it was the largest population center in the Pacific Northwest. Despite its small size, it aspired to commercial greatness during the steamboat and stagecoach era. A local newspaper, the Oregon Spectator, boasted in 1851 that "the New England of the Pacific" would reap "much of the benefit of California treasures, in exchange for its lumber, its wheat, potatoes, and other fruits of the earth and of the orchard." Courtesy Library of Congress.

In the evening we passed many boats and rafts, blazing with great fires, made upon a thick bed of clay, and their crews singing at their sweeps. Twenty miles above Wilmington, the shores became marshy, the river wide, and the woody screen that had hitherto in a great degree hid the nakedness of the land, was withdrawn, leaving open to view only broad, reedy savannahs, on either side.
—Description of a steamboat trip down the Cape Fear River by Frederick Law Olmsted,
The Cotton Kingdom (1861)

Preface

*L*ong Day's Journey is offered as a companion volume to my earlier *Railroad Signatures across the Pacific Northwest* (1993), although either book could easily stand alone. Frankly, I did not originally plan them as companion studies, but working on the railroad volume with the book professionals at the University of Washington Press proved such a satisfying experience that I decided to pursue a second study of transportation in American life, this time focusing on the era defined by the steamboat and the stagecoach. When I recall that among my earliest professional articles were studies of railroad timetables and the literature of canal promotion, my enduring interest in transportation history should not be too surprising.[1] In *Railroad Signatures* the University of Washington Press understood my wish to treat photographs and other illustrative materials on an equal footing with text; in *Long Day's Journey* we have sought to achieve the same harmony between image and word, while adding many firsthand observations that seek to capture the spirit of the age.

Railroad Signatures studied how railroads functioned as engines of regional development and social change. By contrast, *Long Day's Journey* examines how lack of regional development—the scarcity of investment capi-

tal, widely scattered population outposts, and difficult terrain—shaped the earliest forms of commercial transportation. Railroads created a new regional landscape; steamboat and stagecoach pioneers struggled to adapt their respective technologies to the prevailing natural landscape. If they physically altered that landscape in any way, it was incidental to facilitating the movement of people and goods. Given their dissimilar times and financial resources, it would be hard to say who had the more difficult task.

A few words about terminology: the *northern West* as I describe it here includes the three states of the Pacific Northwest—Oregon, Washington, and Idaho—plus Montana and Wyoming, with lesser emphasis on the Dakotas and northern Utah. The designations *Northwest, far Northwest,* and *new Northwest* are synonyms for the Pacific Northwest, the region that is the book's primary focus. Where necessary, I have not hesitated to examine events in San Francisco, Saint Louis, or even Panama when they relate to the transportation history of the Pacific Northwest.

In the preface to *Railroad Signatures* I speculated about childhood influences that shaped my approach to railroad history, a narrative that ranked human actions

The Puget Sound Country
A
WELLS FARGO
COUNTRY

ADOLPH TREIDLER

*P*uget Sound as Wells Fargo country before the company quit the express business in 1918. So popular did this enterprise become that the name Wells Fargo evolved into a household word on the frontier; miners in remote camps of Idaho and Montana in the 1860s wrote of shipping their gold dust "by Wells Fargo." Courtesy Wells Fargo.

DEPARTURE FROM
COLLINS WASH.
FOR PORTLAND

Boarding the Tahoma *on the Columbia River about 1914. The flutter of a white flag from shore signaled a steamboat to stop for passengers or freight. Along isolated stretches of the waterway, passengers waited in sheds, often with no other buildings visible in any direction. Courtesy Oregon Historical Society, CN 105535.*

and choices above abstract and impersonal forces. Many readers responded favorably and shared personal stories of how railroads influenced their lives. I want to continue the surmising, this time by recalling how boats and ships provided the necessary inspiration for *Long Day's Journey.* Even with the needed addition of considerable material on stagecoaching and other forms of overland transportation, I nonetheless viewed this distinct era in American history, at least initially, from the perspective of the water. For example, I think one of my grandmother Ruth Casteen's favorite bedtime stories was about

her experience during a fire aboard a night steamboat traveling up the Cape Fear River from Wilmington, North Carolina; another was about the sinking of the *Titanic,* the White Star liner that supposedly was unsinkable. She always presented the latter story as a kind of morality tale about excessive pride. I got the message, although I was thereafter hooked by the drama of the story itself, buying every new book on the *Titanic* to learn more about Captain Edward J. Smith (who shared my grandmother's maiden name) and his fateful encounter with the iceberg in 1912.

As for her personal narrative of fire on the river (and although I'm certain she never intended it), my youthful reaction was one of carefully suppressed fright. The thought of having to abandon a cozy ship and risk a nocturnal swim through the Cape Fear's dark, tannin-stained waters to reach a none-too-distinct riverbank that was actually a dense cypress swamp infested with water moccasins, snapping turtles, and possibly alligators was for many years my worst nightmare. Now I'm inclined to recall it only as a metaphor for some of the less pleasant aspects of academic committees.

My father, Arnaldo, had his ship tales too. He would relate how in 1937 he traveled aboard the *Buenos Aires*

Maru from the port of Santos, Brazil, to San Pedro, California, and to new opportunities awaiting an eighteen-year-old in "golden America." I believe his favorite story, however, was his description of returning to the United States aboard the aircraft carrier *Lake Champlain* following military service in Italy in World War Two. Despite heavy seas, the captain crossed the Atlantic Ocean to Norfolk in record time; no doubt he was cheered on by the victorious soldiers who were far more homesick than seasick. It was a simple tale, but one with a happy ending for my GI father, who returned having earned his United States citizenship and eager to be reunited with my mother and meet his nine-

An undated image of a fully loaded Concord coach near Helena, Montana. Courtesy Montana Historical Society, 952–942.

DRAIN STAGE MEETING
STR EVA ON UMPQUA RIVER
AT SCOTTSBURG. ORE.

In the early twentieth century, Wesley Andrews photographed the Umpqua River landing at Scottsburg, Oregon, where the steamer Eva *met the stagecoach for Drain to connect the coast with the Willamette Valley. Courtesy Oregon Historical Society, 24161.*

month-old namesake, their personal contribution to the emerging baby boom.

I myself remember distinctly July 26, 1956, the day the luxurious Italian liner *Andrea Doria* sank after its collision with the *Stockholm,* much as other people vividly recall events on the day Pearl Harbor was bombed or when John F. Kennedy was shot. Much later, in the early

1990s, I added to memory's fund of maritime narratives when I had the opportunity to travel numerous times from Lewiston, Idaho, down the Snake and Columbia rivers to the Pacific Ocean aboard the motor vessels *Sea Lion* and *Sea Bird,* and on two occasions to continue around the Olympic Peninsula to Vancouver Island and Puget Sound. During those voyages I was able to observe

*F*rank Matsura photographed the Okanogan, Washington, waterfront at the turn of the century. A fleet of shallow-draft steamers bucked ninety miles of the upper Columbia and Okanogan rivers to connect this agricultural area with Wenatchee. It was one of three widely separated portions of the Columbia River within the United States along which steamboats regularly operated. The other two were from Astoria to White Bluffs (above present Pasco), a distance of about four hundred miles, and from near Northport across the international boundary into southern British Columbia, about two hundred miles. Courtesy Washington State University, Matsura 70-318.

The steamer Hattie Belle *at Rooster Rock, Oregon, at the western entrance to the Columbia River gorge. The indelicate anatomical appellation that pioneers originally gave to the landmark was sanitized during the Victorian era to the present name. Courtesy Oregon Historical Society, 9561 #269–1.*

modern-day life on the Great River of the West and came to know several kindred spirits of Mark Twain and Horace Bixby, the famous author's mentor on the Mississippi River. Again, it is because of personal encounters like these that the human dimension of both transportation and regional history interests me so much.

Speaking of the human dimension: during the process of researching and writing *Long Day's Journey* I received

help of various types from individuals who now deserve special recognition and thanks. My former department chair, Kent Hackmann, supplied much-needed encouragement, as did Elisabeth Zinser and Thomas O. Bell, two former presidents of the University of Idaho, and Kurt O. Olsson, Dean of the College of Letters and Science. My gratitude also extends to Dick Wilson and Rob McIntyre, graduate students at the University of Idaho, to my emeritus colleague William S. Greever, historian and avid student of transportation history, and to Professor Robert Carriker of Gonzaga University, who recommended to Sven-Olof Lindblad's Special Expeditions that I serve as one of their shipboard historians. Having now enjoyed fourteen of their study tours of the Pacific Northwest and Alaska, I want to thank Pamela Fingleton and her colleagues in New York, Seattle, and aboard ship who make Special Expeditions truly special.

I feel fortunate to have become acquainted with Philip Chadwick Foster Smith on a Special Expeditions study tour of the Columbia and Snake rivers. Chad, the former editor of the *American Neptune,* is an enthusiastic practitioner of maritime history who willingly shared his vast knowledge with me. On another of the river tours, David P. Billington, professor of engineering at Princeton University, taught me to appreciate more fully the relationship between machines and their support structures in transportation history.

Thanks go likewise to Charles Rankin, Rebecca Kohl, and Lory Morrow of the Montana Historical Society; Barbara Walton, A. D. Mastrogiuseppe, and Philip J. Panum of the Denver Public Library; Susan Seyl, Todd Welch, Kris A. White, and Elizabeth Winroth of the Oregon Historical Society; Samuel Wegner, Carol A. Harbison, and Jacquelyn Sundstrand of the Southern Oregon Historical Society; Jerry Ostermiller and Anne Witty of the Columbia River Maritime Museum; Marianne Babal of Wells Fargo's Historical Services; Gene Gressley of Laramie, Wyoming; Larry Jones, Judy Austin, and Merle Wells of the Idaho State Historical Society; Lawrence Dodd and Marilyn Sparks of the Penrose Memorial Library, Whitman College, and their invaluable Thomas Teakle Collection; G. Thomas Edwards of Whitman College; Robert Spude, historian of the National Park Service in Denver and now Santa Fe; John Hanks of the University of Wyoming's American Heritage Center; Cort Conley of Boise, Idaho; Rocky Barker of the *Idaho Falls Post Register;* William L. Withuhn, Curator of Transportation, National Museum of American History; Walter Jones of the University of Utah Special Collections; and the staffs of the Buffalo Bill

Historical Center, the San Francisco National Maritime Museum, the California State Railroad Museum, the Wyoming State Museum, the Utah State Historical Society, the University of Idaho Library, the University of Oregon Library, the University of Washington Libraries, and the Library of Congress. For helping me understand more fully the complicated financial history of overland stagecoaching and for his unfailing good cheer, I am indebted to Robert J. Chandler, Assistant Vice-President of Wells Fargo Bank. At the University of Washington

As a teenager in the early 1960s, I enjoyed photographing the working waterfront in Wilmington, North Carolina, but never did I think that my interest in transportation history and photography might later be combined. Author's collection.

After the California gold rush peaked in the early 1850s, photographers followed the mining frontier north to Oregon's Rogue River country. Among the best-known camera pioneers of the Pacific Northwest was Peter Britt of Jacksonville, a Swiss native who arrived in 1852 and remained an active photographer until the end of the century. As this self-portrait reveals, he was also proud of his talents as an artist. Photography during the 1850s and 1860s was a difficult and demanding trade that involved preparing a large wet-plate negative, often working within the confined space of a portable darkroom to apply a light-sensitive colloid to a clean glass plate, and then properly exposing the exceedingly slow film without benefit of a mechanical shutter or light meter. Yet from the hands of a master, the results could be astonishingly good: in 1867, the San Francisco–based Carleton E. Watkins created mammoth albumen prints of Oregon and the Columbia River that are still prized today. The three decades after 1900 were probably the golden age of black-and-white commercial photography. Courtesy Southern Oregon Historical Society, 3658.

Press I want to acknowledge the help and encouragement of Donald Ellegood, Pat Soden, Julidta Tarver, Audrey Meyer, and Veronica Seyd. Once again, Carol Zabilski deserves praise for her diligence in editing my prose. However, I alone must take responsibility for any errors or omissions that appear in the following pages.

I benefited once again from the generous assistance of the University of Idaho's John Calhoun Smith Memorial Committee. For more than a decade my research and writing have received annual infusions of John Calhoun Smith money, yet until recently I had no idea who Smith was. How appropriate it is, then, that Smith was an early-day packer out of Lewiston and Walla Walla, a pioneer of the kind of rudimentary transportation that defined the northern West's steamboat and stagecoach era. Smith's success story reminds me why every trip on the frontier was a long day's journey, both literally and figuratively.

Wells Fargo & Company provided a generous grant to the University of Washington Press to help underwrite the cost of publishing *Long Day's Journey*. The continued interest of Wells Fargo, a major participant in early transportation developments across the northern West, in the region's history is both praiseworthy and magnanimous.

Finally, I want to dedicate this book to four very special people: Aunt Barbara and Uncle Charles Casteen, for the good times at Wrightsville Beach, for boat rides on Chesapeake Bay and the Potomac River, and especially for taking time from your busy schedules to introduce me to the Library of Congress and many other fascinating sites in Washington; and Aunt Mariinha and Uncle Siegfried Schwantes, who by word and deed introduced me to the concept of multiculturalism well before it acquired a commonly accepted name or excess political baggage. When Uncle Siegfried earned his doctorate in Semitic Languages at Johns Hopkins University, he revealed to me for the first time what graduate education demanded, and he has since then inspired me by his enduring love of teaching. Until his late seventies he continued to teach college classes in Brazil. I only regret that I can't read the family history he wrote in Portuguese. Such are the limits of my multiculturalism.

A poster from West Shore *announced the long-awaited opening of the first railroad between Oregon and California. "As the six-horse stagecoach, imposing in its day, crowded off the trail the saddle-horse and pack-mule conveyance, it in turn is driven off the Siskiyou route by the big engines and sumptuous palace cars of the Southern Pacific railroad," observed the Portland Oregonian on December 25, 1887. It was not all gain: "The trip over the mountains between California and Oregon will no longer be invested with the romantic flavor of exciting rides down steep grades, stories and scenes of highway robbery, and views of grizzly bear tracks in the road." Courtesy Southern Oregon Historical Society, 1964.*

LONG DAY'S JOURNEY

The common staples were transported to the country by sea; our pioneers generally did not spin and weave the clothing they wore; such articles as nails, salt, sugar, glass and many others could often be had, and there was less need of resort, in Oregon, to the homely expedients and severe shifts of pioneer life than in the states which had been settled from twenty-five to fifty years earlier. Our access to the ocean kept up some degree of communication with the world of mankind, often at long intervals, it is true, but still we were not wholly shut out. Few, indeed, proposed, and still fewer attempted, to return to the places whence they came, for the double reason that all quickly became satisfied with Oregon, and the return journey was an undertaking hardly to be considered. The labor of getting here was quite enough.
—Harvey Scott, Portland Oregonian *(June 16, 1888)*

After all, do not the cars go too fast, as they pass commercially along where the transit and the level bade them go, and where to the old timer there is no such respect to his command: "Stop driver until we all take a drink"? Where the most beautiful scenery is discernible from the stage coach, the train will quickly round a curve or plunge through a snow shed so rapidly as to lose to the eye the beauteous mountain stream or landscape fair.
—Idaho Scimitar *(August 8, 1908)*

Perhaps in the early history of no part of our country were greater difficulties overcome in moving from one place to another than in the mining districts of Oregon and Idaho. Essentially a mountain region . . . , its surface, besides being broken into deep cañons, lofty ridges, inaccessible precipices, impassable streams, and impenetrable lava beds, was also covered everywhere with the sharp points and fissured hummocks which were cast out during a long and active period of primeval eruption. There were no natural roads in any direction.
—*Nathaniel P. Langford,* Vigilante Days and Ways *(1912)*

Introduction

The steamer Lewiston *on the lower Snake River in the early twentieth century. Except for the grain warehouses, the scene had changed little since Ephraim Baughman piloted the first steamboat through these waters in 1861. Courtesy Idaho State Historical Society, 2435.*

During the summer of 1943 the Oregon Shipbuilding Corporation christened its 199th Liberty ship the *Ephraim W. Baughman* to honor a transportation pioneer of the steamboat and stagecoach era. His long life spanned the rise and decline of steamboating on Northwest waters: on July 11, 1860, he received the first pilot's license issued by the United States government on West Coast waters, and on the Columbia and Snake rivers he was a familiar figure to two generations of travelers. Yet by World War Two, just twenty years after his death, few people could recall Captain Eph Baughman or tell of his significance. He belonged to another time only dimly remembered as the prerailroad era.

In early May 1861 Baughman received the hazardous assignment of finding a new way to move passengers and freight through some of the most difficult terrain in North America. This would be one of the great challenges of his long career. In the normal course of events, Baughman would have been back in Illinois piloting a plow through the dark soil of the corn-country farm where he grew up, but here he was on the uncharted waters of the lower Snake River in the far Northwest attempting to guide a steamboat where none had gone

before. Life was never the same, Baughman recalled, after he attended a Fourth of July celebration back home in Fulton in 1849 and heard Senator Stephen A. Douglas tell of golden opportunities awaiting ambitious young men out west in California. Fifteen-year-old Eph saved $91 during the next nine months, bought an ox team, and headed for the goldfields with two other teenagers. The youths reached San Francisco after three months of hard traveling but soon split up to seek their individual fortunes.

Eph tried placer mining around Hangtown in the Mother Lode country but quickly discovered that earlier arrivals had claimed all the best sites. He then drifted north to Oregon aboard a sailing ship, and after a month at sea he reached the village of Portland. There the teenager took a number of odd jobs; he even farmed for a year in the fertile Willamette Valley before discovering the real love of his life. That was when he hired aboard the steamboat *Lot Whitcomb* as a fireman. His proudest day probably was in 1860 when an inspector traveled all the way from New Orleans to issue him a pilot's license. It was his prized possession, and Baughman displayed it in the wheelhouse of every steamboat he commanded until

he retired in 1915 (ironically as an employee of the Union Pacific Railroad, which owned his last vessel).

In March 1861 the Oregon Steam Navigation Company had sent Baughman together with Captain Leonard White into the sparsely settled interior of Washington Territory to build a small boat at Colville and explore down several hundred miles of the Columbia River to The Dalles. Their assignment was to determine how far inland a steamboat might safely travel with a load of freight and passengers. The men completed their reconnaissance in two months and delivered their findings to company officers based in Portland. Within days the boatmen-explorers received a new assignment: this time they were to sail a steamboat east to the base of the Rocky Mountains where promising new finds of gold had been reported.

On May 1, less than a week before Arkansas and Tennessee sided with the Southern Confederacy in the widening national crisis, the indefatigable Baughman and White steered the unpretentious little *Colonel Wright* up the Columbia above Celilo Falls and through the swift, turbid waters of its tributary, the Snake River. Members of the Lewis and Clark expedition had paddled five dugout canoes along the same route in 1805, and countless fur trappers and traders had followed in their wake, but until now the staccato beat of steam power had never reverberated from the walls of these remote canyons.

By extending its reach several hundred miles inland from Portland, the Oregon Steam Navigation Company hoped to profit handsomely from an army of fortune seekers animated by the peculiar dementia that repeatedly swept through the isolated canyons and gulches of the northern Rocky Mountains in the early 1860s. Some tormented souls whom people described as "gold crazed" had already abandoned prosperous farms and paying jobs in settled portions of Oregon and California for the backbreaking work of transforming pristine mountain streams into muddy rivulets in their quest for the elusive yellow metal. In summertime when water was plentiful and the days were long, miners labored feverishly, often seven days a week. Hour after hour they shoveled and hauled, dug ditches, and built sluice boxes and flumes. Ignore the damage to the environment, forget the ceaseless and generally unprofitable toil. Theirs was a special kind of passion that transcended common sense.

Among these argonauts a gray-haired man was a rarity, although many were already veterans of earlier mining rushes to California, British Columbia, and Colorado. All were participants in a frenetic lottery, and none could predict who would find one of the elusive pockets of gold that would make a poor man a king. "Some pockets held so much that their owners were at a loss as to how to assemble and move it. Typically they poured it into boots and hung the pairs, like panniers, to either side of a mule."[1]

In the Boise Basin, one of a dozen especially promising locations in the northern Rockies, arrastras and stamp mills seldom stopped as they methodically ground gold-bearing quartz into precious powder. At the peak of the excitement, sawmills ran day and night, and lumber was purchased as fast as it could be produced to build houses

Captain Ephraim Baughman. As early as 1861—when the "old man of the river" was only twenty-six years old—it was clear that Baughman was an extraordinarily skilled steamboat pilot. By that time he had already spent nearly a decade aboard steam and sailing vessels of all types. Courtesy Oregon Historical Society, CN 003220.

*T*he steamer Spokane *is near Lewiston, Idaho, in this early twentieth-century view. Courtesy Idaho State Historical Society, 78–203.6.*

A timeless pose on the mining frontier: F. Jay Haynes photographed placer miners in Idaho's newly discovered Coeur d'Alene mining district in 1884. Courtesy Montana Historical Society, H-1387. All Haynes images are from the Haynes Foundation Collection.

Few photographs of Rocky Mountain mining camps survive from the early 1860s, but the roughhewn appearance of mining outposts changed little during the next several decades. This is Grand Forks, Idaho, destroyed by the great forest fire that swept through the Bitterroot Mountains in 1910. Oregon Historical Society, 4689, #678-A.

or sluice boxes. Jerry-built collections of small structures fashioned from rough lumber that took the names of Centerville, Placerville, Idaho City, and Pioneer arose as if by magic. The Boise Basin yielded twenty million dollars' worth of gold by 1866.

The arrival of packtrains and, later, freight wagons laden with merchandise of all kinds brightened the miners' long days. On town streets the braying of mules mingled with fiddle music from the saloons and the

hammering of carpenters. Their ceaseless pounding and sawing often grew so loud that it silenced casual conversations. Town after town sprang up like mushrooms and then faded just as fast, as miners stampeded to new diggings. If a few fortune seekers became rich, most did not. The disappointed ones frequently sought solace in saloons, where they tried to drown their misfortunes in glasses of "tangle-leg," "lightning," and "tarantula juice," descriptive names for whiskey, the miners' favorite drink.

Because white settlers had long avoided the harsh, isolated, and seemingly unproductive country of the northern Rocky Mountains in favor of irrigated farms in Utah, the lush Willamette Valley in Oregon, and proven diggings in California, not a single mile of telegraph wire had been strung in the early 1860s to speed word of mineral bonanzas to the outside world. Yet news of every strike spread rapidly east and west to population centers of the Mississippi Valley and the Pacific coast, where the mixture of half-truths and outright lies animated new legions of fortune seekers. Not far behind the miners followed canny merchants ready to sell them goods of every description. Almost overnight, transportation of all types was demanded to move an unprecedented volume of people and merchandise. The crazy rush to the northern Rockies in the 1860s became the defining event of the region's steamboat and stagecoach era.

Apart from individual success or failure, the miners in their collective quest for gold and silver left behind a legacy still visible in places like Idaho City, Virginia City, Silver City, and Baker City, four very different survivors from among the thousands of mining camps and towns that once dotted the northern West. The *city* portion of these place-names may sound pretentious today, but during the heady optimism of the mining rushes, each settlement aspired to become a real city and sometimes succeeded, briefly. Within three years of its founding in 1862, Idaho City surpassed Portland to reign for a short time as the largest population center in the northern West. Idaho City featured opera and theater houses, music stores, tailor shops, breweries, bowling alleys, bakeries, and other urban amenities, not to mention the numerous saloons found in every mining camp. One hundred thirty years later these four "cities" exist in various states of arrested decline, although all but Silver City have generated newfound prosperity by mining for tourist dollars. Baker City has the added advantage of being located along the old Oregon Trail and modern Interstate Highway 84.

Far less obvious today than the northern West's colorful mining heritage is how gold and silver bonanzas of the 1860s forged lines of transportation and communication across the region during the prerailroad years. This happened along both slopes of the Continental Divide, where two river systems and two cities competed for the burgeoning mining camp trade. Saint Louis extended its already vast network of trade and commerce nearly three thousand miles farther west along the serpentine Missouri River to the head of steamboat navigation at Fort Benton, where miners and supplies continued overland to the widely scattered camps and diggings of Montana and Idaho. Upstart Portland did likewise along the Columbia River and its tributary the Snake until steamboat whistles echoed along navigable waters that stretched more than four hundred miles inland to Lewiston. Both Saint Louis and Portland were themselves important inland links in great commercial systems reaching up the Mississippi River from New Orleans or up the Pacific coast from San Francisco. The two river-based empires finally touched one another near the Continental Divide and then overlapped slightly as they competed for the lucrative mining trade of the northern Rocky Mountains.

This facile pairing of cities and steamboat routes is hardly the whole story of early transportation across the northern West, for apart from the two great river systems there were trails that extended from California and Kansas to Salt Lake City and northward to form a third competing transportation network. The Mormon metropolis actually divided its loyalties between California and Missouri merchants whose trade goods reached Salt Lake warehouses at the speed of oxen and mules that regularly plodded along the overland route.

But this was not all. During the enthusiasm of the 1860s people eagerly competed to blaze shorter and more convenient water and land routes to tap the alluring mineral wealth of the northern Rockies. There were San Francisco merchants who sought to ship goods to the Salt Lake City gateway via an imaginative combination of routes: down the Pacific coast, around the Baja Peninsula, and up the Gulf of California and the Colorado River to a trailhead in northern Arizona from whence they could proceed overland to the Utah entrepôt. From the east, others pioneered a dangerous overland shortcut known

Portland's waterfront in the early twentieth century. The steamboat Dalles City *passes an ocean liner, possibly the* General Sherman. *Courtesy San Francisco Maritime National Historical Park, F11.5, 001n.*

as the Bozeman Trail, which crossed the favorite hunting grounds of the Plains Indians; there was also the Chico route through northern California and across the wilderness of the Great Basin. Most such routes lasted only a short time and were abandoned, but a few succeeded in permanently redirecting the flow of people and goods across the northern West.

Today the states of the northern West—Oregon, Washington, Idaho, Montana, and Wyoming—differ in many obvious ways. As if to emphasize that fact, these five states are usually grouped into at least two separate regions, typically the Pacific Northwest and the Rocky Mountain West. Apart from their Oregon Trail and Union Pacific Railroad heritage, it is difficult to recall now that maritime Puget Sound and the Columbia River once shared a common destiny with the landlocked high

plains of eastern Wyoming. Although geography decreed that no steamboat route would ever link Wyoming to either Oregon or Missouri, distant parts of the northern West were nonetheless bound by their mutual dependency on a complex and evolving system of water and land transportation that antedated America's transcontinental railroads.

Telegraph lines and other forms of communication also forged common bonds between distant parts of the northern West. During warfare that periodically erupted on the high plains of Wyoming in the 1860s, Indians sometimes retaliated against white soldiers by severing the sole telegraph link between the Atlantic and Pacific coasts, halting the flow of news, and thereby underscoring the interdependence of seemingly dissimilar portions of the northern West. Making such disruptions all the

more intolerable for residents of the far Northwest was their anxious desire for any news from distant battlefields where armies of the North and South repeatedly bloodied one another to determine the nation's future. Yet even during the 1860s when the Civil War dramatically redefined the nation's political landscape, in the northern West new modes of communication and transportation had a more immediate impact on everyday life.

Technology Redefines a Landscape

On its historic voyage to the Rocky Mountain gold country in May 1861, the diminutive *Colonel Wright* carried a crew of fourteen men in addition to its officers, Leonard White and Ephraim Baughman. Their navigation of the lower Snake River would be mainly a matter of trial and error: there were no government charts or maps, and Indians living near its confluence with the Columbia, when asked for information, would only exclaim, "Oh, *hias skookum chuck*" (very strong water). There were the journals and maps of Meriwether Lewis and William Clark, although those documents were now almost sixty years old and never intended to aid steamboat navigation.

One of the three names commonly given to the river honored Captain Lewis. The other two, Pohogava and Snake, were descriptive of the waterway's forbidding character. Early fur trappers claimed that Pohogava was an Indian word that meant "Sage Brush River." Freighters and packers insisted on using the name Snake, "since a more snake-infested stream than this does not perhaps exist this side of the tropics." They told tales of huge rattlesnakes that would crawl upon travelers resting along the river's banks or into their bedrolls at night. Others claimed the name came from the river's own tortuous course, always crooked and bending, or from local Indians, the Snakes. Which name was most appropriate was something the crewmen of the *Colonel Wright* would soon learn for themselves. In any case, in the forbidding Snake River country it was their good fortune to serve under two of the most experienced steamboatmen in the far Northwest.[2]

Perhaps White and Baughman prepared themselves

for the voyage by reviewing published accounts of early exploration or by seeking out experienced voyageurs from the fur trade era who had retired to the French Prairie settlement on the Willamette River above Portland. White does seem to have used a skiff for some preliminary exploration (and some accounts claim that he had earlier guided the *Colonel Wright* sixty miles up the Snake to the mouth of the Palouse River), but neither boatman left much of an account of their historic 1861 voyage. Only this much is certain: White and Baughman already knew that any surprises awaiting them on the Snake River would not alter the fact that navigating a single steamboat from Portland through to the goldfields was physically impossible. A series of natural obstacles called the Cascades, the Grand Dalles, and Celilo Falls narrowed the Columbia River and seemed to turn its waters on edge. It would require at least three different steamboats and two cumbersome portages to connect Portland by water to any new settlements along the Snake River.

Construction of portage roads or railroads around obstacles to navigation was a tactical consideration. Extending Portland's commercial hegemony over the interior Pacific Northwest and northern Rocky Mountains was a strategic challenge that energized directors of the newly formed Oregon Steam Navigation Company, who envisioned nothing less than a Portland-based commercial empire of the Columbia. Not without a good fight would they permit San Francisco to establish a competing line of freight wagons and stagecoaches running overland to the interior mines. The Portlanders were even willing to compete with long-established Saint Louis merchants for the mining camp trade of the northern Rockies.

Considering that Portland had only 2,874 inhabitants in 1860 (though it was still the largest population center in the northern West), compared to 56,802 for San Francisco and 160,773 for Saint Louis, the confidence of its early merchants seemed based entirely on fantasy. Yet the interest of the Oregon Steam Navigation Company in probing the navigable reaches of the vast Columbia River system derived from an entrepreneurial vision that encompassed the entire northern West and assessed the money-making potential of freight wagons and stagecoaches no less carefully than that of steamboats.

Corporate strategy was probably not uppermost in the minds of White and Baughman as they methodically threaded the *Colonel Wright* through the twisting canyons of the Snake River. So intently did they study the unknown waters before them that neither man apparently took time to reflect on how steam power came to this remote part of the West, although both knew the story well from firsthand experience. The brief history of their own *Colonel Wright* perhaps summed it up best. Prior to 1859 the Columbia River above The Dalles had been navigated only by Indian canoes, bateaux of the Hudson's Bay Company, and most recently by a few flat-bottomed sailing craft called schooners. These vessels were used to forward freight inland to Wallula, the first white settlement on the Columbia above Celilo Falls. At Wallula was an old adobe fort originally built by the Hudson's Bay Company for the fur trade, but in the late 1850s it was occupied by an army quartermaster who used the building as a warehouse. This was the main jumping-off point for the army's newly established Fort Walla Walla, an outpost located thirty miles farther inland in the shadow of the Blue Mountains and the forward base of operations during Indian wars that convulsed the Columbia Plateau in the late 1850s. Strings of pack animals also carried some military freight through to Fort Walla Walla from the portage around Celilo Falls, located farther down the Columbia River near Dalles City (or The Dalles today).

When two frontier entrepreneurs, Lawrence W. Coe and R. R. Thompson, obtained a federal contract to carry freight to Fort Walla Walla, they used bateaux or schooners like everyone else. Soon, however, their business grew large enough to justify construction of a small stern-wheel steamboat at the mouth of the Deschutes River, near the head of the portage around Celilo Falls. Steamboats were not new to the lower Columbia River, but none had yet been used above The Dalles. Because their freight business depended so heavily on carrying supplies for the army, Coe and Thompson wisely named

their new craft for George Wright, colonel of the Ninth Regiment, United States Infantry, in command at Fort Dalles.

Coe and Thompson launched the *Colonel Wright* on October 24, 1858. The homely, half-cabined craft was about 125 feet long. The following April the pioneer steamer made her maiden upriver trip and thereafter settled into a regular schedule of voyages between Celilo and the mouth of the Walla Walla River at Wallula. Like all early steamboats, the *Colonel Wright* burned wood; but to maintain steam along a hundred-mile stretch of river where even driftwood was scarce, the boat was compelled to haul along enough fuel for a round trip from Celilo, and thus firewood at times composed the bulk of her cargo. Perhaps Coe and Thompson had the fuel problem in mind when they ingeniously rigged the *Colonel Wright* with a mast that carried a huge square, or lug, sail to provide an advantage during seasons when prevailing winds blew up the river.

Without the lugsail, White and Baughman could never have ascended the Snake River in the *Colonel Wright.* Captain Baughman (for Oregon Steam would soon reward him with that title) later recalled their historic trip: "As pilot, I directed that we travel very slowly and only during the day time, for rocky reefs and shoals were numerous and the waters were not deep. Each stream which we thought had not theretofore been named we took it upon ourselves to christen; likewise every other natural feature, and even to-day many of the landmarks and creeks bear the names which we gave them."[3]

A reporter for the *Oregon Weekly Times* who happened to be in Wallula when the *Colonel Wright* steamed up the Snake River on its "voyage of experiment" supplied some of the details Baughman left out. Lawrence Coe, having become the local agent of the Oregon Steam Navigation Company, invited him along for the ride. The *Colonel Wright* cast off from the landing at the old fort at three o'clock and reached the mouth of the Snake River two hours later, having traveled about eleven miles. The steamer continued for another six miles before tying up for the night along the bank. Starting early the next morning the *Colonel Wright* paddled slowly up the Snake

On the upper Columbia River, October 27, 1915, the Twin
Cities *heads west near Wallula. In May 1861, when the first
miners came this way by steamboat, much of their talk was
of sluice boxes, long toms, rockers, pans, pay dirt, and bedrock. Courtesy Washington State Historical Society, 33645.*

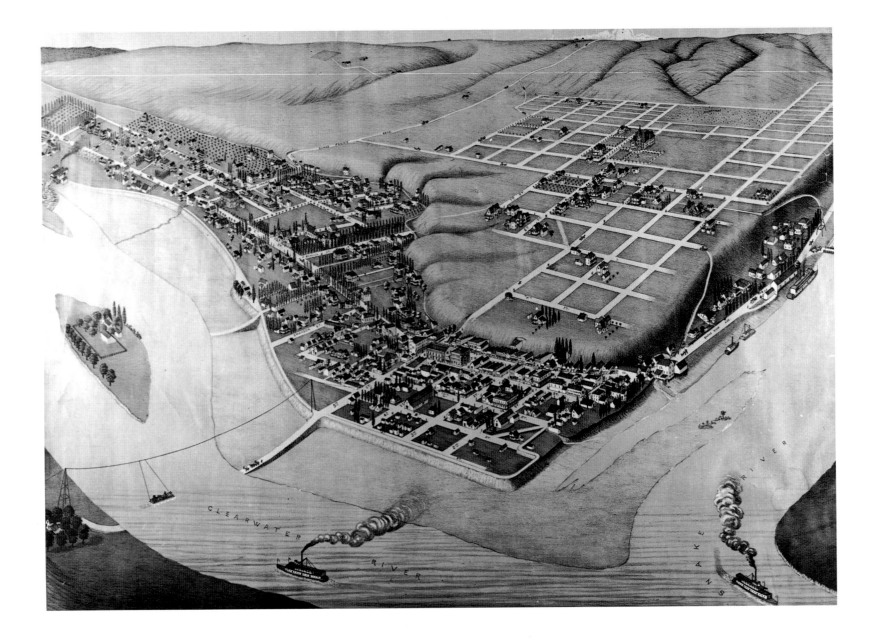

as far as the Colville Road ferry, where the operator tried to persuade Captain White that any further progress upriver was impossible.

The cable used by the tiny ferry was lowered into the water, but not deep enough, because when the *Colonel Wright* attempted to cross over, the cable snagged and damaged the paddle wheel. The steamboat remained at the ferry landing overnight to make repairs. By sunrise

on the morning of May 3 the *Colonel Wright* had reached Palouse Rapids, one of several challenges on a river that stair-stepped its way down from the Rocky Mountains by means of foaming cascades alternating with long, relatively quiet stretches of water. With 135 pounds of steam, the vessel walked up the Palouse Rapids without difficulty, but at Tucannon Rapids, a rope had to be run out and tied to a large rock and the lugsail set. But before White or Baughman could take advantage of the strong wind blowing upriver, the rope worked loose and wound itself around the paddle wheel. Fortunately, the lugsail held the steamer steady against the current while its engines were stopped so crewmen could cut the rope away. The lugsail would be used frequently during the voyage, and by the union of wind and steam power the *Colonel Wright* worked its way inland to reach the Clearwater River, 150 miles from Wallula and 375 miles from Portland. The bank was much gentler here than in the canyons downriver, and horses and cattle belonging to Nez Perce Indians grazed in large numbers. This was where a new town soon arose and was named for Captain Meriwether Lewis.[4]

Baughman's own recollections fail to mention the difficulties of the historic voyage but dwell at length on the more ordinary pleasures of the task assigned him. "In due time, we swept around the big bend in the Snake just below where Lewiston now stands and were met by the rushing waters of a stream clear as crystal and broad enough to be classed as a river. Before us spread out a beautiful bunchgrass valley, or rather a series of plateaus, reaching away to a high prairie to the southward: This Indian paradise was occupied here and there by a tepee. Several Nez Perce Indians loitered about and a few bands of ponies grazed contentedly upon the luxuriant grass. The picture was indeed a pretty one."[5]

Baughman noticed that "the sound of the steam whistle and the pounding of the engines naturally attracted the attention of the Indians, who flocked to the water's edge to gaze on the wonderful fire boat." He steered the vessel's prow into the crystalline waters of the Clearwater River. "Slowly the little steamer propelled itself onward in the direction of the Oro Fino mines. We had to line the vessel over the Lawyer and several other rapids and about thirty miles up the Clearwater we found an obstruction which we could not pass. This was what has since come to be named Big Eddy. Throughout our entire journey on the Clearwater thus far we were accompanied by Indians riding along the shore on horseback. By many little acts and signs did these children of nature manifest their friendliness, no one of their num-

ber, so far as I can now remember, giving the slightest evidence of other than kindly sentiments."

At Big Eddy on May 6 the *Colonel Wright* could make no headway through the foaming rapids. "Twice we lined her and moved slowly up stream but the vessel did not have power enough to keep herself in the channel, so finally we gave it up for the time being, came on ashore and began making explorations. The result was not favorable." The steamboatmen had climbed to within forty-five miles of the mines but were unable to surmount these rapids. "There was therefore nothing to do but to unload the freight."

Most of the goods belonged to Seth Slater, one of several businessmen who rode along as passengers. Slater had been so confident of getting within easy distance of the Oro Fino diggings that he brought along ten to fifteen tons of merchandise to sell to the miners. "Slater thought the site a good one as it was the apparent head of navigation so he and a few others remained there establishing Slaterville," a village of five tents and fifty inhabitants, which lasted only a few weeks until Slater relocated to Lewiston.

The *Colonel Wright* steamed rapidly back to its base above Celilo Falls. Along the way the vessel paused briefly at the mouth of Lapwai Creek, and most of the crew went ashore to visit Chief Lawyer, whose lodge was on benchland overlooking the Clearwater River. From the steamboat, recalled Baughman, "we could see his tepee and before it a tall pole on whose top the Stars and Stripes floated in the breeze. This display of patriotism by the brave and friendly old chief touched a responsive chord in our hearts and we never forgot it. Lawyer, who had been educated in the East and could talk good English, received us most cordially and we chatted with him a long time. His hospitality was especially praiseworthy when it is remembered that we were invading his territory and opening the way for thousands to follow."

Indeed, thousands of miners, merchants, and eventually settlers did follow in the steamer's wake. They traveled aboard the *Colonel Wright* as well as on the *Okanagan, Tenino,* and other vessels built in rapid succession to profit from the largest Pacific Slope gold rush since California in 1849. And as officers of the Oregon Steam Navigation Company had hoped, Portland became the newcomers' main West Coast gateway to the mines.

Despite its historic consequences, the voyage of the *Colonel Wright* went almost unnoticed outside the far Northwest. With the Union in crisis, most Americans cared little that a steamboat had opened a distant waterway to passengers and freight. In any event, even after the Pony Express shortened the time between Missouri and California to ten days in 1860, news from remote corners of the northern West still required almost a month to reach the East Coast, and passengers and freight took even longer.

The nation's isolated northwest corner had always marched to a different rhythm, one that was wholly unrecognizable in longer-settled portions of North America. During another great war, when American revolutionaries assembled in Philadelphia in 1776 to write their Declaration of Independence, Captain James Cook set sail from England that same July on a voyage that had profound consequences for the far Northwest. Until his two ships reached the coast of future Oregon almost two years later and returned home in 1792 bearing word of the region's fur riches, there had been no sustained contact between the Pacific Northwest and the East Coast or Europe.

In later decades when North and South wrestled with weighty questions of industrial growth and human bondage, the Pacific Northwest remained a land apart. As early as 1792 the Spanish had sought to establish a base on the Olympic Peninsula of future Washington, but they abandoned Núñez Gaona in frustration and disgust after only a few months. Apart from scattered trading posts and mission stations, as late as 1840 not a single non-Indian population center existed across the region. With the exception of the landing at Wallula and the village that arose outside Fort Walla Walla after the army established the outpost in 1856, Euro-American settlement in the interior Northwest was negligible when the *Colonel Wright* first steamed up the Snake River in 1861.

Only three years earlier, in 1858, the ship's namesake, Colonel George Wright, had led a punitive expedition from Fort Walla Walla to crush the latest Indian uprising on the Columbia Plateau. His nearly six hundred well-armed regulars proved a ruthless adversary, using new long-range rifles and slaughtering seven hundred Indian horses to demoralize their foe. Wright then marched grimly through Indian country near present-day Spokane, peremptorily hanging sixteen chiefs and others considered guilty of fomenting what was then termed the Yakima War. Ironically, the man whom white settlers revered as a military hero perished in a naval disaster along with 224 others traveling aboard the steamship *Brother Jonathan* when it struck a rock and foundered off Crescent City, California, in July 1865. That same *Brother Jonathan* had brought Oregonians the glad news of statehood in 1859 and transported many of them to and from business and pleasure in San Francisco. The tragic sinking of a popular steamship no less than the death of a popular soldier must have seemed like a personal loss in many a Pacific Northwest household (Native American ones excepted).

Two Kalispel Indians use a sturgeon canoe on the Pend Oreille River in northeastern Washington about 1908. Courtesy Eastern Washington State Historical Society, L. 84–327.762.

Not without reason did it appear that transportation, or lack thereof, played an inordinately large role in shaping the early Pacific Northwest. So much of the region's history during the century after 1778—from the time of Captain Cook to the days of the Oregon Trail and Ben Holladay's stagecoach empire—could be written in terms of evolving networks of transportation and communication by water and land. Even the Columbia River itself (originally Columbia's River) owed its name to a ship, Robert Gray's *Columbia Rediviva,* which in 1792 sailed a short distance up the waterway in search of furs and thereby gave the United States a modest claim to the region. Almost seventy years later, in the spring of 1861, the pioneering voyage of the *Colonel Wright* up the Columbia and Snake rivers continued the quest for commercial advantage in the far Northwest and opened the latest Northwest passage.

Northwest Passages

Today the dirt-and-gravel road that winds across the Continental Divide at Lemhi Pass bears little resemblance to the vital portage Thomas Jefferson must have had in mind when he emphasized to Meriwether Lewis that the "object of your mission" is to explore the Missouri River and determine whether it together with the Columbia or any other river of the West "may offer the most direct & practicable water communication across this continent for the purposes of commerce." When Jefferson penned those words in mid-1803, not even the best maps could reveal to the nation's third president exactly where the Missouri and Columbia rivers ran or that a snow-covered range of mountains separated their headwaters. Nor could he guess what names might ultimately define the western landscape. The entire area was unknown to all but its Native American inhabitants. Yet in Jefferson's orderly and informed mind a Lemhi Pass or, more likely, some less rugged connection between waters flowing to the Atlantic and Pacific oceans must almost certainly exist to permit a far-flung American commerce in furs to compete with the British and Canadian one farther north.[6]

One year and four months after they left Saint Louis,

the first members of the Lewis and Clark expedition at last surmounted the continent's great divide on August 12, 1805, at the place on the Idaho-Montana border now called Lemhi Pass. Private Hugh McNeal, a Pennsylvanian, saluted their feat by triumphantly standing astride the tiny spring he believed to be the headwaters of the great river that had been his lifeline and constant companion these many months. In Lewis's words, "McNeal had exultingly stood with a foot on each side of this little rivulet and thanked his god that he had lived to bestride the mighty & heretofore deemed endless Missouri."[7]

Beyond the 7,373-foot-high pass, one of the highest points on their journey, Lewis and the three other members of his advance party left the Louisiana Purchase territory (and the western boundary of the United States) and became the first non–Native people to enter the rugged land now called Idaho. A few hundred yards farther down the steep western slope of the divide, they came to a clear, cold stream where the captain "first tasted the water of the great Columbia River." The explorers could easily hike between waters flowing east and west in less than fifteen minutes, but Jefferson's hoped-for passage to the Pacific in this area did not exist and never would. A labyrinth of mountain ranges and the single most difficult month of their entire journey severely tested members of the Lewis and Clark expedition before they at last reached a navigable tributary of the Columbia. Successful in so many ways, the two captains failed to find an easy portage between the rivers; nonetheless, fur brigades and mountain men would occasionally cross through Lemhi Pass.

Other sojourners in the West would piece together enough geographical information from personal observations and Native American informants to make regular travel by covered wagon possible through South Pass in future Wyoming to connect the Missouri Valley with Oregon and California in the 1840s. It was at South Pass, not Lemhi, that the waters of the Atlantic and Pacific nearly clasped hands and where the nation's reach extended westward. Crossing the Continental Divide at South Pass were thousands of gold seekers hurrying west in 1849 to the Sierra Nevada and the Mother Lode diggings, thousands more farm families bound for Oregon's Willamette Valley, and Mormons eager for their new promised land in the valley of the Great Salt Lake. By the late 1850s regularly scheduled stagecoaches made commercial travel overland to the Pacific coast along the central route possible for the first time.

A few years later a local stage line threaded its way through Lemhi Pass to carry passengers and freight between Salmon City, Idaho, and Red Rock, Montana, during a mining boom, but as decades passed, Lewis and Clark's overland link became largely forgotten, especially after the Gilmore and Pittsburgh Railway began to serve Salmon City through nearby Bannock Pass. Apart from local ranchers and an occasional history-minded tourist, few people travel that way at all today, although the tiny spring that fed into the Missouri River and the clear, cold rivulet destined for the Columbia are still there in their natural states. To the west, range after range, mountains still define an empty landscape and provide a vivid reminder of why transportation links were so difficult to forge across the northern West.

Over the years Jefferson's dream of a portage between the navigable waters of the Missouri and Columbia rivers was not forgotten. Sixty years after the president issued his special instructions to Lewis, another military man, Lieutenant John Mullan, finally forged the missing link. After the first steamboats managed to push their way 3,100 miles up the Missouri River from Saint Louis to the headwaters of navigation at Fort Benton in future Montana, a troop of soldiers set out for the Columbia River. Their journey took fifty-seven days, and the 624-mile-long route across the Bitterroot Mountains was hardly the practicable portage Jefferson had envisioned. Yet, long as it was, the Mullan Road formed the only such portage in the entire West.

The Mullan Road neither lived up to expectations nor justified the $230,000 that Congress invested in the project. Little freight and few travelers ever made the entire journey. For several years after 1860, steamboats provided regular service from Saint Louis to Fort Benton east of the Rocky Mountains and from Portland to

*W*here the northern West met the Pacific rim: the barque Eilbek *loaded lumber for distant markets through her stern ports at Port Blakely, Washington, in this turn-of-the-century photograph. Some of the timber measured twenty-two inches square and nearly eighty feet long. Courtesy Washington State Historical Society.*

Lewiston west of the mountains, but never did stagecoaches or freight wagons run regularly along the length of the Mullan Road to connect traffic on the two waterways.

Not until the fall of 1883 was a commercial freight and passenger link at last forged across the northern West from the Great Lakes to Puget Sound, and then only by rail. When the final spike was driven alongside a remote and nonnavigable reach of the Clark Fork River in Montana Territory to complete the Northern Pacific line, the nation's *second* transcontinental railroad provided service fully independent of steamboat and stagecoach connections. Often during the years that followed, the railroad used various forms of advertising to salute itself for completing what Lewis and Clark had begun: "Explored by Lewis and Clark in 1804–6 and developed by the Northern Pacific Railway" was the subtitle of a pamphlet called *The Storied Northwest*.[8]

In May 1869, when Union Pacific and Central Pacific officials met at remote Promontory in the Utah desert to drive home a final spike to complete the nation's *first* transcontinental railroad, they did not immediately end stagecoach and steamboat transportation to the northern mines. But their new east-to-west line along the central overland route between Omaha and Sacramento dramatically altered established patterns of water and land transportation across the West, affecting places seemingly as distant from one another as the Isthmus of Panama and the prairies of western Canada.

Even so, in the vast hinterland that stretched north from the rail towns of Wyoming and Utah to the Canadian border and beyond, commercial transportation of passengers and merchandise continued to depend almost exclusively on steamboats, stagecoaches, freight wagons, and packtrains for another fifteen years. The few miles of track that existed there prior to the early 1880s belonged mainly to short-portage railroads built around obstacles to navigation on the Columbia River, to a line that joined the navigable waters of Puget Sound and the Columbia, and to a handful of feeder lines in the Willamette and Walla Walla valleys intended primarily to supplement river traffic.

Only with the opening of the Northern Pacific line in 1883 did the railway age really dawn for much of the northern West, but preceding this major advancement in transportation was a fifty-year span that can accurately be described as the steamboat and stagecoach era. Its beginnings were tentative: in 1831 the first steamboat in the northern West reached Fort Union on the upper Missouri River (at the present border between Montana and North Dakota), and in 1846 the first stage line within the same geographical area advertised for passengers between Oregon City and the Tualatin plains west of there.

The main features of the new era grew more distinct during the 1850s when common-carrier steamboats increased in number on the Columbia River and reached another thirteen hundred miles up the Missouri from Fort Union to Fort Benton, and during the 1860s when stagecoaches first threaded their way through the canyons of the northern Rocky Mountains. The era faded when an expanding network of railroads came to dominate commercial transportation across the West during the 1880s and 1890s. The end of steamboat and stagecoach service usually happened with little fanfare at different times in widely scattered locations, although in several places too remote or too sparsely populated to attract railroads, stagecoaches continued to fill a need until the early 1930s. A few freight-and-passenger-carrying steamboats still plied the waters of the Columbia and Missouri rivers until about the same time. But by then their era was long past.

Because of the widespread use of sail and steam to power ships along the Pacific coast and of horses, mules, and oxen to haul freight to remote corners of the interior West, this was their age, too. The construction of a short but vital railroad across Panama in the mid-1850s, the earliest railroads of the northern West during the following two decades, and even an expanding network of telegraph lines are likewise part of the lost world recalled in *Long Day's Journey*. But it was the steamboats—more than five hundred of which were built for Pacific Northwest waters and hundreds more for the Missouri—and

stagecoaches that symbolized most vividly this distinctive era of commercial transportation.

Steamboats and stagecoaches were the offspring of two vastly different technologies; yet they had much in common, and together they would redefine time and space across the northern West. They regularly dispatched the United States mail, small packages, magazines, and newspapers across the continent to link western mining camps, farm villages, and military outposts with the nation's centers of population and commerce. The steamboat captain and stage driver, like the locomotive engineer of later years, were respected figures across the West and heroes to many a youngster growing up in prerailroad times. Even now, when theme parks seek to invoke the Old West, they rely on replicas of steamboats or stagecoaches (in addition to narrow-gauge, steam-powered passenger trains). The ubiquitous Wells Fargo stagecoach has become a popular icon of the old West,

The steamers Idaho *and* Colfax *at the waterfront in Saint Maries, Idaho. From here passengers could travel by boat up the Saint Joe River, one of the highest navigable waterways in the world, to a series of lumber camps in the Bitterroot Mountains or north to Lake Coeur d'Alene. Courtesy Brigham Young University, P3839 McKay.*

much as have false-front wooden buildings and mock shoots-outs in the streets of places named Tombstone and Virginia City, or Knott's Berry Farm and Disneyland.

Peculiarities of Western Transportation

The transportation network that gradually extended across the West did not follow the pattern that evolved earlier in the East. The main reason was that the West lacked water, navigable and otherwise, and hence population centers, across the thousand miles of arid land that separated the hundredth meridian and the Cascade and Sierra Nevada ranges. Rivers and lakes of the East and Midwest—the Hudson, Delaware, Potomac, Mississippi, Ohio, and so many others with mellifluous names celebrated in history and song—formed early highways across a well-watered land. Unlike settlers in so much of the West, Americans on the eastern seaboard usually lived near rivers, inlets, bays, and other waterways that facilitated transportation and travel. Brigs, barques, schooners, sloops, and ships carried passengers and cargoes across oceans and to neighboring coastal towns. Even farmers without direct access to seaports used water transportation—flatboats, rafts, and other river craft—to carry their produce to market. Beyond the reach of navigable rivers, an extensive network of canals extended the influence of New York City, Philadelphia, and other growing centers of manufacturing and commerce.

When the 364-mile-long Erie Canal was completed in 1825 to link the Hudson River and Great Lakes, it reduced the cost of shipping wheat or flour from Buffalo to New York City from $100 to $10 a ton and fostered a popular frenzy known as the "canal craze" or "canal mania." A nation that counted fewer than a hundred miles of canals when construction of the Erie Canal began in 1817 recorded 3,325 miles in 1840 and a peak of 4,500 miles during the decade of the 1850s, almost all of them located east of the Mississippi River. Canals, however, were a deceptively simple form of transportation technology: in addition to the locks and towpaths that were so much a part of the canal landscape, they required an extensive but far less obvious system of reservoirs and aqueducts to maintain the water level.

Without a steady supply of water, all traffic ground to a halt. But water presented a fundamental problem in much of the West.

Unlike communities in the East, settlements west of the hundredth meridian tended to resemble island outposts surrounded by miles of arid and almost empty space. Aridity, in fact, defined more than two-thirds of the western landscape. The prevailing pattern was less distinct in well-watered portions of the Pacific Northwest, but even settled areas west of the Cascade Range still tended to resemble islands separated by miles of dense forests, and much of Oregon and Washington east of the Cascades was as dry and lightly populated as the rest of the rural West. The essence of this often high and windswept interior terrain where winters were cold and harsh, summers were hot and dusty, and water was always scarce was captured in the names that pioneers left behind: Hard Rocks, Alkaline Lake, Cactus Flat, and Skull Valley. In such country, water to maintain canal traffic was not only scarce but would have required far more elaborate feats of engineering than the region's sparse population warranted or its rudimentary economy permitted.

Apart from log flumes and various conduits used to channel water from mountain lakes and reservoirs to where it was needed elsewhere for irrigation, mining, electric power, and household plumbing, westerners built few canals during the nineteenth century, and these consisted mainly of short channels to facilitate navigation around waterfalls and rapids. Most notable was the Cascades Canal opened in 1896 to aid steamboat transportation along the middle Columbia River. Even with such bypasses, major western rivers that supported steamboat navigation could be counted on the fingers of both hands: these included the Columbia and Snake rivers as far inland as Lewiston, Idaho, the Missouri from Saint Louis to Fort Benton, the Willamette from Portland to Eugene, the Colorado north from the Gulf of California to several desert mining settlements in northern Arizona, and the Sacramento and San Joaquin rivers in California's Central Valley, and none of these came any closer than the Missouri and Columbia in the northern Rocky

Mountains to forming any kind of regional or transcontinental system of river transportation. A few less well known rivers like the Rogue in Oregon, the Cowlitz in Washington, and the Kootenai in Montana supported at least modest amounts of steamboat traffic for varying lengths of time.

In addition, steamboats plied the waters of several large inland lakes, including Flathead in Montana, Klamath in Oregon, Coeur d'Alene and Pend Oreille in Idaho, and Tahoe in the Sierra Nevada, and the tidal currents of San Francisco Bay, Puget Sound, and a few other Pacific estuaries. Along the coast, a large fleet of ships powered by sail and steam linked the Pacific Northwest to California, Alaska, Hawaii, and the Far East, even

to the Isthmus of Panama or around Cape Horn to reach the East Coast and Europe. But in interior portions of the northern West, steamboat traffic was always confined to a small number of rivers and lakes. It was for this reason that stagecoaches, freight wagons, and other early modes of overland transportation provided vital supplements to water connections, and in many cases (as in landlocked Wyoming) operated completely independently of river traffic.

It should also be noted that the work of building railroads across the West differed from that in the East, where even the earliest carriers generated freight and passenger business by serving already established population centers and markets. Western lines, by contrast, had

Charles R. Pratsch photographed the turn-of-the-century steamer Harbor Belle *in Grays Harbor, Washington. Courtesy Washington State University, Pratsch #234.*

to build across hundreds and even thousands of miles of rugged and lightly populated countryside. They would need to generate passenger and freight revenue by running from nowhere in particular to nowhere at all. In other words, the railroads of the West would have to create entirely new towns and markets and foster settlement of countless miles of farmland by promising investors a share of future wealth, a task that sobered even the most optimistic westerner.

Vast distances, the predominance of small and widely scattered centers of population, and a general lack of navigable water meant that the West in the nineteenth century must necessarily forge its own distinctive pattern of transportation links, especially during the era of the steamboat and stagecoach. These were challenges faced by visionaries like Thomas Jefferson, roadbuilders like John Mullan, and hard-driving entrepreneurs like Ben Holladay, "the Stagecoach King," and John C. Ainsworth, the steamboat captain and prime mover behind the powerful Oregon Steam Navigation Company. The pages that follow will examine in detail the steamboat and

stagecoach era and, in addition, illustrate how these and related modes of water and land transportation responded as railroads extended their hegemony across the landscape of the northern West.

Although the Rocky Mountain gold fever of the 1860s highlights the main features of the steamboat and stagecoach era in the northern West (and these mineral bonanzas figure prominently in *Long Day's Journey*), any study of how early transportation and communication shaped the destiny of the region must actually begin much earlier with a frenzied quest for gold of another sort. Well before miners diverted the creeks and streams of the mountain West, an earlier generation of wealth seekers and their employees had regularly plundered the same valleys and meadowlands in search of furs. The pursuit of fortunes in pelts had spurred intense national rivalries in a portion of North America that remained almost wholly unknown to outsiders as late as the era of President Thomas Jefferson. At that time, as was also true during the 1860s gold rushes, the slopes on either side of the northern Rockies had much in common.

*P*eter Britt photographed these gold miners in 1894 one-half mile up the Rogue River near Gold Hill. Courtesy Southern Oregon Historical Society, 758.

Good-bye, driver—Good-bye, mustangs and donkeys! Good-bye stagecoaches and ambulances! Two thousand four hundred miles of their drag and shake, of their rattle and bang, across the Plains and over the Mountains, have given us our fill of them. We had had runaways, we had had breakdowns, and about every stage experience except a general upset, and how we happened to escape that will always remain a mystery. Our romance of stage-coaching, I must say, was long since gone. There before us now lay the lordly Columbia, with visions of steamboats and locomotives. And looking back on our long jaunt with all its discomforts and dangers, it seemed for a moment as if nothing could induce us to take it again. Hereafter, we felt assured, we should appreciate the comfort and speed of eastern travel more, and pray for the hastening of our Pacific railroads.
—James F. Rusling, Across America; Or, The Great West and The Pacific Coast *(1874)*

Golden Years, 1831–1869

The old stage coach certainly has its interesting story to tell; its beautiful memory to keep green in the hearts of those who have familiarized themselves with this interesting and unique, ancient mode of travel. The Pullman car with its plush upholstery, its steam heat and white electric light, falls short in the joy and mirth and freedom which is to be found on the hard leather covered seat of the stage coach; a hill to walk up or down to keep warm, and the star of heaven's canopy to give light to the eye.
—Idaho Scimitar *(August 8, 1908)*

The Beaver rests at anchor in the harbor at Nanaimo, Vancouver Island, May 20, 1858. Courtesy Hudson's Bay Company Archives, Provincial Archives of Manitoba, E. 36/4 fo. 6.

The Missouri river has been from the early settlement of this Territory regarded by its citizens as one of the main arteries through which flow the means of subsistence, and the machinery and materials necessary for carrying on the great industrial pursuits of the country. Long before the advent of the gold hunting whites, an occasional boat disturbed its turbid waters, bringing up supplies for the American Fur Company, and articles with which to barter for furs, then the only known product of this country.
—Helena Montana Radiator *(June 16, 1866)*

Soft Gold Defines a Distant Land

The age of steam dawned in the Pacific Northwest on May 16, 1836. That was when the aptly named *Beaver,* a diminutive side-wheeler built on the Thames near London and purchased by the Hudson's Bay Company, first fired up her boilers at Fort Vancouver. The British fur monopoly intended the *Beaver* to be a working vessel, a small cog in a large and complex economic machine that encompassed dozens of trading posts and farms, several thousand employees, and operations that extended along the Pacific coast from Spanish California to Russian Alaska. The company's primary interest was the pursuit of profits from furs—fittingly described as soft gold—but first a few excursions seemed an appropriate way to celebrate the power of steam.

Guests of the Hudson's Bay Company boarded the *Beaver* on June 14 for a day-long cruise from Fort Vancouver down the Columbia River into the much narrower Multnomah channel of the Willamette River, around low-lying Sauvie Island and into the main channel, then back to the Columbia and the company's district headquarters. For the most part the passengers must have seen only trees and water, for signs of human habitation were few. Among the lighthearted group that pleasant summer day was the missionary Samuel Parker, for

whom the novelty of a steamboat on the Great River of the West "awakened a train of prospective reflections upon the probable changes, which would take place in these remote regions, in a very few years." For Parker and other guests, the *Beaver* represented a "forerunner of commerce and business. The animation which prevailed was often suspended, while we conversed of coming days, when with civilized men, all the rapid improvements in the arts of life, should be introduced over this new world, and when cities and villages shall spring up on the west, as they are springing up on the east of the great mountains, and a new empire be added to the kingdoms of the earth."[1]

The excursionists aboard the *Beaver* in 1836 were better prophets than they knew. Travelers who retrace that historic voyage today would begin in the modern city of Vancouver, Washington (pop. 46,380), where a multilane highway and railroad embankment isolate the United States National Park Service's re-created Fort Vancouver from the Columbia River that once was its lifeline. Heading downriver, the modern excursionists would pass several industrial complexes, one for shipping grain to Asia and another where the first aluminum plant in the Pacific Northwest was built in 1940. Turning southeast into the still heavily forested Multnomah channel, they would pass a large wood products plant at Saint Helens, Oregon.

Sauvie Island retains a bucolic appearance, but farther up the serpentine channel a houseboat suburb of Portland crowds both sides of the waterway. Along the main part of the Willamette River, drydocks, oil storage facilities, warehouses, and large ships line the modern channel all the way to Portland, a city of 437,319 people in 1990. When the *Beaver* first steamed along the Willamette, Portland did not exist (and would not for another nine years). In fact, apart from fur traders and trappers and several missionaries, of whom Samuel Parker was the vanguard, the Euro-American presence in the Pacific Northwest was negligible. To put the plodding pace of development and population growth in perspective, it might be noted that Parker's 1836 excursion aboard the *Beaver* occurred almost midway through a century bracketed by the first sustained contacts between Europe and the Pacific Northwest in the early 1780s and completion of a northern transcontinental railroad linking the region to the Midwest and East Coast in 1883.

Less than a week after the historic excursion, Parker took passage aboard the *Beaver* to Fort George (the site of modern Astoria), near the mouth of the Columbia River, where a few days later he transferred to a barque bound for the Hawaiian Islands. Parker was pleased to reached Honolulu only sixteen days later, from whence in mid-December he sailed back to the East Coast. His ship followed the usual route around South America and reached New London, Connecticut, the following May 1837. Although he prepared the way for several missionary couples who followed him to the Pacific Northwest, Parker himself never returned.

Neither did the *Beaver* return to the Columbia River or Fort Vancouver. The pioneer steam vessel kept busy serving the needs of the Hudson's Bay Company along the North Pacific coast to Alaska and had no time for any general commerce that might have developed the country but would have interfered with the almighty fur trade. Thirteen more years elapsed before another steam-powered vessel churned the waters of the Columbia

River. Although the *Beaver* was important as a symbol of the coming age of steam, she did little to hasten commercial transportation by steam power.

On the upper Missouri River (the portion above Sioux City, some nine hundred miles above the confluence with the Mississippi, and an area still very much a frontier in the 1830s and 1840s), steam power arrived only slightly earlier than on the Columbia. On both waterways the lure was the same—soft gold—although it was Americans based in Saint Louis who controlled the trade on the Missouri and its tributaries. Towering above a host of would-be competitors in what was then the biggest business in the northern West was John Jacob Astor's American Fur Company, which by the mid-1830s had gained near-monopoly status east of the Rocky Mountains. Astor's empire was responsible for the historic voyages of the *Yellow Stone* on the upper Missouri.

During the summer of 1831 the *Yellow Stone* (with approximately the same modest carrying capacity as the *Colonel Wright* on the Columbia River) steamed as far north as Fort Tecumseh, where, on the bank opposite, Pierre, South Dakota, later arose. The *Yellow Stone* headed south to Louisiana to spend the winter in the sugar trade but returned to the upper Missouri the following spring to probe much farther upriver. Writing from Paris during the summer of 1832, John Jacob Astor asked, "How did the *Yellow Stone* behave and what said the Indians about her?" The experiment was a success, he soon learned. On June 17, after defying the current of the Big Muddy for more than thirteen hundred miles, the *Yellow Stone* successfully completed a voyage to Fort Union, the high-plains trading post located near the confluence of the Missouri and Yellowstone rivers. After an exchange of supplies for furs and pelts, the *Yellow Stone* paddled back to Saint Louis, having proved that steamboats offered a practical means of transportation in a distant part of the American West. What began as an experiment quickly became a regular feature of the Missouri River fur trade. Every spring until it sold its operations in 1864, the American Fur Company dispatched one or more steamboats to its upriver posts.

ss *Beaver*

Built largely of "English oak of good quality, well squared and free from sap" and capable of a top speed of slightly less than ten miles per hour, the Beaver *was launched May 2, 1835. Together with the barque* Columbia *and manned by a crew of thirteen, she left Gravesend under sail for the Columbia River on August 29. After traveling around South America and pausing at Oahu in the Hawaiian Islands, both the* Beaver *and the* Columbia *passed Fort George on March 26, 1836, and arrived at Fort Vancouver on April 10. Two low-pressure boilers built in England by Boulton and Watt and each producing thirty-five horsepower were installed there during the next few weeks. David Home, captain from 1835 to 1837, pronounced the* Beaver *an "excellent sea boat, & should the engines go wrong will answer as a sailing vessel perfectly well." The* Beaver, *usually described as a schooner-rigged side-wheel paddle steamer with two masts and a funnel, was a hundred feet long, twenty feet wide, and eleven feet deep. She drew little more than eight feet of water when fully loaded.*

After the 1836 excursion on the Columbia River, the Beaver *spent most of her long career working on Puget Sound, mainly to carry supplies north from Fort Nisqually to Russian Alaska at Sitka and to trade with natives at intermediate ports of call. At first the* Beaver *carried thirteen woodcutters aboard to supply forty cords of fuel a day: they might work two days to cut the amount of wood burned in twelve to fourteen*

*C*hurning along the Colorado River in 1854, this pioneer vessel exposed the vital machinery common to all steamboats. Lithograph by J. Young after a sketch by H. B. Möllhausen. Courtesy Oregon Historical Society, 91703, #1201.

Gateways to the Northern West

hours of travel, or a distance of about 230 miles. Following the discovery of coal on Vancouver Island in the late 1840s, the little ship rarely burned wood again. After forty years in Hudson's Bay Company service, the Beaver *was sold to new owners. The pioneer steamer ran aground on July 26, 1888, while heading out of Vancouver Harbor in British Columbia and was wrecked.*
—Adapted from *"S. S. Beaver,"* Hudson's Bay Company Archives, Winnipeg

On both sides of the Rocky Mountains the fur trade attracted the first Euro-Americans to the northern West. From the 1780s to the 1840s in the Pacific Northwest, and until the early 1860s in the mountains and high plains of the upper Missouri River, the fur trade remained the dominant economic activity. So great were profits from selling the warm and fashionable furs that commerce in soft gold defined a globe-girdling system of communication and transportation and was responsible for introduction of steam power on both the Columbia and upper Missouri.

In early March 1804, when upper Louisiana first became American territory and shortly before the Lewis and Clark expedition headed west from Saint Louis, the budding frontier metropolis consisted of about two hundred dwellings. Deteriorating Spanish fortifications and European-style houses that rose tier upon tier from the waterfront gave Saint Louis a distinctly Old World look. Although tributary to New Orleans, which was located a thousand miles farther down the Mississippi River and which had long served as the main outlet for commodities from the interior West, upstart Saint Louis cultivated a cosmopolitan life-style that visitors compared favorably to that of the seaport metropolis.

For Saint Louis the fur trade remained the single most important commercial activity for a decade or more after statehood in 1821. The city's sprawling warehouses annually received a flood of furs to process and distribute to world markets. During this time Saint Louis emerged as the "capital of the far west," presiding over the fur trade of the Rocky Mountains, the lead industry of Illinois and Wisconsin, and the growing commerce of Santa Fe in northern Mexico. The key to maintaining commercial control of this vast hinterland was the growth and improvement of transportation facilities. For thirty years—from the 1840s through the 1860s—Saint Louis was home to a steamboat fleet that transported over-landers to trail heads at Independence, Council Bluffs, and other jumping-off points for the Rocky Mountains and Pacific coast. Eventually special "mountain steamboats" bucked the muddy Missouri all the way to Fort Benton in central Montana. Where river commerce once crowded the Saint Louis waterfront, Eero Saarinen's stainless steel arch now soars majestically across the skyline to symbolize the city's historic role as gateway to the West.

Before the railway age, the steamboat served as the main mechanism for introducing and spreading steam power throughout the United States. At the time of Robert Fulton's celebrated first voyage of the *Clermont* in 1807, the nation's few steam engines were all imperfect and cumbersome machines; thirty years later the technology had evolved into a generation of efficient steamboat engines that composed almost three-fifths of America's total steam power. Steamboating on western waters dated from 1810 when Nicholas Roosevelt relocated from New Jersey to Pittsburgh, where, with eastern financial backing and his own engineering know-how, he built an engine for the *New Orleans.* That first steamboat west of the Appalachians descended the Ohio and Mississippi rivers during the fall of 1811, the same year that Oliver Evans sent his son George to Pittsburgh to build high-pressure engines for western rivercraft. The new engines were compact, relatively simple to build and repair, and according to Evans, ten times more powerful than the low-pressure Boulton and Watt models imported from England.

The first steamboat to reach Saint Louis was the *Zebulon M. Pike,* which arrived from New Orleans in 1817. Steamboat operations on the Missouri River itself commenced two years later when the *Independence* ascended to Franklin and Chariton, Missouri, a distance of about 250 miles. Also in 1819 a military and scientific expedition under Major Stephen S. Long steamed out of Saint Louis in four boats to explore distant parts of the trans-Mississippi West. Long's flagship, the *Western Engineer,* was a fantastically designed craft with a bow resembling a serpent's head and a stack arranged to pour smoke from the mouth of "Long's Dragon." Planned with the apparent intent of frightening the Indians, this strange monster under the white man's control almost certainly startled them (and probably any other casual onlookers as well).

A few years after Long's trip—which was plagued by mud from the turbid waters that accumulated in boilers—steamboats made regular runs between Saint Louis and Independence, Westport, and Saint Joseph, where trails headed across the Great Plains to the Rocky Mountains and farther west. Even so, throughout the twenties and thirties steamboat activity on the Missouri River, as compared to the Ohio or Mississippi, remained insignificant because settlement along the frontier waterway was too sparse to support more than limited commerce. It required several more years, furthermore, to adapt the new technology to the shallow water, strong currents, and other hazards of Missouri River navigation. The number of steamboats reported in regular operation on the lower Missouri increased only slowly, from five in 1831, to twenty-six in 1842, and to fifty-nine in 1858. But there was also considerable traffic from other great rivers of the Midwest that passed through Saint Louis. By 1850 the booming metropolis could claim a population of 77,860.

West of the Continental Divide, on the Columbia River, no city played a role comparable to Saint Louis's in the Missouri River–based fur trade. In fact, in the sprawling Oregon Country (comprising the modern states of Oregon, Washington, Idaho, the western portions of Montana and Wyoming, and southern British Columbia), there were no urban centers at all prior to the mid-1840s. There was, however, Fort Vancouver,

*F*ort Vancouver in 1845. In addition
to a sawmill that provided lumber for
building construction and repairs, the
Hudson's Bay Company operated a shipyard, two gristmills, two dairies, an
orchard, and a farm of several hundred
acres, where employees planted crops and
raised herds of cattle and other domestic
animals. Sailing ships from distant ports
brought news and books and periodicals
to stock the post's library. H. J. Warre
lithograph, from Sketches in North
America and the Oregeon Territory
(1848). Courtesy Oregon Historical
Society, 803, #409–1.

for two decades a vital workshop in the wilderness and
regional headquarters of the Hudson's Bay Company, the
oldest and most prominent of all fur companies in North
America. Chartered by King Charles II in 1670 (and thus
of such ancient lineage that humorists claimed its initials
stood for "Here Before Christ"), the Governor and Company of Adventurers of England Trading into Hudson's
Bay had dominated the Columbia River country since
the early 1820s. Trade routes from Fort Vancouver
extended inland to the mountain headwaters of the
Columbia and its major tributaries, up the coast to Russian Alaska, and across the Pacific to Asian markets. An
overland canoe route reached across North America to
connect the Columbia and Saint Lawrence rivers.

For two decades, from 1824 to 1846, Fort Vancouver

functioned as the nerve center of a vast and complex
commercial system based not only on furs but also on a
lively trade in deer hides, prized shells, gold dust, and the
various products of farm, forest, and stream. Here was a
small, almost self-sufficient European community that
included a hospital, school, several churches, thirty to
fifty small houses where employees (*engagés*) lived with
their Indian wives, storehouses for furs, trading goods,
and grain, and workshops where artisans and laborers
engaged in blacksmithing, carpentry, barrel making, and
other crafts.

On a map the Great River of the West that flowed past
Fort Vancouver's busy wharves somewhat resembled a
gnarled oak tree resting on its side, with its topmost
branches reaching far inland into what is now southern

British Columbia, western Montana, and northwestern Wyoming. From its source high in the Canadian Rockies, the Columbia River extended a distance of 1,243 miles to the Pacific Ocean and, together with numerous tributaries like the Snake and Willamette rivers, drained 258,000 square miles, an area larger than France, Belgium, and the Netherlands combined. More than any other physical feature, it knit together the various landscapes of the far Northwest, crossing deserts, high plains, and grasslands as it threaded its way through four major mountain ranges to pour more water into the ocean than any other river in North America except for the Saint Lawrence, the Mississippi, and the Mackenzie. In the gorge where its waters breached the Cascade

Range, the agitated Columbia posed a formidable challenge to Fort Vancouver's fur traders (and to steamboat traffic in later years).

On a typical journey upriver in the early 1840s, the men of the Hudson's Bay Company used special wooden bateaux noted for their great strength and buoyancy: "In building them, flat timbers of oak are bent to the requisite shape by steaming; they are bolted to a flat keel, at distances of a foot from each other; the planks are of cedar, and generally extend the whole length of the boat." Going to upriver posts from Fort Vancouver, each bateau typically carried eight or nine crewmen and about three tons of clothing, flour, powder, bullets, groceries, and other supplies that were packed into ninety-pound bales.

The Dalles of the Columbia River near the head of Five Mile Rapids. Joseph Drayton of the Wilkes expedition described the site in the early 1840s as "one of the most remarkable places upon the Columbia." Courtesy Oregon Historical Society, 67073, #373-A.

Joseph Drayton, an artist who accompanied the Wilkes expedition, noted in 1841 that a typical flotilla consisted of nine boats, rowed by sixty voyageurs, mostly French Canadians and some Iroquois Indians (occasionally accompanied by their wives), who used heavy oars and sometimes a square sail to muscle their way upriver against the swift current.[2]

Drayton observed that in setting out on a lengthy journey the voyageurs usually traveled "only a few miles the first day, in order that they may discover if anything has been neglected, and be able to return for it." For this reason their first night's encampment was often at the sawmill. The first obstacle they encountered going upriver from Fort Vancouver was the stretch of white water known as the Cascades, the location of two portages, each requiring that voyageurs unload and carry a staggering weight of goods. "To a stranger, unacquainted with navigation of this river, the management of these boatmen becomes a source of wonder; for it is surprising how they can succeed in surmounting such rapids at all as the Cascades." Men pulled their empty boats through the foaming waters while the loads were "secured on the back of a voyageur by a band which passes round the forehead and under and over the bale; he squats down, adjusts his load, and rises with ninety pounds on his back; another places ninety pounds more on the top, and off he trots, half bent, to the end of the portage," observed Drayton.

An officer of the Hudson's Bay Company told Drayton that he had once seen a voyageur carry "six packages of ninety pounds on his back (five hundred and forty pounds); but it was for a wager, and the distance was not more than one hundred yards. The voyageurs in general have not the appearance of being very strong men. At these portages, the Indians assist for a small present of tobacco. The boats seldom escape injury in passing; and in consequence of that which they received on this occasion, the party was detained the rest of the day repairing damages."

Another, even more difficult passage was located at the Grand Dalles. On the morning of July 4, Drayton observed in amazement as the voyageurs began the mile-long portage. "It is very rugged, and the weather being exceedingly warm, many of the Indians were employed to transport articles on their horses, of which they have a large number. It required seventy men to transport the boats, which were carried over bottom upwards, the gunwale resting on the men's shoulders. By night all was safely transported, the boats newly gummed, and the encampment formed on a sandy beach. The sand, in consequence of the high wind, was blown about in great quantities, and every body and thing was literally covered with it." Ahead a few miles more were the Chutes (or Celilo Falls), where they made yet another portage.

Depending on seasonal variations in the volume of water, voyageurs used different methods to surmount the rapids. In 1836 the missionary Narcissa Whitman stood at the Grand Dalles and watched as fur traders continued upriver without unloading their boats. Indians walked along the edge of the precipice and used long ropes to pull them through. Two men remained in each boat to guide it around obstacles in the raging waters. Ropes sometimes snagged on basalt projections, leaving the bateaux temporarily trapped in the wild current. During these moments of mortal danger, it is likely that prayers or oaths, not their characteristic lighthearted songs, issued from the lips of voyageurs.

"After passing the Dalles," continued Drayton, "an entirely new description of country is entered, for the line of wood extends no farther. The last tree stands on the south side of the river, and is named Ogden's Tree [for Peter Skene Ogden] on our map. . . . The brigade, as usual, set out early, and with the sun there arose a fine breeze, which carried them briskly onwards. . . . After passing John Day's river, the country becomes much lower and more arid, and the current comparatively less. The weather was exceedingly hot, and the drifting sands were in greater quantities than before, so much so that whole islands were passed entirely composed of the sand."

East of the Continental Divide, goods and passengers traveled along the upper Missouri River by canoe, mackinaw, keelboat, and the smaller bullboat that Indians and fur traders made by stitching together a covering of buffalo hides that when thoroughly soaked was stretched over a framework of willow poles shaped like an oversized washtub. No nails or pins were used for fastenings, only buffalo sinew. Hides would then dry and shrink until they drew as tight as a drumhead. Carefully rubbing a mixture of buffalo tallow and ashes into all seams or cracks made the covering watertight. Skilled builders used only the tough skins of buffalo bulls (hence the name), which formed the covering best able to resist abrasion from scraping along the bottom of the shallow river. Typically two men poled the awkward craft along. At night these bullboatmen would land, dump out their furs, turn the boat over to let it dry, and then sleep under it, as if it were a tent.

The most efficient of all nonsteam rivercraft was the keelboat, the principal vessel used to haul supplies to fur posts along the upper Missouri River until 1832. Ranging in length from fifty to seventy-five feet, and often twenty feet wide, keelboats were typically manned by twenty to forty crewmen and were capable of hauling cargoes both with and against the current. Going upriver, a keelboat could transport twenty tons at a rate of ten to fifteen miles a day. Even so, it still required an entire summer to reach the upriver posts, and not infrequently ice choked the Missouri before keelboaters reached their farthest inland destinations.

Keelboats utilized a variety of power sources, including oars, poles, sails, and the cordelle, a long line that crewmen used to pull the boat upriver as they trudged along the shore. Where water was too deep for the poles and where cordelling was impracticable, boatmen resorted to oars. Sometimes, however, they would simply run the boat close to shore and grab bushes to pull themselves along. Not without reason did onlookers commonly call these early boatmen *bushwhackers,* a term not to be confused with the bloodthirsty guerrilla bushwhackers of Civil War days. Occasionally the wind blew hard enough to permit keelboaters to use sails—they rigged a mast with a square sail spreading about one hundred square feet of canvas, which often provided enough power to propel the boat against the swift current of the river—but mostly they had to pull, pole,

or row their heavy cargoes against the current for two thousand miles from Saint Louis to Fort Union, the major upriver post of the American Fur Company.

Not only was hauling freight by keelboat slow and laborious, but the vessels themselves were expensive to operate because they required such large crews to haul comparatively small payloads. Yet it was by keelboat that the American Fur Company sent its annual cargoes of merchandise upriver from Saint Louis and brought furs back. Arrival of steamboats on the Missouri River did not immediately displace the keelboat or other vessels, but steam power's greater efficiency soon enabled it to dominate river traffic and quicken the tempo of economic life by greatly reducing upstream travel time.

Big Muddy

The two great rivers that offered access to the northern West were studies in contrast. Until the 1840s the Columbia served mainly as an avenue for British enterprise, while on the Missouri, American fur traders prevailed. But even more pronounced than national allegiances were the physical contrasts: massive falls and chutes split navigation on the Columbia River below its confluence with the Snake into three distinct segments. During the early decades of steamboat traffic, wagons and special railroads portaged passengers and freight around the churning stretches of water that made life so difficult for voyageurs.

The Missouri River, forming part of the longest navigable waterway in North America, was by contrast a natural stairway leading from the ocean to the mountains. Historically only that portion of the Missouri from its confluence with the Mississippi near Saint Louis to Fort Benton was of great importance to steamboaters. During the years of steam navigation after 1860, Fort Benton was considered the head of navigation because the thirty-seven miles from there to the Great Falls were, for all practical purposes, nonnavigable. Steamboatmen, who measured the river by tracing its meandering channel, calculated the distance from Saint Louis to Fort Benton to be about 3,100 miles. However, army engineers who measured across the meanders computed the distance

Jolly flatboatmen on a midwestern river in 1846. On the Missouri, the first substantial freight carrier was the mackinaw, which could haul as much as fifteen tons and travel more than a hundred miles a day. Limited to downstream use only, the craft was sold for lumber at the end of the trip. This image is by Thomas Doney after Caleb Bingham. Courtesy Library of Congress, 484.

to be around 2,300 miles. Regardless of its actual length, the Missouri's many bends reduced the slope and slowed the current enough to permit specially constructed steamboats to conquer it.[3]

The main hazards to navigation on the Missouri River were not rocks or chutes but unstable banks and constantly shifting sandbars. After emerging from foothills and badlands east of the Rocky Mountains, the current chafed a zigzagging channel through silt plains that accumulated to a depth of fifty feet or more above the bedrock. Steamboatmen described the 160-mile stretch from Fort Benton to Cow Island as "the rocky river," and from there to the Mississippi as "the sandy river."

The Missouri's unimpeded meandering from bluff to bluff across the prairies created distinctive bends that varied in length from one to thirty miles, with land travel across their necks being much shorter than continuing around by water. At the Great Bend in South Dakota where the course of the river was comparatively stable, the neck was only a mile and a half across while the dis-

For all its fame the Oregon Trail was essentially a private passage to the Pacific. Neither stagecoaches nor other public conveyances followed the overland route to Oregon prior to 1864. It played no part in the *first regularly scheduled commercial* transportation between Oregon and the rest of the United States. That distinction belonged to the Pacific Mail Steamship Company, which inaugurated monthly service in 1850 between the lower Columbia River and San Francisco. Before this time, oceangoing vessels had called on the far Northwest only at irregular intervals, and with the exception of the *Beaver,* none was powered by steam. Because of its geographical isolation—bound on one side by the Pacific

Ocean and on the other by the Great Basin desert, snow-capped Rocky Mountains, and Great Plains—early Oregon was essentially an island that could be reached far more easily by sea than by land. It was part of a maritime frontier that included Hawaii and California.

For more than a quarter century, beginning with the Oregon Trail in the early 1840s and ending with completion of the first transcontinental railroad in 1869, the most popular commercial mode of passenger and freight transportation between the two coasts was by ship. The water journey, which often included a short portage across Panama after 1849, was "the main, almost sole route for business and pleasure travel between the Pacific

A steamboat on the Missouri River near the landing at early Kansas City, one of several jumping-off points for the far West. Courtesy Library of Congress, 3666.

The port of Honolulu in the Sandwich Islands in 1849. In the age of sail this was a logical port of call because prevailing winds and currents swung away from the South American continent to carry mariners far out into the Pacific Ocean. It was easier to sail to Hawaii than to hug the Pacific coast and buck often fierce headwinds. Only after discovery of gold in California did San Francisco tend to replace Honolulu as a way station on the long voyage to Oregon. Courtesy Hudson's Bay Company Archives, Provincial Archives of Manitoba, P-349, N5566

and Atlantic Coasts. Two or three thousand persons pass each way by it every month. Where one goes overland, hundreds take this route," recorded the journalist Samuel Bowles in the mid-1860s.[3]

Around Cape Horn

At first the only practical alternative to the overland trail was a tedious ocean voyage around Cape Horn, a distance from coast to coast of at least eleven thousand miles. Life aboard ship was different from but rarely any easier than the journey west to Oregon by wagon. Many a midwesterner selected the shorter land route without hesitation, thus avoiding the unfamiliar and often dangerous ordeal of a lengthy ocean voyage. But in settle-

ments along the Atlantic coast, westering Americans took the opposite view: they looked naturally to the sea as the easiest and safest way to reach distant lands. For them a trip by sea avoided the expense and difficulty of obtaining all the equipment required for a long overland trek and eliminated the risk of attack from hostile Indians (a possibility that haunted the imaginations of travelers on the Oregon and California trails).

Usually it took six to eight months to sail down the eastern seaboard, around South America, and north to the Columbia River. Ships often made intermediate stops at Rio de Janeiro, Brazil; Valparaíso, Chile; and Honolulu, Hawaii. The time needed to round Cape Horn varied according to wind and weather, a ship's sailing qualities, the skill and daring of her captain, and the direction of travel. A voyage from Atlantic to Pacific was typically far more time-consuming than one heading in the opposite direction. A lucky few mariners completed the westbound passage around Cape Horn in less than a week; others, battling contrary winds and lashed by unremitting storms, were tossed about for more than a month before they finally emerged into the Pacific Ocean. Both crew and passengers approached Cape Horn with trepidation: "The billows rolled over the waist of the ship; almost every wave passed over the vessel. Day came, the same weather continued. Toward noon, it became impossible to hold to the cape any longer," recalled Jean-Nicholas Perlot. The topsail, "fully reefed, the only sail which had been left set, was torn by the winds, as if someone had tried, with a machine made expressly, to make it into a canvas sieve. It was necessary to fly before the storm and we put the wind astern." [4]

It was tempting for mariners to take a shortcut through the Strait of Magellan. Though this route reduced the length of a voyage to Oregon by hundreds of miles, the narrow, storm-lashed passage posed so many hazards that prudent captains usually avoided it. From end to end the strait was nearly three hundred miles long, but prevailing winds were unfavorable for travel from east to west, currents were swift and treacherous, and the confining channel made navigation for sailing ships extremely hazardous.

Food was always a problem on long sea voyages. Ships stocked many of the same staple items found in covered wagons on the overland route: flour, hardtack, cornmeal, molasses, coffee, and dried fruit. Lack of refrigeration excluded most fresh fruits and vegetables. Ships instead carried a menagerie of pigs, chickens, and ducks for food, and sometimes a cow or goat for milk. Passengers and crew occasionally caught fresh fish for the dinner table. Fresh drinking water was always a dilemma at sea: even when stored in watertight compartments below deck, saltwater seepage and warmth from the tropical sun often tainted it.

To pass time during a tedious voyage, passengers might play chess and backgammon or cast a line over the side to try fishing. A few travelers succumbed to boredom or too much alcohol or to tropical diseases. There was simply no way to escape it: disease was an unwelcome companion on the way west, whether traveling by land or sea.

After 1855, when a railroad portage opened to speed passengers and express across Panama, the Cape Horn route continued to be used mainly by slow, ponderous sailing vessels of the type that had long hauled heavy freight, plus the new clipper ships that during the early 1850s sped valuable cargoes to California in record-shattering times. In 1851 the famous clipper *Flying Cloud* on her maiden voyage raced from New York around Cape Horn to San Francisco in an unprecedented eighty-nine days. She was the fastest vessel on long voyages ever to sail under the American flag, but this was primarily of benefit to California. Transporting goods and people north along the Pacific coast from the Golden Gate to Oregon remained an expensive, difficult, and time-consuming ordeal, and especially so because of the dangerous bar at the mouth of the Columbia River; yet until completion of the first transcontinental railroad to California, sailing vessels plying the Cape Horn route formed the vital freight connection between East and West.

Pacific Mail Steamship Company

With a long-standing controversy over national boundaries in the far Northwest finally resolved with England in 1846, Congress for the first time gave serious thought to establishing regular mail service between the East Coast and Oregon. At about the same time a treaty with New Granada (Colombia)—of which Panama was then a part—granted the United States free transit across the isthmus and in return guaranteed New Granada's sovereignty. The next step followed in March 1847 when Congress passed the Mail-Steamer bill authorizing $290,000 in annual subsidies for a line of steamships sailing twice a month between New York and Chagres on Panama's Atlantic coast.

To establish the remaining portion of the lengthy new mail route to Oregon, a ten-year contract was issued

Nanaimo in 1859 showing one of the West Coast's early coal mines. All coal used by Pacific Mail steamers originally had to be transported around Cape Horn. No adequate source of supply existed on the West Coast until coal began to be mined commercially on Vancouver Island in the late 1840s. Courtesy British Columbia Provincial Archives, PDP 64.

to subsidize three steamships providing once-a-month service from Panama north along the Pacific coast to Astoria on the lower Columbia River, the location of the first post office west of the Rocky Mountains. The rate for a letter from Astoria "to the United States" was forty cents (compared to ten cents for letters traveling more than three hundred miles on the East Coast), if a way could be found to carry the mail expeditiously. That same year, 1847, also saw the first federal postage stamps.

Out of a complicated shuffle of contracts and subcontracts, two New York entrepreneurs emerged with winning hands in the contest to establish mail service to the Pacific coast. Obtaining the Atlantic coast connection was a group headed by George Law, a man previously identified mainly with railroad projects but now head of the newly formed United States Mail Steamship Company. The Panama-to-Oregon route went to William Henry Aspinwall, a man of wide mercantile experience and ample means (a fortune estimated to be $400,000 in 1846), who had earlier pioneered in the construction

and operation of clipper ships to China. Aspinwall was elected president of the Pacific Mail Steamship Company following its incorporation in New York in April 1848.

The two steamship companies teamed up to provide through service between coasts, yet many observers regarded Aspinwall's Pacific Mail Steamship Company as the far weaker partner because it shouldered the heavy burdens of a transportation pioneer. Aspinwall would need all his New York financial connections and organizational skill—and considerable luck—to succeed on the West Coast where Pacific Mail proposed to serve a population that was small, scattered, and so impoverished that many settlers resorted to barter instead of money. There were no western cities comparable to New York, Philadelphia, Charleston, or New Orleans to generate traffic, or even any settlements one-tenth their size. There were no aids to navigation, and even something so basic as coal to fuel Aspinwall's steamships posed a major problem.

There was simply no precedent for what Aspinwall

was attempting. In the late 1840s the sole example of steam power on the West Coast of North America was the *Beaver,* and at this time it still burned prodigious quantities of wood and did not attempt to make a profit hauling passengers and mail. As far as Pacific Mail or anyone on the East Coast knew, no commercial deposits of coal existed anywhere along the far shore of the Americas. Aspinwall would have to establish coaling stations and haul the precious black diamonds from mines as far away as England. Historically there had been so little contact between the two coasts that no established commercial connections or patterns of travel existed for Pacific Mail to exploit.

Despite many unanswered questions, Pacific Mail progressed toward inaugurating regular mail service on the West Coast by launching the first of its three steamships, the SS *California,* on May 19, 1848, in New York. The *Panama* followed on July 29, and the *Oregon* on August 5. Nearly sisters in design (each having an overall length of two hundred feet, a beam of thirty-three feet, and a draft of twenty feet), the three ocean-going steamships were elegant vessels with masts, yardarms, sails, and state-of-the-art engines that drove huge side-wheels. Each ship cost $200,000.

The *California* cleared New York harbor on October 8, 1848, and began the long voyage around Cape Horn. Her intended destination was Astoria. She was expected to operate a monthly round-trip schedule carrying mail, passengers, and cargo between her home port of Panama and the Northwest Coast, but fate intervened in the form of a golden opportunity for Aspinwall and Pacific Mail investors. When the *California* steamed out of New York harbor, her passenger cabins were nearly empty because Americans had so little faith in rumors of fantastic gold deposits in California. Only seven passengers were aboard, none destined for points beyond Callao, Peru. Much the same thing happened when the *Falcon* cleared New York with only ninety-five passengers aboard to establish the Atlantic coast connection of the United States Mail Steamship Company.

Nothing lessened the nation's prevailing skepticism until President James K. Polk's message to Congress

on December 5, 1848. The *Falcon* was steaming down the Atlantic seaboard on the first leg of her voyage to Panama when Polk emphasized that "accounts of the abundance of gold" in California had been "corroborated by the authentic reports of officers in the public service who have visited the mineral district and derived the facts which they detail from personal observation." The president's message described the find as "extraordinary" and something that "would scarcely command belief." [5]

Polk's electrifying affirmation helped launch the mad rush to California. When the *Falcon* docked at New Orleans, another hundred passengers swarmed aboard clutching tickets to San Francisco or at least expecting to secure passage from Panama aboard the *California* when she steamed north to inaugurate the Pacific coast leg of the mail route. By a stroke of good luck, the inauguration of Pacific Mail's new mode of travel coincided with the California gold rush.

The *California* rounded Cape Horn without incident and dropped anchor off Panama City on January 17, 1849. Here Captain Cleveland Forbes found some fifteen hundred gold seekers who had recently slogged across the isthmus on jungle trails and now demanded speedy passage to San Francisco. The *California* was designed to accommodate only about 250 passengers in cabins and in steerage, and so it seemed certain that many argonauts would be left behind. What really irritated the Yankees sweltering in Panama was that when the ship had anchored earlier at Callao, Captain Forbes had filled his empty cabins with seventy passengers headed north in response to news of California gold. Many of the *Falcon*'s passengers had sailed with the understanding that they were to board the *California* at Panama for a quick trip to the goldfields. Some even brandished through tickets to California.

Tormented by heat, humidity, and fear of tropical diseases, the Yankee argonauts were simply in no mood to permit Latin Americans to beat them to California. Determined that Peruvians and other foreigners should not reap fortunes from the diggings while Americans remained behind to suffer in Panama, they staged noisy

public protests and raised the possibility of mob violence. Yankees congregated outside the shipping agents' office to protest transportation of greedy "greasers" in preference to American citizens on their way to their own country. "Throw them off," they shouted. Apparently none of the unruly crowd noted that a majority of the hated Latin Americans aboard the *California* had English surnames and were probably New England Yankees already in Peru.[6]

Pacific Mail finally resolved the ugly confrontation when it relegated passengers from Peru to hastily constructed berths and opened the *California*'s staterooms to voyagers from the United States. On February 1, after two tense weeks in Panama and with another 250 argonauts crowded aboard, the *California* weighed anchor. Her sails unfurled to catch a favorable breeze and, paddle wheels churning the Pacific into a foamy wake, the

steamer carried more than four hundred passengers and crew slowly up the coast. "Ship filled to cramnation with passengers & stores & everyone looking out for himself with peculiar aptness," Captain Forbes complained to his diary. Having become so ill that he temporarily relinquished command of the *California*, he emphasized, "I am heartily sick & tired of this life of vulgar deportment & if the present is a sample of Passengers in general bound to California, I would not command this ship for $10,000 a year, for one cannot handle pitch without soiling his hands."[7]

The *California* reached San Francisco a month later after a voyage of fourteen thousand miles that lasted 144 days. Adding to the time in transit were five stops, including another tense one, this time at Acapulco, where insubordination among firemen caused passengers to fear that the crew might desert en masse and pre-

maturely end the voyage. When the *California* finally steamed through the Golden Gate on February 28, it was cheered by residents who had gathered atop a hill to greet the ship. Thus ended the first steamer voyage between the two coasts, and thus arrived the first steamship on the Pacific coast north of Panama since the *Beaver* weighed anchor at Fort Vancouver in 1836.

Before the *California* could return to Panama for another load of passengers, all officers and crew with the exception of Captain Forbes and one of the engine-room boys deserted the ship. The steamer had also exhausted her supply of coal on the northbound trip, and the collier that Pacific Mail dispatched from England had not yet arrived. So not until May 1 did the *California* leave San Francisco for Panama. However, on the return voyage, the ship ran out of coal, and crewmen burned wooden spars, bulkheads, and even lifeboats to raise steam. Only later did they discover about a hundred sacks of the precious fuel stowed away in the keel as ballast.

All the while, congestion in Panama remained severe. Three weeks elapsed after the departure of the *California* on her maiden voyage north before the *Oregon* rounded Cape Horn and finally dropped anchor off Panama City on February 23. By then more than twelve hundred gold seekers had crowded onto the beaches, and the *Oregon*, which already carried a number of through passengers, was able to take aboard only about two hundred more.

The third and last of the Pacific Mail steamers, the *Panama*, followed two months later, sailing north on May 18 with hundreds more emigrants.

Some stranded argonauts so despaired of finding other transportation that they gave up and booked passage for home. Others bought small open boats and attempted to sail to California. Even so, Panama City remained badly overcrowded through the first half of 1849, until the three Pacific Mail steamers adopted regular schedules to San Francisco and thinned the crowd of gold seekers. The three vessels were taxed to the limit to accommodate passengers at rates that soon rose to $300 for cabin class and $150 for steerage passage from Panama to San Francisco. This was also the heyday of the ticket speculator, who could resell steerage passage for as much as $1,000. This hefty sum equaled about two years' wages in many factories in the United States.

When the *California* sailed into San Francisco on her maiden voyage in February 1849, there were no wharves. Passengers, baggage, and cargo were all transferred to shore in small boats and lighters. Thus did the first forty-niners arrive by sea. By late summer the vanguard of the long caravans from across the parched plains and the Sierra Nevada finally reached California to swell its population further. By the end of the year the number of residents had soared past the hundred thousand mark.

The great irony was that Pacific Mail had originally

A view of San Francisco from Telegraph Hill in 1850. The greatest boomtown of the California gold rush was formerly a small, somnolent pueblo named Yerba Buena. In this rapidly changing urban landscape, the ironworks and machine shops of the Pacific Mail Steamship Company at nearby Benicia emerged as the Golden State's first large-scale industrial enterprise. Courtesy Library of Congress, 408866762.11537.

been awarded a contract to provide coast-to-coast mail service to Oregon, a technicality overlooked in the rush to California. With discovery of gold in California, it was Oregon that was nearly forgotten. Finally in January 1850, an exasperated secretary of the navy ordered the Pacific Mail Steamship Company to forward mail from San Francisco to Oregon by sea no later than June 10. He further mandated that the northern terminus of the route be Fort Nisqually on Puget Sound, with a stop in each direction at Astoria. Pacific Mail balked at serving remote Puget Sound with its tiny population and proposed instead to forward mail from Astoria up the Columbia River to Portland as soon as a steamboat could be placed in service. The navy secretary reiterated that Puget Sound service must begin with the three original steamships, but Pacific Mail sent the *Carolina* to Oregon in June 1850 despite his objections. In January 1852 a subsequent navy secretary finally agreed to Astoria as the northern terminus, and there mail was put aboard steamboats for passage upriver to Oregon's main centers of population.

Though seemingly cobbled together, Pacific Mail's service was infinitely better than that offered when Oregon's nearest post office was located in Missouri. Despite its many shortcomings, the Pacific Mail Steamship Company did provide more or less regular passenger and mail connections between Oregon and the eastern states. In addition, a growing number of sailing vessels, especially the fast clipper ships serving California, strengthened commercial freight links between the nation's Atlantic and Pacific coasts.

Jungle Fever

Given the boredom and the risks of a voyage around Cape Horn, it is not surprising that most people bound for Oregon preferred the long trail overland prior to 1849, the year that a third route to Oregon—via the Isthmus of Panama—became possible. Like a journey over the Oregon Trail, the way west via the popular isthmian route evolved over time. In the early years of the land crossing, ships leaving Panama for the California goldfields were unable to accommodate more than a

fraction of the people clamoring to board them. Argonauts became idle and frustrated guests of Panama City, a place in which chauvinistic Yankees could find few redeeming values.

As if to underscore the crush of passengers it handled between Panama and California, the Pacific Mail Steamship Company in mid-1850 paid its stockholders a 50 percent dividend. The payout would not remain that high for long because so lucrative an investment opportunity quickly attracted competitors. As fast as ships reached their home ports, owners put them on California runs. Ships of all descriptions, both steam and sail, called at San Francisco Bay, where they unloaded tons of merchandise and thousands of passengers. Some were destined to sail again once their captains recruited crews, but many were either dismantled or allowed to rot at their moorings. Some, sold at much less than cost, were placed in the coastal trade between California and Oregon. By 1851, the Pacific Mail Steamship Company alone had a fleet of thirteen ships on the West Coast.

For a time Nicaragua seemed to offer a pleasant alternative to the arduous Panama crossing. The Nicaraguan isthmus was wider than that of Panama—165 miles compared to about 50 miles—but by being located farther north it shortened the length of an ocean voyage between New York and San Francisco by 1,000 miles. The crossing was further eased by Lake Nicaragua, more than 100 miles long, which extended almost to the west side of the isthmus where it was separated from the Pacific Ocean only by a ridge of hills about 16 miles across.

Fascinated by the moneymaking possibilities of a Nicaragua route, Commodore Cornelius Vanderbilt envisioned a grandiose monopoly with his steamships providing connections on both oceans to a trans-Nicaragua coach, wagon, and steamboat service. In 1849 at the age of fifty-five, the wily Vanderbilt had already accumulated a fortune by operating a fleet of ferries and steamers in the waters around New York City. The first of Vanderbilt's Independent Line ships, the *Pacific*, reached San Francisco in the summer of 1851 and prepared to challenge Aspinwall's Pacific Mail line. Fierce rate wars dropped the cost of a first-class cabin from New York to

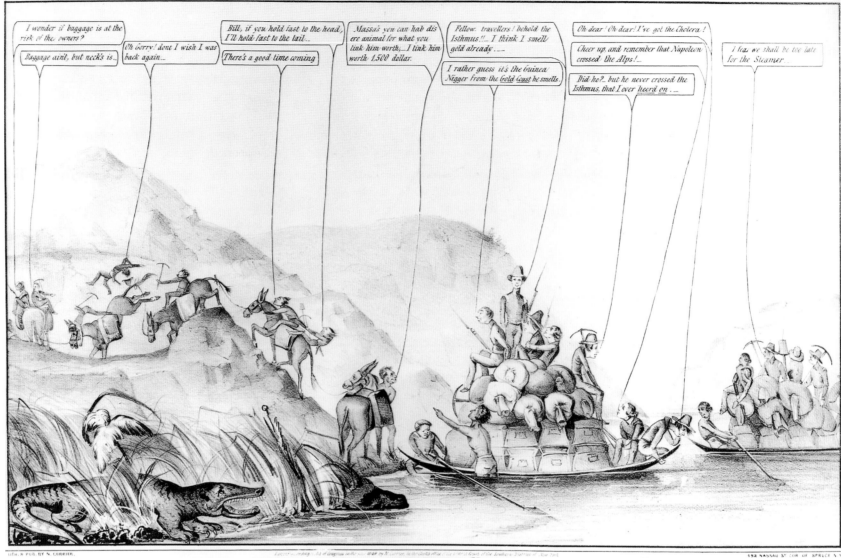

THE WAY THEY CROSS "THE ISTHMUS".

San Francisco, which had been $450 or more only a few months earlier, to as little as $100.

William Walker, a soldier of fortune, greatly complicated the commodore's economic life by conquering Nicaragua in 1855 and plunging the country into political chaos that fostered anti-Yankee xenophobia. Nicaragua remained in disorder until a firing squad in neighboring Honduras executed Walker in 1860. A short time later Vanderbilt withdrew from the contest, but not before the cutthroat competition led to races among rival vessels along the Pacific coast and to inevitable disasters at sea.

During one fifteen-month period in 1852 and 1853, four of the six Vanderbilt steamships on the Pacific coast were wrecked. Pacific Mail fared better: from 1849 to 1860 its ships carried, at a conservative estimate, a quarter of a million passengers, all without the loss of a single life by shipwreck (though some of its ships were wrecked). This feat was credited largely to the fact that Pacific Mail chose

A satirical view of the difficulties of crossing the Isthmus of Panama during the early days of the California gold rush. Courtesy Library of Congress, 408866 762 26405.

its captains with great care: most of them had been officers of the United States Navy and knew how to maintain rigid discipline over well-trained crews.

Disaster finally overtook even Pacific Mail when, on July 21, 1862, the 2,100-ton side-wheeler *Golden Gate* caught fire off the Mexican coast. Of 338 passengers on board, 223 perished; of all the disasters that befell West Coast gold rush ships, this was the most costly in terms of life and treasure ($1.4 million in specie was lost). The fact that steamers were seldom beyond the sight of land along the entire Pacific coast apparently created a false sense of security in an area that lacked accurate charts, lighthouses, buoys, and other aids to navigation and was bound by steep cliffs that made any type of emergency shore landing difficult and dangerous. Over the years dozens of vessels plying the Panama route exploded, foundered, or simply disappeared, but for most travelers the voyage remained fairly routine. The single greatest threat to life was disease. And for all who traveled by steamship between opposite coasts of the United States, the most memorable part of the trip was usually the passage through Panama, where the threat of disease was greatest.

Bayard Taylor, who headed west with the first wave of gold rushers in 1849, left behind a particularly vivid account of his troubled portage across Panama. Because no public transportation was available at that early date across the isthmus, each argonaut arranged for the services of a guide or porter in Chagres, a village of about seven hundred inhabitants, where Atlantic steamships docked. The steamy climate at Chagres was reputed to be the most uncomfortable and unhealthful on the isthmus, and since accommodations for travelers were poor and any food available was proverbially bad, Yankees tried to avoid spending even one night there by arranging for river transportation as quickly as possible.

From Chagres travelers headed across the isthmus in dilapidated canoelike boats called bungos, propelled by local residents using crude oars or poles along the narrow Chagres River to Gorgona. From there they continued by horse, mule, or foot along jungle trails to Panama City on the Pacific. During the three- to five-day trek,

no real accommodations existed at any point along the way, and torrential downpours often punctuated the tropical heat.

Taylor and his party agreed to pay a canoeist fifteen dollars to paddle them up the Chagres River toward Cruces, a village near the crest of the divide between the Atlantic and Pacific oceans. "We were scarcely out of sight of the town before he demanded five dollars a day for his labor. We refused, and he stopped working. Upon our threatening to set him ashore, in the jungle, he took up the paddle, but used it so awkwardly and perversely that our other men lost all patience. We were obliged, however, to wait until we could reach Gatun, ten miles distant, before settling matters." Before long, however, their canoeist struck up "Oh Susanna!" which he sang "to a most ludicrous imitation of the words, and I lay back under the palm leaves, looking out of the stern of the canoe on the forests of the Chagres River." Everyone relaxed for the remainder of the ride.[8]

After leaving the river, Taylor and the other argonauts traveled uphill for several days, then "came to a level tableland, covered with palms, with a higher ridge beyond it. Our horses climbed it with some labor, went down the other side through clefts and gullies which seemed impassable, and brought us to a stream of milky blue water, which, on ascertaining its course with a compass, I found it to be a tributary of the Rio Grande, flowing into the Pacific at Panama. We now hoped the worst part of our route was over, but this was a terrible deception. Scrambling up ravines of slippery clay, we went for miles through swamps and thickets, urging forward our jaded beasts by shouting and beating. Going down a precipitous bank, washed soft by the rains, my horse slipped and made a descent of ten feet, landing on one bank and I on another." At last Taylor sensed the salty air of the Pacific Ocean.

Upon reaching the city of Panama, he discovered that the ancient port had no harbor as such, that "vessels of heavy draught cannot anchor within a mile and a half of the city, and there is but one point where embarkation, even in the shallow 'dug-outs' of the natives, is practicable. The bottom of the bay is a bed of rock, which at low tide lies bare far out beyond the ramparts." Small boats transferred passengers and freight to and from steamships across these shallow waters.

Within a year, by the middle of 1850, conditions that had deterred all but the hardiest souls from attempting the trip had largely disappeared. Shipowners and agents began soliciting family groups and providing accommodations designed to assure some degree of privacy and comfort. They established regular transportation between the two coasts via small steamboats and packtrains as well as facilities for meals and shelter.

The head of the Pacific Mail Steamship Company built a new port, Aspinwall, on Panama's Caribbean shore to supersede Chagres in 1852. Three years later, after workmen completed the Panama Railroad, daily trains shortened the transit time between Aspinwall and Panama City to a matter of mere hours. During the following decade, some 400,000 passengers rode through the jungle, ocean to ocean, in only four hours—an achievement that nurtured American pride and brought huge profits to the Panama Railroad.

However, for passengers traveling through Panama between Oregon or California and the East Coast, three things did not change: the steamy weather, the ever-present possibility of contracting a fatal disease, and vegetation so lush that residents of more northerly homes groped for words adequate to describe it: "Here is the richest, densest vegetation in the world—an impenetrable tangle of mangoes, plantains, palms, oranges, bananas, limes, India rubber trees, and thousand of shrubs and parasites new to northern eyes," wrote the American newspaperman Albert D. Richardson. "Monkeys and parrots chatter on the branches," he added, and "wild beasts hide in the dingles; insects swarm in the swamps; huge reptiles drag their slow lengths along the oozy soil, darkened by thick foliage which shuts out the light of the rich tropical heavens."[9]

The main blemish in this portrait of paradise was disease. It always added to the risk of traveling across Panama. Bayard Taylor wrote in 1849 that "as we neared Gorgona, our men began repeating the ominous words: 'Cruces—mucha cólera.' We had, in fact, already heard

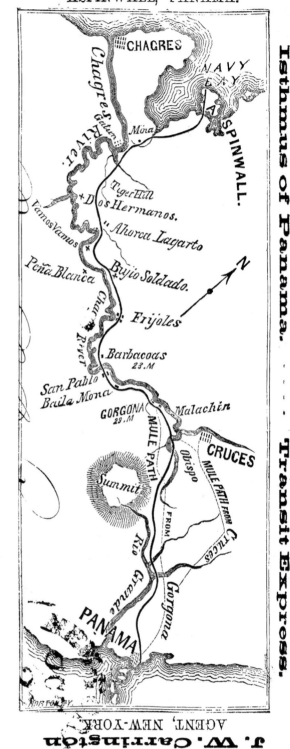

A map of the Isthmus of Panama in 1854, a year before the railroad opened. Bayard Taylor, like many of the American sojourners who followed him, found that no landscape in the world compared to the lush jungles of Panama. "No description that I have ever read conveys an idea of the splendid overplus of vegetable life within the tropics. The river, broad, and with a swift current of the sweetest water I ever drank, winds between walls of foliage that rise from its very surface. All the gorgeous growths of an eternal summer are so mingled in one impenetrable mass that the eye is bewildered." Courtesy Wells Fargo Bank

Life aboard a crowded steamer during the California gold rush. Even in the mid-1860s, when Samuel Bowles made the trip, the crush of passengers remained the main source of discomfort on Pacific steamships: "We are as thick as flies in August; four or five in a stateroom; we must needs divide into eating battalions, and go twice for our meals: would we have chairs to sit in shade around the deck, we must buy and bring them: there is no privacy; gamblers jostle preachers; commercial women divide staterooms with fine ladies; honest miners in red flannel set next my New York exquisite in French broadcloth." Courtesy Wells Fargo Bank.

of the prevalence of cholera there, but doubted, none the less, their wish to shorten the journey." There was also the threat of yellow fever (commonly called Panama or Chagres fever.) [10]

"I was well satisfied to leave Panama at the time," emphasized Taylor; "the cholera, which had already carried off one fourth of the native population, was making havoc among the Americans, and several of the *Falcon*'s passengers lay at the point of death." The ubiquitous Panama fever struck untold thousands more, many of them fatally, as did malaria and a veritable encyclopedia of other tropical diseases. In 1852 the passenger steamer *Philadelphia*, bound for New York City from Panama, lost one-third of those aboard to cholera. The bodies of the victims, many of them prominent West Coast citizens, were unceremoniously heaved overboard in a hapless effort to halt the spread of the plague. Oregon's first delegate in Congress, Samuel R. Thurston, died of a tropical fever off the west coast of Mexico in 1851.

Pacific Coast Connections

Like early crossings of Panama, the trip along the Pacific coast presented additional challenges to passengers bound for California or Oregon. "A voyage from Panama to San Francisco in the year 1849 can hardly be compared to sea-life in any other part of the world or at any previous period," recalled Taylor. His ship, the *Oregon*, "was crowded fore and aft; exercise was rendered quite impossible and sleep was each night a new experiment, for the success of which we were truly grateful. We were roused at daybreak by the movements on deck, if not earlier, by the breaking of a hammock-rope and the thump and yell of the unlucky sleeper. Coffee was served in the cabin; but many of the passengers imagined that, because they had paid a high price for their tickets, they were conscientiously obliged to drink three cups, [so] the late-comers got a very scanty allowance." [11]

As the *Oregon* steamed up the coast, Taylor observed a "succession of lofty mountain ranges, rising faint and blue through belts of cloud. . . . We were within sight of the Coast Range of California all day, after passing Cape Conception. Their sides are spotted with timber, which in the narrow valleys sloping down to the sea appeared to be of large growth."

At last Taylor's fifty-one-day odyssey drew to a close. "All is excitement on board; the captain has just taken his noon observation. We are running along the shore, within six or eight miles distance; the hills are bare and sandy, but loom up finely through the deep blue haze. . . . An hour later; we are in front of the entrance to San Francisco Bay."

Following the same route as Taylor, but sixteen years later and in the opposite direction, the newspaperman Samuel Bowles complained to his readers that "steam-ship service on the Atlantic side, between Aspinwall and New York, has been very poor for years; a disreputable monopoly, and greatly aggravating the perils and discomforts of the California voyage." He granted that "lately the management has been changed, and the service much improved; and we were in the luck to connect with a new and elegant steamship, on her first voyage." The company that Bowles praised for upgrading service on the Atlantic portion of the trip was none other than Pacific Mail, winner of the contest to dominate the Panama route and a name that became as venerable in the western transportation lexicon as the names of Wells Fargo, Ben Holladay's Overland Stage, and the Union Pacific Railroad. "The whole line of this service, on both sides of the Continent, has now passed into the hands of the

The coastal steamer Columbia *in 1855 near Port Orford Rock, one of the hazards to navigation along the southern coast of Oregon. Courtesy Oregon Historical Society, 77942, 353 P01.*

Pacific Mail Steamship Company, heretofore controlling only the steamers on the Pacific Coast. This event is hailed with delight by all California travelers, old and new," claimed Bowles. "The Pacific Company is the most notable triumph of our American steam marine, and is as popular as it has been successful." [12]

Bowles's account of his trip emphasized that, although he had spent one day longer on the Pacific side than was typical, his entire journey from San Francisco to New York took only twenty-one days. In other words, his journey from coast to coast in the mid-1860s took about a week's less time than when Taylor made the same trip in 1849. "The whole distance is five thousand miles; with fine weather and crowding the steamers up to their fullest power, it can be passed over in eighteen or nineteen days," claimed Bowles; but the trip ordinarily required from twenty-two to twenty-four days.

Even with the all risks, the Panama route had much to recommend it until the transcontinental railroad offered a suitable alternative. "No one's knowledge of California life is complete who does not go or come by the steamship and Panama route," concluded Bowles. "It offers as strange and interesting and instructive an experience as any other feature of our summer journeyings over the Continent."

For travelers Oregon-bound by steamship, however, there remained the 661-mile journey from San Francisco to Portland. Until a stagecoach line opened in 1860, they had little choice but to continue by sea, and not until late 1887 was a through railroad line opened between the two

The wreck of the Peter Iredale *lies south of the Columbia River on Clatsop Beach in 1906. Courtesy Columbia River Maritime Museum, 1984.36.5.*

cities. Over the years many thousands of people made the voyage by sea, but perhaps no one penned a more evocative account than Theodor Kirchhoff, a German who called Oregon home during the 1860s and 1870s. Being inclined to notice mundane details that most Americans took for granted, and blessed with a wry sense of humor, Kirchhoff compiled a vivid narrative of travel in the northern West during the age of steamers and stages, much as Bayard Taylor did for the early isthmian route.

One of Kirchhoff's several trips north from San Francisco to Portland began on Sunday, September 10, 1871, when he boarded the *Idaho,* a steamship belonging to Ben Holladay's North Pacific Transportation Company. "Unfortunately the steamers that ply this coast are among the world's worst," complained Kirchhoff. "Americans properly call them old tubs. Antiquated, they have been retired long ago, sold in other countries, sent here, given new names, superficially renovated, and pressed into service in these dangerous waters—to sail bravely until an accident does them in. With prodigal generosity they could be called second-rate but no generosity can make them seaworthy. Even the biggest, the old *John L. Stephens* (also referred to, tellingly, as 'the Grasshopper'), is nothing less than the arch second-rater." The *Idaho,* to which Kirchhoff entrusted his life, "though at least supposed to be safe, looked like an old tub in questionable condition." Heightening his concern was that between San Francisco and the mouth of the Columbia River the ancient vessel encountered "extensive, disagreeable, dangerous fog."[13]

Groping its way along the Oregon coast, the *Idaho* almost hit a reef. The captain then headed for the safety of open waters and waited through the night for the fog to lift. "These coastal Oregon fogs are peculiar," observed Kirchhoff. "Whence they come nobody knows. They appear in the best weather and often surprise ships in

places of greatest danger. Moreover, forest fires rage frequently here this time of year; sometimes it's hard to tell what blankets the ocean, smoke or fog. When the two mix, the smog is so dense that nothing can be seen a ship's length ahead."

On the morning of September 13, the *Idaho* steered east to regain the coast and was once more swallowed up by fog. "The captain, thinking we stood at least five miles from shore, proceeded at twelve knots. Suddenly some passengers spotted land and screamed a warning. Dead ahead loomed the rocky coast, surf breaking against it. In minutes the ship was turned and headed back to open water. The rocky coast disappeared equally fast. The pallor of officers and crew told us our escape had been narrow. Had the ship not reversed so quickly, we would have crashed. Rescue there, where cliffs thrust steeply out of waves? Impossible. Never shall I forget the terror of rocks suddenly towering black out of fog and how narrowly we had missed smashing into them." The location of Kirchhoff's near-disaster was Tillamook Head, about sixteen miles south of the mouth of the Columbia River. "What a disagreeable 'good morning' its 500-foot cliff bade us." The *Idaho* "circled again in open sea for twenty-four hours. The morning of the 14th we returned to the coast once more, in search of the Columbia, in fog. The pilot we had brought from San Francisco guided us through pea soup with more luck this time, straight into the mouth."

During the 1850s and 1860s the Isthmus of Panama loomed far larger in the transportation geography of the average resident of the Pacific Northwest than it does today. The same is true of the place where the Columbia River meets the sea, the treacherous bar that once symbolized all the geographical impediments that bound early Oregon residents within their distant and isolated corner of the United States.

Next morning the sea was calm, the boat was "running nearly on an even keel," and the rest of the voyage was delightful. Our third day on the ocean, the table was full again and everybody jolly. So I stick to my original conclusion: Take a day's sea-sickness on the way to Oregon, rather than go by stage. There is another argument in favor of this route. The fare from "Frisco" to Portland is only $25.00, while from Sacramento there by land is $45.00, both in gold.

—J. H. Beadle, The Undeveloped West *(1873)*

Oregon Unbound, or the Formative Fifties

Commercial transportation between Oregon and the rest of the United States during the 1850s meant a long and circuitous trip. Leaving the Willamette Valley for the distant east coast of North America, the traveler first sailed west. Passengers, mail, and express journeyed down the Columbia River and south along the Pacific coast to make steamship or stagecoach connections in San Francisco. For better or for worse (and for most travelers it was unquestionably for worse), anyone who entered or left the Oregon Country by commercial transportation had to overcome fear of the entrance to the Columbia River. Dangerous sandbars and currents caused much dread then; and even at the end of the twentieth century, with modern aids to navigation, dredging, and Coast Guard protection, the area still commands respect from masters of small and medium-size vessels who must carefully calculate winds, tides, and currents to predict the best time to cross the Columbia bar safely.

Not until 1860 did stagecoaches at last connect Portland and California; and not until 1864 did a combination of steamboats and stagecoaches provide travelers a shortcut east from Portland along the Columbia River and Oregon Trail to a connection with overland stage-

coaches at Salt Lake City. Until then, just about the only travelers who managed to avoid the dreaded Columbia bar were settlers in scattered villages along Puget Sound and in the Rogue River gold country just north of the Oregon-California border.

"Mere description," the navy explorer Charles Wilkes emphasized to Congress, "can give little idea of the terrors of the bar of the Columbia: all who have seen it have spoken of the wildness of the scene, and the incessant roar of the waters, representing it as one of the most fearful sights that can possibly meet the eye of the sailor." It was in July 1841 that the *Peacock,* one of several ships of the United States Exploring Expedition that Wilkes commanded, ran afoul of the Columbia bar and broke apart in the pounding surf. All lives were saved, but the loss of the sloop-of-war was more than an embarrassment for her commander, Lieutenant William L. Hudson, her one-hundred thirty officers and men, and three civilian scientists.[1]

Wilkes used the fate of the *Peacock* to dramatize the importance of Puget Sound as the only truly valuable harbor in the American Northwest. "Nothing can exceed the beauty of these waters, and their safety," he asserted, adding that no country in the world possessed a water-

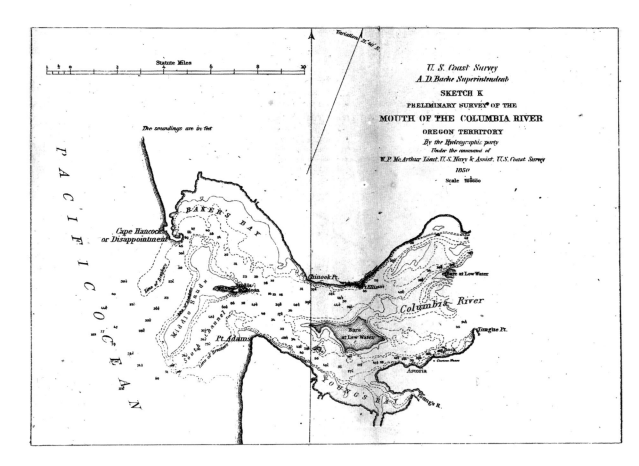

way equal to it. Because the United States had not yet acquired California, Wilkes's timely warning probably stiffened the resolve of American negotiators, who extended the international boundary north of Puget Sound in 1846 and not down the Columbia River as the British preferred.

One traveler who observed the Columbia bar and penned a vivid recollection that captured the unspoken fears of all who crossed it was Theodor Kirchhoff. Steaming north from San Francisco aboard the *Brother Jonathan* in 1863, he wrote: "At sundown we approached that interesting spot and the so-called Columbia River Bar. From a distance its breakers were imposing: foaming mountains like wild titans roaring and crashing into one another. Yet our captain claimed that the passage was quite calm then. He had been forced to stand off the Bar before daring to enter for days on end. I was glad when a pilot guided us through those 'calm' waters where, in some places, safe distance between submerged sandbars is but a steamer's length; indeed, where many a ship has gone down to a miserable end. During our 'calm' entry our *Brother Jonathan* groaned in every joint, as if the waves wanted to extinguish the fires. A couple of waves met like lovers in a kiss above the deck and my enthusiasm for the romance of those waters cooled considerably." This frightful aquatic gateway seemed to symbolize all the ways that nature had bound and isolated the Oregon Country.[2]

Working to free scattered settlements from the restraints imposed by distance and natural barriers was a generation of pioneer entrepreneurs who took their first halting steps toward providing better communication and transportation during the 1850s. From a national perspective, the key events of the decade foreshadowed

The wreck of the Peacock *as illustrated in Charles Wilkes's narrative of his* United States Exploring Expedition of 1838–1842. *Courtesy Day-Northwest Collection, University of Idaho Library, Q115.W55 1845.*

the Civil War. One dismaying episode after another—the Compromise of 1850, Bleeding Kansas, Dred Scott, and John Brown's Raid—strained the bonds of nationhood. In the West, the 1850s opened with California becoming the thirty-first state in 1850 and closed shortly after Oregon became the thirty-third state in 1859. This was also the formative decade for transportation and communication on the Pacific Slope, an accomplishment often obscured by all the noisy political confrontations that dominated the nation's consciousness. Even for settlers who seldom traveled far from their new homes in the Pacific Northwest, the enlarged and improved network of United States mail service during the 1850s redefined the spatial relationship between East and West. This proved crucial during the dark days of early 1861 when the disunited states lined up on opposing sides.

Steaming through Northwest Waters

Because of their isolation, early Oregonians dressed in styles that outsiders considered peculiar. "The men all wore black, broad-brimmed, soft hats, and long hair combed back behind their ears, covering their necks," noted one observer. Odder still were their clothes: canvas tents and wagon covers that had seen service from Missouri to the Columbia were commonly remade into raincoats. "Lined with the remnants of an old woolen garment, and with a broad collar and cuffs faced with fur of beaver or otter, these garments would pass without criticism even though their ancestry might be known to everyone by indelible marks that had been on the tent or wagon cover."[3]

The homespun ways of pioneer Oregon began to change as a result of California gold. Perhaps as many as ten thousand Oregonians rushed off to the diggings,

Length 230 Feet.
Beam 36
Hole 23
465 Tons

THE CENTRAL AMERICA & CALIFORNIA STEAM SHIP COMPANYS.

Steamer Brother Jonathan.

abandoning or neglecting their farms and creating the possibility of a severe labor shortage to hamper trade and industry in the territory. When the argonauts returned, many brought fortunes with them ranging from $1,000 to $10,000 or more. A considerable amount of the precious yellow metal started circulating in Oregon during the early 1850s, primarily in the form of "slugs," or $50 gold coins minted in San Francisco, and $5 "beavers," or gold pieces minted in Oregon. One laborer, formerly indigent, returned from California reportedly worth the princely sum of $100,000; but too many of Oregon's successful gold seekers relied solely on their stash until it was gone, and some died poor. Still other Oregonians returned from the diggings more impoverished than before: in September 1861 the Salem *Register* published a parody of the popular "Oh Susanna!" called "The Returned Californian's Song," the chorus of which claimed:

Oh, California!
You're not the land for me,
I've been and *left* the wash-bowl
I had upon my knee.

Mining fever nonetheless stimulated agricultural, milling, shipping, and mercantile enterprises in Oregon, and improved transportation to and from California. Four bushels of Oregon apples brought $500 in gold dust in San Francisco, and tons of eggs sold for a dollar apiece in the gold camps. Not far behind was the price of wheat, which soared from one dollar to six dollars a bushel; and in 1850 Oregon produced a total of 208,000 bushels of wheat, mostly in the Willamette Valley. California remained a lucrative market for Oregon-grown food and lumber well after the gold rush subsided and despite the fact that agricultural production and flour and lumber milling advanced in California also.

Although at one time during the fall of 1849 as many as twenty sailing ships awaited cargoes along the Willamette and Columbia rivers, the use of steam power to carry Oregon commodities to California markets was hardly considered. When the first non-Indian towns and villages emerged in the Willamette Valley in the 1840s, it was wind and muscle power, not steam, that linked Oregon to California and the world beyond. Not until thirteen years after the *Beaver* first fired up its boilers at Fort Vancouver in 1836 did that change.

Offering a tantalizing glimpse of the new age of steam was the *Massachusetts,* which entered the Columbia River under her own power in May 1849. Arriving from Honolulu and the East Coast, the screw-propeller army transport brought fresh troops to fight in the Cayuse War then raging east of the Cascade mountains. Constructed in Boston in 1845, the *Massachusetts* was the earliest *American* steamer to reach Oregon. She paused at Fort Vancouver where the brass cannon fired a welcoming salute, then she steamed up the Willamette River to Portland before heading back down the Columbia to load lumber for army bases in California.

Of even greater importance in the history of commercial transportation was the Pacific Mail Steamship Company's diminutive *Carolina,* which entered the Columbia River in June 1850 on her maiden voyage up the West Coast. Carrying letters, cargo, and a few passengers, she paused at Astoria, six days out from San Francisco, then continued another two days to reach Portland. The *Carolina* brought the first mail to Oregon by way of the Isthmus of Panama. Until this time mail had been dispatched north to Oregon in sailing vessels, and service was irregular. The arrival of the screw-propeller *Carolina* marked the beginning of fairly regular monthly service between California and Oregon.

For the rest of 1850, Pacific Mail steamship service extended north as far as Astoria, the mail distribution center for Oregon; but early in 1851 the company's new steamship *Columbia,* a 777-ton side-wheeler built especially for the Oregon route, inaugurated regular runs between San Francisco and Saint Helens, a new town located on the Columbia near its confluence with the Willamette. Twice a month the sturdy *Columbia* connected with Panama-bound steamships. Pacific Mail now guaranteed to make the entire run between Panama and Astoria, including all intermediate stops, within twenty-five days. In return the federal government increased its annual mail subsidy to $348,250.

The *Columbia* enjoyed a long and successful career linking California and Oregon. Though one of Pacific Mail's other ships occasionally supplemented her schedule, the *Columbia* completed 102 trips between Oregon

and California and a trip to Panama during her first five years of service. During this time she carried ten thousand passengers and eighty thousand tons of freight over a total distance of 220,000 miles. The Pacific Mail ship, incidentally, was one of two steam-powered pioneers on Northwest waters called the *Columbia.*

When the *Carolina* first reached Astoria in May 1850, an observer might have noticed the Pacific Northwest's first home-built steamboat taking shape on the riverbank. The following July the *Columbia's* maiden voyage took her upriver to Portland and later to Oregon City, where the citizenry gathered to celebrate Independence Day and welcome the first true steamboat on Oregon waters. Except for the symbolism, though, the *Columbia* offered little to brag about: only ninety feet long, doubled-ended, and resembling a ferryboat, this strictly utilitarian vessel lacked both style and comfort. Her speed seldom exceeded four to five miles an hour. The *Columbia* made two runs a month to Astoria to connect with Pacific Mail steamers from California. For passage, the travelers paid $25 each way and had to bring along their own blankets and lunch baskets.

Soon half a dozen steamboats joined the *Columbia* on Northwest waters, although the first of any size was the *Lot Whitcomb* (160 feet long with two side wheels 18 feet in diameter). Built at Milwaukie, Oregon (and named for the town's founder and pioneer merchant-miller), it utilized technology developed in Europe and on the rivers of the East and Midwest. Launched on Christmas day 1850 amid great festivities, the *Lot Whitcomb* churned between Portland and Astoria twice a week and charged passengers a fare of $12. Another steamboat plied the Willamette River between Portland and Oregon City, making one round trip a day, not including Sundays.

The *Lot Whitcomb* was a big, Mississippi-type steamboat that soon proved too expensive to operate on Oregon waters given the meager returns of the Columbia and Willamette trade. In 1853 it relocated to California in search of a more promising volume of traffic. The *Lot Whitcomb* was nonetheless significant because it launched the careers of both Ephraim Baughman, who began as a fireman, and John C. Ainsworth, its first captain and a man destined to set the pace for steamboating in the far Northwest. Ainsworth brought to Oregon the skills he had gained in Iowa, where he piloted steamboats on the upper Mississippi River.

He subsequently served as captain of the *Jennie Clark,* the first stern-wheeler to ply Northwest waters. Built at Milwaukie in 1854, she entered service the following year and steamed regularly for several years between Portland and Oregon City. Before the *Jenny Clark,* all steamboats on Northwest waters had employed either small propellers or side wheels, but propellers fouled in shallow water, bent their blades, and snapped their shafts, while side-wheelers were hard to manage in swift currents and winding channels. The *Jennie Clark,* a stern-wheeler with rudders located close to the paddle wheel, could maneuver easily through narrow channels and tricky currents.

Steam Propels Municipal Rivalries

Not long after the *Carolina* entered the Columbia River in 1850, the independent steamer *Gold Hunter* arrived at Portland to haul goods and passengers between there and San Francisco. A side-wheeler built originally for Sacramento River service, she was the first Portland-owned steamship in Oregon waters. The pride that Portlanders took in the *Gold Hunter* illustrated how municipal rivalries fueled transportation rivalries, and vice versa.

When the 1850s dawned, it was not clear which of several small settlements clustered near the confluence of the Willamette and Columbia rivers—Milwaukie, Portland, Oregon City, and even Saint Helens—would emerge to dominate water transportation in the Oregon Country. Each fledgling community aspired to become the transshipment point where workmen transferred cargoes between steamboats and oceangoing ships. At first the edge went to Oregon City. In 1844 it became the first American municipality incorporated west of the Rocky Mountains. Located at the falls of the Willamette a few miles upriver from Portland, Oregon City also served as territorial capital from 1849 to 1852. It was Oregon's largest settlement in 1850, when its 933 residents

accounted for about one-tenth of the fledgling territory's non-Indian population. Blessed with a growing population and abundant water power to run its two flour mills and five sawmills, Oregon City's prosperity and future prospects seemed assured.

But Portland was soon to cast a permanent shadow across Oregon City's aspirations. A slightly younger and smaller community, it was positioned nearer the confluence of the Willamette and Columbia rivers at a site better able to capitalize on the rapidly expanding fleet of steamboats and steamships. In 1850, though, nothing was certain about Portland's future. Then a mere village of 821 residents, it had been founded five years earlier by two New England merchants, Amos L. Lovejoy of Massachusetts and Francis W. Pettygrove of Maine. The town was located on the west bank of the Willamette River about halfway between the falls at Oregon City and the river's mouth. To one observer it seemed to huddle along a narrow stretch of lowlands between the river and the tall, dark forest that almost overshadowed the jumble of partially cleared lots and wooden buildings, brush, trees, logs, and stumps: "The site was carved out of the great forest of heavy timber which covered the whole region; the soil was deep, almost bottomless, especially after the great winter rains commenced."[4]

Giving Portland fortunes a boost were men who returned from California diggings with well-filled purses, and California dwellers who demanded all sorts of food. When the Pacific Mail Steamship Company temporarily located its northern terminus at Portland, proud residents greeted the *Columbia* as she tied up at the dock on May 1, 1851. Thereafter the regular arrival of a Pacific Mail steamship with mail, passengers, and goods from San Francisco and more distant points was a gala event for Portlanders. Thus when Pacific Mail announced late in 1853 that it would implement a plan to establish its northern terminus at Saint Helens, where the company developed a large tract of land and built a fine dock, a ripple of fear spread through Portland. The company promised to use its river steamer *Multnomah* to make connections between Saint Helens and lower Willamette towns, but that was not good enough for Portlanders.

St. Portland in 1852.

*T*his photograph shows Portland in 1852, when it had no improved streets or pavement. The outpost's main thorough-fare was Front Street, seen here, a rough dirt road, frequently muddy, that ran parallel to the river and along which stretched Portland's entire business district. Courtesy Library of Congress, 20146.

Local businessmen grew alarmed, and some of the more hot-headed ones hanged the Pacific Mail agent in effigy on Front Street. They labeled him an "enemy of Portland" and accused him of intending to fill his "private purse" at the expense of the company and the public good. Leading merchants drew up a set of resolutions that condemned Pacific Mail's relocation as "antagonistic to the best interests of Portland" and agreed to give an opposition steamship, the *Peytona*, all their freight. Without ever explaining why in public, Pacific Mail soon resumed direct service between San Francisco and Portland.[5]

As its merchants understood clearly, Portland as Pacific Mail's northern terminus gained a decided advantage over all rivals, which would remain centers merely of local transportation. When W. S. Ladd erected the first brick store in Portland in 1853, the solid structure seemed to symbolize the local business community's growing confidence in the city's future. The following year

Portland was incorporated. By the late 1850s the great merchant families—the Ainsworths, the Corbetts, the Failings, the Ladds, and the Reeds—had all begun to amass their fortunes. Nevertheless, Portland remained a curious mixture of virtuous, churchgoing New England townsfolk—for a majority of its merchants and settlers came from the American Northeast—and brawling miners and lumberjacks who frequented the port city's saloons and brothels between jobs.

During the formative decade of the 1850s, Portland won the contest to become the largest urban center north of San Francisco. It also established effective control of an immense hinterland that encompassed both the Willamette Valley and the Columbia Plateau east of the Cascade Range. By dominating the main water routes, Portland maintained an advantage over all rivals even after the coming of railroads and the emergence of new population centers in Idaho's mining districts and on Puget Sound. Only Seattle, which got off to a much slower start in 1852, would eventually surpass Portland in population and regional importance—although the latter assertion remains a matter of heated debate and the basis for an ongoing urban rivalry.

Portland's busy wharves formed the heart of a rapidly expanding transportation network that linked lofty sailing vessels and oceangoing steamships from distant ports with the steamboats that shuttled cargoes and passengers along the Columbia and Willamette rivers. Freight destined for upriver points was transferred to river steamers or to the wagons that congested Portland's muddy streets. At the docks, during busy seasons, was where merchants, farmers, and ship captains met to trade information and goods and discussed business prospects. Portland businessmen eagerly sought news of prices and market conditions from "below" (San Francisco), or "home" costs from New York.[6]

Portages: Steamboats Extend Portland's Reach

The lower Columbia River is deep and broad, forming a water thoroughfare a hundred-miles long between Portland and the sea. River transportation above Portland is a different story. The falls at Oregon City required passengers and freight traveling to and from Eugene City and other upper Willamette landings to portage at that point. In 1851 steamboats commenced service above the falls, joining with a motley fleet of flatboats, keelboats, and other craft to haul grain and produce downriver. Captain Leonard White extended steamboat navigation when he took the *Fenix* upriver to Harrisburg in 1854; three years later he pushed the *James Clinton* all the way to Eugene City. For the next forty years, stern-wheelers regularly worked their way along the Willamette to the head of navigation at Eugene, if water conditions permitted. The trip was seldom easy, even with federally funded improvements to navigation.

By the time steamboats first appeared on the Willamette, portages along both sides of the falls were well established: freight wagons and then a horse-powered railroad hauled a swelling volume of goods, produce, and passengers. The new town of Canemah, located just above the falls on the Oregon City side where there was a good natural harbor and relatively calm water, gained importance as the point where the river's commerce was transferred. In 1872 work on a lock and canal began at Oregon City, and this structure opened the following year to eliminate the tedious portage.

Steamboats plying the Columbia River above Portland faced even more formidable natural barriers than the falls on the Willamette River. About forty miles east of Portland was the first of three stretches of white water that forced Hudson's Bay voyageurs to undertake their risky and time-consuming portages. Until 1896 it required three separate steamboats to travel nearly four hundred miles up the Columbia and Snake rivers from Portland to Lewiston, gateway to the mines and forests of northern Idaho. Except for a rough, summer-only cattle trail pioneered in the late 1840s and known as The Dalles and Sandy Road, precipitous cliffs where the Columbia cuts through the Cascade Range made a land route prohibitively expensive to build.

In 1850, just below present Bonneville Dam, the town of Cascades was founded. At the mouth of Mill Creek the brothers Daniel F. and Putnam Bradford built a

large store, warehouses, a sawmill, and a wharf. In 1851 Dan Bradford extended steamboat service to the middle Columbia by building the *James P. Flint,* which shuttled between the Cascades and The Dalles. But commerce and population had not yet caught up with the ambitious new technology. Because the boat lacked enough business to turn a profit, workmen put it on skids and hauled it below the Cascades, where it resumed service in 1852.

Steam returned to the middle Columbia with the small side-wheeler *Mary,* built and launched above the Cascades in 1854. Soon, steam from the *Wasco* also wafted across the waters of the middle river. A person could travel from The Dalles to the Cascades aboard either the *Mary* or *Wasco* and connect there via a portage road with the *Belle* or *Fashion,* each of which made several trips a week between the Cascades and Portland. Soon, however, an unanticipated chain of events disrupted this schedule even as they dramatically increased the steamboat business. In the fall of 1855, one of the most serious Indian wars in the history of the Pacific Northwest erupted when tribes in distant parts of the region rose simultaneously. One major conflict burst forth east of the Cascades and another in southern Oregon, and

An advertisement for the steamer City of Eugene. *The Willamette River formed an essential artery of transportation and commerce in the early Northwest, connecting a number of towns and landings with Oregon City, Portland, and the outside world. In addition, Dayton and Lafayette were located along a navigable stretch of the Yamhill River, a Willamette tributary; Hillsboro and Forest Grove were on the Tualatin River, another navigable tributary. Courtesy Oregon Historical Society, 91836.*

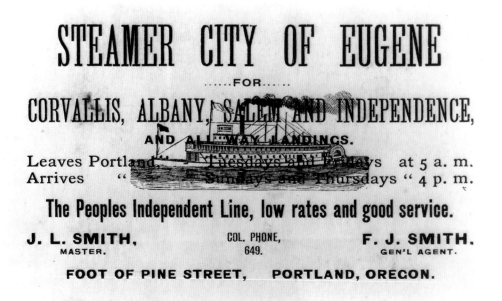

STEAMER CITY OF EUGENE

......FOR......

CORVALLIS, ALBANY, SALEM AND INDEPENDENCE,

AND ALL WAY LANDINGS.

Leaves Portland ...... Tuesdays and Fridays at 5 a. m.
Arrives " ...... Sundays and Thursdays " 4 p. m.

The Peoples Independent Line, low rates and good service.

J. L. SMITH,
MASTER.

COL. PHONE,
649.

F. J. SMITH.
GEN'L AGENT.

FOOT OF PINE STREET, PORTLAND, OREGON.

there were skirmishes on Puget Sound, but the conflicts apparently derived from the same basic cause. Native Americans everywhere became increasingly sullen and fearful as a growing number of settlers threatened their traditional way of life.

In treaties signed in the Walla Walla Valley and other places during 1854 and 1855, the Indians of newly formed Washington Territory (1853) had ceded considerable land on the Columbia Plateau and elsewhere that was soon to be opened to settlement by newcomers. But scarcely was the ink dry before news of promising new gold deposits near the old Hudson's Bay post of Fort Colville lured several small groups of prospectors up the Columbia River and across land still jealously guarded by Indians. "The settlers think the Indians will not dare attempt to prevent the Americans working the mines, *treaty or no treaty,*" reported the *Democratic Standard.* The *Oregon Argus* described the excitement among packers, miners, and townspeople at Oregon City as so great that even if President Franklin Pierce himself came to town, his presence would have attracted little attention unless he happened to bring "news from the mines." The rush to the Colville diggings threatened Indian culture east of the Cascades in a way that fur traders and missionaries never had.[7]

An incident that occurred in eastern Washington during the summer of 1855 illustrated the potential for cultural misunderstanding and conflict. When a small party of gold seekers camped for the night near the confluence of the Snake and Palouse rivers, each man scattered in search of wood to build a fire; most returned with driftwood from the riverbank. But two Indians soon appeared in camp and kicked out the fire. One of the wood gatherers hastily unfastened a gun from his saddle, but before he could shed any blood, his companions had the presence of mind to ask the Indians what the trouble was. "This is our country, and you white men pass through it. You take our grass and water, and burn our wood. For that we do not care; but this man comes to our burying-ground and cuts down the monuments on the graves of our fathers." The trigger-happy miner had made firewood from the scaffolds that Indians erected for their dead.[8]

More generally, the Indians of the Columbia Plateau insisted that Americans had no right to be there until Congress ratified the recently negotiated treaties and met their provisions concerning annuities (the federal compensation to Indians for loss of their land). Until then, Indians were determined to block all travel and settlement in the area, and they would do more than merely kick out campfires. Thus did incursions by prospectors touch off warfare and generate military business aplenty for steamboats above the Cascades. At the tiny but strategic settlement at the Cascades, Indian raiders in late March 1856 burned cabins, warehouses, and freight and left eleven civilians and three soldiers dead.

The attack at the Cascades surprised workers making improvements to the portage road. They dropped their tools and fled in all direction: "The Indians were now pitching into us right smart," recalled a man who sought shelter in Fort Rains at the middle Cascades. An Indian armed with an iron bar jumped aboard the *Mary* as she was getting up steam, but he was knocked down, scalped, and thrown overboard by agitated crewmen. After raising enough steam, "Hardin Chenoweth ran up into the pilot house, and, lying on the floor, turned the wheel as he was directed from the lower deck. It is almost needless to say that the pilot house was the target for the Indians." The *Mary* hastened to The Dalles for more troops.[9]

Three days later both the *Mary* and *Wasco,* blue with soldiers from Fort Dalles and towing a flatboat load of dragoon horses, steamed back to the upper Cascades. "The soldiers, as they got ashore, could not be restrained and plunged into the woods in every direction, while the howitzers sent grape after the now retreating redskins." About 350 regulars routed all Indians at the Cascades, losing only two soldiers in the process. The confrontation, incidentally, was Second Lieutenant Philip H. Sheridan's first taste of battle. The army recognized the strategic importance of controlling the vital portage by building a blockhouse, Fort Cascades, at the middle landing and Fort Lugenbeel at the upper Cascades. Completion of the new fortifications by late 1856 seemed to secure the area militarily, though sporadic warfare

erupted on the Columbia Plateau for another three years.[10]

Following the scare at the Cascades, a small fleet of steamboats regularly plied the middle Columbia River, hauling mainly army supplies and soldiers, except in autumn when they added emigrants who had reached The Dalles via the Oregon Trail. Many a road-weary traveler was delighted to find aboard the *James P. Flint* "articles we had not seen served at meals for many days, cold slaw, potatoes, onions, pickles, fresh beef, and butter." Sometimes the overcrowded little steamboats towed a barge loaded with more passengers, wagons, and baggage. On the upper Columbia above The Dalles there was little traffic prior to the late 1850s; but offering a hint of the dramatic changes soon to overtake the upriver trade was the flurry of mining excitement known as the Fraser River Rush of 1858. Many goldseekers from California shipped to The Dalles, which served as an outfitting point for the upper Columbia River route to the British Columbia diggings.[11]

When the Indian wars of the Columbia Plateau ended

in 1859, a well-organized steamboat service existed between Portland and The Dalles, even as attempts to probe the rivers of the upper country were just beginning. At the same time, a competitive free-for-all at the Cascades encouraged steamboatmen to forge a monopoly embracing the entire Columbia River between Astoria and The Dalles. To that end they organized the Union Transportation Company in April 1859, a combination that quickly proved too loose to withstand challenge. The Oregon Steam Navigation Company came into legal existence on December 20, 1860. Into this grand consolidation went a pool of a dozen steamboats (including the pioneer *Colonel Wright*) serving all portions of the Columbia River below its junction with the Snake. The value of Oregon Steam Navigation Company steamboats, sailboats, wharf-boats, and miscellaneous property was stated at $172,500. Enjoying a stroke of luck comparable to that of the Pacific Mail Steamship Company before the gold rush to California, the Oregon Steam Navigation Company was ready when the great rush to Idaho began in the spring of 1861.[12]

The side-wheeler Oneonta *meets the portage train at the Upper Cascades in 1876. The peaceful scene photographed by Carleton Watkins sharply contrasts with the battle that Indians waged here two decades earlier. Courtesy Oregon Historical Society, 1458 #1100a.*

Early Land Transportation in Oregon

Roads and postal service in the Oregon Country were consistently bad. Throughout the decade of the 1850s, residents complained bitterly about slow and irregular mail delivery. When separation-minded settlers living in the portion of Oregon north of the Columbia River joined in protest at Cowlitz in August 1851, beginning the process that led to the creation of Washington Territory, they stressed their transportation troubles, emphasizing that "it costs more for a citizen in the North of Oregon Territory to travel to a clerk's office or to reach a District Judge than it does a man to travel from S. Lewis, Missouri to Boston, Massachusetts and back; and much longer." [13]

At best it took a month, but usually between thirty-five and forty-five days, for mail from New York to reach Portland via Panama, and several more days passed before steamboats or stages delivered mail to upper Willamette towns. During winter months even the best roads of Oregon were practically impassable: one farmer who held back his wheat crop until the price climbed to $2.00 per bushel found the roads so bad during the winter of 1858 that he could not move his grain to the nearest steamboat landing.

Commercial transportation by land seemingly inched its way across Oregon. When an announcement for what may have been the first "stage line" west of the Missouri River appeared in the *Oregon Spectator* in late 1846, it promised to address the problem:

TELEGRAPH LINE
EIGHT OX POWER

The subscriber begs leave to announce to the public that he proposes to run an express—rain or no rain—mud or no mud—load or no load—*but not without pay*—from Oregon and Linn Cities to Tuality Plains during the ensuing season—leaving the two former places on Mondays and Thursdays, and the Plains on Wednesdays and Saturdays. The 'cars' will be covered and every accommodation extended to passengers. For freight or passage, apply to the subscriber, proprietor and engineer, at Linn City.

October 29, 1846   *S. H. L. Meek*[14]

Meek's brave announcement, however, did not herald the dawn of a new day for commercial transportation by land. Rather, it was typical of the crude and piecemeal development of early stagecoach lines across the northern West. Perhaps more promising were developments in southern Oregon where the mining frontier extended north from California.

Throughout 1851, prospectors from California's Shasta area had crossed the Siskiyou Mountains to probe for pay dirt in the gulches and crevices of the Rogue River country. Two packers, late in 1851 or early 1852, made a rich strike, and at the site of their discovery the town of Jacksonville, at first only a tent camp, sprang into existence. Perhaps as many as two thousand people, mainly Californians, had collected in the vicinity of Jacksonville by the summer of 1852.

Demand for provisions increased along with the population, but because of severe drought local farmers were initially unable to reduce Jacksonville's dependence on distant suppliers. Later, when winter snows closed mountain trails, prices for life's necessities rose sharply. Seasonal price hikes would become familiar to miners in every camp in the northern West that depended on pack-trains. Wagon freighting soon supplanted the packers, but hauling freight and passengers through the mountainous terrain of southern Oregon remained difficult and expensive.

In Oregon west of the Cascades, freight service continued to improve during the 1850s, as did an expanding network of stagecoach lines. Most early stage lines were small outfits that provided only local service, but beginning in 1855 the Pioneer Line offered tri-weekly overland transportation between Oregon City and Corvallis: "The Stages are of Concord manufacture," assured the proprietor, and are "comfortable and safe. The horses are capable, and make good time, and the drivers are reliable." The following year, pioneer stagemen extended service still farther south by establishing weekly schedules between Corvallis, Eugene City, and Winchester on the Umpqua. From that point to Jacksonville, freight continued by pack train and wagon. During the rainy season the roads between Eugene City and Winchester

were so bad that mail and passengers had to be conveyed by horseback. Poor as the road was between Jacksonville and the towns of the Willamette Valley, freighters favored that route over the hazardous but shorter one from Crescent City. Southern Oregon thus remained part of Portland's commercial hinterland.[15]

North of the Columbia River in newly created Washington Territory, the evolution of stagecoaching was not unrelated to transportation improvements in the Willamette Valley—where by 1857 a stage line between Portland and Salem regularly covered the fifty miles in a single day—but it was far more limited in scale. The waters of Puget Sound provided a magnificent transportation link among all communities of any consequence and diminished the need for an extensive

network of roads and stagecoach lines. That was not the case, however, for the land bridge between Puget Sound and the Columbia River.

The first overland passenger service out of Olympia, southernmost port on Puget Sound, began in 1853, although it seemed at first to have been only an adjunct to wagon freighting. Outfits from Olympia usually met Cowlitz River boats coming north from the Columbia Valley, and seeking to augment their freight business, they offered to transport passengers to and from the river landing. As the number of through passengers increased, stagecoaches supplanted freight wagons. The first regular stage vehicles running in western Washington Territory were mudwagons, a name appropriate for the conditions: Ezra Meeker, a prominent pioneer, noted how early trav-

Jacksonville in 1856: the principal trading center of southern Oregon's mining country was accessible only by narrow pack trails that extended from northern California over the Siskiyou Mountains, south from the Willamette Valley, and east from Scottsburg near the mouth of the Umpqua River, and later from Crescent City on the California coast. Mexican packers and their mule trains laden with merchandise became a familiar sight as they filed into the little mining center. Courtesy Southern Oregon Historical Society, 14685.

elers to and from Olympia were conveyed "over either the roughest corduroy or deepest mud, the one bruising the muscles the other straining the nerves in anticipation of being dumped into the bottomless pit of mud."[16]

In 1860 the first close connection between Portland and Olympia was established with steamboat service between Portland and Monticello, or sometimes nearly forty miles farther inland to Cowlitz Landing, and thence by stage to Olympia. The trip still required two to three days because of the quagmire called a road. When Speaker of the House Schuyler Colfax visited the Pacific Northwest in 1865, a reporter complained that "in all our journey of more than three thousand miles from the Missouri, the road from the Cowlitz to Olympia is by far the worst we have traveled. It is even now unfit for anything but pack animals to pass over." The ordeal of the portage did not end until the Northern Pacific opened a railway line between Tacoma and Kalama in the early 1870s.[17]

Trend Setter of the West Coast

Several stage companies provided local transportation within Oregon and Washington during the 1850s, but the first move to connect the Pacific Northwest with anywhere else came from California, the transportation trend setter of the West during the formative fifties. Any technological or financial innovation pioneered there would invariably influence early transportation entrepreneurs in the Oregon Country. California steamboat and stagecoach lines served as models for Oregonians to emulate.

During the palmy days of the California gold rush, from 1848 to 1854, miners extracted more than five million troy ounces of gold from the diggings, and this new wealth fueled the growth of San Francisco. Prior to 1849 its population had been a mere 810 people; during the next five years it grew to over 50,000 people and emerged as the commercial metropolis of the West Coast. During the boom years a virtual revolution in transportation occurred on Pacific waters with the rapid expansion of a fleet of steamships and tall clippers. Only a few months after the Pacific Mail's steamship *California* landed the

first forty-niners in San Francisco, steamboats in ever increasing numbers churned across the bay and up inland waters to Sacramento and other jumping-off points for the gold country. Some sternwheelers probed up the Sacramento River as far north as Red Bluff, where they loaded golden cargoes of grain from valley farms and ranches.

Early in 1854 several owner-captains concluded that collaboration earned them bigger returns than unrestrained competition, and thus they formed a combination known as the California Steam Navigation Company. For many years it dominated steamboat traffic on the Sacramento and San Joaquin rivers. It was so profitable that it paid dividends of 300 percent before being sold in the early 1870s to the Central Pacific Railroad. Critics denounced the steamboat monopoly, but formation of large-scale corporate enterprises to manage public transportation was clearly more than a passing fad. In fact, only months before the steamboatmen united, most of California's stagecoach operators formed a monopoly of their own; and soon similar cartels appeared on the Columbia and Willamette rivers.

Like the steamboatmen, stagecoach operators rapidly extended their lines outward from San Francisco and Sacramento to remote corners of California during the early 1850s. In dry weather the flat bay shore extending south from the Golden Gate to San Jose provided a natural roadway for the first stagecoaches in California, but it was Sacramento that emerged as the primary hub of activity. As early as 1851, long-distance stage lines extended north from there to Shasta City, a mining boomtown located west of present Redding that soon became the main jumping-off point for diggings in southern Oregon. Shorter lines extended east from Sacramento into the Mother Lode country.

By 1856 Sacramento had emerged as the stagecoaching capital not just of California but of the entire nation, and the California Stage Company became the largest transportation enterprise of its kind in the United States. A joint-stock firm with a capitalization of a million dollars, it was organized in December 1853 to combine at least five-sixths of all stage lines in California and commenced

Lith. & Pub.by.J.Childs152.late 84.S.9.3.St.Phil.a

WRECK OF THE STEAMSHIP CENTRAL AMERICA.

APPALLING DISASTER.

On Saturday, September 12th, 1857, Capt. Herndon, bound to New York, from California, with the Pacific Mails, Passengers and Crew, to the number of 592 persons, and treasure to the amount of over $2,000,000, foundered in a hurricane, off Cape Hatteras.

operations on New Year's Day. Within three years the young giant operated twenty-eight daily stage lines over nearly two thousand miles of road; had federal contracts for carrying the mail on about two-thirds of that distance; owned 1,500 horses and 205 Concord stagecoaches and mud wagons; and employed 300 drivers, agents, relay station keepers, hostlers, and others. Not until a decade later, when Ben Holladay gained control of nearly all staging over the central overland route from the Missouri River to Salt Lake City and northwest into Montana and Idaho, was there a stagecoach operation equal to this enterprise. Yet, remarkably, though California Stage linked San Diego in the south to Yreka in the north and

maintained numerous feeder routes in between, not a single one of its coaches (or those of any other company) linked California with another state. Like Oregon, California was an island isolated by an ocean of land.[18]

Presiding over the fortunes of the California Stage Company was young James E. Birch, a native of Providence, Rhode Island. Having conquered all competitors in California, this ambitious twenty-five-year-old dreamed of breaking the bonds of geography by extending a stage line across three deserts to link East and West for the first time with regularly scheduled commercial transportation by land. As the head of a stagecoach empire large enough to distribute the equipment and stock needed to maintain service between Sacramento and St. Louis, Birch became obsessed with the dream of improved land transportation between the two coasts. In the Far West he championed what only a few years earlier would have been considered a fantastic project. His main instrument of conquest was to be the Concord coach, which when pulled by four- or six-horse teams symbolized the stagecoach era, if not the frontier West itself.

Commercial transportation within California, where free-spending miners paid outrageous sums for fast and frequent service to and from the diggings, required no federal subsidies, but running a successful line across the West would be impossible without help from Capitol Hill. But during the 1850s the wheels of Congress turned slowly, and often not at all because of the growing sectional enmity that stymied rational consideration of the best overland route between East and West. Invariably the question arose: would the route extend through southern or northern territory?

When Birch took the first concrete steps to run a mail coach line across the desert Southwest, he had a personal as well as financial interest in the venture. For several years the rising entrepreneur had frequently commuted by ship between his home in New England and his business on the Pacific coast. He dreamed of an alternative route by land, but because of congressional dithering on the mail subsidy, Birch was doomed to ride the steamships a while longer.

And doomed he truly was. On September 12, 1857, thirty-five days after the news first broke in New York City, California learned of the sinking of the palatial sidewheel steamship *Central America* in a hurricane off Cape Fear on the North Carolina coast. Among the 491 passengers lost at sea was the energetic young president of the California Stage Company. At least a stagecoach passenger was unlikely to drown at sea, a simple fact not lost on would-be travelers between Portland and California who yearned for a land alternative to seasickness and the dreaded Columbia bar.[19]

During the formative 1850s public transportation on the West Coast expanded outward from two hubs—Portland and San Francisco–Sacramento. From north and south, stagecoach lines advanced ever so tentatively toward one another in the mountainous country separating Oregon from California. In 1856 the California Stage Company extended a line from Yreka to Jacksonville. The tri-weekly stage to Jacksonville ran only during the summer months until 1859, when an Oregon company completed a road over the Siskiyou range, enabling stage service to continue all winter. At last, in 1860 the California Stage Company forged an overland link between Sacramento and Portland. The giant of West Coast staging had in hand a four-year federal contract to carry mail daily between California and Oregon for $90,000 per year, paid in gold. The running time from April to December was seven days; during the rainy months from January to March, it was twelve to fourteen days, or about one hundred miles every twenty-four hours. Support for the land route came mainly from Oregonians who had long complained about poor mail service by the Pacific Mail Steamship Company.

The *Sacramento Union* undoubtedly spoke for many travelers when it anticipated that a person "who has no desire to risk his life on the rough coast of Oregon, can take a quiet seat in a stage, pass through a most interesting section of the country, and reach Portland at his leisure." For this reason the paper urged that the starting of a daily mail stage to Portland "should be announced by the firing of cannon and other indications of enthusiasm."[20]

On September 15, 1860, the first coach, drawn by four horses, reached Portland from Sacramento. Thereafter, every morning at six o'clock, Concord coaches marked "Overland Daily Mail" above and "California-Oregon Stage Company" below left their respective terminals to begin the 700-mile journey to Oregon or California. Along the route were some sixty stations where stages stopped to allow passengers some measure of rest. To stock the line had required twenty-eight coaches, thirty stage wagons, and five-hundred head of horses, in addition to fourteen district agents, seventy-five hostlers to care for the stock, and thirty-five drivers. Except for the Butterfield line recently opened between Missouri and

*W*ell *after the 1850s mining rush was over, Ashland, Oregon, exuded prosperity, as this late nineteenth-century photograph shows. Among the businesses to be found in any respectable town was the livery stable, which boarded horses and offered carriages for hire. The equivalent at that time of a modern service station combined with a rental car agency, livery stables not only catered to special-occasion customers, such as wedding and theater parties, but also often sold or traded saddles, wood, and grain. These places were redolent with the odors of horse liniment, manure, hay, leather, tobacco, and the ammonia smell that some claimed aided the tubercular. Courtesy Southern Oregon Historical Society, 7399.*

California, this was the longest run in the United States. In the opinion of the *Sacramento Union,* this connection was the beginning of "an important era in the history of California staging." Its main value was that it did away with "the delays of the uncertain Ocean mail service." That was true, but for speed the coastal voyage was still best. In 1862 the record for steamships between Portland and San Francisco was 69 hours, considerably less than half the stage's 151-hour time.[21]

Daily mail service also extended north from Portland to Puget Sound in 1860. Thus with the California Stage Company's system as the vital link, the growing network of Pacific Northwest steamboats and stage lines connected to overland stages reaching east from the Golden State to clasp hands with lines reaching west from hubs in Missouri. Oregonians at last had commercial transportation by land, and not just to California: now they could continue across the West from San Francisco to Saint Louis on stage lines established by successors to the visionary James Birch.

Steam has placed Oregon within two days of San Francisco, and within a few hours of the Upper Columbia. Steam carries us over the interior railroads, and for hundreds of miles, even to the base of the Rocky Mountains, through the intricacies and maelstroms of the Snake system, lands us in the heart of a distant region so beautiful, so well adapted to the homesteads of millions, so rich in mineral and agricultural wealth, as to throw into the shade even the visionary dreams of the great Pathfinder himself [John C. Fremont]. Steam has done this for Oregon, and is destined to do still more. Even as I write, the mountains are being excavated and crushed 'neath the power of steam.

—C. Aubrey Angelo, Sketches of Travel in Oregon and Idaho *(1866)*

The Pulse of a Continent

Steam power and an expanding network of telegraph lines noticeably quickened the pulse of North America during the late 1850s, making communication between East and West faster than ever. Even so, only in mid-March 1859 did Portland residents learn that Oregon had become the nation's thirty-third state, although President James Buchanan had signed the legislation a month earlier, on February 14. The welcome news traveled to Oregon in the fastest way possible: by telegraphic dispatch to the end of the wire in Saint Louis, by overland stage to San Francisco, and by the coastal steamship *Brother Jonathan* to Portland. The elapsed time was twenty-nine days. The announcement continued by horseback to the capitol in Salem.[1]

The speed of communication between East and West improved dramatically the following year when on April 3, 1860, the Pony Express commenced between Saint Joseph, Missouri, and Sacramento, California. A letter could now dash between those two places within ten days. The cost was five dollars per half ounce, but the elapsed time was ten days less than the circuitous overland mail route that stretched across the desert Southwest from Missouri to California. A transcontinental telegraph line was completed to California in

October 1861, but news from the East still traveled north from the Golden Gate to Portland at the plodding pace of a stagecoach or coastal steamer.

Finally, on March 5, 1864, the first through telegraph message from California and points east reached Portland, and the *Oregonian* commemorated the event with an extra edition containing news from New York *only twenty hours old!* In a formal celebration three days later, the mayors of Portland, Oregon, and Portland, Maine, exchanged telegrams. For residents of the far Northwest the new telegraph link ended an era of isolation, but until 1869, when a transcontinental railroad finally joined California and the East, travel between Oregon and the Atlantic seaboard for both passengers and freight still required at least a month. Still, many Oregonians recalled when the same journey took six or seven months. The pulse of the continent—the flow of information, goods, and people—was visibly quickening.[2]

The First Transcontinental Railroad

During the 1850s, improvements in transportation and communication usually occurred within two separate but related spheres of activity. On one hand were upgraded land and water links between hubs like Sacramento and

GRAND PATENT INDIA-RUBBER AIR LINE RAILWAY TO CALIFORNIA.
COMPETITION DEFIED.

Portland and their hinterlands; on the other were better overland connections between East and West. After steamship service first linked both coasts of the United States via Panama in 1849, the most notable improvement to the route was the completion six years later of the 48-mile-long Panama Railroad, which transformed a five-day jungle ordeal into a jaunt of only four or five hours. North America's first transcontinental railroad inaugurated service in 1855 with 10 woodburning locomotives, 22 passenger cars, and 123 freight cars and offered a vista unlike any other in the Western Hemisphere: "Eleven miles from Panama we crossed the summit, through a natural gap three hundred feet above the ocean. From these mountains one can see both Atlantic and Pacific at once." Only the most jaded traveler was not impressed.[3]

Even with the ever-present threat of disease, a railroad journey across the isthmus became something of a romantic adventure for passengers from West Coast steamers who upon arriving in Panama, "hastened down

Quickening the pulse of the continent: a cartoon of the "Grand Patent India-Rubber Air Line Railway to California" satirizes the desire of Americans for faster, better public transportation to the West Coast. Courtesy Library of Congress, 408866 762 768.

An accident in 1856 on the Panama Railroad near Gatun, nine miles from the new port of Aspinwall. The tropical landscape just outside the cars never ceased to awe travelers from northerly latitudes. Courtesy Library of Congress, 408866 762 1636.

the hot, narrow, winding streets to the railway station at the water's edge; and elbowed through the dense, panting crowd into the cars, which have cane seats, and wooden blinds instead of glass windows. The locomotive shrieked, and we moved out of the city, following endless curves, slowly winding around foot-hills and through jungles, toward the summit of that narrow neck of land which divides two unbounded seas."

Although the Panama Railroad cost $6.5 million to build, it had the distinction of returning to its owners profits far greater than those generated by any other rail-

road its length in the world. But construction and maintenance costs were also inordinately high. "The railroad itself seemed well built, and fairly managed. It was said, indeed, to rest literally on human bodies, so many poor fellows perished in the deadly miasmas, while constructing it," said General James Rusling, repeating an often told horror story. The journalist Albert D. Richardson, who rode the line when returning from a West Coast trip in the mid-1860s, emphasized that "again and again its work was suspended; for the fever-breeding air poisoned all who breathed it. Natives, West Indians, Irish, French,

Germans, Austrians, Coolies, and Chinese were successively employed as laborers, and to all it proved fatal. The forty-eight miles, ridged with graves, are said to have cost a man's life for every sleeper [tie]. Jamaica negroes and whites from our northern states bore the climate best, and finished the work. Think of men breathing fever, penetrating cane-brakes, wading swamps, fighting noxious insects, dodging boa-constrictors, cougars and crocodiles, and constantly braving death, for one or two dollars per day!"

The popular myth claimed that during five years of construction one man died for every tie, but this was nonsense. As John H. Kemble calculated, there were 99,294 ties and the number of men employed was about fifteen thousand, "requiring that each man should have died over six times to make 'a life for every tie.'" Among white laborers, of whom there were about six thousand, there were 293 deaths from the beginning of construction until completion of the railroad.[4]

On Panama's Atlantic coast, trains met ships at the recently constructed port of Aspinwall located on Navy Bay about four miles from the mouth of the Chagres River. The terminus was named for the New York magnate who headed both the Panama Railroad and the Pacific Mail Steamship Company. The government of New Granada never recognized the Yankee name, and on official maps it was always Colón, yet not until some forty years later did the name Aspinwall disappear from common usage. By either name, the town became a stop familiar to a generation of coast-to-coast travelers, though few found it pleasant.

Surrounded by pestilential swamps and shut off from the cooling sea breezes, Aspinwall was extremely depressing to most voyagers. Hubert Howe Bancroft said of it in 1851 that the "very ground on which one trod was pregnant with disease, and death was distilled in every breath of air." Glued furniture fell apart, "leather molds, and iron oxidizes in twenty-four hours." Some American travelers who paused in Aspinwall's motley hotels were afraid to eat any meat, fearing that it might be cooked monkey. Later travelers found the port only slightly less oppressive. "Aspinwall has no past like Panama [City],

no present and no future but what the railroad and steamships make for it," avowed Samuel Bowles.[5]

The Panama Railroad not only quickened the crossing of the isthmus—two trains, one passenger and one freight, operated daily from each terminus—but also reduced the cost of transportation dramatically, although heavy freight continued to go by way of clipper ships around Cape Horn. Valuable cargoes invariably went across the isthmus. A total of $710 million in gold and silver was shipped east from San Francisco by way of Panama from 1849 to 1869, and such shipments were particularly important during the Civil War when West Coast gold helped to boost the Union's struggling economy. Embattled Confederates laid plans to capture some of the treasure ships and trains but apparently never carried them out.

For nearly fifteen years the isthmian route experienced

PACIFIC
Mail Steamship Co's

THROUGH LINE
—FROM—
SAN FRANCCISO TO NEW YORK!
CARRYING THE U. S. MAIL, BY
STEAMERS OF THE PACIFIC MAIL STEAMSHIP CO.
ON THE PACIFIC AND ATLANTIC,
AND BY
THE PANAMA RAILROAD FROM PANAMA TO ASPINWALL.
FROM SAN FRANCISCO,
Leaving the COMPANY'S WHARF, foot of FOLSOM Street,
AT 11 O'CLOCK, A. M.,
ON THE 10th, 19th AND 30th OF EVERY MONTH,
EXCEPT WHEN SUCH DATES FALL ON SUNDAY, WHEN THE DEPARTURE WILL BE ON THE SATURDAY PRECEDING.
CHILDREN BETWEEN 6 and 12 years,.....HALF FARE.
"   "   2 and 6 years,.....QUARTER "
"   UNDER   2 years,.............FREE.
100 lbs. Baggage allowed each adult passenger. For all over this weight, 10 cts. per lb. must be paid to the Purser on board.
No Merchandise or Bedding will be taken as Baggage. Baggage checked through in charge of Baggage Master, over the entire route.
Passengers berthed through. An experienced Surgeon attached to each ship. Medicines and professional services free of charge.
OLIVER ELDRIDGE, Agent, P. M. S. S. Co.,
CORNER SACRAMENTO AND LEIDESDORFF STS.

An advertisement for the Pacific Mail Steamship Company in 1866 misspelled San Francisco but otherwise gave a clear picture of ocean transportation between Oregon and the East Coast. Courtesy Oregon Historical Society, 91758.

heavy traffic, with an annual average of thirty thousand passengers and considerable express and high-value freight. The number of people rose year after year, peaking just before the rails of another transcontinental railroad met at Promontory, Utah, in 1869. Until then, the distant passage through the jungles of Panama formed an integral part of the transportation geography of a generation of Oregonians.

Oregon and the Southern Overland Route

During the 1840s the stream of settlers moving west increased from a mere trickle that slowly made its way to Oregon each year to a mighty river that engulfed California during the gold rush. An estimated 100,000 people went to California in 1849 in pursuit of wealth. When California became a state the following year, it claimed a population of around 300,000 residents. The pace of immigration to the arid interior West was much slower, but by 1848 the Mormon pioneers had established Salt Lake City, soon to become the largest settlement between the Missouri Valley and the Pacific coast. Little more than a decade later the Pike's Peak gold discoveries drew thousands of miners and settlers to Colorado and the new boomtown of Denver. Because water transportation did not serve the fastest growing settlements in the interior, and railroad connections remained yet another decade in the future, stagecoaches and freight wagons became the two vehicles that won the hinterland West during the 1840s and 1850s.

Stagecoaching in California and Oregon originated with numerous small operators, most of whom managed to obtain federal contracts to carry mail (and an occasional passenger) between steamboat landings and inland settlements. Small outfits created to meet local transportation needs often coalesced into giant statewide enterprises like the California Stage Company, and coaching across other parts of the West made significant strides as well. In July 1850 mail stages commenced running between Independence, Missouri, and Santa Fe, New Mexico, then a newly acquired part of the United States and terminus of the important trade route between that region and Missouri.

However, not until 1856 did the Post Office Department subsidize transcontinental mail service along a land route to the Pacific coast. That contract went to the California stage magnate James E. Birch to support semimonthly runs between San Antonio and San Diego on a thirty-day schedule. For an annual subsidy of $149,800 he was to begin service in mid-1857 and continue it for four years. Until that time California and Oregon had only semimonthly, thirty-day mail service by steamship from the East Coast via Panama or a trickle of letters carried on muleback via Salt Lake City.

Birch made arrangements to stock the new route, but on August 20, 1857, shortly before commencement of the first mail and passenger service, he bade his California associates goodbye and boarded a steamer bound for Panama on the first leg of what he mistakenly thought would be a routine journey to attend to business and family matters on the East Coast. He was traveling on the last day of August when the pueblo of San Diego enthusiastically greeted the safe arrival of the first mail from San Antonio. "An old cannon in the plaza was booming away, bells and 'a hundred anvils' were ringing, there was cheering from an ecstatic crowd. Mail through from San Antonio! Thirty-eight days! Thirty-four days' traveling time!"[6]

Any more desolate country than this route crossed would have been difficult to imagine, as would be two terminal points more remote from population centers. Critics called it a line that extended from "from no place through nothing to nowhere." With the exception of Tucson (a cluster of adobe buildings that probably had perhaps as many as two hundred residents), the only settlement of consequence along the entire line was El Paso, at the border with Mexico.[7]

Mail and passengers were scheduled to leave both ends of the line at six o'clock on the mornings of the ninth and twenty-fourth of each month. The fare was $200, which included meals along the road. Passengers were supplied with provisions during the trip, except when coaches stopped at one of the infrequent public houses scattered along the line, where the travelers paid for their own meals. Each person was allowed thirty pounds of personal baggage, "exclusive of blankets and arms." An advertisement promised that passengers and express would travel in new coaches "drawn by six mules over the entire length of our Line, excepting from San Diego to Fort Yuma, a distance of 180 miles, which we cross on mule back." An escort of six mounted guards traveled through Indian country with each mail train. At San Diego the California Steam Navigation Company offered steamship connections north to San Francisco. Passengers arriving at San Antonio could transfer to "a Daily Line of Four-Horse Coaches to Indianola, from which place there is a Semi-Weekly Line of splendid Mail Steamers to New Orleans." The significance of the San Antonio and San Diego Mail Line was that it was the first stage outfit to haul both passengers and mail across the full breadth of the American West.[8]

Rudimentary as the San Antonio and San Diego Mail Line was, the thirty-year-old Birch expected this first transcontinental stage link to function as part of his future expanded system, but his untimely death at sea was the first of two misfortunes that overtook what was popularly and satirically known as the Jackass Mail line. The second occurred when the administration of President James Buchanan awarded a lucrative mail contract along a major portion of the existing line to John Butterfield and Company, a group of seven New Yorkers that included William G. Fargo, who would establish the first truly transcontinental stagecoach service. Butterfield himself was one of the founders of the American Express Company and a personal friend of President Buchanan's; his associates were all executives of the nation's four giant express companies: Adams, American, United States, and Wells Fargo. The enterprise receiving the federal subsidy was to be officially designated the Overland Mail Company, but it was always known and remembered as the Butterfield Overland Mail.

The postmaster general Aaron V. Brown, a proslavery Tennesseean, specified that he would accept as eastern terminals only Saint Louis, Missouri, and Memphis, Tennessee. The routes from these two places converged at Fort Smith, Arkansas, and ran from there south and west, following much of the southern route pioneered by the Jackass Mail to reach San Francisco. However,

when news of the Butterfield contract was released, showing its $600,000-a-year subsidy and 2,795-mile southwestern route, newspapers of the North and West howled in protest. The *Chicago Tribune* labeled it "one of the greatest swindles ever perpetrated upon the country by the slave-holders." The *Sacramento Union* blasted it as "a foul wrong; a Panama route by land." New York editors, protesting that the "Oxbow route" managed to avoid every population center and ran through impassable savage-infested deserts, predicted that it would prove too expensive to operate even with its "scandalous subsidy." Though these critics would have preferred the central route through South Pass and Salt Lake City, the southern route did have the advantage of fewer mountains to cross and far less snow.[9]

The federal government granted John Butterfield's Overland Mail Company a full year to prepare for operation of its semiweekly service. Although most of the route ran through wild and semiarid territory, the terrain was not particularly difficult for wheeled vehicles to cross, for the trail was mostly across open prairies and deserts, with few large rivers or high mountains. Butterfield needed time to establish a support structure for his stagecoaches by building, stocking, and maintaining relay stations at frequent intervals, especially west of the Pecos River where the route crossed elevated tablelands nearly devoid of wood and water. At places where Indian raids on the stock seemed likely, corrals had to be surrounded by thick sod or adobe walls six to eight feet high.

Finally, on September 16, 1858, the Overland Mail Company simultaneously dispatched its first coaches from East and West on their transcontinental journeys. (The one from Missouri actually left Tipton, the western end of the Pacific Railroad that connected to Saint Louis.) When the mail coaches reached their respective destinations, they were greeted by brass bands, loud hurrahs, and even louder speeches. In Saint Louis a long procession led by brass bands escorted the first overland mail through city streets to the post office. There was much to celebrate in California: from 1849 to 1858 the press depended on Pacific Mail steamships for eastern

and European news, but the inauguration of Butterfield's stagecoaches now meant receiving news twice a week instead of semimonthly by ship. The travel time was only three weeks compared to twenty-five to thirty-five days previously. Saint Louis became the clearinghouse for all eastern and European news bound for the West Coast.

Butterfield's stages regularly crossed the western half of the continent in "a period of time not to exceed twenty-five days" at an average speed of four miles per hour, although the company's first published schedule in September 1858 contained this caveat from Butterfield:

"This Schedule may not be exact—Superintendents, Agents, Station-men, Conductors, Drivers and all employees are directed to use every possible exertion to get the Stages through in quick time, even though they may be ahead of this time. If they are behind this time, it will be necessary to urge the animals on to the highest speed that they can be driven without injury."[10]

Butterfield stagecoaches hauled passengers, mail, and express (including the news that Oregon had become a state). The overland mail line gradually gained in favor until by 1860 more letters were sent via the Butterfield route than via ocean steamers. Even the British regularly shipped sealed bags of letters overland to San Francisco and British Columbia during the intervals between departure dates of the Panama steamers.

Despite its record of success, Butterfield's operation across the Southwest was as doomed as Birch and his Jackass Mail, which actually managed to outlast the Overland Mail Company across parts of the desert by a few months. Northern opposition to the so-called Oxbow route intensified along with sectional controversy. Without waiting for formal disruption of the Union, a bill introduced in the United States Senate early in 1861 directed the postmaster general to take steps to shift mail service to California from the southern to a central route that would extend from Saint Joseph, Missouri, to Sacramento. Both houses of Congress would approve the measure by March 12, but the line had already ceased running six days earlier because pro-Southern raiding parties drove off Butterfield's livestock, claimed his rolling stock, and destroyed bridges along the route. In short, Confederate zealots in Texas ripped out the stage line "by the roots" and halted service. After following the Oxbow route for nearly three years, Butterfield's remaining stagecoaches relocated to the new central overland route where on July 1, 1861, they commenced daily service.

The Central Overland Route

Unlike the southern overland route, which originated with James Birch and California stage interests, the central route was shaped in large measure by the growing volume of freight and passenger traffic heading west across the Great Plains. Located on high ground with a commanding view of the Missouri River was Independence, for many years the best known of the trail heads. Since the early 1830s it had been the outfitting and departure point for the immense ox-wagon caravans hauling merchandise to Santa Fe; it also evolved into the eastern starting point for several frontier mail routes that extended west across the prairies from the Missouri River.

The first vehicular transportation of United States mail across the Great Plains under a congressionally autho-

rized contract dated from July 1, 1850, when Waldo, Hall and Company's mule-drawn mail wagon left Independence on an 800-mile journey to Santa Fe. That same day, Colonel Samuel H. Woodson used pack animals to inaugurate monthly mail service between Independence and Salt Lake City. Woodson's route extended west along the Oregon Trail via Forts Kearny and Laramie, through South Pass, and past Fort Bridger to reach its western destination, where a post office was established in 1850. He utilized no way stations at first: the same teams or sets of pack animals made the entire round trip to Salt Lake City. Woodson's federal contract called for covering the 1,400-mile route in thirty days, for which he received a subsidy of $19,500 per year from 1850 to 1854. But delays of all types were common: Brigham Young noted in mid-April 1853 that because of mountain snows Salt Lake City had received no mail from the East Coast since the previous November, almost six months earlier.

Another mail route linked Salt Lake City with the Pacific coast. After California became a state in 1850, its senators had demanded speedy overland mail service. Federal officials advertised for bids to furnish a monthly connection between Sacramento and Salt Lake City to connect there with Woodson's once-a-month mail service to Independence. They received numerous bids, including one for four-horse coach service with a guard of six men at $135,000 annually. A lower and more practical bid submitted by Absalom Woodward and George Chorpenning was for pack-mule service along the 900-mile-long route at $14,000 per year.

After federal officials accepted their low bid, Chorpenning, several men, and a string of pack mules left Sacramento on May 1, 1851, headed east over the Sierra Nevada to Salt Lake City. In the high mountains they encountered snow so deep that the men used wooden mauls to pound it down so that their animals could continue. They struggled on for sixteen days. There was no through service yet, and no passengers accompanied the mail, but this was a beginning of sorts for transcontinental mail service on what became known as the central overland route. Primitive though this arrangement was, mail service along the route continued to evolve during

Outside a Medford, Oregon, livery stable. Although mules (and rarely a team of oxen) pulled some stagecoaches, the horse was king of nonrailroad passenger transportation by land across the West from the 1840s until the coming of the automobile in the early twentieth century. Courtesy Southern Oregon Historical Society, 7399.

the 1850s to pave the way for the first coaches carrying mail and occasional passengers.

During the early years, the separate mail routes extending east and west from Salt Lake City proved difficult to maintain. Both of them changed hands several times until 1858, when George Chorpenning and John M. Hockaday received a federal contract to provide weekly mail service between Missouri and California. The first coach of the Hockaday line left Saint Joseph on May 1 carrying eight hundred pounds of mail and two passengers. The fare included meals, and the coaches featured fold-down seat backs that formed a mattress to enable passengers to rest.

It was now possible for mail to travel between Saint Joseph and Sacramento in thirty-two to thirty-four days. Passengers could, too, but they found stagecoaching across the continent by the central route to be even more of an ordeal than travel by steamer on the isthmian route

or by John Butterfield's new line through the desert Southwest. One added hazard was the possibility of war in Mormon Utah, which would disrupt travel along the central overland route.

Mail and freight to Salt Lake City received a big boost in 1857 when President James Buchanan dispatched 2,500 troops, or about one-sixth of the nation's regular army, to quell a reported insurrection by Mormons against the authority of the federal government. The Utah Military Expedition, or Army of Utah, was small by Civil War standards, but its purpose was to crush the supposed rebellion. On June 28, 1858, when the federal troops and another thousand civilian employees marched into the Salt Lake Valley, the city's 15,000 residents greeted them with stony silence. Soldiers established their base, Camp Floyd, southwest of Salt Lake City.

The threat of war in Utah greatly benefited the West's premier freight-hauling firm of Russell, Majors and

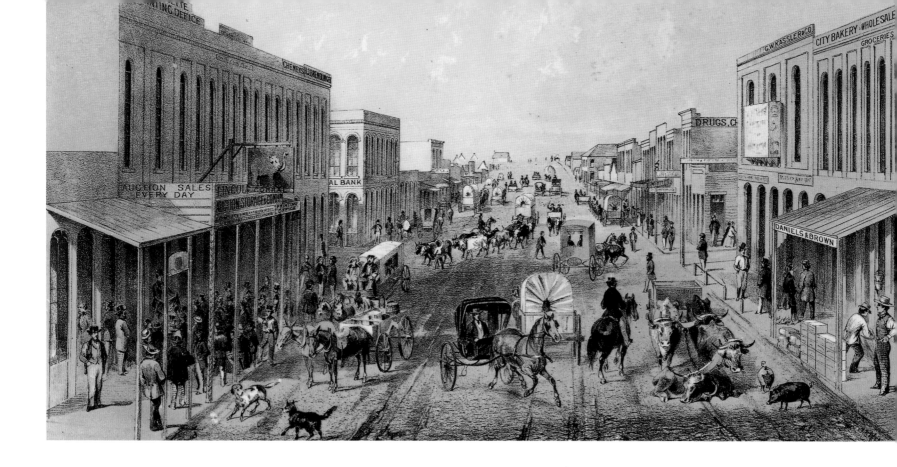

Waddell, which enjoyed a near monopoly on the central overland route. In the late 1850s these three partners—William H. Russell, Alexander Majors, and William B. Waddell—were widely regarded as the most substantial and most influential businessmen in the West. The value of their contribution to the settlement of the Rocky Mountain region in terms of passenger transportation, express and mail facilities, and the freighting of essential supplies is inestimable. More than any other enterprise, this partnership bridged the gap between the Missouri River and the Rocky Mountain West using various modes of transportation during the years between the Mexican War in 1848 and the Civil War.

While the great freight wagons of Russell, Majors and Waddell churned along the dusty roads to Salt Lake City during the summer and fall of 1858, hauling supplies to General Albert Sidney Johnston's troops, prospectors discovered gold in the Pike's Peak region of what was then western Kansas. To capitalize on the rush, a staging outfit

called the Leavenworth and Pike's Peak Express Company organized early in February 1859 with Russell as president. The irrepressible Russell proposed to provide daily service between Leavenworth on the Missouri River and the fledgling settlement of Denver City, and despite vehement protests from his two worried partners, he borrowed and spent money freely. Russell purchased one thousand Kentucky mules, about fifty new Concord coaches, and other necessary equipment, all with notes payable in ninety days.

About a week after the first coaches rolled out of Leavenworth for Denver, the ever-optimistic Russell assumed yet another heavy financial burden. On May 11 he bought the unexpired sixteen months of Hockaday's 1858 contract to transport United States mail between the Missouri River and the Pacific Slope. The purchase price was $50,000 plus the appraised value of the company's mules, corrals, farming utensils, coaches, wagons, harness, and other equipment, or a total of about $144,000

Blake Street in Denver, Colorado, in 1866. About a decade earlier, news of gold in the Rocky Mountains reached Leavenworth when a prospector walked into a bank with a goose quill full of gold dust. The frenzied dash to the diggings of what was at that time western Kansas gave rise to Denver during the winter of 1857–1858, at first a mere tent encampment on Cherry Creek. Courtesy Library of Congress, 5350.

for the none-too-robust Hockaday operation. Even with its federal subsidy, the Leavenworth and Pike's Peak Express Company remained a money-losing venture; but its financial affairs and those of Russell, Majors and Waddell were so inextricably entwined that if the former sank into bankruptcy it would certainly drag the mighty freighting outfit down with it. Waddell and Majors watched with growing concern what their partner was attempting to do.

Late in 1859 the worried owners of the Leavenworth and Pike's Peak Express Company formed an alliance with the Salt Lake and California Mail Company, which operated mail and passenger coaches between Salt Lake City and the West Coast. As the Central Overland California and Pike's Peak Express Company, they hoped to improve their grave financial prospects by operating a daily transcontinental stage line along the central overland route. Apparently it was Russell who chose the encompassing new name to improve his chances of securing a million-dollar federal subsidy for daily California mail service.

The Central Overland California and Pike's Peak Express Company struggled to maintain stagecoach mail and passenger service along the central route. For a time it seemed as if the sprawling enterprise might actually succeed, especially after the company gained a share of the million-dollar federal contract that subsidized the Overland Mail Company when it relocated its route northward in 1861 to avoid Confederate guerrillas. The old Butterfield firm, effectively controlled by officers and stockholders of Wells Fargo after 1860, shouldered responsibility for operations between Salt Lake City and Virginia City, Nevada, but sublet the section of the federal mail route between Virginia City and Placerville (and later Sacramento) to a California concern, the Pioneer Stage Company. It sublet the third segment of the central overland route—between the Missouri River and the Mormon capital—to the central overland California and Pike's Peak Express Company. There was not, strictly speaking, a through stage line under one ownership and management, though practically it functioned as such. The relocation was a stroke of good luck

for Russell, Majors, and Waddell, who were jubilant for a time over their brightened financial prospects.

It required about three months to transfer Butterfield's stages and stock from the southern route and to build new stations, secure hay and grain, and get everything in readiness for operating a six-times-a-week mail line. Finally, on July 1, 1861, the first through stages on the new 2,000-mile line—officially designated by the Post Office Department as the Central Overland California Route— left Saint Joseph and Placerville simultaneously. The westbound mail reached San Francisco eighteen days later. That was at least three days faster than the best time on the southern route. "At each end of the line the event was celebrated with much pomp, it being regarded as an undertaking of vast importance, not only to the east and west ends, but also an enterprise of considerable magnitude to the entire country." Supporters hailed the triumph of the central overland route. The main dissenters were stubborn champions of the old Butterfield route, who were quick to declare the new one a failure.[11]

The Express Business

Good overland stage connections quickened the pace of communications across the West, and among the prime beneficiaries were the express companies. For a fee, they would arrange for the rapid shipment of valuables, newspapers, and even important letters. This service was not necessarily a luxury. In the early 1850s there were no banks in the Oregon Country, and without them there was no exchange. As a consequence, express messengers had to shuttle money to and fro to permit the conduct of daily business affairs. By the time of the heady days of the 1860s gold rush, Portland alone was responsible for huge express shipments, which reached a peak of $6.2 million in 1864.

The express business in the Pacific Northwest dates at least from the summer of 1851 when Adams and Company opened an office in Portland. Within two years the Adams firm, which was generally regarded as California's leading business organization, dominated the numerous small express companies in Oregon. It handled more money, dealt with more people, and furnished more services to industry and commerce than any of its competitors. Adams messengers regularly traveled from Portland to San Francisco aboard ocean steamers, and thence to the East Coast with their precious cargoes.

Adams and Company died after the 1855 panic when the firm's bank failed in San Francisco, but taking its place was Wells, Fargo and Company, soon the biggest name in western express. Henry Wells and William G. Fargo were among the founders of the American Express Company in 1850; two years later, on March 18, 1852, they gathered with business associates at New York's famed Astor House and organized a new banking and express company that they named for themselves. On July 13, Wells, Fargo and Company opened its home office on Montgomery Street in San Francisco and later that same year a branch office in Portland. The firm built a thriving business serving West Coast immigrants who wanted to receive letters and packages from home and send back their wealth and who needed their gold protected and exchanged for specie.

Wells Fargo agents handled most gold dust in transit from Idaho and Montana, via steamboat, ocean steamer, or stagecoach, to the federal mint in San Francisco. No frontier community of any consequence was without its Wells Fargo office, which was as universal an institution as the saloon. The express company became legendary for its efficiency in safely transporting both messages and millions of dollars in precious metal across remote parts of the mining West.

Perhaps the most famous of all pioneer communication links—certainly the one most steeped in western lore—was the Pony Express, which originated to fill the need for quicker transmission of information between the Pacific coast and the rest of the Union. Financially, however, the Pony Express was a shaky enterprise because the federal government provided it no subsidy as a mail route. Planning for the Pony Express dated from late 1859, just as the firm of Russell, Majors and Waddell was struggling to make a go of its Leavenworth and Pike's Peak Express Company. Once again the architect of the dubious new venture was William Russell, whose announcement early in 1860 of a new express

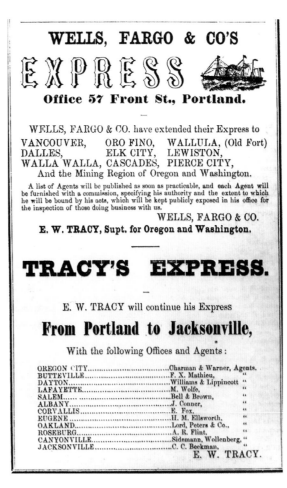

startled and amazed Americans, who were accustomed to the idea of weeks and sometimes months being required for communication between the Atlantic and Pacific coasts. Any promise to reduce that time to ten days seemed incredible if not irresponsible. But that was Russell's way of doing business.

Little more than two months elapsed between the announcement of the Pony Express and its first formal day of operations. During that interval a remarkable amount of necessary organization was completed along the 1,966-mile-long route. Saint Joseph was the point of departure, and there a big send-off for the first rider took place. Flags floated in the breeze as a great throng of people gathered at Patee Park across the street from the stables that housed the horses. Russell and Majors were present. Perhaps Waddell was also. A brass band played,

*P*ony Express! 10 Days to San Francisco." As the rider straddled his horse, there was a locked pocket in front of and behind each thigh. Only the agents at either end of the line and specially designated officials had keys to open these pockets, which contained matter going the complete distance, but a "way" pocket was left open for any messages taken or delivered along the route. The reason for so many pockets was that the weight (no more than twenty pounds) had to be evenly distributed. Important business letters and press dispatches from eastern cities and San Francisco were printed on tissue paper. Courtesy Wells Fargo Bank.

became more valuable than ever. It was via Pony Express that West Coast residents learned of Abraham Lincoln's election in November 1860, and read President Buchanan's last message to Congress the following month. News of both events was transmitted in eight days. Setting the all-time fastest record, however, was the transmission of President Lincoln's inaugural address of March 4, 1861, which traveled from Saint Joseph to Sacramento in a record seven days and seventeen hours. Without question, the most stirring news carried west by Pony Express was the outbreak of war between the states.

Word of the bombardment of Fort Sumter in April 1861 reached California in eight days, fourteen hours. At no time was news more anxiously awaited on the Pacific coast than during the hostilities that raged between the North and South. California businessmen and public officials paid a bonus to the Pony Express company, to be distributed among the riders, for conveying the war news as fast as possible. Copies of eastern metropolitan newspapers, printed on special tissue paper and placed in letter envelopes, were carried across the continent by the fleet pony riders to the leading San Francisco dailies, which could furnish the news to their readers at least two weeks ahead of overland mail coaches and nearly three weeks in advance of the Pacific Mail Company's ocean steamers.

It has been claimed that the cost of the Pony Express ultimately ruined the partnership of Russell, Majors and Waddell, but this was not true. It was only one financial burden among many that contributed to the collapse of the parent enterprise. The Central Overland California and Pike's Peak Express Company, which operated the Pony Express (along with Wells Fargo after mid-April 1861), was a much larger failure as a money-making institution. So too were most partnerships involving Russell, Majors, and Waddell. Both Majors and Waddell knew that the Pony Express would not pay any dividends, yet they hoped that by favorably influencing public opinion and members of Congress it would gain them a lucrative contract for carrying the United States mail. But no horse, no matter how fast, could match the speed of the "lightning of heaven" flashed across the

and there was speech-making. As the sound of cannon fire echoed through the streets, the first Pony Express rider headed west on April 3, 1860. In his saddlebags he carried forty-nine letters wrapped in oiled silk to exclude moisture, five telegrams, and a few special editions of New York newspapers for Salt Lake City, Sacramento, and San Francisco. In California the event was celebrated on an even grander scale than in Saint Joseph.

The Pony Express had been in operation mere months when the entire country began trembling on its foundation. In California and Oregon, news from the East

continent by telegraph, and an overland telegraph meant the end of the Pony Express.

Local Communications Span the Continent

What was probably the first telegraph line on the West Coast opened in October 1853 to link San Francisco, San Jose, Stockton, Sacramento, and Marysville. The first telegraph line in Oregon joined Portland and Oregon City on November 16, 1855, and was soon extended as far south as Corvallis. Most of the line was strung from trees and was susceptible to damage from storms. Any breaks were only slowly repaired. Various other local telegraph lines extended out from Portland during the 1850s. By 1858 a line was in operation between Sacramento and Yreka, California, from which point news reached Oregon by horse or stagecoach. There were also coastal steamships to deliver news from San Francisco. "The *Pacific* steamer arrived yesterday morning bringing news received by Pony at San Francisco from the States up to the 27th June," wrote the *Daily Oregonian* on July 12, 1861.

Not until June 16, 1860, did Congress offer federal support for a new telegraph link between East and West. Starting in midsummer the following year, a company in Nebraska and another in California extended lines toward each other until they met in Salt Lake City late in October 1861. The first transcontinental message was sent to President Lincoln from Stephen J. Field, chief justice of California; but anyone willing to pay about a dollar a word could now speed messages to the East.

Regardless of cost, the transcontinental telegraph dramatically reduced the time of communication even to Oregon, although direct communication from there to the East Coast was delayed until 1864. The four and one-half days required for news to travel to Portland from the northern end of the wire at Yreka was a vast improvement over the month it took via Panama, the standard during much of the 1850s. Local investors, meanwhile, incorporated the Oregon Telegraph Company at Portland on March 26, 1862, with capital stock of $75,000, to join Portland and Yreka. This line was in operation between Portland and Salem as early as April 1863, but the disastrous loss of wire in a shipwreck delayed completion of a line through to Yreka until March 5, 1864, when Portland at last received its first direct message from San Francisco. Until then the *Oregonian* ran a pony express of its own to speed news between the ends of the wires at Yreka and Salem. To celebrate the new age in

San Francisco's busy Green Street Wharf about 1890. As early as the formative decade of the 1850s, steam power expanded beyond the shipping lanes between Oregon and California. The first steam-powered sawmill commenced operation in Portland in 1850. Courtesy San Francisco Maritime National Historical Park.

communications, Governor Addison Gibbs wired President Lincoln: "Our telegraph completed. Let the great *Pacific* railroad with a branch to Oregon soon follow. We want no Pacific republic, no compromise with rebels in arms, and no more slavery." The region's telegraph network was soon extended from Portland to Puget Sound towns and New Westminster, British Columbia, in 1864 and 1865, and inland to Boise in 1868. But even the vital trunk line between Portland and San Francisco was hardly perfect. Falling trees caused occasional breaks, and as late as 1880 the line remained out of service for as long as ten days at a time.[12]

Even with improvements in communication, Oregon's main commercial lifeline remained the route via the Panama Railroad for passengers and express or via Cape Horn for bulky, nonperishable freight. Ships of the Pacific Mail line continued to dock at Portland at regular fortnightly intervals, and "Steamer Day" continued to be a time of excitement for merchants and other residents. As important as the new transcontinental links were in quickening the pace of life in the Pacific Northwest, events closer to home—the discovery of major gold deposits throughout the northern Rocky Mountains—had a far greater energizing effect than all the remarkable economic and technological developments of the 1850s and early 1860s.

Falls

Practicable for Steamers for eighty Miles

Parks Crossing

Cabinet M.ᵗ

Mountains

Clarks Fork

Wagon Road to Black's Fork

Spokane Prairie

Tohnotoge Cr.

Cress

Antoine Plante's

Ferry

Cœur d' Alene R.

Cœur d' Alene Mission

Thomson's Prairie

Spokane Plain
th 1858

Territory

Cœur d'Alene

Cœur d'Alene R.

Horse Plain

Camas Prairie

Cañ Jordan 1858

of kes 1858

Hangman's Cr.

of Washington

North Fork St. Joseph's River

BITTER ROOT

Prairie

Steptoe battleground
May 17 1858

Ingossomen Cr.

South Fork

MOUNTAIN

PYRAMID PEAK

St. Joseph's R.

Patoose River

IDAHO

DIVIDE

Boundary

Tah-to-nah Hills

Fishery Cr.

Lo-Lo Fo

TERRITORY

Mountains

108

May 27, 1862: Mounted my horse at 6 a. m. and started alone for Florence City. The snow was piled so high on either side of the trail for several miles that I could not see over it—in some places it was ten feet deep. I reached Florence at 4 p. m. and was the first man to enter Florence on horseback. When I reached the mining district and the miners caught sight of my horse, they threw down their picks and shovels, tossed up their hats and shouted and yelled as if they were crazy. This din of shouts followed me until I reached the town. The sight of a horse was an announcement of cheaper food and all sorts of merchandise.
—*Preston W. Gillette in* An Illustrated History of North Idaho *(1903)*

Rocky Mountain Gold Fever

A detailed map of a portion of the route traversed by the Mullan Road. The land bridge—624 miles long from river to river—officially opened in August 1862 at a total cost of $230,000. John Mullan hoped to reduce the nation's dependence on long and dangerous ocean voyages to the West Coast and thus benefit both civilian and military travelers. Courtesy Day-Northwest Collection, University of Idaho Library, UA 963 A5 1863.

Lieutenant John Mullan, military engineer, left Fort Walla Walla during the summer of 1859 at the head of an expedition of 230 men, 100 of them soldiers and the rest mainly artisans and laborers. The force was considered strong enough to repel any Indian attackers who might interfere with its work of surveying and constructing the missing link in the transportation geography of the northern West: a military wagon road to join steamboat navigation on the Missouri and Columbia rivers. It would be the longest road of its kind in the United States, and the first in the West to be built on sound engineering principles.

In 1861 when the route was still half finished, Major George Blake and three hundred soldiers traveled by steamboat from Saint Louis to the trail head at Fort Benton and from there completed the overland trek to Fort Walla Walla in fifty-seven days. Ironically, because there were no further Indian uprisings on the Columbia Plateau, this was the only time the army used its new road to relocate a large body of troops. The Mullan Road never realized its potential as a grand portage facilitating transcontinental civilian travel either. Few people used it from end to end. Apart from a small number of emigrants who accompanied Major Blake's men, and another party

that Captain James Fiske escorted to Walla Walla in 1862, the Mullan Road failed as a northern alternative to overland trails farther south.

Nonetheless, as Mullan's road builders stubbornly hacked their way across the Bitterroot divide, they anticipated the immediate future of the northern Rocky Mountains by unearthing small deposits of gold. When prospectors located much larger ones in gulches farther south, steamboats on both the Columbia and Missouri rivers competed for the burgeoning commerce of the Rocky Mountain mining camps. Portions of the Mullan Road served gold seekers heading to what became Idaho and Montana—from the Pacific coast to Montana the trail was lined with men and animals in 1865—although most of the major mining districts were located south of the portage route.

Because it was little better than a pack trail in many locations, few wagons ever attempted to use it; nor did stage lines travel it to link steamboat traffic on the two great rivers of the West. After the 1860s gold rushes, the Mullan Road quickly deteriorated. In the Bitterroot Mountains, washouts and downed timber made it nearly impassable even for packtrains and foot traffic. Yet during this time, hordes of gold seekers continued to reach diggings in the northern West by other routes. In the northern Rockies, gold was the first real stimulus to non-Native settlement. A series of discoveries in the 1860s had a lasting impact on transportation and communication, as had the California bonanza a decade earlier.

Gold Crazy

After the California rush, many a prospector grew bent and gnarled in the continuing quest for gold. Wandering the West with a pick, pan, and shovel on a pack mule, these searchers dreamed of future riches but meanwhile ate canned beans and wore clothes that fell away in rags. Rumors of gold in the northern Rocky Mountains had circulated since 1849. All through the 1850s, prospectors probed remote coulees and gulches for the elusive yellow metal and occasionally found enough to spark some excitement. All it took was the mere talk of gold to cause men otherwise apparently sane and possessed of good business sense to join a stampede. While "stampede fever raged it was as contagious as smallpox," recalled one aging pioneer.[1]

"Gold by the Ton in the Grand Coulee," proclaimed a newspaper headline in 1858, although the story had little basis in fact. The number of bogus diggings became legendary. Yet occasionally a prospector unearthed just enough gold to make a few of the first arrivals wealthy and keep hope alive in all others. "Who of the old times does not pick up his ears at the mention of 'Stampede' even as a retired war horse that hears the sound of battle again? There is a mysterious fascination in it almost irresistible, and the most sybaritic and sensuous spring from downy beds and luxurious tables with a wild anxiety to grease their innards with bacon and repose their exteriors on mother earth with nothing above them save the brilliantly bespangled firmament and a thin blanket." The Portland *Oregonian* offered a less romantic explanation for mining stampedes when it claimed that "these men are willing to rush off to the first excitement and 'play to double or break.' There are many connected with agricultural employment, who have lands mortgaged or debts hovering over them, which they hope to liquidate speedily by a successful season in the mines."[2]

Regardless of the cause, at least once a year following the discovery of the precious yellow metal in California, an epidemic of gold fever had swept across the northern West. Theodor Kirchhoff summarized the popular delusion by noting that "as soon as word-of-mouth or the local papers spread news of a strike, prospectors by the hundreds and by the thousands rush from every point of the compass to the new fields to try their luck. With the prospectors come, not only adventurers of every kind, but also merchants. Long pack trains follow one hard upon another, carrying the components of brand-new towns, and food, and tools to work the mines."[3]

The biggest rush of the decade was to the Fraser River in southern British Columbia in 1858. During a span of only two weeks, from May 15 to June 1, some 10,000 men raced north from California and Oregon to the Fraser River; by year's end an estimated 25,000 to 30,000 men had participated in the brief stampede. Also located north of the international border were the Similkameen gold mines. Discovered during the fall of 1859, they sparked a flurry of excitement the following spring. "If the mines prove productive, we shall have a market for our produce," the Portland merchant Henry Failing sighed hopefully.[4]

*Placer miners in southern Oregon.
In the wake of early gold miners came
farmers, merchants, and transportation
entrepreneurs. Courtesy Southern
Oregon Historical Society, 8525.*

But as West Coast businessmen knew all too well, most rumors of precious metals failed to pan out. "The semi-annual excitement for gold humbugs is now at hand, and there is a rush for the northern mines: Frazer river, Canal river, Similkameen, and now Rock Creek! The attention of many is now turned to the Santiam silver mines. Anything but steady home labor! Will such wild schemes pay?" wondered one skeptical Oregonian, David Newsom, in March 1861. Probably among the shiftless gold seekers and adventurers that Newsom scorned was Elias Davidson Pierce, a 35-year-old prospector. In the spring of 1860 Pierce claimed to have discovered gold near the Clearwater River on the Nez Perce reservation in eastern Washington Territory (now central Idaho). An account of his find circulated in Walla Walla in April, and some mention of it appeared also in the *Oregon Argus* of Portland. Most people only scoffed at Pierce's claim, thinking it just another of the many humbugs that had caused them to grow skeptical of all such stories.[5]

Thus Pierce created no special excitement. He could not immediately return to verify his discovery because of opposition both from the Nez Perce and military authorities who sought to enforce provisions of an 1855 treaty setting aside the reservation for Native Americans. They understood all too well that discovery of gold and the consequent rush onto Indian land would cause considerable trouble. But what none realized was that the full extent and richness of gold deposits in the northern Rocky Mountains had, despite the many earlier rushes, remained a mystery until now.

Together with twelve companions, Pierce slipped out of Walla Walla in August 1860 and again traveled quietly and illegally across the Nez Perce reservation to investigate the Clearwater country in more detail. Pierce later wrote, "On the 1st of Oct. commenced our labor. Found gold in every place in the stream, in the flats and banks and gold generally diffused from the surface to the bed rock. I never saw a party of men so much excited. They made the hills and mountains ring with shouts of joy." Returning to Walla Walla in November, one of the illicit prospectors sent word of the apparent bonanza to Alonzo Leland, publisher of the *Portland Times*. From this information, Leland penned a series of enthusiastic articles during the remainder of 1860 and into early 1861. Critics at first charged Leland with fanaticism or worse, of being a hireling of the newly formed Oregon Steam Navigation Company, which wanted to spark a stampede if only to fill its fleet of steamboats. Yet rumors persisted, and newspapers published what they heard.[6]

Pierce persuaded a party of adventurers to leave Walla Walla with him again and spend the winter in the Oro Fino basin. There they built cabins, whipsawed lumber for sluice boxes, and searched for still more gold deposits. Their prospecting proved very satisfactory, although Pierce himself was not unduly optimistic. He was positive they were probing only the fringe of a rich mining region that lay farther south; indeed, fabulous new discoveries in the Salmon River country soon validated his belief. Meanwhile, nobody in Walla Walla or elsewhere received word of what was happening in the Oro Fino basin until March 1861.

Tramping out through deep snow, the prospectors returned to Walla Walla with a considerable amount of gold dust. When a sample reached Portland it confirmed

Leland's claims in the *Times* and "caused a blaze of excitement. Steamships sped the news south to San Francisco and other points in California; northward, the glad tidings flew to Puget Sound, to Victoria, and through the Fraser River country in British Columbia. Very soon every locality was converted into a scene of confusion, bustle, and activity." Newspapers sent special correspon-

Detail from the "New Map of the Mining Regions, Oregon & Washington Territory, 1863," prepared by Alonzo Leland. Courtesy Oregon Historical Society, 24085, #717-F.

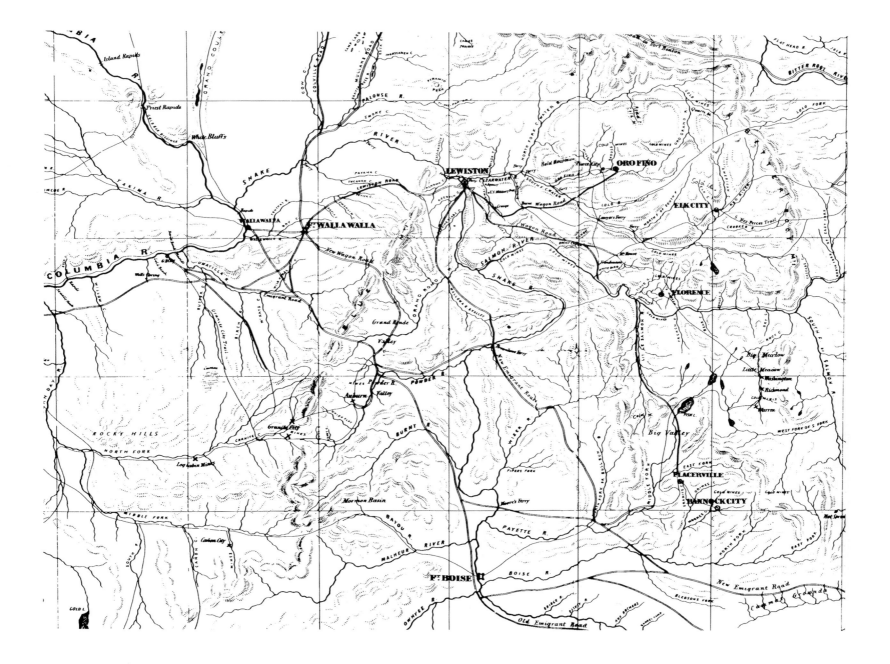

The quiet main street of Pierce, Idaho, after the gold rush was over. By the first of June 1861, thousands of eager gold seekers had pitched their tents along the alluvial bottoms of Oro Fino Creek and along the streams and gulches that empty into it, far up into the heart of the Bitterroot Mountains. One of these pioneers, William A. Goulder, added that "Oro Fino and Pierce City, two model mining towns with houses built of pine logs and roofed with 'shakes,' had already taken up their positions within a mile and a half of each other on the banks of the same stream which had given a name to the new camp and to one of the new towns." Oro Fino by July 1861 had a population of about twelve hundred; Pierce City was as large or larger. Courtesy Idaho State Historical Society, 548-B.

dents into the northern Rocky Mountains, and their stories heightened already feverish interest in the mountainous terra incognita of eastern Washington Territory.[7]

"In the spring of 1861 came the mad rush up the Columbia, simultaneously with the booming of cannon on the coast of South Carolina. The Civil War was on in the east, and a new golden era had opened in the west," recalled William Armistead Goulder, one of the thousands who joined the rush. Prospectors idle in California and drifters who had been chasing elusive yellow nuggets since the days of 1849 swarmed north in search of gold. Argonauts came from all over the United States as well as from Mexico, Canada, Great Britain, Italy, France, China, and the Hawaiian Islands; and their ranks included churchmen, merchants, laborers, and lawyers, virtually anyone capable of handling a pick and shovel.

Henry Failing and other Portland merchants could rejoice that "the mines are no longer a supposition but a reality." Indeed, Pierce's discovery sparked a rush that "exceeded in eagerness and volume any mining rush in

the Pacific Northwest, until the 'rush to the Klondike' burst upon an astonished world in 1897, and distanced anything in that or any other similar movement, in history, since that to California." Pierce's find thus launched a truly golden decade that defined the high point of the steamboat and stagecoach era in the northern West.[8]

A Land Abounding in Resources

New strikes, some of them far richer than Elias Davidson Pierce's original discovery, followed in rapid succession. Collectively they swelled the population of eastern Oregon and Washington and what soon became Idaho and Montana territories. Joaquin Miller noted how "two wild and stormy streams of humanity, one from California and the other from Oregon, had joined and flowed on tremulously together. They were on their way to the new mines of Idaho."[9]

As a rule the richest placers were discovered where least expected. Theodor Kirchhoff recalled a group of prospectors from the Yreka goldfields who headed north to Oro Fino across the expansive landscape of eastern

Oregon in 1862. They paused "on a hot summer day in a deep and shady canyon, beside a swift stream. That tributary feeds the John Day River, which flows north to the Columbia. One prospector dipped a pan of sand from the creek and washed it. He had no particular hope of finding gold here; every stream met in the wilds is routinely checked. Imagine the joyous astonishment when, after a little easy effort, forty-three dollars' worth of beautiful nuggets glittered in the pan. An unexpected strike! At once our friends from Yreka, expert miners, recognized a bonanza. Food nearly gone, shoes in rags, they nonetheless set to work forthwith, hungry and barefoot. They explored the area and found gold abundant. Nearly every canyon teemed with it. A prosperous mining town quickly appeared [a half-mile south of the original strike], in a mountainous wilderness where no white man had set foot: Canyon City on gold-rich Canyon Creek." [10]

Prospectors found more placer deposits along eastern Oregon's Powder and Burnt rivers in 1861 and 1862 and sparked a rush to the diggings unequaled in the state's history. Millions of dollars in gold came from eastern Oregon during the 1860s, but the bonanza there never matched that in Idaho and Montana. In the rugged and remote Salmon River country about a hundred miles southeast of Lewiston, prospectors discovered the riches of "fabulous Florence" almost by accident late in the fall of 1861—so late, in fact, that few gold seekers were able to reach the diggings that season before deep snow blocked their way through the surrounding mountains. The discoverers of the new goldfield had arrived at Oro Fino after the choicest ground was taken. Their persistent search for the elusive yellow metal led them south about eighty-five miles where they discovered rich placers at Elk City and Florence. The claims around Florence were easily worked, and some offered rich rewards: using a small rocker a man could often wash out more than one hundred dollars a day.

News of gold in the Salmon River country quickly spread. Around Walla Walla, "I found everything up there in a state of excitement about the Salmon mines— in fact, I found a second edition of California in '51–2,

revised and improved." During the fall and winter of 1861 California newspapers circulated rumors of gold discoveries on the Salmon River; and though the exact location was fuzzy, many argonauts prepared to head there as soon as warmer weather permitted. [11]

From the first of February 1862 until the last of May, gold seekers crowded aboard every steamship headed north from San Francisco to Portland, from whence they journeyed inland to join like-minded people from all over the West who converged on Florence. Among these pioneers, incidentally, was Alonzo Leland, the Portland newspaperman who first spurred interest in the gold of the northern Rockies. Florence was located in a high mountain basin where winter snows accumulated to great depths and lasted a long time: during the winter of 1861–1862, snow drifted fifteen feet deep in the mountains and five feet on level ground, and the temperature hovered around twenty degrees below zero. Cut off from the rest of the world, early residents of Florence faced starvation.

Supplies normally arrived by packtrains from Lewiston, the head of steamer navigation on the Snake River, but because of immense snowdrifts, animals hauled goods only to the base of the mountains. From there, men on snowshoes carried the cargo on their backs or on small sleighs and toboggans. As a result, whatever merchandise reached Florence commanded a very high price. At one time late in 1861 and again early in 1862, the price of flour climbed to one dollar per pound; some groceries, such as sugar, tea, coffee, bacon, and tobacco, sold for even more.

During the spring of 1862, after most of the snow had melted, on every road leading to Florence was a column of men and animals. Among those who trekked inland from Portland was Preston W. Gillette, who finally reached his destination in late May. He discovered "a continuous stream of people . . . pouring into Florence, which gives it an exceedingly busy appearance. There is still some snow on the ground, but it is rapidly melting away. Having never been in a mining camp before, it is very interesting and new to me. Everyone but the newcomers are as busy as bees, digging, ditching and washing out gold in cradles and sluices. Immense heaps of fresh earth are piled up at every direction and the whole country is so full of prospect holes that it seems totally ruined."[12]

By summer an estimated eight thousand people had reached Florence, but few of them remained there for any length of time. On June 8, just days after he arrived, Gillette witnessed one of the sudden population shifts common in northern Rocky Mountain mining regions during the early 1860s: "This morning reports were circulated that exceedingly rich diggings had just been discovered in the neighborhood of Buffalo Hump, about sixty miles in a northeasterly direction from here. A few miners who seem to know where the new discoveries are started off in the night to prevent the crowd from following them. All day people by hundreds, and perhaps by thousands, are getting ready as fast as possible to go. Many start with packs on their backs, while others take horses well laden with food to last weeks."[13]

John Hailey, a transportation pioneer in the northern Rockies, recalled that the Buffalo Hump excitement "furnished a good market for provisions which had been packed to Florence in large quantities. Many men left Florence for Buffalo Hump and each one had to have a small outfit of grub and tools, tobacco, etc. Merchandise went up to a high figure. Those who had no means to purchase an outfit, would get some friend who could not go to outfit them with the promise of a division of what they found. This is commonly called 'grub staking.' It is understood that the prospector is to divide whatever he finds with the man who 'staked' him, and do the necessary legal recording and work to hold the claim or claims." Buffalo Hump proved a disappointment, but among the promising new sites was Warren's Diggings, located across the rugged Salmon River divide about twenty miles southeast of Florence. Even better was the Boise Basin still farther south. There in August 1862, prospectors discovered rich diggings located about thirty-five miles northeast of the present city of Boise.[14]

Persistent gold seekers made yet one more major discovery in 1862, this time across the Bitterroot Mountains in future Montana, where Colorado prospectors seeking a shortcut to diggings west of the Continental Divide found gold on Grasshopper Creek, so named because of the clouds of grasshoppers that swarmed into the valley. Located high on a tributary of the Missouri River, the Grasshopper diggings resulted in the creation of yet another boomtown, Bannack City, and helped spark competition among transportation pioneers on both sides of the Continental Divide to serve the gold camp trade.

The December 6, 1862, issue of the Walla Walla *Washington Statesman* claimed that the year was without parallel in the history of the northern West. "Where, but a short time ago it was a barren wasteland now sounds the busy hum of almost every brand of industry, and a land that was once thought useless for any purpose whatsoever has proven itself abounding in resources." Fortunes also slumped, as happened when once-booming communities collapsed; yet during the first half of the 1860s, new gold discoveries always seemed to renew hope.[15]

Prospectors in mid-1863 stumbled on a second major gold deposit east of the Bitterroot Mountains. That was Alder Gulch, where 27-year-old Bill Fairweather discovered yellow metal on May 26 and sparked yet another stampede. In short order, speculators sympathetic to the South had laid out a townsite and named it Varina, after the wife of Jefferson Davis, but pro-Northern miners changed it to Virginia City, which became the capital of newly created Montana Territory in 1864. As productive as the ground around Virginia City was, its fidgety miners were not immune to the siren call of gold elsewhere. "About the middle of January, 1864, a regular stampede craze struck Virginia City. The weather had been quite cold and work in the mines was temporarily suspended. A large number of idle men were about town and it required no more than one man with an imaginative mind to start half the population off on a wild goose chase. Somebody would say that somebody had found a good thing and without further inquiry a hundred or more men would start out for the reported diggings."[16]

Finally, on July 21, 1864, prospectors unearthed still more gold, this time in Last Chance Gulch, now the heart of Helena, Montana, in what proved to be one of

the last great discoveries of the decade. As its fame spread by word of mouth, the site became a beehive of activity. Six months later, Helena gave the appearance of a "narrow street between double files of straggling log-cabins." It had "five hundred buildings and ten times that number of inhabitants, was well supplied with its hurdy-gurdy and gambling houses, Sunday street auctions, an active 'Vigilance Committee,' and various other attributes of a mining camp, all in complete running order." But Helena, the future capital of Montana Territory, proved a conspicuous exception to the usual ephemeral mining town.[17]

Gold Camps and Silver Cities

In the mid-1870s the journalist J. Mortimer Murphy estimated that there were three hundred mining camps in Idaho Territory alone, most of them dependent on placer mining. In mining country of the northern West, as was true of California earlier, towns appeared and vanished

as quickly as the morning dew when miners stampeded to new diggings. Some observers discerned a pattern to their rise and decline: "In a favorable location in the new mining district, some clever Yankee lays out a town, gives it a pompous name, and offers real estate for sale. Soon there is a board shack, purveying hard liquor. A restaurant follows. Then in a crude smithy, miners picks are produced and obstinate mules shod. Before two months pass, a smart infant city graces the wilds with saloons, stores, hotels, cafes, dance halls, billiard parlors, and so forth, à la mode."[18]

Early camps in the Boise Basin resembled an army bivouac with little groups of men scattered across the flats, gulches, and hills as far as the eye could see; at night, campfires dotted the landscape in all directions. Much the same was true of early Florence, described by G. H. Atkinson in midsummer 1862: "On either side of the trail in the woods you see prospect holes. Soon you come to a ditch, which had appeared at a distance

Virginia City, Montana Territory, in 1868. The first census taken four years earlier revealed that 11,493 people had settled in the goldfield that extended fourteen miles along Alder Gulch, from a head in the Gravelly Range to a broad alluvial fan of the Sinkingwater Creek (later renamed Ruby River). Within three seasons, these miners would remove gold dust worth $30 million. The district was unusual in that almost every claim yielded something. Evidence of mining was everywhere: all along Virginia City's main street lay huge, unsightly mounds of dirt fringed by sagebrush and cactus. Courtesy Library of Congress, GM 1868/412070.

PERSPECTIVE MAP OF THE CITY OF

HELENA, MONT.

CAPITAL OF STATE, COUNTY SEAT OF LEWIS & CLARKE CO.

1890.

Helena, Montana, in 1890. A major reason why Helena did not wither like most gold camps and silver cities of the northern West was its location along several major trade routes, including the eastern portion of the Mullan Road. Well before it became Montana's seat of government, Helena had evolved into a transportation hub and supply center for several outlying placer diggings. Courtesy Library of Congress, GM 1864/412070.

like a road winding among the hills. It is to bring the water from Meadow Creek into Smith's Gulch, and still further on. It is nearly completed. Here on either hand the gulches and ravines are dug up. . . . The woods are cleared off about town, and about two hundred wood and canvas buildings constitute the city." Its suburbs extended for three or four miles over the hills dotted by miners' cabins and tents. The trail was impeded everywhere by ditches and holes. "The town is simply made for the mining business. If that fails it will go to decay. Corner and front lots are valuable now but all the buildings are temporary. Every man feels that he is merely a

sojourner. His home is elsewhere and he does with the smallest amount of comfort."[19]

Even early Lewiston, a supply center and not a true gold camp, at first amounted to little more than a jerry-built collection of tents because a local army officer barred merchants from erecting permanent structures on what was then still Nez Perce land. But so many newcomers arrived each day that stopping them proved hopeless. In Lewiston, stores quickly prepared for business by stretching canvas over a frail and hastily erected framework; inverted goods boxes or a plank extending from one barrel to another served as a counter. Thus arose a "city of cotton," with a population in the thousands. The walls of its buildings were so translucent that at night they seemed to newcomers to be as transparent as glass.[20]

Lewiston and the mining camps of Pierce City, Oro Fino, Elk City, Florence, and Warren were all located on Nez Perce land. Despite the obvious injustice done to them, the Indians did not retaliate with violence, as sometimes happened in other parts of the American West. The Nez Perce desired to maintain peaceable relations with newcomers, all of whom seemed determined to bring an instant version of their civilization to the frontier. Lewiston pulsed with the incessant ringing, rattling, and grating of the anvil, hammer, and saw. Trains of pack animals plodded through the streets, carrying loads of clothing and provisions and casks of whiskey destined for outlying camps. Drivers hollered at their animals; elevated on a platform, half a dozen musicians further enlivened the scene with songs and the sound of banjo, fiddle, guitar, and tambourine.

Precious metal, usually gold (or rumors thereof), was the lifeblood of all the new settlements of the northern Rocky Mountains. Gold dust was the money of the era. In bustling gambling halls in Virginia City, great stakes of gold and silver lay on every table. The trousers of roughly dressed miners bulged with buckskin pouches of gold. The contents purchased the miner's food, clothing, tools, newspaper, and drink and paid his postage, express charges, and fares; a measure bought him an evening at the theater or the hurdy-gurdy houses or a place at the gambling table, compensated his lawyer for legal work, paid his taxes, or was his donation at church.

"Weigh out," a bartender would say. Wherever business was done, small pocket scales or larger box scales were at hand, and the gold was weighed out to close each transaction. Occasionally a scoundrel tried to mix heavy yellow sand with gold dust to cheat the unwary. The *Walla Walla Statesman* reported that "Mr. Jones has exhibited several ounces of counterfeit gold dust found near Klamath Lake. It appears to be a compound of copper and some other metal. It is heavy in weight, about the same as gold, and has the same color. It should be

noted that an unaware person could be tricked by it." Because a good deal of bogus dust was created from metal filings galvanized to resemble real gold, merchants sometimes used nitric acid to test samples in a transaction. A few drops on false dust caused it to simmer and fry; in two minutes, it turned black as carbonized sugar.[21]

Greenbacks, or Northern paper money created to finance the Civil War, were unpopular in western mining centers. In the East, the daily press gave quotations of greenback values, but this information took several weeks to reach Montana camps, and frontier merchants were loath to accept money when its current value was unknown. Thus greenbacks circulated only at deep discounts. Besides, the large Southern population in Montana and Idaho camps was unwilling to accept the national government's currency on principle.

Large numbers of Confederate sympathizers arrived

F.Jay Haynes photographed Black Tail Gulch and Gayville, Dakota Territory, in 1877. The look of a mining landscape differed little from Alder Gulch to the Black Hills. "Trees that might have softened the bleakness were gone, fed into the saws of local mills, converted into timbers and rough planking for crude buildings and sluice boxes, used as logs for cabins," wrote Larry Barsness in his history of Virginia City. "There was no beauty to be seen from any spot in the camp." Courtesy Montana Historical Society, H-157.

A hurdy-gurdy house in Virginia City, Montana. In hurdy-gurdy houses across the northern West a man paid half a pennyweight in gold to hire a partner for one dance and an equal amount to the barkeep for drinks for himself and his temporary lady friend. When Albert Richardson visited a Virginia City hurdy-gurdy he noticed "at one end of the long hall, a well-stocked bar, and a monte bank in full blast; at the other, a platform occupied by three musicians; between, many lookers-on, with cigars and meerschaums. The orchestra leader shouted: 'Take your ladies for the next dance.' Half-a-dozen swarthy fellows fresh from the diggings, selected partners from the tawdry, bedizened women who stood waiting." He noticed how, publicly, decorum was preserved, "and to many miners, who had not seen a feminine face for six months, these poor women represented vaguely something of the tenderness and sacredness of their sex." Courtesy Library of Congress, 408866 762 99734.

during and after the Civil War, and they occasionally indulged in barroom brawls with Northern sympathizers. But far more troublesome were the dedicated lawbreakers from both North and South. It seemed that in mining towns some people believed they had "passed out of all worldly experience into a new and unexplored phase of existence," that all normal restraints were removed. The old California miners had long since "shaken off the shackles of an effete civilization" and had been living for many years "free from the trammels and restraints of Sunday-school influences." The greenhorns and tenderfeet were not slow in learning how to follow in the footsteps of those who had so long enjoyed that larger liberty that comes from a wild, free life lived so far away in remote mountain regions." Like the camps themselves, lawlessness went through predictable phases, evolving from the unrestrained wildness of the stampede to the

more settled state that prevailed when the yield of precious metal and the business interests that grew up around the mines became "so important that lawlessness and tomfoolery cease to be possible, and then the men of will and worth get together and enforce good order," recalled one observer of the West.[22]

Even after a mining camp had "purged itself of ruffian rule," there long remained a tendency "towards prodigious drinking among the people of nearly every class. What must have been the amount of drinking when there was neither law nor order you can perhaps imagine. Men without the restraint of law, indifferent to public opinion, and unburdened by families, drink whenever they feel like it, whenever they have the money to pay for it, and whenever there is nothing else to do." Among Lewiston's numerous saloons were the the Gem, New Eden, the Rose, and the Miners' Rest. Barkeeps sold glasses of whiskey to miners for as much as fifty cents apiece. Of the saloons in Florence, the *Oregon Argus* wrote, "As bees on a warm summer day are almost continually jostling and jamming one another on the way into and out of their hives, so with the frequenters of these saloons." Regarding drinking in Oro Fino, it was "accounted no murder" to sell whiskey to a man "if he survives long enough to get out of doors." They called this fluid "tarantula juice" or "Extract of Scorpions."[23]

"In the settlement of New England," claimed Julian Ralph (with pardonable exaggeration), "it is said that the first thought of a new community was towards the establishment of a school-house and a church. In the mining regions the first institutions of a public character were a piano and a billiard-table. Of course, in the mountains (and especially before the railroads began to run all over them as they do in Colorado and other States) such bulky things were not hauled in, and a hurdy-gurdy or a banjo took the place of the piano, while a roulette-wheel or a simple lay-out for faro or craps served instead of the billiard-table. The billiard-table represented the gambling-house, and also served, in some places, for

Views of Idaho's new Wood River mines were printed in West Shore *in October 1885 to highlight the latest boom in the northern Rocky Mountains. The mines eventually played out, but because of their scenic setting, Ketchum and nearby Sun Valley are today prosperous resort communities. Courtesy Oregon Historical Society, 91790.*

a theatrical stage, if a strolling company of actors or minstrels happened along." [24]

Gambling, guns, and liquor formed a potent combination. And, curiously enough, Sunday was when this trio seemed most often on display. In Florence in mid-June 1862, Preston Gillette noted how miners observed Sunday in a typical Rocky Mountain camp: "The town is alive with people today. Everybody goes to town on Sunday to lay in supplies, see the sights, get and send letters, buy newspapers and take a rest. Newspapers cost $1 each. I can only afford three a week. On almost every corner an auctioneer is selling horses, goods, and merchandise of every sort. Great clumps of people stand in the streets discussing the 'new diggings.' The saloons are full of people. Many are gambling, hundreds drinking, while some are simply idling away the time and listening to the alluring chink of coin on the gaming tables. Frequent quarrels occur at the gaming tables which almost always culminate in shooting, and often killing. Not infrequently some drunken ruffian draws his revolver and begins to shoot in the midst of the vast crowd, often killing and wounding some one and creating a fearful stampede. Such is Sunday in Florence." [25]

From his vantage point in the Willamette Valley, David Newsom had observed of the miners in 1861 that "two-thirds of them return back for *winter quarters*— 'strapped,' and then what? Why each miner and his Indian pony must be taken in somewhere—for they are inseparable companions. After a bill is made, the settlers are generally pretty glad to allow them their price for labor—forty or fifty dollars per month!" On the other hand, the *Oregonian* claimed that "while the repulsive accompaniments of a miner's life are numerous, there are charms in its rugged independence and its daily fluctuations." And apparently many agreed, because a generation of gold seekers seldom tired of their quest. [26]

This was the rowdy, evanescent world that pioneer transportation entrepreneurs tried to serve. The task was seldom easy: not only did highwaymen lie in wait for packtrains and stagecoaches but the rapid relocation of population made long-term business prospects uncertain. John Hailey noticed during the Buffalo Hump excitement that "many of the men engaged in running packtrains between Lewiston and Florence bought cargoes of goods in Lewiston at greatly increased prices and hurried them into Florence on their pack animals, expecting to get big prices. But unfortunately, when they reached Florence, they learned that the Buffalo Hump placer mines were a complete failure. The demand for goods in Florence was very limited and the prices offered by the merchants [were] about the same as the packers had paid in Lewiston. This was very discouraging, so many of the packers went to other fields, myself among the number." Some transportation enterprises, however, notably the Oregon Steam Navigation Company, managed to thrive despite the uncertainty. [27]

Ho for Idaho! Steamboats to the Gold Country

In May 1861, only two months after Elias Davidson Pierce's gold caused a stampede to the northern Rocky Mountains, the *Colonel Wright* probed the navigable reaches of the Columbia and Snake rivers and dropped off Seth Slater at Big Eddy to start a new supply outpost for miners headed to the Oro Fino diggings. Returning several days later to the confluence of the Snake and Clearwater rivers after loading additional passengers and freight at Celilo, the *Colonel Wright* found a messenger from Slater waiting. He requested that the steamer continue to Big Eddy and retrieve the merchant, who had now decided to move his store to a location from whence several trails headed inland to the mines. "The vessel steamed up to the eddy, got Slater and his goods," recalled its pilot, Ephraim Baughman, "and brought them safely to the shores of the Snake where Slater again pitched his tent. So he had opened near the confluence of the rivers the first store in what is now Lewiston and perhaps the first in the Clearwater country." [1]

Immediately after the *Colonel Wright*'s second trip, the Oregon Steam Navigation Company placed an additional boat in service on the upper Columbia and Snake rivers, the much larger and better-equipped *Okanagan.* Captain Leonard White commanded the new vessel; Captain Baughman took charge of the now venerable *Colonel Wright.* Only a month later, Oregon Steam added the *Tenino,* even larger than the *Okanagan,* to its rapidly expanding fleet and made Baughman its captain. None of this growth happened any too quickly; in fact, demand for steamboat transportation to the interior diggings nearly overwhelmed the Oregon Steam Navigation Company.

Henry Miller, a California newspaperman, joined the throng headed up the Snake River aboard the *Okanagan* in late May 1861. Where the Palouse River joined the Snake he described an ascent of at least six feet in three-quarters of a mile. "The water is lashed into billows capped with foam, and the feat of ascending them looks fool-hardy. But we take a running jump right into the centre of the rapids; and inch by inch the boat goes bravely up. The waves strike her sides as if she were thumping on the rocks." The *Okanagan* churned

The steamer DeSmet *on the upper Missouri River. Courtesy State Historical Society of North Dakota, A-4242.*

furiously for an hour and a quarter to gain three-quarters of a mile. Steamboatmen learned to pull upstream through these rapids by means of lines, winches, and deadmen buried deep in the shore. With a steam-driven capstan they would slowly reel in a cable attached to one of the deadmen and in this way inch their boat upstream.[2]

Such feats were all in a day's work, additional examples of how boatmen on both sides of the Rocky Mountains adapted technology of all types to steam upriver as close as possible to the mines. In no other part of the United States would steamboats penetrate so far inland or

encounter such hazards as they did on the upper Missouri, with its shallow and tortuous channel, or on the churning waters of the Columbia and Snake rivers. The northern West was blessed with numerous streams and rivers, but steamboats were unable to navigate all but the largest of them, and then in some cases only for a relatively short distance. Packtrains, freight wagons, and stagecoaches continued where steamboats could not.

Prior to the mining rush of 1861, messages, people, and goods all crossed the sprawling northern Rocky Mountain country no faster than a horse or canoe. The advent of steamboats changed that, bringing in their wake the improvements that some observers equated with civilization. Not fifteen years earlier the Clearwater Valley "was a howling wilderness, and a white man carried his life in his hands, who dared to venture in these parts"; now, in 1861, "gentlemen seated on the forward guard view the scenery, smoke Havana cigars, and quaff Champagne cock-tails. The daily papers penetrate here, and St. Louis news is read here in seventeen days after date." It was a strange feeling, "that of whirling along by steam where so few years before the Indian and the trader had toiled through the virgin forest, bending under the weight of their canoes."[3]

Mountain Steamboats on the Missouri

With gold as the lure, steamboat traffic increased rapidly along the upper Missouri River to Fort Benton, trailhead to the mines of Idaho (which until early 1864 included all of Montana). Before the rush, it had been the ongoing search for fur wealth, soft gold rather than the elusive yellow metal, that enticed steamboaters into shallow waters so far inland. Back in 1832 when the *Yellow Stone* first reached Fort Union, the voyage added another seventeen hundred miles to the navigable inland waterways of the United States. After this, steamboats made annual trading trips to the fort, but the volume of traffic above Sioux City remained small. Because the sparsely settled Great Plains country supported only a limited amount of commerce, not many steamboats plied the upper Missouri River prior to 1840. Those that did were small, sluggish, and of heavy draft, often one-boiler side-wheelers that lacked modern conveniences for the comfort and safety of passengers.

The formative decade of the 1850s witnessed both the rapid expansion of steamboat traffic along the Missouri River and its extension into areas hitherto beyond the reach of steam. Settlement of the Missouri Valley as well as emigration to land farther west continued practically unabated. By 1856, newcomers had rapidly filled the lower valley of the Missouri and pushed upriver as far as Sioux City, by which date all the modern towns below that point had been established. There were fifty-nine

steamboats working the lower Missouri River in 1858, and more than three hundred steamboats arrived that year at the port of Leavenworth, Kansas, soon to emerge as the starting point for overland mail stages to the northern Rocky Mountains and California. Within another two years, more steamboats left Saint Louis for ports on the Missouri River than departed for ports on both the upper and the lower Mississippi River. During the half decade from 1855 to 1860—before railroad competition and the dark days of the Civil War—the lower Missouri River witnessed the golden age of steamboating. This was the era of palatial side-wheelers fitted up more for passengers than for freight, a time of fast boats and exciting races between favorites.[4]

A far different world existed on the frontier river above Fort Union. For nearly thirty years the challenge of extending steamboat navigation from Fort Union all the way to Fort Benton had occupied the attention of the American Fur Company. As early as 1834 the *Assiniboine* reached a point near the mouth of the Poplar River, a hundred miles above Fort Union, but there it remained trapped by low water all winter. For another nineteen

The Oregon Steam Navigation Company issued special tickets to Chinese passengers. Courtesy Oregon Historical Society, 91834.

Oregon Steam Navigation Co.

DECK PASSAGE.

PORTLAND TO LEWISTON.

1870 ONE CHINAMAN.

years this was the farthest point reached by steamboats. In 1853 the *El Paso* probed inland another 125 miles to a point 5 miles above the mouth of Milk River. For the next six years El Paso Point, as this place came to be called, marked the limit of steamboat progress up the Missouri.

In 1859 the final step, or very nearly so, was taken toward reaching the head of navigation. On May 28 the American Fur Company dispatched two vessels from Saint Louis with its annual outfit: its own steamer, the *Spread Eagle,* and a chartered one, the *Chippewa,* which her owner had contracted to take to Fort Benton, or as far as it was possible to navigate. At Fort Union he defaulted on his contract and sold the boat to the fur company for just about the cost of the charter. From Fort Union the *Chippewa* made her way successfully, and without any notable incident, to within fifteen miles of Fort Benton, and discharged her freight at Brule bottom, where Fort McKenzie had once stood. She reached this high point on July 17, 1859, forty years and two months after the *Independence* first brought steam to the Big Muddy. Because the Missouri was falling rapidly, freight from the *Chippewa* traveled overland the remaining distance to Fort Benton.

The *Chippewa* was a specially constructed "mountain boat." Steamers of this type used a powerful high-pressure engine to drive a large stern wheel, and most important of all, they drew only about thirty inches of water when fully loaded. Stern-wheelers could thread a narrow channel that would have beached the more traditional side-wheelers, and paddles placed at the rear were far less exposed to damage from snags and floating objects. This arrangement also allowed more space for cargo and made loading easier. The *Chippewa*'s shallow draft proved especially important in 1860, when it and the *Key West* finally overcame the hazards of shallow water to reach Fort Benton. On July 2 they made fast to the bank in front of the old fur post. This was the last quiet summer before the outbreak of war between North and South and the discovery of gold on Oro Fino Creek that launched a rush to the Rockies. It was also fifty-five years since Lewis and Clark had passed this way.

The *Chippewa* and *Key West* had reached a point farther from the ocean by a continuous watercourse than any other steamboats in American history: they had climbed to a port nearly half a mile above sea level, along a river entirely unimproved by locks, canals, or mechanical portages. Six summers later, on June 16, 1866, the *Peter Balen* climbed the river another thirty miles to the mouth of Belt Creek, six miles from the Great Falls of the Missouri (twelve miles of rapids and cataracts that churned the river and dropped it a total of 383 feet); however, the steamer accomplished this feat only during the June flood. For all practical purposes Fort Benton remained the head of navigation on the Missouri River.

Within five years after the *Chippewa* and *Key West* reached Fort Benton, an unanticipated series of events, not just the gold rush, dramatically changed the nature of transportation on the upper Missouri. When the American Fur Company dispatched its first steamers to Fort Benton, it did so not just to pursue fur trade profits but also to make money transporting military supplies to upriver outposts. This business only increased after Dakota Territory was organized in 1859, and an army of settlers crowded onto land in what is now South Dakota, greatly heightening tensions with the Indians. A Sioux uprising in western Minnesota in 1862 led to extensive military campaigns in the upper Missouri area. Even before this date, with the coming of the Civil War the army's primary mission on the upper Missouri became to protect the river route and its commerce; consequently, its major posts were all located on or near the river. The work of transporting military wagons, arms, ammunition, and construction supplies upriver from Saint Louis provided steamboatmen considerable freight and substantial incomes. At the same time, booming gold traffic ended the primitive era of steamboat travel along the river above Sioux City.

Starting with the *Chippewa* in 1859, from two to eight boats ascended the upper Missouri each year to 1865 (except for 1861 when the *Chippewa* burned at Disaster Bend). A thousand passengers, six thousand tons of merchandise, and twenty quartz mills reached Fort Benton in 1865. Two years later, seventy-one steamboats left

Saint Louis for the upper Missouri, of which thirty-five were loaded entirely and eight in part with government freight. There was not much downstream traffic, although all the boats carried gold dust. One steamer, the *Luella,* had on board in 1866 more than a million dollars' worth of the precious dust.

The rapidly increasing volume of mining supplies, equipment, and passengers bound for Fort Benton encouraged the formation of competing steamboat companies and provided numerous new jobs. In steamboat operations that served the mining regions by way of the upper Missouri, there was no monopoly such as the Oregon Steam Navigation Company on the Columbia River. But among the several important companies was the Montana and Idaho Transportation Line, formed in 1865 and destined to became the largest steamboat enterprise serving the upper Missouri River during the post–Civil War boom.

Steamboats going to Fort Benton and the gold country typically departed Saint Louis in late March or early April to take advantage of high water created by melting snow in the mountains and spring rains on the prairies. The upriver journey usually required about sixty days— going about fifty miles a day against the current—but because of the fluctuating level of the water and various impediments to navigation, the time of travel for the annual struggle between steamboatmen and the ever cantankerous Missouri could never be stated with certainty. During most years the boats reached Fort Benton late in May, but sometimes they did not arrive until June or July; they remained at the inland port only long enough to load outbound passengers and freight. Generally a good boat could make a hundred miles a day going downriver, and more if she ran all night. Like the travel time to Fort Benton, passenger fares between there and Saint Louis fluctuated according to the season, nature of accommodations, and volume of traffic, although $150 was about the average price of a one-way journey.

Departure of a packet for the Rocky Mountain goldfields was always an exciting event, even in a port as busy as Saint Louis, where steamboat arrivals and departures were commonplace. "So, when the *Wm. J. Lewis,*

not at 12 noon precisely as the newspaper advertisement had promised, but at 4:30 P.M., on March 27 [1866], backed out into the channel of the Mississippi, swung about with her bow to the north, and headed toward the junction with the Missouri, a large crowd had gathered on the levee to watch." A group of African-American roustabouts, or common laborers, collected at the stern of the *Wm. J. Lewis.* As the boat's steam whistle sent up a deafening thunder and the crowd on the bank answered with a cheer, the black roustabouts sang of the prowess of the great new steamboat on her way to fame and fortune, or possibly disaster, in the northern West, all of which added to the excitement of departure.[5]

It was primarily the rush to the Montana goldfields that drew Saint Louis entrepreneurs into the upper Missouri River transportation business after the Civil War. Their main rival during the early years of the Montana mining boom was the overland route that extended west from trail heads along the lower Missouri. This competition was not hard for rivermen to meet despite the fact that steamboating was a seasonal business: the overland route to the mining regions by freight wagon or stagecoach was long and difficult, and it passed through country inhabited by Indians who grew increasingly hostile to white encroachments. But there was also the Columbia River from the West, and no one could predict how much competition that route might offer.

Financial Wonder of Its Day

Each year on the West Coast during the first half of the 1860s, the annual rush to the northern Rocky Mountain diggings commenced with the spring thaws. During the winter of 1861–1862, when deep snow and subzero weather prevailed throughout the Pacific Northwest, miners who wintered in the mile-high Salmon River camps suffered severely, and some fell victim to disease and the bitter cold. Still others froze to death when they tried to travel overland from The Dalles to the mining regions. None of these tragedies seemed to deter thousands more from converging on the mining country from all directions. Heavy passenger loads burdened coastal steamships headed north from San Francisco, and the *Brother Jonathan* of the California Steam Navigation Company once carried as many as a thousand people on a single trip. Passenger traffic similarly taxed the boats of the Oregon Steam Navigation Company bound for Wallula and Lewiston but also provided a lucrative source of revenue.

Portland, already established during the 1850s as the terminus for oceangoing ships, was well situated to command the trade of the Columbia and extract a share of the gold pouring from the mines of Idaho and eastern Oregon. During the years from 1861 to 1865, when successive waves of miners swept up the Columbia each spring to Oro Fino, Florence, the Boise Basin, and Alder Gulch, Portland rapidly evolved from a village into a city; her merchants and other capitalists built up their aspiring metropolis and expanded facilities for trade and commerce as they supplied the valuable new hinterland. Miners enjoyed returning to Portland for the winter, freely spending their earnings and helping to build a robust local economy. The city's numerous gambling establishments lured the restless and largely male population with music and tempting lunches, inducing all comers to bring gold dust or coin and take a chance on the games. Though it had only about six thousand residents in 1862, Portland was by far the busiest place in the Northwest.

During the 1862 rush, as was true the year before, the primary beneficiary of Pacific coast traffic to and from interior goldfields was the Oregon Steam Navigation Company. Its fleet carried prospectors and gamblers and axes, shovels, tents, foodstuffs, whiskey, and all kinds of other freight to the trailheads; downriver Oregon Steam vessels brought returning passengers and the yellow dust that was the source of all the activity. As a result of the mining boom that dropped a windfall into its corporate lap, after only six months in operation, the "financial

A classic image of steamboating on the upper Missouri River: the Rosebud *as photographed in 1886 between Bismarck and Standing Rock, Dakota Territory. Courtesy Montana Historical Society, 955–147.*

wonder of its day" declared a 20 percent dividend, and that was only a promising beginning for what emerged as the far Northwest's premier business enterprise.

By gaining control of all steamboats on the middle Columbia River, managers of the Oregon Steam Navigation Company raised rates to suit themselves. From Portland to The Dalles, a distance of less than a hundred miles, a ticket cost eight dollars (some years with meals included and others with each meal costing seventy-five cents additional); from Portland all the way to Lewiston, passage cost thirty dollars. All freight cost $120 a ton by measurement. An "O. S. N. ton," except for heavy articles such as nails, measured forty cubic feet, always from widest or highest point. In the case of a wagon, the tongue was extended to get the full length, then raised to get the full height.[6]

Because of the steamboat monopoly, the cost of moving a ton of freight up the Columbia River averaged about ten times higher than that on the Missouri River. Even so, the line of freight wagons at Oregon Steam Navigation's Portland docks was so great that it remained unbroken day and night, seven days a week. The crowds of passengers were no less impressive. Typically at 4:30 every morning but Sunday, passengers gathered for the voyage to The Dalles. When the freight was at last stowed, the pilot climbed into the wheelhouse, and deckhands cast off the lines promptly at 5:00; an hour later, downstream boats for Kalama and Astoria pulled away. The rest of the morning was quiet until about 11:00 when the boat from the Cascades arrived.

When the Oregon Steam Navigation Company was reorganized under the laws of Oregon in 1862, it had a declared capitalization of two million dollars. That year and the next the company paid no dividends but invested heavily in additional steamboats and improvements to its portage railways. In 1861, the first full year of operations, Oregon Steam carried 10,500 passengers between Portland and The Dalles and 6,290 tons of freight, but in 1864 at the height of the rush, its boats hauled some 36,000 passengers and 21,834 tons of freight. During the years from 1861 through 1864, the Oregon Steam Navigation Company transported a total of 60,320 tons of freight and nearly 100,000 passengers. New boats purchased from profits scarcely kept up with the crush of traffic.

The mining boom brought enormous profits to Oregon Steam Navigation but soon inspired a flurry of competition. Two rival carriers, the Independent Line and the People's Transportation Company, vigorously battled for a share of the lucrative business. The resulting rate war lowered the passenger fare between Portland and The Dalles in 1863 to one dollar, but Oregon Steam merely dropped its rates too. The competitors came to

An advertisement for the Oregon Steam Navigation Company in 1863. Some idea of the flood of money created by the gold rush to Idaho and eastern Oregon may be gleaned from the fact that steamboats commonly collected fares totaling $1,000 to $6,000 a trip, and sometimes as much as $11,000 for passengers, freight, meals, and berths. Courtesy Oregon Historical Society, 91798.

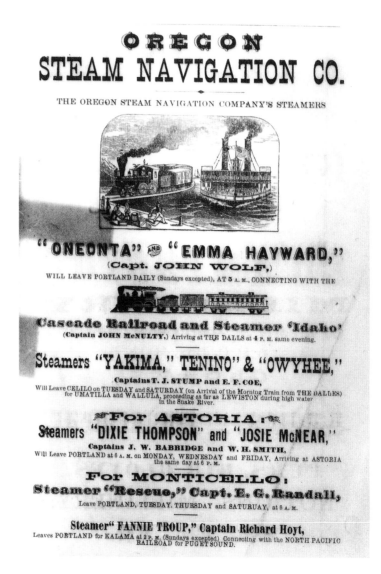

*C*aptain John C. Ainsworth (1822–1893) was the primary architect of the Oregon Steam Navigation Company monopoly on the Columbia River, serving as president during all but one of its nineteen years in business. His remarkable career began on the Mississippi River where he was a steamboat pilot. He joined the rush to the California mines in 1850 but soon headed north to Oregon to take command of the new Lot Whitcomb. *Courtesy Oregon Historical Society, CN 004235 307 P207.*

terms when the People's Transportation Company retired to the Willamette River, after which freight and passenger rates on the Columbia soon more than tripled. When the Merchants' Transportation line entered the competitive fray, Oregon Steam promptly undercut it, charging twelve dollars a ton from Portland to The Dalles and four dollars for passengers, with a dollar more for meals. When the rival kept up the struggle, the freight rate fell to as low as five dollars a ton. Then, after the Merchants' line gave up the fight, the Oregon Steam Navigation Company hiked its charges to twenty-five dollars a ton.

During its two-decade existence, the Oregon Steam Navigation Company spent more than three million dollars for equipment and improvements and paid out dividends of nearly five million dollars. The final inventory of its property included twenty-six steamboats and large real estate holdings in The Dalles, Astoria, Portland, and Vancouver. The Portland capitalists who organized the company in 1860 succeeded beyond their wildest dreams. One of them, Simeon G. Reed, went on to invest in various enterprises, including mines in northern Idaho and livestock breeding, and thereby vastly enlarged his wealth. His widow willed three million dollars toward the founding of Reed College, which opened in Portland in 1911. The Oregon Steam Navigation Company became a millionaire-making machine.

In the eyes of many Pacific Northwesterners, high profits combined with monopoly power to make the Oregon Steam Navigation Company an object of envy and hatred for two decades after 1860. Yet Oregon Steam did not always depend on competition to lower rates, and it often passed on lowered costs of operation to its customers. Nor were the rates particularly outrageous for either the times or the conditions; the Civil War caused inflation, and the primitive nature of travel throughout the inland Pacific Northwest made it expensive. The Oregon Steam Navigation Company gained a reputation for good service. Its white boats were distinguished for their speed, good accommodations, and regularity of service. At first most of its fleet was nondescript, with the exception of the *Carrie Ladd,* a truly elegant steamer for the pioneer era. Built in 1858, the *Carrie Ladd* was a stern-

wheeler with inside cabins that opened onto a parlor that doubled as a dining room. A ladies' saloon at the forward end provided a special refuge for women and children. Even when Columbia River steamers became larger, faster, and more elegant, they only elaborated the design pioneered by the *Carrie Ladd.*

Oregon Steam's first real floating palace was the *Oneonta,* built at the Cascades in 1863 for the run to The Dalles. Somewhat imitating the architecture of a Mississippi River steamer, she featured massive side wheels and two tall stacks. Impressive as the *Oneonta* was, the big boat made so little money that in 1870 Captain John C. Ainsworth himself piloted her through the Cascades to use on the more heavily traveled Portland routes. Among the other elegant boats that the Oregon Steam Navigation Company acquired elsewhere was the *Wilson G. Hunt,* a big side-wheeler built on the Hudson River and sailed around Cape Horn to the West Coast.

Oregon Steam was also a corporation with a soul, readily giving free passage to an old soldier or to a fisherman or rancher who came aboard without funds. The captains, pilots, and pursers of the gold rush years "were as fine a set of men as ever turned a wheel. Bold, bluff, genial, hearty, and obliging they were, even though driven to occasional outbursts of expletives and possessing voluminous repertoires of 'cusswords' such as would startle the effete East."[7]

Columbia Connections

A key element in maintaining the Oregon Steam Navigation Company's monopoly on the Columbia River was its dominance of the two portages that separated Portland from its interior hinterland. The profitability of steamboat traffic to the goldfields depended in large measure upon control of these portages, and without a portage road or railroad, opposition carriers had little chance to succeed. Thus it was at the portages that the Oregon Steam Navigation Company fought some of its biggest battles. Its directors realized that if steamboats were moneymakers, the portages were even more so. At the Cascades during the great rush, steamboats discharged such enormous quantities of freight that traffic sometimes clogged the whole portage from end to end.

The oldest of these improvements dated from 1850 or 1851 when F. A. Chenoweth and others constructed a six-mile wooden tram along the north bank of the Columbia at Cascades Rapids. They used a mule to haul freight on a single flatcar. When workmen erected a storehouse at the lower end of the portage in 1852, it was clear that the little tram had created a distinctive transportation landscape. The Bradford brothers, Daniel F. and Putnam, acquired and rebuilt the north-bank line in the fall of 1856 to handle an increasing volume of military and emigrant business. Their financial success only inspired competition, however, and W. R. Kilborn advertised a rival portage road in 1858 on the Oregon side of the river. The Bradfords fought back by naming their line the Cascade Railroad, while the south-side rival became the Oregon Portage Railway and was soon acquired by Colonel Joseph Ruckle and Harrison Olmstead.

Horses and mule-powered trains of four or five flatcars rumbled over the six-inch-square wooden tracks of the Cascade Railroad. One hundred pounds of "emigrant effects" would be portaged around the rapids for seventy-five cents. As the volume of traffic grew, the technology used at the portages improved: in the early 1860s, a bearing surface of sheet iron was affixed to the wooden tracks, and the primitive horse trams and horse-drawn wagons yielded to freight and passenger trains pulled by a succession of ever more powerful steam locomotives.

The portage lines were not originally owned by any steamboat company, though each railroad acquired its own steamboats or allied itself with steamboat interests to offer through service between Portland and The Dalles. In any case, the portage owners reaped the larger share of the profits on river traffic. After the flood of 1861 when Olmstead and Ruckle's portage railroad on the Oregon side of the Cascades enjoyed a monopoly of the business, it pocketed one-half of all freight income between Portland and The Dalles. This financial advantage was something the directors of the Oregon Steam Navigation Company would not long tolerate.

When Oregon Steam was originally formed, it amounted to little more than a loose alliance of former competitors. John C. Ainsworth became increasingly annoyed with Ruckle and the Bradford brothers, important figures in the company, because they retained ownership of their respective portage lines at the Cascades yet refused to pay for damages to any goods in transit. By clever manipulation, Ainsworth and Oregon Steam soon acquired the portages from these competitors within company ranks.

When Oregon Steam dispatched work crews to rebuild the Bradfords' Cascade Railroad after the devastating flood of 1861, Olmstead and Ruckle sold their Oregon Portage Railway—two wharf boats, twelve mules, five horses, twenty freight cars, one passenger car (a flatcar with benches under a canopy), three wagons, and Oregon's first steam locomotive, the Oregon Pony—to the expanding company. After most portage business shifted across the river to the rebuilt and improved Cascade Railroad, the Oregon Portage Railway fell into ruin and ceased operation. Later the Oregon Pony was transferred upriver to help construct Oregon Steam's new portage railroad around Celilo Falls.

Finding a real railroad in the wilderness occasionally surprised first-time passengers: "Yes, reader, we found right here on the north bank of the Columbia, in Washington Territory, five miles of as good railway—thanks to the Oregon S. Nav. Company, as there are anywhere in the country, and a locomotive all the way from Paterson, New Jersey, to take us onward at railroad speed."[8]

The tracks of the rebuilt Cascade Railroad ran mainly on wooden trestles built well above the high-water mark, in contrast to those of the Dalles and Celilo Railroad, which were built on shifting sand. The latter carrier originated when Orlando Humason established a portage road from Dalles City to Celilo, a distance of about fifteen miles, and used oxen, mules, and any available freight wagons to ferry passengers to boat connections on the upper river. The Humason road, replaced by a portage railroad in 1862, climbed above the river and wound around the highlands until it descended again to the landing near the mouth of the Deschutes where

*C*arleton Watkins photographed the Oregon Steam Navigation Company's operations at the lower
Cascades of the Columbia River in the 1860s. To ease a staggering load of passengers and freight using their
portage, Harrison Olmstead and Joseph Ruckle acquired the Oregon Pony, a woodburning steam locomo-
tive built at the Vulcan Iron Foundry in San Francisco, the first one to operate in the Pacific Northwest.
Beginning in 1862, every day it hauled an average of two hundred tons of freight from Bonneville up to the
Cascades and took miners and their precious gold down. Courtesy Oregon Historical Society, 21103, #1100-A.

Lawrence W. Coe and Robert R. Thompson operated their bateaux and the *Colonel Wright* for Wallula. In the early days of the mining rush to Idaho and before the portage railroad opened, passengers boarded Concord coaches drawn by four or six horses. Sometimes as many as four coaches left The Dalles at one time, all packed with passengers.

In 1862 the Oregon Steam Navigation Company prepared to build a portage railroad east from The Dalles, incorporating the Dalles and Celilo Railroad in October and acquiring rails in California. The rebuilt Cascade Railroad and the Dalles and Celilo Railroad began operations together on April 20, 1863. Each used a single locomotive, named respectively Ann and Betsy, grown-up versions of the Oregon Pony. The portage railroads soon bought more locomotives and added to their rolling stock. Unlike the wagon road, The Dalles–Celilo Railroad stayed close to the river under the bluffs where winds occasionally piled sand dunes across its tracks.

To link its two portage railroads along thirty-eight miles of the middle river, the Oregon Steam Navigation Company operated three steamboats: the *Hassalo,* the *Mary,* and a new side-wheeler called the *Idaho,* which is probably the source of the name of the modern state of Idaho. Even together the steamboats were inadequate for the job. Much traffic still followed the Barlow Road through the Cascade mountains. As long as the Rocky Mountain mining boom lasted, Oregon Steam had trouble providing boats enough to carry all the traffic. By 1865, when the excitement finally diminished, the Oregon Steam Navigation Company operated a fleet of nearly thirty steamboats, thirteen schooners, and four barges on the Columbia River alone.

Up the Broad Columbia

Despite the crush of passengers during the early 1860s, a steamboat trip through the Columbia Gorge meant traveling through a landscape that was (and still is) magnificent. "The admirers of mountain scenery will be constantly on the deck, admiring the ever varying battlements of basalt which shoot up several thousand feet high on either side. To gaze on them was really a perpetual feast to all of us." [9]

On a typical summer morning during the gold rush years, a traveler would leave Portland at daybreak, perhaps aboard the *Wilson G. Hunt,* and reach the lower Cascades six hours later. Theodor Kirchhoff, who penned a vivid description of travel up the Columbia River in the early days of the Oregon Steam Navigation Company, was "pleasantly surprised" to find the *Wilson G. Hunt* "appointed in luxury for which American riverboats are justly famous but which I had not expected in this remote region. If not quite as sumptuous as steamers plying the Sacramento, this one roared through Oregon's wilderness in elegance and comfort equal to some European counterparts and was a floating palace compared to the 'hotel' I had just left in the famous city of Vancouver. Still, a sign in my cabin declared in gold letters: Passengers are requested not to go to bed with their boots on. Which says something about the state of domestic manners here. Our inn-on-the-water was soon underway and carrying us rapidly upstream." [10]

As the *Wilson G. Hunt* steamed east, Kirchhoff observed that "here and there along the Columbia's thickly wooded banks were clearings cut with axes, and in them the cabins of hardy pioneers, agents of the inexorable advance of civilization. Slowly the scene grew wilder, signs of white society less frequent." A few miles beyond Cape Horn, "a stream plunged from a dizzying height over a thickly wooded mountainside and billowed like a silvery veil among green firs in the depths below: Multnomah Falls, 800 feet high and 20 wide. To the left other falls greeted us. Swollen by the last rains, they raced and roared to spill over the edges of crags, to the valley below."

At the lower Cascades, steamboats docked at eleven, and passengers made a leisurely transfer while all fast freight was trundled on handcarts out onto the wharf boat and into the stubby freight cars, a job that usually took an hour. Here, as C. Aubrey Angelo noted in 1862, passengers "immediately seat themselves in the cars; the locomotive is attached, a shrill whistle is heard, and off

Multnomah Falls as portrayed in the West Shore in February 1882. Of this portion of the scenic gorge General James Rusling wrote, "Some have compared the Columbia to the Hudson; but it is the Hudson many time magnified, and infinitely finer. It is the Hudson, without its teeming travel, its towns and villas, its civilization and culture; but with many times its grandeur and sublimity." Courtesy Oregon Historical Society, 91784.

ROOSTER ROCK

MULTNOMAH FALLS, COLUMBIA RIVER, OGN.

LITH. BY THE WEST SHORE, FROM PHOTOS BY I.G.DAVIDSON.

we go. The foaming cascades are at our sides; the fragile bridges groan as we pass over them; women and children cling to their kindred, and even those who have faced the battle-field close their eyes and gaze no longer." [11]

The vista at the upper end of the five-mile-long Cascade Railroad (a place later called Hamilton Landing and located just downstream from present Stevenson, Washington) "is wondrous," emphasized Kirchhoff: "the river spreads wide and its green waters mirror superb forests on surrounding mountainsides. In the Cascades downstream, the green turns suddenly to silvery foam. Steam-

boats that ply the Columbia's middle stretch tie up right at the end of the tracks, which follow an incline to the water's edge." [12]

After transferring to the *Oneonta* or *Idaho* for the trip to The Dalles, passengers began the transition from the humid, low-lying, heavily timbered western slopes of the Cascades to the dry, breezy, hilly land east of the mountains. "Rounding a bend ninety-three miles from Portland, we suddenly saw rows of houses: Dalles City. The sun was setting brilliantly behind mountains clad sparsely in fir, when our steamer rendezvoused with The

Carleton Watkins photographed Dalles City from the east in 1867. The settlement, which boasted about two thousand residents in the mid-1860s, ranked second only to Portland among Oregon's population centers. Courtesy Oregon Historical Society, 21578, #1100-A.

The village at Celilo, in this view by Carleton Watkins, was the location of the largest warehouse in the United States, "over eleven hundred feet long, built to receive the heavy Idaho freights," claimed Albert Richardson. Here was where the Tenino, *the* Yakima, Nez Perce Chief, *or perhaps* Owyhee *would be waiting to take passengers to upriver points. Courtesy Oregon Historical Society, 21587, #1180-A.*

Dalles' wharf boat." Kirchhoff climbed aboard a baggage wagon for a short ride to the fashionable Globe Hotel. "I headquartered temporarily in its hospitable accommodations. Still, I had trouble finding a place for my suitcase; and I had to make do as circumstances permitted in a room so small the bed occupied over half of it. A sheet of unbleached cotton covered the low ceiling, doubtful protection for my head."

The chief purpose of The Dalles during the 1860s was to facilitate connection between steamboats on the middle and upper Columbia River. It was at this inter-

ruption of navigation that the canny Kirchhoff set up his business and watched the ebb and flow of humanity. "When there is nothing to do in the store, we sit in the ever-open door, puff meerschaums, and watch the amusing bustle in the streets. Railroad tracks run through the center of town, on the way to the wharf at Celilo, above the rapids from which The Dalles takes its name. A mere ten feet from the store a locomotive puffs past. Its bell warns everybody to stay clear. Horses, alarmed by the hullabaloo, run away with driverless carriages. Stubborn mules and evil-tempered cayuses kick

and paw, bite at their drivers, lie down, or rear and prance until the ropes holding their packs break—and boxes and bundles roll in the street in wild confusion."[13]

Kirchhoff's pen captured the excitement that greeted the portage train. "Here it comes, bell clanging, engine roaring, thundering through the streets, all cars packed with vile-looking miners. The minute it stops, a dense, seething crowd surrounds it. Hotel runners, on hand to shout at arrivers the merits of respective houses, raise a

hell of a racket. Friends meet here and there; those bearing heavy pouches of gold are greeted with hurrahs. Through the crowd push miners and merchants from the fields, half-crushed under loads of gold. How sad to see people so burdened."

The next morning at five o'clock the downriver boats pulled out, while other travelers boarded the train that wound east through the center of town for about fifteen miles to reach slack water above Celilo Falls about ninety

The locomotive S. G. Reed *caught the eye of the photographer Carleton Watkins as it hauled a Cascades portage train in 1867. In the background are the ruins of an earlier bridge and the middle Cascades blockhouse. Courtesy Oregon Historical Society, 21108.*

minutes later. Pack mules and then wagons and stage-coaches had formerly made this portage; but the railroad was built after much hard blasting and costly wall-work, and now "riding on a rail" to Celilo, with the Columbia "boiling, swelling and hissing" alongside, like the rapids above Niagara, was exhilarating and superb. "On the bank, immense drifts of sand, white as snow, prove most serious obstructions to the locomotives." [14]

Proceeding inland from Celilo in the 1860s, "there is uninterrupted navigation, and daily or tri-weekly steamers running, to Umatilla, eighty-five miles, Wallula, one hundred and ten miles, and to White Bluffs, one hundred and sixty miles, farther up the stream. For six months in the year, boats can and do run way on to Lewiston, on the Snake River branch of the Columbia, which is two hundred and seventy miles beyond Celilo, or five hundred miles from the mouth of the Columbia, as White Bluffs, the head of navigation on the main river, is four hundred miles from the mouth." [15]

At the earliest light of the morning, the steamer from Celilo would head right to the impetuous current of the river, bound for Lewiston, 280 miles farther yet, taking two days, sometimes three, but usually only one day to return. Here the landscape changed too, much to the amazement of first-time travelers. "Above the Dalles the woods disappear; the banks are smooth, hills of velvet grass, without leaf or shrub in the whole range of vision. The entire country, watered by the upper Columbia, embracing eastern Oregon, Washington, Idaho, and a portion of Montana, looks a dreary desert; but its grasses are rich and nutritive." [16]

The upriver boat reached Umatilla by late afternoon or Wallula a couple of hours later. Beginning in 1864, a traveler could take a stage from Umatilla to Boise and Salt Lake City for points east. Other stage lines offered connections from Wallula to Walla Walla and from there to Lewiston or Boise. Umatilla, Wallula, Walla Walla, and other upriver towns initially lacked the commercial importance of The Dalles, but they rapidly gained stature as a result of a growing network of stage and freight lines that extended into hinterland mining camps from steamboat landings along the Columbia River.

*O*n the Washington side of the
Columbia River, the Dalles City loads
horses at Hamilton Landing near the
upper Cascades. Courtesy Oregon
Historical Society, 12399.

The steamer continued to come up the river three times a week loaded down with passengers and freight for the Boise Basin. The rush for this mining district was greater than at any time before. The road from Umatilla to the mining district was literally lined with travel, the larger portion on foot, while some had horses, some wagons and teams. Many came by saddle trains and the stages were crowded with passengers.
—*John Hailey,* The History of Idaho *(1910)*

Via Shank's Mare and Stagecoach

Vital as steamboats were, the shallow rivers of the Rocky Mountains denied them direct access to the main mining regions. Thus at numerous wharves, levees, and landings, water and land transportation intersected. At The Dalles, Umatilla, Wallula, and Lewiston, all located along western approaches to the mines, and at Fort Benton on the east side, steamboats dropped off gold seekers with their heavy carpetbag suitcases. Crowds of onlookers invariably gathered at such places to watch every movement of the deckhands as they carried ashore shovels, picks, and other mining equipment and heavy sacks filled with coffee, sugar, potatoes, dried apples, flour, meal, beans, and other basic foods. "More often than otherwise, when unloading a steamboat, things would go wrong and greatly annoy the captain and mates. It was the hardest kind of work to discharge from the boat a heavy cargo of freight. From long hours of labor some of the deckhands naturally would be completely played out, and this seemed to exasperate the officers in charge. Apparently they had no mercy for the worn-out toilers. It didn't take much to annoy the first or second-mate of a Missouri River steamboat, and if in an unpleasant mood they would let off a volley of cuss-words."[1]

Gateways to Golden Hinterlands

Nature placed The Dalles astride the main commercial route between Portland and the mines of the northern West and made it a necessary stop for all passengers and freight. At this location miners either portaged around a stretch of white water to continue their journey upriver by steamboat or switched to horses (and later stage-coaches) and followed trails that wound across the Columbia Plateau to reach the gold regions farther east.

The 1860s boom made The Dalles the second largest city in Oregon. Not only did it emerge as a primary supply center for mines of the interior, but miners frequently returned there to spend the winter and their money. Until the decline of the diggings after 1868, The Dalles was a popular meeting place for miners from the northern Rockies, British Columbia, California, and even Mexico. During the height of the rush as much as two million dollars in gold dust might reach The Dalles in a single month, and its saloons and stores readily accepted gold dust as payment for goods and services. Perhaps no other place along the Columbia River offered a better view of the "immense number of people deriving their supplies from Portland," noted C. Aubrey Angelo.

"For months past, a daily average of one hundred tons of goods have been landed at the Dalles, the principal portion of which has been immediately forwarded to the various localities above."[2]

The Dalles was a wide-open town, easily boasting the biggest gambling houses in eastern Oregon. "The 'tenderfoot' visitor saw more gold piled on the gaming tables—twenty dollar pieces almost exclusively—than he ever dreamed of in his limited philosophy." One visitor in 1862 "watched operations until midnight and saw scores of infatuated victims to the gambling fever skinned with neatness and dispatch." Traffic to and from the green-covered tables was constant, "an endless chain of sheep to be shorn."[3]

Theodor Kirchhoff was one of those who perceived an opportunity to mine the miners passing through The Dalles, and it was here that the astute German opened his store. From this vantage point, Kirchhoff penned a vivid account of everyday life in The Dalles during the city's golden years. "Ragged miners crowd the dining-room tables, bolt hot food with amazing speed, and look like misfits in civilized society. People's appearance is nowhere more disappointing than in the gold fields. Often you meet, especially among seasoned California miners, cultivated men who consider grooming anomalous to this, their new lifestyle. At first glance you would take them for backwoods Indians—or worse." Kirchhoff recalled that "nearly every miner at the tables carries a long knife and a revolver. Orders, talk and the sound of eating emanated in a jumble from the crowd: a din that roars as if each member is narrowly escaping death by starvation. Here, for example, in a sonorous voice, a mountain of a man orders mutton chops and roast beef, and snarls at the waiter because he doesn't bring them fast enough."[4]

Of his own commercial venture, Kirchhoff mused: "Sometimes, after unstinting effort and a display of eloquence brilliant enough to surpass Calhoun or Webster, you sell something to one of these Webfeet who has been sniffing and snooping around the store. When it comes to payment, he questions the accuracy of the scale, then offers dust of the worst sort. He wants the best price, even though the dust is either half-full of reddish-brown sand or laced with bits of copper. The alloying with copper, done in his spare time, is called doctoring. Unless you pay the closest attention when taking dust, and test it carefully with nitric acid, you can be easily and terribly fooled by bogus dust that deceptively resembles the real thing."

It was at The Dalles that the Oregon Steam Navigation Company located its main machine shops in 1863, creating there an impressive industrial landscape. Angelo observed that the facilities covered several acres of ground; "they are erected on a gigantic scale, and rather puzzle the visitor to know for what purpose so much steam power can possibly be used. These buildings have been erected regardless of expense, and possess an availability for mechanical purposes that will bear comparison with the best workshops in California. With the exception of casting and foundry work, the Company manufactures everything they require, either for water or railroad travel." Upon entering the company's office, the first thing that attracted Angelo's eye was the posted list of rules and regulations governing employees. One of these strictly forbade card playing, while another read, "Any person attached to this employ found drunk, to be immediately dismissed."[5]

Among the argonauts who traveled overland from The Dalles to the Salmon River mines was Preston W. Gillette; he and his companions packed their horses with nearly two hundred pounds of provisions and camp equipment in anticipation of a long and difficult journey. He noted in the late spring of 1862 that all roads running east from The Dalles were "full of people and vehicles of every description, while the steamboats were more than full. There was a great tide of immigration and commerce, rolling up the Columbia Valley like an irresistible torrent." The Powder River mines of eastern Oregon had recently been discovered, and many gold seekers were hurrying in that direction; others were headed to Florence. But upon reaching the town of Umatilla, Gillette also encountered a number of miners returning from the Powder River diggings, all glad to get back, declaring that there was no gold there worth the getting.

Lorenzo Lorain photographed The Dalles in the mid-1860s. During the boom years of the first half of the decade, the town's streets thronged with people going to or coming from the mines. There was more activity in The Dalles than in Portland, some local boosters claimed. The Umatilla House, with its thick carpets and piano, bustled in both lobby and bar, and "bed-time brought no hush." Fitz-Hugh Ludlow wrote in the Atlantic Monthly *in 1864 that the ceaseless activity gave visitors the impression that The Dalles was "sitting up all night to be fresh for an early start in the morning." Courtesy Oregon Historical Society, 5345-a.*

It was here he found a tent restaurant that advertised: "Meals $1; with dessert $1.75." As Gillette recalled, "We all took a full meal of bacon and beans, hardtack, coffee, and a small piece of the poorest sort of dried apple pie."[6]

At Umatilla in the mid-1860s it was "astonishing to see the immense quantities of freight landed here by every steamer," most of it destined for the Boise Basin. "Pack trains and bull trains are constantly coming and going from this place." It cost one and one-half cents a pound to ship freight from Portland to Umatilla by water; but continuing from there to the landlocked Boise Basin, located about three hundred miles farther inland, the rate jumped to as high as twenty cents per pound. Angelo emphasized that the beaches at Umatilla and Wallula were "covered with mill machinery and merchandise, and all the stores are filled to their utmost

capacity with goods awaiting transit to the various mining, grazing, and agricultural districts in the upper country. These two points will continue the entrepots and forwarding depots. The number of quartz mills lying on the beach, and going forward, has exceeded all previous calculations. Several mills have also been transported overland."[7]

Umatilla had the advantage of being the highest point on the Columbia River to which steamboats could ascend during all stages of water, but the settlement's glory was brief. By 1867 it was already possible to describe Umatilla as "a dilapidated specimen of a town, with one principal street running along the bank of the river and having but one side to it." Among its eight hundred inhabitants were many who earned a living by providing cheap lodgings and whiskey. Yet, it could be predicted that at Umatilla

UMATILLA. OR. 1864.

W.S. BOWMAN COPY PHOTO PENDLETON OR

"stage and water travel will be so combined that neither will be irksome and a great passenger traffic must thus spring up."[8]

Continuing another thirty miles upriver from Umatilla, steamboats reached Wallula, a second terminus of navigation for Idaho-bound travelers. Freight charges from Portland to either place were the same, and for a time the number of travelers was very nearly equally divided between them. Wallula and Umatilla were rivals; each town had its partisans who claimed it was the better jumping-off point for inland mines. At Wallula, "good stages, with steady drivers await your arrival, and convey you over a good road to Walla Walla," the transportation hub located about thirty miles east and at that time the largest city in Washington Territory. This settlement, less than a decade old, originated with Fort Walla Walla, which dated from 1856 and the Indian wars that convulsed the Columbia Plateau.[9]

The clutter of tents and shacks around the military outpost gradually evolved into a small trading center that supplied the needs of soldiers and the few settlers who arrived from the Willamette Valley. They relocated mainly to graze their cattle on the tall grasses, seeing at first little possibility of farming the land. Military purchases subsidized producers of grain, horses, and cattle—with most such products still arriving from distant locations—and provided jobs for local teamsters; but the small population and the lack of local transportation discouraged the growth of agricultural or livestock production around Fort Walla Walla. Thus the Walla Walla Valley remained lightly populated and economically unappealing to would-be settlers. As recently as 1859 Walla Walla had been described as a village having a population composed mainly of traders and gamblers. "There are ten or twelve houses, including canvas-houses, in the place." The six drinking establishments outnumbered all other businesses. That same year a line of weekly stages was established between Walla Walla and The Dalles. But soon the Rocky Mountain mining booms, beginning with the Oro Fino diggings, reconfigured the northern West.[10]

"I got in sight of the City of Walla Walla," recalled

Umatilla in 1864. C. Aubrey Angelo noted that steamboats on trips upriver usually stayed at Umatilla overnight to unload mountains of freight, but on the way back down the Columbia, "they scarcely remain long enough for a man to kiss his wife, pay his bills, and take a drink!" It was from here that a trail led inland across the Blue Mountains to the numerous mines of eastern Oregon and southern Idaho. Courtesy Oregon Historical Society, OrHi 9909.

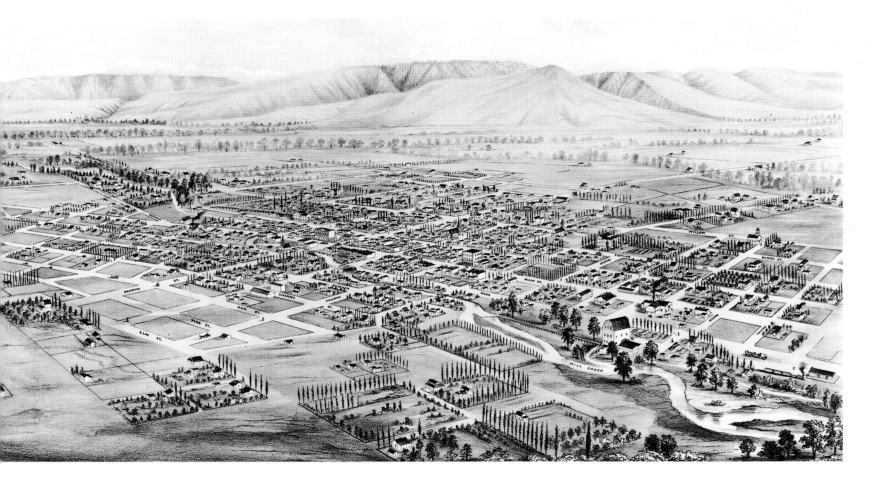

Prosperous Walla Walla in 1876. Preston W. Gillette, who passed through Walla Walla in May 1862 at the beginning of its rapid transformation into Washington's largest city, described this supply center for the inland mines as "a row of stores and small houses on either side of the road." The country around Walla Walla and Lewiston was only just beginning to attract settlers in large numbers. Courtesy Library of Congress, GM 2978/412070.

Randall Hewitt of his 1862 journey: "it was a lively little place of about two or three thousand inhabitants, mostly transient miners, teamsters, packers and land-seekers," who formed a "considerable army of rough men" crowded together on its dusty streets. "One would naturally conclude, to judge from the numerous places where gambling was in progress day and night, with an orchestra and free lunch as additional attractions in each establishment, that this was the chief occupation" and that "all the games known to the guild were running in full blast unceasingly." Despite Walla Walla's many coarse qualities, the new settlement's boosters claimed that there "can be no comparison between Walla Walla and the little catch-penny towns that seek to contend with us for the mining trade. The center of a rich agricultural valley,

the development of which is but just commenced, there is a stability and firmness about our town that is not to be found at any of the mere 'portages' where the traveler lays over the night and hastens away in the morning." And they were right.[11]

Though not located on a navigable river itself, Walla Walla quickly evolved into the main supply center for mining camps in the Clearwater, Salmon, and Boise river drainages; in western Montana; and even those as far north as British Columbia's Kootenay region. Long trains of mules and horses laden with supplies for all these distant diggings filled Walla Walla's streets, and stagecoaches arrived and left every day. The *Walla Walla Statesman* wrote on December 13, 1861, that during the "week past not less than 225 pack animals heavily ladened with provisions have left this city for the mines," and that was just the beginning.

Several local firms extended express service between Walla Walla and the mines. The largest of these was Tracy and Company, which Wells Fargo succeeded during the 1860s. That same year, about 150 freight wagons remained busy hauling merchandise from steamboats at Wallula to Walla Walla and Lewiston. It was from Walla Walla that Major Pinckney Lugenbeel set out in 1863 to locate a new military base called Fort Boise to help protect travelers on the Oregon Trail (and around which the modern Idaho city of Boise grew). From Walla Walla, too, Lieutenant John Mullan completed his 624-mile-long road to link steamboat navigation on the Missouri and Columbia rivers and provide a faster route for the movement of soldiers and mining supplies. For miners from all over the inland Northwest, Walla Walla, like Portland and The Dalles, became a popular winter haven, and their hard-won fortunes became fair game for the merchants who ran the city's numerous saloons, hotels, restaurants, and stores.

Gillette continued overland from Walla Walla to Lewiston in 1862, where he observed that "the mighty flood of human life still rushes on with restless steps and eager hopes. Pack trains and vehicles of every sort come laden with provisions, merchandise, and lots of whiskey. The town still grows, houses spring up like magic, saloons and gambling houses are numerous and are full of people day and night. Here fools and their money part to meet no more. There is much crime and frequent murders here." Lewiston thrived as the prospectors unearthed one fabulous discovery after another. When Congress created the new territory of Idaho in 1863, Lewiston briefly served as its first capital.[12]

Across the Continental Divide, at the opposite approach to the Rocky Mountain mining camps, was Fort Benton. To early observers the place seemed cut from the same ragged cloth as the several Columbia River gateways. Any traveler from Saint Louis who, after enduring a month or more aboard a river steamer, expected to find a thriving metropolis was invariably disappointed in the Chicago of the Plains, as the village styled itself. One weary sojourner in 1865 noted first the old adobe fort of the American Fur Company and then commented scornfully on "a dozen uncouth houses of logs and adobes, lemonade made with syrup at thirty-eight cents per glass, full-breed squaws, suggestive half-breed children in abundance, and a village, considered in all its parts, about as picturesque as a hole in the ground." Not much changed during the 1860s and 1870s to soften travelers' harsh assessments of Fort Benton's rough appearance, lack of accommodations, and the tough-looking habitués of its innumerable saloons and gambling halls. Yet during the spring boating season, when steamer after steamer brought boatloads of freight and expectant fortune seekers, a positive change of sorts did come over the outpost after a long winter's hibernation.[13]

With every steamboat arrival, Fort Benton's levee became a noisy hive of activity as deckhands unloaded cargoes of chickens, horses, barrels of flour, buggies, stoves, and whiskey. There were boxes of dry goods and clothing, barrels of liquor, sacks of provisions, cases of mining tools, and bulky quartz mills. For the downriver trade they took aboard cargoes of buffalo hides and peltries of all sorts. Every Fort Benton warehouse was jammed with goods, and even private dwellings were sometimes pressed into temporary service as warehouses. The safes of the town bulged with gold dust as it was brought in, and precious packages of the yellow metal were sometimes carelessly left in stores. Freight wagons hauled by mules, horses, and oxen crowded the treeless, dusty streets. In early days, when the unkempt settlement offered little to comfort the travel-weary, most new arrivals lingered in Fort Benton only long enough to secure transportation to the mines of Virginia City or Helena, a distance of from one hundred to two hundred miles, or north to Canada. Fort Benton not only supplied camps scattered through western Montana but also functioned as the hub of a sprawling overland transportation network that radiated out to reach settlements as distant as Calgary and Edmonton on the Canadian prairie.

Hit the Road

The earliest and simplest form of passenger transportation heading inland from steamboat landings was the Foot and Walker's Transportation Line, as some people jokingly referred to the long hike overland. Some gold seekers shouldered their own packs and started out afoot, while others banded together and purchased a single pack animal to load with their blankets and a small supply of provisions. Other groups walked to the diggings with pack animals enough for all. A variation on hiking to the mines, or travel by shank's mare, was the system known as ride and tie. Two men who had only one horse between them would often take turns riding. The first would ride for some distance, find a place to tie the horse, then proceed ahead on foot. When the second man reached the horse, he would ride until he overtook the first and then continue some distance ahead. Then he would tie the horse for his companion to ride and take his own turn at walking. It was a slow

method but better than having no horse at all. A cut above travel by shank's mare or by ride and tie was the saddle train, probably the earliest and certainly most primitive mode of public conveyance, by which owners furnished horses to carry riders, a small amount of baggage, and provisions.[14]

Early in 1863 when gold seekers hurried up the Columbia River to the Boise Basin mines, some brought along their own saddle horses. A few more had pack animals, but the great majority arrived without any animals, nor could they afford to purchase any once they reached Umatilla or Wallula. Every time a steamer landed two hundred or more miners at Umatilla, at least half would have heavy packs already strapped to their backs and be ready to move as soon as the gangplank touched the shore. "Each one appeared to want to be in the lead for fear the other fellow might get there first and get the best claim."[15]

Many argonauts would buy a lunch, "roll it up in

their blankets, shoulder them and 'hit the road' in a few minutes after they landed from the steamer, trusting to replenish their stock of grub at some packer's camp or at some of the temporary stations established on the road for the purpose of collecting toll on some trail or horse-bridge and also for selling something to drink. We cannot say it was whiskey, although called by that name; at any rate, a little of it went a long ways." Most of the pilgrims who set out in so casual a fashion suffered greatly long before reaching their destinations, and many arrived footsore and half-starved. At first all went well, as the trail headed east across the rolling Columbia Plateau, but where it climbed the steep slopes of the Blue Mountains, nature would torment the greenhorns unmercifully. "There was snow on many parts of the road and the sun shining brightly on the snow, made many a poor fellow snow-blind." [16]

Given the dangers that faced any individual or party unfamiliar with the rugged terrain, many gold seekers preferred to hire transportation for themselves and their baggage from someone familiar with the road who would pack a sufficient supply of provisions for the trip and, when the time came to camp, care for the animals. Aboard every steamboat were some gold seekers who had money enough to buy passage overland. They would always stop and inquire about local transportation, but until 1864 the only conveyance available from Umatilla was a saddle train. These outfits generally consisted of about twenty horses or mules, sixteen with riding saddles and four that carried blankets, small grips, and provisions to feed sixteen passengers.

The owner supplied each rider with a horse and saddle plus food enough for the trip, along with all the necessary cooking utensils. Passengers did the cooking in camp and took turns standing guard at night, while the train master would care for the animals and pack up the baggage and camp outfit daily. He also paid all tolls en route. For this service, the usual passenger fare from Umatilla to the Boise Basin was fifty dollars in gold, paid in advance. Saddle trains often left Umatilla within two hours of a steamboat's arrival and reached the Boise Basin camps

eight days later. Among the pioneers of this primitive form of commercial transportation were William Ish and John Hailey, partners who in mid-April 1863 inaugurated saddle train service across the Blue Mountains to the Boise Basin. "Very soon other saddle trains started to carry passengers and the fare was reduced to forty dollars and later to thirty dollars. By September the travel to the Basin was almost over for the season, so we engaged in packing." [17]

By February 10, 1864, the ice broke up on the Columbia River, and four days later the Oregon Steam Navigation Company dispatched one of its steamboats from Celilo to Umatilla. Even at that early date it carried a large number of passengers who were eager to return to the mines of the Boise Basin. As soon as the boat docked at Umatilla, many of the men rushed to the office of Ish and Hailey in the Orleans Hotel to book saddle train transportation. Ish and Hailey's operation was closed for the winter, and their horses and mules were still out on winter range nearby. But the weather was so warm and pleasant that many of the argonauts pleaded for a ride, so a saddle train was driven in and quickly rigged for the journey. Gold seekers continued to flood into Umatilla, and Ish and Hailey sent out a saddle train loaded with passengers every time a steamboat came up the Columbia, which was three times a week. "There were also hundreds along the road on foot, carrying their blankets and lunches. These men had a hard trip." The saddle train business blazed a trail for the stagecoach lines that soon supplanted it. The successive modes of land transportation to the Rocky Mountain mines evolved in much the same fashion on the Missouri River side.[18]

Prior to the spring of 1866 there were no regular stagecoach connections between Fort Benton and the diggings at Helena or elsewhere. Travelers had to purchase outfits of their own or make use of whatever irregular facilities existed. John Mullan advised sojourners as late as 1865 to purchase light wagons in Saint Louis and horses or mules in Fort Benton. Apparently it was C. C. Huntley who offered the first reliable public transportation by land out of Fort Benton when he dispatched a stagecoach to Helena on a semiweekly schedule starting in mid-May 1866. The volume of passenger traffic was so great that he instituted triweekly service in August and then daily service in September for the remainder of the season. The following year, Huntley won a contract to carry the United States mail between Fort Benton and Helena for a six-month period beginning in April. Huntley's success soon attracted other operators, notably Wells Fargo, to serve the route.

Stagecoaches to the Rocky Mountain Diggings

In mining centers of the northern West, the first stage lines extended inland from one of the river gateways or north from Salt Lake City, where coaches had operated along the central overland route since the late 1850s. Not long after prospectors discovered gold in Grasshopper Gulch, in what is now southwestern Montana, in 1862, Andrew Jackson (Jack) Oliver, a former California miner, provided a vital service by carrying letters between Salt Lake City and Bannack at one dollar each. The following year he switched to a primitive covered wagon, providing much-needed mail service where none existed and hauling an occasional passenger.

During the spring of 1863, news of still more gold discoveries in Idaho caused a stampede along the central overland route rivaled only by the California rush of 1849 and the Pike's Peak boom a decade later. Ben Holladay, "the Stagecoach King," put on extra coaches to haul the crush of passengers west from Missouri River landings, but he also more than doubled the fare. Those who were in a hurry and had money enough took Holladay's coaches to Salt Lake City, but "it was impossible for the stage line to carry one-fourth of the big rush." In some instances, seats had to be reserved well in advance. Holladay profited greatly from the mining traffic, and so too did local operators like Jack Oliver and his several competitors who offered passage north from Salt Lake City. Oliver stocked the 400-mile trail between Salt Lake City and Virginia City with mules and a few secondhand coaches and offered triweekly service, charging passen-

gers \$150 each. Other transportation pioneers of less ambitious reach mined for profits by hauling passengers on the local routes between Virginia City and outposts like Prickly Pear, French Gulch, and Silver Bow.[19]

Stage lines commenced service between Umatilla and Wallula and inland points such as Walla Walla and Lewiston within a year or two of the first gold discoveries on Oro Fino Creek. Beginning in mid-March 1864, Ish and Hailey's Pioneer Stage ran triweekly coaches between the steamboat landing at Umatilla and the base of the Blue Mountains, a distance of about fifty miles. Beyond there deep winter snows made the road impassable for wheeled vehicles. "In the meantime, stations had been established on the remainder of the route from twenty to twenty-five miles apart. Relays of horses were at each

An advertisement for the Walla Walla and Lewiston Stage Line in 1864. Courtesy Idaho State Historical Society, 75.228.83.

WALLA WALLA
AND
LEWISTON
STAGE LINE!

Carrying U. S. Mails and Wells, Fargo & Co.'s Express.

THROUGH IN ONE DAY!

Leaves WALLA WALLA and LEWISTON every other day, connecting with stages to

WALLULA, BOISE AND FLORENCE,
AND EXPRESSES TO
ORO FINO AND ELK CITY.

PASSENGERS Leaving LEWISTON in the Morning reach the Steamers at WALLULA the SAME DAY.

Passengers' Fare, \$15.00.

☞ TWENTY-FIVE pounds of BAGGAGE allowed each passenger. EXTRA baggage, on freight, 12 cents per pound.

STAGE OFFICES:

In Lewiston, at . . . . HILL BEACHY'S.
In Walla Walla, at . . . . KOHLAUFF & GUICHARD'S.
SEPTEMBER 3d, 1864.

station and arrangements were made for passengers to get meals at these stations. Two of these routes were traveled over each day. Dinner was had at the noon station and a change of horses. While this was not so comfortable as riding on the cars, it was certainly quite an improvement on the camping out and riding the same horses over the whole road." By the first of May, and after most of the snow had melted and road conditions improved, coaches traveled seventy miles east from La Grande to Express Ranch. Operators were ready to provide through coaches to Boise about the first of June.[20]

Hailey, one of the few stage pioneers ever to write a detailed history of his enterprise, described the troubles he and Ish had to overcome to begin service. "Harness was scarce and often had to be changed from one team to another for a short time. Stations were established from ten to fifteen miles apart, with relays of horses and a stock tender at each station to have the horses ready so as to have as little delay as possible." Ish and Hailey did not have barns or stables at all of their relay stations at first. "It was impossible sometimes to do more than build corrals and the horses were driven into these corrals and caught and harnessed there. The grass was good at the majority of the stations, so the stock could live well on the range. Stock had to be kept up and fed at two stations on the Blue Mountains, one station at Placerville, and two at the Umatilla end of the route. This was rather expensive, as hay and grain was very high." Many of the same start-up troubles afflicted other pioneer operators.

Ish and Hailey were not without competitors. That same spring of 1864, two other stage companies joined forces to operate a line of coaches between the steamboat landing at Wallula and the Boise Basin: George F. Thomas and Company stocked the road from Wallula through Walla Walla to Express Ranch on the Burnt River, and Henry Greathouse and Company continued from there to Placerville, Idaho Territory. This company's route crossed the Blue Mountains over what was commonly called the Thomas and Ruckles road, located about twelve miles north of the route followed by Ish and Hailey between Umatilla and the Boise Basin. The two companies on the Wallula route hauled passengers and Wells Fargo express, but no mail, which at this time was still carried on saddle or pack horses.

There was a great deal of rivalry between the Umatilla and Wallula lines, but in the end the Thomas company won the contest; and from 1864 to 1866 it carried the mail for Ben Holladay between Boise and The Dalles. In this way Holladay and his subcontractors expanded the options available to overland stage passengers. For hardy travelers from Oregon who had to reach the East, the fastest route became by steamboat to Wallula, by stage from there to the Utah capital, and thence via Holladay's Overland stages.

Yet, the Columbia River gateway had no monopoly over stagecoaching or any other form of transportation to the moneymaking mines of Idaho. In addition to the routes that extended from Salt Lake City and Fort Benton, other stage pioneers, including John Mullan, stretched lines north to Idaho from Nevada and California in the mid-1860s to forge bold new passenger and freight links that bypassed Portland entirely and thus greatly worried the Oregon Steam Navigation Company. During the vicious contest that followed, one of the Portland company's big steamboats could actually be seen steaming through the empty sagebrush country of southern Idaho to capture trade from California. Even that was not the strangest episode to result from transportation rivalries during the northern West's steamboat and stagecoach era.

A freighter is not necessarily a bad man; he is often generous to a fault, but his language will not bear repeating here. . . . A freighter accumulates a vocabulary that would start almost any balky horse. His oaths pour through his lips like water down a hill. With every crack of the whip as it cuts into the sage-brush, or into the flank of the leader, or the wheelhorse, there is an accompaniment of profanity long, loud, and strong that dies away in mutterings of the same hot stuff, until Rock, or Pete, or Jim, lags a bit behind the other sturdy pullers, then he begins anew his oration of oaths as he snaps the whip on the ears or haunches of the delinquent animal.

—Carrie Adell Strahorn, Fifteen Thousand Miles by Stage *(1911)*

Long Hauls Overland: The Freighters

Lloyd Magruder left California in search of a better life in the gold camps of the northern Rocky Mountains. With the elusive goal of personal success almost within his grasp, the 37-year-old packer headed his string of mules west over the Bitterroot Mountains from Virginia City toward Lewiston. Disposing of trade goods in the booming mining camps of Bannack and Virginia City had netted him a personal fortune worth at least ten thousand dollars in gold dust, maybe more, which he now carried home to Lewiston through the lonely, mountainous terrain traversed by the South Nez Perce Trail.

Ahead lay some of the most rugged mountain country in the entire northern West, where seven grueling ascents to ridge tops were followed by seven equally steep descents into creek bottoms. Even in the 1990s, more than 130 years later, the United States Forest Service warned motorists who contemplated driving the back-country dirt trail now called the Magruder Corridor that they could "encounter a variety of dangerous conditions. It is your responsibility to inform yourself about these inherent risks and take appropriate precautions." John Mullan once considered converting the Indian trail into

a military road but decided against it because of the deep winter snows and other obstacles.[1]

Samuel Parker, who followed the trail with a party of Indians in the fall of 1835 on his way west as an advance agent of American missionary activity, complained that they were "constantly ascending and descending." He described the forbidding topography as "mountain raising above mountain, and perpendicular above perpendicular." Suffering from high fever, headache, and general fatigue, Parker feared for a time that he might die in the Bitterroot Mountains. He later "rejoiced to find myself wholly through the Salmon river mountains, and convalescent. These mountains were far worse to pass than the Rocky Mountains, as we could not take advantage of any valley, excepting one in which we journeyed only two-thirds of a day. Excepting the middle of the days, the atmosphere was cold, and frequently ice was formed during the night."[2]

Even encountering these formidable natural obstacles, Lloyd Magruder might well have returned home with his treasure and life intact had his luck not run out during the night of October 11, 1863. In a grisly crime that shocked the entire Rocky Mountain West, four men who had volunteered to accompany the mule train shot or axed to death the popular Magruder and four of his companions, hid or burned the evidence, including several pack animals, grabbed the gold, and hurried west.

William ("Hill") Beachey, a Lewiston hotelkeeper and friend of Magruder's, became suspicious when he learned that four strangers had passed through town using a saddle and horse that belonged to Magruder's packtrain. On the strength of this evidence and his recent strange dream that some harm had befallen Magruder, Beachey set out in hot pursuit, armed with a temporary commission as deputy sheriff, a warrant for the arrest of the four suspects, and an extradition warrant from Idaho's territorial governor (then residing in Lewiston). The highwaymen had five days' advantage, but when Beachey learned that the quartet had boarded a coastal steamer for California, he turned south at Portland and raced overland by horse and buggy and stagecoach to his former hometown of Yreka, which he knew was the northernmost end of the telegraph line. From there he urged the San Francisco chief of police to apprehend, arrest, and hold the fugitives until he arrived.

In this manner Beachey intercepted the four suspects, and after four weeks of legal wrangling he returned with them to Idaho. After a short trial in Lewiston, three of the four murderers were hanged, largely on the basis of evidence provided by the fourth, though not before newly formed Idaho Territory discovered that it actually had no criminal law. Despite this technicality, few if any Idahoans regretted the "illegal" hanging of Lloyd Magruder's killers. Soon, extralegal vigilantes in Virginia City and Bannack, then located within the sprawling territory, would hang a far greater number of chronic lawbreakers than these three. When persistent searchers located the scene of the crime the following spring, they found what little remained of Magruder: "a few bones, some buttons from Magruder's coat, some fire-arms, etc. The coyotes had been too busy to leave much." [3]

This bizarre tale of crime and punishment underscores the wave of lawlessness that swept across the northern Rocky Mountains after 1861 and the perils it posed to packers and others who risked their lives hauling precious cargoes of gold. Lloyd Magruder was only one of many victims. There was also John Welch, a packer held up at Grass Valley, Oregon, who, upon turning over a sizable amount of gold dust to his robbers, burst out, "I'll see you again." "No you won't," was the highwayman's reply as he casually shot off Welch's head with a double-barreled shotgun. [4]

Freight charges and wages were always paid in gold, and as a result the typical packtrain carried large amounts of the precious dust. But at times it became too dangerous to pack any gold at all, and honest citizens complained that "all the jail doors have been opened in the states and the bad men come here." In remote camps and along secluded sections of numerous trails, thieves imperiled the life of anyone who carried gold. "In the wilderness, highwaymen (who liked to call themselves road agents) ambushed and murdered California-bound miners loaded with riches, and plundered the treasure, whenever opportunity knocked." At one time on the heavily used yet lonely trail that stretched across the Blue Mountains from the Columbia River to the Boise Basin, highwaymen, or "toll collectors," as Theodor Kirchhoff called them, "were said to be in control of the road, their behavior most impolite. Not satisfied with relieving peaceful travelers of the usual tribute—'superfluous' gold watches, chains, rings, brooches, gold dust, coins, currency, and other luxuries—the highwaymen were reputed to treat male travelers roughly and take pleasure in shooting at them with revolvers in disagreeable ways." Yet, brave entrepreneurs could make fortunes for themselves by transporting precious cargoes safely through the gauntlet of robbers. [5]

Before 1870, considerable gold was hauled from the interior to Fort Benton in wagon trains and then shipped down the Missouri River. Express companies commonly charged 5 percent of its value to ship gold safely to the States. With some three million dollars worth of gold dust transported down the Columbia River in 1861, and Alder Gulch alone yielding over ten million dollars' worth two years later, the temptation to acquire what seemed like an easy fortune simply overwhelmed some thieves. Express companies responded in kind. Wells

Fargo, which opened its first office in Lewiston in 1861, often dispatched its messengers armed with a six-shooter or sawed-off shotgun (frequently both) to accompany shipments of the precious metal by stage or steamboat.

More than anything else, it was the traffic related to gold mining, if not always the transport of gold itself, and the surging population growth in widely scattered camps that encouraged packers like Lloyd Magruder, stagecoach operators like Ben Holladay, and the various steamboat companies to forge a network of transportation lines to serve the needs of the hitherto isolated northern West. From Fort Benton to Helena during the freighting season of 1866, an estimated twenty-five hundred men, three thousand teams, twenty thousand oxen and mules, and six hundred wagons were engaged in the business of hauling freight. This traffic hit a peak in 1867 when some thirty-nine steamboats carried approximately ten thousand tons of freight up the Missouri River to Montana.

Commercial wagon freighting never became extensive in those portions of Oregon and Washington west of the Cascade mountains. But until the coming of railroads to the Columbia Plateau and northern Rocky Mountains, it remained vital to inland settlements, where freight and express outfits were needed to haul everything from writing paper to mining machinery, from barrels of molasses and whiskey to a few pounds of perishable butter, and even oranges. Miners headed to the Oro Fino diggings in 1861 noticed that along the fertile bottomlands of the Clearwater and Snake rivers were farms where the Nez

Perce had planted corn and vegetables; some also raised chickens and cattle that they offered to sell to newcomers. "These Indians have some fine farms here and apparently well cultivated. I had not seen either chicken or egg since June last, but there we saw both chickens and eggs—chickens for three dollars apiece, and eggs four dollars a dozen." Some Nez Perce farms were quite large. Even so, Indians were unable to raise enough food to feed the rapidly growing mining camps, nor did they necessarily want to. Until the output of local farms and ranches (those of Indians as well as newer settlers) increased significantly after the mid-1860s, enormous quantities of flour, meat, and other foodstuffs had to be imported from the Willamette Valley and elsewhere, thus creating freighting opportunities on the Pacific Slope comparable to those out of Fort Benton.[6]

Freight traffic to the interior mines, no less than passenger transport, boosted the fortunes of Portland and placed its economy on a solid footing. Judge Matthew Deady recalled standing at the city's wharves in 1861 "when the drays were loaded going to the boats of the Oregon Steam Navigation Co. and stood in line it seems to me half a mile long; unloading at night so as to go on in the morning up the river."[7]

Not all freight traveled up the Columbia River in barrels and crates. In the spring of 1860 the first rates for shipping livestock by steamboat were published. The following year the Oregon Steam Navigation Company outfitted the *Julia* for carrying cattle and offered special low rates to shippers. Willamette Valley farmers drove herds of cattle to Portland for shipment to the mining camps. During the first eight months of 1862, 46,000 head of cattle went upriver, mostly for beef, but some went to breed new stock on ranches that sprang up in the Walla Walla Valley to feed the miners. By 1864 Oregon Steam had a stock-carrying fleet that hauled sheep, hogs, cattle, and horses. Cattle were driven from Lewiston to Florence to be slaughtered for meat. Livestock traffic to the mines by steamboat and trail remained significant until 1868, when farms and ranches east of the Cascade Range at last produced enough meat on their own to

eliminate the need to import it on the hoof from the Willamette Valley.

Hippah, Mulah!

The population of Boise Basin mining camps during the excitement of 1863 may have swelled to as many as twenty thousand people, mostly men, and all of them hungry. Except for small amounts of freight, mainly flour, that came from Salt Lake City, all food had to be packed overland from steamboat landings at Umatilla or Wallula or from farms newly planted around Walla Walla. For a time even a fish wagon prospered by hauling loads of fresh salmon to Boise Basin miners. Numerous mules and horses were required to transport supplies during the busy spring and summer months because it was necessary to pack in enough food not only to satisfy current needs but also to last through the winter until packtrains arrived again the following spring.[8]

Even so, starvation always remained a possibility in isolated camps during winter months, and personal survival often required making difficult decisions. One group of prospectors who reached the Boise Basin in December 1862 found themselves trapped by a winter storm: "There stood our nice old steers, all covered with white snow looking imploringly at us for something to eat. They had been our best friends, had carried our loads, had been our best companions, while lost in the mountains, had slept at our bedside. To kill and eat them looked like cannibalism, but what else could we do? Shoot them?" Because not one of the six prospectors would volunteer or be hired to shoot their steers, they had to cast lots.[9]

When scurvy broke out in Florence during its first winter of isolation, the only way to get edibles into the camp was on the backs of "Boston jackasses," a term used for strong men who shouldered loads of provision weighing from sixty to seventy-five pounds. "Not until May could the pack trains get to within a dozen miles of Florence" because of the snowdrifts, and so the Boston jackasses earned forty cents a pound carrying provisions the last part of the way. With each round-trip a man might clear as much as thirty dollars.[10]

Packtrains still served Clarkia, Idaho, and many other small towns of the northern West in the early twentieth century. A typical mule would carry 300 to 500 pounds of flour in burlap sacks and liquor in 28-gallon kegs. Occasionally the sturdy animals hauled quartz mills, burial caskets, cans of blasting powder, and even pianos on their backs. One particularly husky mule carried a crescent-shaped steel plate weighing 667 pounds more than a hundred miles from Lewiston to Warren over the steep and difficult terrain of the Salmon River watershed. The plate was needed for a stamp mill. Courtesy Idaho State Historical Society, 80–37.34.

Even the more conventional packtrains of horses or mules, while offering simple and reliable transportation, were an exceedingly expensive way to haul freight. A large train consisting of several dozen animals could not carry as much cargo as would fit into two ordinary freight wagons. In addition, grain usually had to be hauled along to supplement the meager forage found along mountain trails, and this feed for draft animals further reduced the total volume of merchandise freight. Wages for the minimum of four or five men required to handle a train of fifty mules added more expense because each muleteer received from $100 to $125 a month, in addition to board. But at first there were simply no alternatives to packtrains. Most early diggings were located

far from farms and practical wagon roads. Bulky agricultural products could not be easily and economically packed on the backs of mules, but the lower-priced alternative of wagon freighting was not usually available until a camp had survived its first tenuous months.

Given the high demand and the low initial costs—the average pack mule sold for about $250—it was not difficult to launch a packing or express business, but success in either enterprise depended on different personal qualities. The express business prized speed, integrity, and the good marksmanship needed to protect valuable cargoes. The work of hauling heavy or bulky freight by packtrain required other skills, although packers always armed themselves with rifles and revolvers. In addition

to the brute strength it took to load and unload several animals each day, packers needed expert judgment to match the weight of cargo with an animal's carrying ability. The average load for a mule was approximately 350 pounds, with as many as forty or fifty, sometimes even a hundred, animals forming a pack string. "Having to lift heavy weights sheer from the ground onto the pack saddle, 'packers' are very muscular men, with grand chests and shoulders. They have also many savage accomplishments: are good farriers, can accomplish marvels with the axe, a screw key and a young sapling for a lever. But they are a godless race both actively and passively," complained the minister James Reynard in 1869. "They earn considerable wages, and after a few years settle down in some of our beautiful valleys, surrounded by an Indian clientele."[11]

After each mule took its accustomed place in line, the packtrain started out and kept going until time to make camp for the night. Packing and unpacking mules each morning and evening was a lengthy job, and drivers felt that going through the process again at noon wasted too much precious time and human energy. If an adjustment had to be made to a pack or if there was a problem with a particular mule on the trail, the entire train kept moving while the mule involved was stopped and the difficulty remedied. The mule caught up with the train later.

Packs had to be adjusted often. No matter how carefully a packer prepared the load each morning, it invariably settled as the mule jogged along, loosening the lashings until the pack had to be rearranged and the lashings tightened again. It took an expert to balance the load while placing the pack saddle and cargo on a mule, and blindfolds were often used to keep the mule from getting skittish. When camp was reached at last, the packs and saddles were removed and the mules turned out to graze. Only the bell mare was hobbled

A pack train pauses in Crawford, Idaho, about 1908. Packing by donkeys (pictured here) or by mules was not without its problems. Mules sometimes lost their footing and fell, as happened in dramatic fashion when one stumbled at a steep place and scattered a load of women's garments through the treetops. Some mules would attempt to rub off their heavy packs against trees. There were also problems with liquid cargoes, usually whiskey, that sloshed around too much and sprang mysterious leaks in the wilderness (no doubt with a little help from packers). Courtesy Idaho State Historical Society, 61.23.7.

or staked out, since other mules would not stray very far from her.

A typical outfit included several riding mules for the packers and a bell mare to lead the way and to carry a rider who also served as cook. All muleteers understood the importance of a bell mare. Usually a light-colored horse that the mules could see in the dark, she wore a bell that tinkled reassuringly whenever she could not be seen. This sound was a great attraction for trained pack animals, and they would follow her docilely anywhere they could hear the bell. In this way a packtrain covered from fifteen to twenty miles a day. Most started by six o'clock and made camp for the day by early afternoon. If it stormed or rained heavily, the train remained in camp another day. Heavy snows usually ended packing in the mountains around November.

Along narrow trails of the northern Rocky Mountains there was no real alternative to hauling freight on the backs of mules or horses, although some packers experimented with camels, believing they would travel much faster, carry heavier loads, and be more likely to frighten Indians, thus enabling trains to escape any raids. But camels posed problems of their own. Granville Stuart described the fiasco that resulted when promoters of camel power staged a public demonstration in Virginia City to illustrate how a single dromedary could carry several children or a thousand pounds of freight and to show that the animals would kneel and rise on command. "One young lady of sixteen summers perched comfortably on one of the kneeling animals, but when the awkward beast attempted to regain its feet she was wholly unprepared for the sudden dip forward and was pitched head first into the street, but fortunately escaped serious injury. This mishap brought the exhibition to a close and as the strange animals frightened every horse that came in sight of them, causing serious runaways, the owner was ordered to take them out of town." Two small camel packtrains of about six and twelve animals respectively made a trip from Umatilla to the Boise Basin, but after they stampeded a large freight outfit and caused considerable damage, they had to be withdrawn and sent elsewhere.[12]

In March 1863, after the rush to interior mining camps commenced again, steamboats disgorged large amounts of freight at Umatilla and Wallula where packers loaded it on their animals for the long haul to the Boise Basin mines. It required about thirteen days to complete the three-hundred-mile journey. In the Blue Mountains, where the trail was narrow and cut through deep snow, the number of pack animals was so great that they created severe bottlenecks. "An average of one hundred and fifty pack animals pass over this trail daily, sometimes forming a string a quarter mile long," observed C. Aubrey Angelo. "An unloaded train coming from the opposite direction is invariably compelled to give way to a loaded one; must either diverge into the snow, or, if the latter is too deep, must retrace their way to some spot better adapted for the purpose. For this reason, return trains usually push through during the night."[13]

John Hailey had a similar experience when he headed back to Umatilla for another load. "Night came on and found us sitting out in the snow with the result of not having made more than five miles. We resolved to travel all night while those going in the opposite direction were in camp." Hailey opined that "the trip was rough and disagreeable and none but strong, energetic men could stand the work in stormy weather. We earned all we got."[14]

During the summer of 1864, roads were at last completed so that freight could be hauled from Umatilla to the Boise Basin by wagon. This development reduced rates by up to 50 percent and made it possible to haul items that could not be cheaply or easily packed by mule, such as large stoves and household furniture. The change benefited consumers during the summer and fall months, but packtrains still prevailed during the winter and spring seasons for several more years because snow and mud made roads impassable for wagons. In the late fall, likewise, packtrains continued to reach camps in Idaho and Montana for weeks after early snows had closed roads to wheeled vehicles.

The *Montana Post* estimated that as many as ten thousand pack animals hauled freight to various parts of the territory as late as 1866. And even after railroads finally extended their tracks across the northern West during the 1870s and 1880s, pack mules and horses continued to haul freight to many isolated camps where miners hailed the muleteers' echoing cries of "Hippah, mulah" as synonymous with the arrival of welcome supplies and food.

Wagon Wheels

When wagonloads of merchandise finally rolled through the northern Rocky Mountains in the mid-1860s, they represented the latest phase in the evolution of commercial freighting across the American West. This industry dated from the 1840s—during the early days of the Oregon Trail across the Great Plains—and grew quickly into a giant enterprise. "Few persons except those who saw with their own eyes can have a correct idea of the enormous amount of traffic on the overland route in those early days. There were trains constantly outfitting and crossing the plains from Omaha, Nebraska City, St. Joseph, Atchison, Leavenworth, and a few other points. This, it should be remembered, was before the railroads had passed west of the Missouri river, and everything had to be hauled by oxen, mules, and horses."[15]

For nearly three decades, until completion of the transcontinental railroad in 1869, ox and mule teams, and a smaller proportion of horse teams, hauled millions of tons of supplies across the American prairies and into the mountains for military and other expeditions and for emigrants on their way to California, Oregon, or the Great Salt Lake valley. By one estimate, the freighting business across the high plains in 1865 employed 8,960 wagons, 14,620 mules, 59,440 cattle, and 11,220 men to move 54,000 tons of freight to various destinations.[16]

A regular pattern of travel developed. Each spring during the 1850s and 1860s freighters hastened to be the first to head west from Missouri River landings. Long trains of heavily loaded wagons, drawn by mules or oxen, moved out daily; but immense warehouses and large yards remained full of massive machines for working the mines, goods for feeding and clothing the miners, and agricultural implements to cultivate the prairies,

all awaiting the trip west. Samuel Bowles reported in the mid-1860s that the "mule trains have been in progress for a month, but the ox-teams have had to wait till now, so that the animals could be fed on the grass *en route*."[17]

It was during the late 1850s and early 1860s that the ox trains of Russell, Majors and Waddell of Leavenworth were most conspicuous. William Russell, Alexander Majors, and William Waddell formed a remarkable partnership, and the volume of business done by their freighting firm was enormous. Much of their transport consisted of hauling supplies from the Missouri River to isolated army posts such as Forts Union, Laramie, Bridger, and others scattered across the West. The so-called Mormon War vastly increased their cargoes when they transported General Albert Sidney Johnston's army, together with its vast military stores and subsistence, from Fort Leavenworth west across the Great Plains and Rocky Mountains to Utah. "The supplies sent to Utah in the year 1858 were enormous," recalled Majors, "being over sixteen million pounds, requiring over three thousand five hundred large wagons and teams to transport them. We found it was as much as we could do to meet the Government requirements with the two points in full operation."[18]

Most of the ponderous freight wagons of Russell, Majors and Waddell were constructed in Saint Louis to carry as many as seven thousand pounds of merchandise each. While engaged in the transportation business, and when commerce was brisk, this partnership owned and operated as many as 6,250 wagons pulled by as many as 75,000 oxen. Animals and equipment, yoked together and hitched, would have formed a train forty miles long. Theirs was a million-dollar enterprise that over the years employed thousands of men.

None of the other freight outfits serving the mining camps of the northern West was as large as Russell, Majors and Waddell. At first, many small companies competed for the lucrative gold camp traffic. Prior to 1865, freighters out of Fort Benton could command their own terms, sometimes receiving as much as ten cents per pound in gold to haul goods to Helena. Such high rates spurred competition, with firms such as the Diamond R

MISSOURI RIVER

*T*he Missouri River entrepôt of Leavenworth, Kansas, in the late 1860s. Courtesy Library of Congress, GM 1420/412070.00

Transportation Company, E. G. Maclay and Company, Garrison and Wyatt, Carrol and Steel, Hugh Kirkendall, and scores of smaller ones churning along the dusty roads leading to and from the steamboat landing at Fort Benton. The largest was the Diamond R Transportation Company, which originated in Virginia City in 1864 as a freighting outfit to ship goods, mainly hides, to Helena. Within a few years the company's wagons were hauling

cargoes from Fort Benton overland to Missoula, Virginia City, and Helena. Its business really took off in 1869 with the beginning of a major freight haul from the newly completed transcontinental railroad at Corinne, Utah, to settlements in Montana.

As the territory's premier freighting outfit, Diamond R became as important to Montana in the 1860s and 1870s as transcontinental railroads were to the state in later

decades. At one time the equipment of Diamond R consisted of 350 mules, 500 yoke of oxen, and 300 wagons, besides countless saddles, harnesses, and buildings, having a total value of about $250,000, a huge sum on the frontier. Every wagon, animal, and saddle was branded with a large R in a diamond, which led some employees to joke that they too were tattooed with the familiar mark.

After a steamboat docked at Fort Benton, freighters worked quickly to transfer goods to freight wagons or warehouses, since boat officers were nervous about remaining in the river port any longer than a few days. They realized only too well that a slight drop in the water level could leave them stranded, perhaps until high water the following spring. A large fleet of freight wagons soon lumbered out of the river bottoms that surrounded Fort Benton and creaked slowly across the plains and mountains toward the diggings a hundred or more miles away. Still more of the heavy wagons traveled north from Utah.

The glory years of wagon freighting across the north-

Freighting in Silver City, Idaho, during the 1890s. All over the northern West the change from packtrains to wagons enabled consumers to purchase their groceries and other supplies much more cheaply than before and prevented merchants from claiming that high prices reflected mainly the high cost of packing freight. Courtesy Special Collections, Utah State University Library, A-3440.

ern West occurred during the two decades bracketed by 1864 and 1884, and not just in western Montana and eastern Idaho. When roads were in good condition, large wagons hauled freight east over the Blue Mountains. Usually three wagons were coupled together, loaded with twenty thousand pounds of freight, and drawn by twelve good mules, or six or seven yoke of oxen. This mode of transportation lowered the cost of hauling freight to about one-half of what it had been when everything was transported by pack mules or horses.

Much wagon freight continued to enter the Boise Basin from Umatilla until the summer of 1869 when completion of the transcontinental railroad opened a new gateway into southern Idaho from Kelton, Utah, the total distance being about forty miles less than from

Umatilla to the Boise Basin, with better grass to feed draft animals and fewer tolls for bridges and ferries. (It sometimes took half the earnings of a pack animal to pay tolls along the Blue Mountains route). The major exception to this pattern was Silver City, where much freight was hauled by wagon from the Central Pacific Railroad at Winnemucca for four to six cents a pound, a rate comparable to that charged from Kelton. Packtrains simply could not compete with this low rate. Some packers left for more promising diggings, some sold their mules and quit the business altogether, while a few specialized in hauling small cargoes to remote mountain mining camps where there were still no wagon roads.

Transportation of a commodity as basic as flour could present major problems in a mining community, especially when it had to be hauled through winter snows. Nothing, perhaps not even gold, approached flour in importance, yet it was not until 1869 that Montana was able to produce enough flour locally to satisfy demand. Until then, flour was the main commodity shipped north from Utah, and its price fluctuated wildly as a result of seasonal impediments to freighting. The winter of 1864–65 began in October and did not relent until the following April. Temperatures remained extremely low, and snow on the Continental Divide reached eighteen feet deep. As a result of early storms, the worried editor of Virginia City's *Montana Post* remarked that "flour went up four dollars the morning of the snow. If it continues to go up as the snow comes down, where will it stop?" The wholesale price for flour on October 29 was listed as twenty-six dollars. Eventually the high price combined with scarcity to cause a food riot. Several years later, during the summer of 1871 in Helena, the arrival of a much-delayed wagon train prompted public rejoicing because it dropped the price of tobacco and prevented a sugar and coffee famine. Helena residents attributed the delay to a monumental drinking binge by bullwhackers in Corinne.[19]

Perishable delicacies such as fresh fruit could not wait until bullwhackers sobered up. Instead, such merchandise often reached Montana and Idaho via express wagons that also handled letters and small packages of high value, such as gold dust, bullion, and jewelry, rather than be subjected to delay and extensive bruising in a freight wagon. Ripe peaches and pears sometimes arrived on stagecoaches taxed to capacity with fruit shipped north from Utah orchards at enormous transportation costs.

Mule Skinners and Bullwhackers

The plodding ox transported a considerable amount of the freight that crossed the Great Plains before the railroad, and the sight of a bull train seldom failed to impress travelers from outside the region. "They are not unpicturesque from afar, these long-winding trains, in early morning like lines of white cranes trooping slowly over the prairie, or in more mysterious evening resembling dim sails crossing a rolling sea."[20]

Early plains freighters learned to fasten two wagons together and pull both with one team, thereby cutting their payroll expenses in half and substantially reducing the number of draft animals needed for a train. One driver and his helper could handle both wagons, and while a single wagon might require a six-horse team to pull it, two together could be pulled by eight or ten horses at most. This tandem arrangement proved so successful that freighters soon were using three wagons to a team instead of two. But on steep grades or where mud or deep sand made the going difficult, drivers had to uncouple the wagons and haul one over at a time, then go back for another. When the laborious crossing was completed, they would couple all their wagons together again and continue on. Sometimes, however, wagon freighting completely bogged down.

All across the Blue Mountains, General James Rusling found freight trains bound for Boise City and the mines "hopelessly 'stalled.' Some of the wagons with broken wheels or axles had already been abandoned. Others were watched over by their drivers, stretched on their blankets around huge fires by the roadside, smoking or sleeping, patiently awaiting their comrades, who had taken their oxen or mules to double-up on some team ahead, and would return with double teams for them to-morrow or next day, or the day after—whenever they themselves got through."[21]

Wagon freighting evolved into a business that developed its own specialized lingo, skills, and work force. A teamster was commonly called a bullwhacker and mule skinner. Typically three heavy wagons—lead, swing, and trail—were linked together behind ten to twelve yoke of oxen. Heavy loads, often as high as 9,000 pounds of freight, filled each wagon; a single train often hauled more than 200,000 pounds of cargo.

In a typical Russell, Majors and Waddell train, the number of wagons was twenty-five. These were under the command of a captain, who acted as wagon master, and the outfit usually included an assistant wagon master, a night herder, a *cavallard* driver (whose duty it was to attend to the extra cattle), and various laborers. There was a driver for each team, making a complete force of

L. A. Huffman photographed a bull train jamming the main street of Miles City, Montana Territory, in 1880. Oxen required very little night herding because they would eat the grass until their paunches were full and then lie down and chew their cuds. The veteran bullwhacker Lafe Rose explained to C. S. Walgamott that in the morning "we were able to put these teams, making in all one hundred and twelve head, in the yoke and be ready to roll in as short a time as it would take the same number of men to harness and start three six-horse teams." Courtesy Montana State Historical Society, 981–543.

thirty-one men per train. Every one of them was thoroughly drilled and knew what to do in case of an Indian attack.

Most outfits serving northern Rocky Mountains settlements were considerably smaller. "Our outfit consisted of three drivers and a swamper whose duty it was to cook," one early freighter recalled of his days on the trail from Utah to the Boise Basin. "Each ox had his particular place in the team and was known by his individual name, and was usually so christened on account of some characteristic, such as color, size, action, and so on. But

I have known many hundred oxen, or bulls as they were usually called in those days, to be named Brigham in honor of Brigham Young, the Big Chief. We had three Brighams in our outfit, designated as Big Brigham, Little Brigham, and Brigham With The Big Horn." Bullwhackers invariably walked alongside their plodding teams, swinging long whips at the animals' flanks, snapping the air with an explosive report that from a distance sounded like the crack of a pistol shot, and turning the team to the left or right by loud cries of "Gee" and "Haw." [22]

Bull trains did not operate according to a set schedule,

although there was some pretense of regularity about each day's routine. They commonly started soon after sunup and remained on the move until noon; then after about two hours or so for the animals to eat and rest, they continued until nightfall. "To see a big train go into camp was a great sight. Every one, including the bulls, was under more or less excitement, hungry and in a hurry; the bulls were thirsty, of course, and if there was water within a mile of camp, the moment the yoke was dropped from a bull's neck he was headed, on a trot, for the creek or river, into which he would wade and stand belly deep to cool his overheated flesh." Ten to fifteen miles constituted a good day's journey with oxen, for which the freighters earned an average salary of one dollar plus expenses.[23]

Teamsters considered the patient ox, though slow moving, to be always reliable. "In performing their work the mules were next to oxen. They were tough, could endure fatigue, and were nearly always reliable. Besides, they could be kept much cheaper than horses. Horses were all right for mounting cavalrymen and in maneuvering artillery at the forts along the Platte, but, simmered down to the important matter of transporting army supplies, the mule invariably stood at the front." Many small freighters in Montana Territory used both horses and mules. Much of the flour, bacon, canned goods, groceries, dry goods, and clothing went by horses or mules, for they could cover the same distance significantly quicker than oxen. But many other freighters always insisted that the ox was best. "Nearly all who thoroughly understood the freighting business regarded the ox team as the cheapest and best method of transporting ordinary merchandise." Heavy deadweight, such as mining and other machinery, stoves, hardware, and salt, except in very rare cases, was shipped by ox train.[24]

Freighters might disagree about the relative merits of oxen, mules, and horses, but they all loved the great Murphy wagon with its sixteen-foot bed, six-foot-high sides, and seven-foot-high rear wheels. These behemoths could carry almost five tons and frequently did. Built by Joseph Murphy of Saint Louis, these wagons contained only well-seasoned wood that did not shrink and fall apart on the trail, as did the wood of some other makes. In many other ways, too, the Murphy Wagon bore evidence of the craftsmanship of a master wagon builder, as did the Concord coaches used by stage lines. A second choice of freighters, especially those in the Utah-Montana trade, was the smaller Chicago wagon, which could carry between one and two tons.

Mule skinners and bullwhackers were certain that their animals responded better to profanity than gentle persuasion. "The vocabulary of the bullwhacker when he was driving or handling his team was full of profanity, but he was not necessarily a crude or cruel man." One man recalled, "I worked one season with a bullwhacker who had command of and used as many profane epithets as any bullwhacker that ever wielded a gourd-stick. He was a college man, and in conversation around camp and at meals his English and manners were scholarly."[25]

Regardless of his background, the freighter endured a harsh life. Not only was he exposed to all kinds of weather, but herding animals was a dangerous and often unpleasant task, especially on nights when he was exposed to chilly winds, fog, or the possibility of an Indian raid. Richard Burton claimed that the typical freighter hailed from one of the old East Coast cities, "and, like the civilized man generally, he betrays a remarkable aptitude for facile descent into savagery." He could do nothing "without whisky, which he loves to call tarantula juice, strychnine, red eye, corn juice, Jersey lightning, leg-stretcher, 'tangle-leg,' and many other hard and grotesque names; he chews tobacco like a horse." After 1865 many freighters were veterans of the Civil War. Camp life continued the rough life of the army, emphasizing similar qualities that carried the force of a code in a masculine community.[26]

Every crossing of the Blue Mountains posed a formidable challenge to bullwhackers and mule skinners. "On the fourth day we commenced to go up the Blue Mountains. We fell in with some other teams that were crossing, and we all had a fearful time, such rough roads and hard pulls. Sometimes we would hitch on 15 or 20 yoke of big oxen to one wagon. We had to sleep on the ground or snow under the wagons for shelter, for the insides of the wagons were full of goods to the tops of the bows, and the snow and rain kept us continually wet, and our blankets were soaking wet, but we would dry some to put next to our bodies by the campfires at night after we stopped," recalled Herman Francis Reinhart.[27]

General Rusling thought he knew "mule-drivers in the army in Virginia and Tennessee; but a harder or rougher set, than the ox-men or 'bull-whackers' (as they call themselves) of the Plains and Mountains, it would be difficult perhaps to find, or even imagine. On the road here in the Blue Mountains, with their many yoked teams struggling though the mud and rocks, of course, they were in their element. *Outré*, red-shirted, big-booted, brigand-looking ruffians, with the inseparable bowie-knife and revolver buckled around their waists, they swung and cracked their great whips like fiends, and beat their poor oxen along, as if they had no faith in the law of kindness here, nor belief in a place of punishment hereafter. And when they came to a really bad place— in crossing a stream, or when they struck a stump or foundered in a mud-hole—it is hard to say whether their prodigious, multiplied, and many-headed oaths were more grotesque or horrible. To say 'they swore till all was blue,' would be but a feeble comparison; the whole Mountains coruscated with sulphur!"[28]

Rusling observed twenty or thirty yoke of straining oxen, "with the 'bull-whackers' all pounding and yelling like mad, their huge whip-lashes thick as one's wrist cracking like pistols, was a sight to see—'muscular,' indeed, in all its parts. The noise and confusion, the oaths and thwacks and splashing of the mud, made it indeed the very hell of animals; but, for all that, the wagon was sure to reach *terra firma* at last, no matter how heavily loaded, or pull to pieces."

Alexander Majors would tolerate no such rough language by his employees, and he even formulated a moral code that included this promise: "While I am in the employ of A. Majors, I agree not to use profane language, not to get drunk, not to gamble, not to treat animals cruelly, and not to do anything else that is incompatible with the conduct of a gentleman. And I agree, if I violate any of the above conditions, to accept my discharge without any pay for my services." The boss proudly claimed not to have remembered "a single instance of a man signing these 'iron-clad rules,' as they called them, being discharged without his pay. My employees seemed to understand in the beginning of their term of service that their good behavior was part of the recompense they gave me for the money I paid them." What happened out of Majors's hearing was another matter. He nonetheless believed he could state "with truthfulness that never in the history of freighting on the plains did such quiet, gentlemanly, fraternal feelings exist as among the men who were in my employ and governed by these rules."[29]

During the long hauls overland, the freighters functioned as foot soldiers in battles for the trade and commerce of a vast hinterland that were waged by merchants of Portland, Saint Louis, Salt Lake City, and San Francisco. During the last half of the 1860s, it was uncertain which of these four cities would prevail. Ironically, when the contest abruptly ended, the primary winner was Chicago, a dark horse not even ranked among the original contenders.

In the early twentieth century, horses hauled steel pipe for an irrigation system built across Montana's Bitterroot River. Courtesy University of Montana Library, 69–58.

The subject of securing to California generally, the trade of Idaho and Montana, which now bids fair to be of vast and growing, as well as of lasting importance, is one which should excite the attention of the merchants and citizens of San Francisco at the present time. The People of Portland, Oregon, (strangely, too), have awakened to a lively sense of the importance of the trade, and are actively engaged in devising ways and means to obtain more speedy and direct communication to those Territories.

—C. Aubrey Angelo, Sketches of Travel in Oregon and Idaho *(1866)*

Contested Terrain

Among the more improbable places to hear a steamboat whistle was along the Snake River in the Great Basin desert. There, during the vertiginous days of gold and silver booms in the Boise Basin and Owyhee Mountains, the Oregon Steam Navigation Company constructed the *Shoshone* near old Fort Boise in hopes of intercepting traffic bound from Utah and California to the Idaho camps. So landlocked was the construction site that when the vessel took shape during the winter of 1865–1866, all of its machinery, fittings, and hardware had to be fabricated in The Dalles and then hauled overland from the Columbia River and across the snowy Blue Mountains on sleighs; all lumber was whipsawed on site.

The floating palace in the sagebrush was such a strange spectacle that for the *Shoshone*'s maiden voyage on May 16, 1866, many sightseers came by stagecoach from Boise and Ruby City to Owyhee Ferry, about forty-five miles south of Boise, just to witness this wonder for themselves. It was not an auspicious beginning because a strong wind whipped the 136-foot stern-wheeler completely around two or three times, as if to signify that the mighty Oregon Steam Navigation Company had lost its bearings with this project.

Captain Joseph Myrick completed the *Shoshone*'s inaugural voyage from old Fort Boise to Olds Ferry and Farewell Bend in four hours and forty minutes. The boat's regular triweekly run was to be from Olds Ferry to the Owyhee ferry, although Captain Myrick hoped eventually to reach Lower Salmon Falls. The total distance of about two hundred miles was still well short of the main road linking Salt Lake City and the Boise Basin. The journey thus began nowhere and ended nowhere. Apart from the lack of any substantial cargo to haul between these points, the simplest of miscalculations soon beached the *Shoshone*. Oregon Steam Navigation had forgotten one important thing about a desert environment: "Our Snake boat is laid up for want of wood," Captain J. C. Ainsworth lamented to his colleagues. "We do not think of starting her again before next spring at which time, if we succeed in getting wood, and making the proper connections we will do a fair business and indirectly be of great service to our company."[1]

The misbegotten *Shoshone* languished until May 1869 when the Oregon Steam Navigation Company finally worked out a salvage plan. Cy Smith, an experienced river captain, and a skeleton crew eased the *Shoshone* into the current of the Snake River to begin a tempestuous journey through Hells Canyon. But when they reached the chasm's churning waters at Copper Creek Rapids, about twenty-five miles above the confluence with the Salmon River, an eddy violently spun the steamboat around. Short of wood and unwilling to risk drowning, Smith and his crew tied up the boat and hiked out. They had history on their side: the fur trader Donald ("Perpetual Motion") Mackenzie had explored Hells Canyon in 1819; he even ascended as far as the Boise River in a barge manned by six French-Canadian voyageurs, but his journey did nothing to confirm the Snake River as a transportation artery. In the early 1860s when steamboats first appeared on the waters of the inland Northwest, they probed up the Snake River as far as Lewiston and even a little beyond, but it was obvious that they would be able to navigate only a few stretches of Idaho's most important waterway.

The Oregon Steam Navigation Company hired another captain and more boatmen to free the *Shoshone* from Hells Canyon. In the spring of 1870, a new crew and Captain Sebastian Miller hiked into the remote location. An Ohioan who relocated to Oregon in 1852, Miller eventually became the master of more than forty different steamboats on the Columbia River system. He would certainly need all his accumulated skills, and more, to survive a voyage through the Grand Canyon of the Snake, one that no steamboat had made before.

Miller and his crew overhauled the *Shoshone*'s machinery on the spot, got up a head of steam, and began their wild voyage toward Lewiston, about seventy-five miles downriver. The *Shoshone* would lurch first one way and then another, at times seeming totally out of control as its paddle wheel rose completely out of the churning water. At one point the river's whirling vortexes whipped the vessel around and smashed off her jack staff against one of the pillars of basalt that rose vertically for hundreds of feet above the tortuous channel. To keep abreast of any leaks, Miller placed lighted candles in the darkened hull and paused when necessary to make repairs at one of the canyon's rare beaches.

For two weeks the bluffs and rock walls echoed with

the pant and churn of pipe and wheel. When the *Shoshone* finally rounded the last bend and steamed triumphantly toward Lewiston, Miller shouted through his speaking tube to the engineer Daniel Buchanan, "I say, Buck, I expect if this company wanted a couple of men to take a steamboat through hell they would send for you and me." Lewiston residents, many of whom feared that the vessel had been battered to bits, were amazed to see her arrive in a "badly demolished" but still serviceable condition. The *Shoshone* worked the lower Columbia and Willamette rivers until 1874 when she foundered on a sandbar in the latter waterway. The only salvageable part was the cabin, which drifted ashore in high water and served for years as a chicken coop on a Willamette Valley farm.[2]

The *Shoshone* was only one example of how the Oregon Steam Navigation Company probed the extreme limits of Portland-based trade. During the expansive 1860s, Captain Leonard White constructed a steamboat at the Little Dalles, close to where the Columbia River tumbles across the Canadian border at the forty-ninth parallel. At Colville Landing on the evening of November 18, 1865, he launched the *Forty-Nine* by the light of torches and candles. Within a few days the diminutive steamer was ready to capitalize on a mining rush that seemed imminent in the West Kootenay region of British Columbia. The stern-wheeler steamed upriver from Colville Landing on December 9 through Lower Arrow Lake to reach a point about forty miles above the international boundary two days later. Here White put miners and their supplies ashore. Ainsworth soon reported to his business associates, "White has made four successful trips from Little Dalles to the foot of Death Rapids, a distance of 260 miles. His prospects are good. His success will give us a large share of the Big Bend trade."[3]

Caroline Leighton described what it was like to steam to the far reaches of the Columbia River. She returned to Fort Colville in July 1866 after a voyage "extending two hundred miles north into British Columbia, on the little steamer built in this vicinity for the purpose of carrying passengers and supplies to the Big Bend and other mines

The Oregon STEAM NAVIGATION COMPANY'S Steamers
"WILSON G. HUNT" or "CASCADE," CAPT. JOHN WOLF.
WILL LEAVE PORTLAND DAILY,
(Sundays excepted,) at 5 o'clock A. M. connecting with the
Cascade Railroad,
And Steamers
"ONEONTA", or "IDAHO," CAPT. JOHN McNULTY,
Arriving at the DALLES the same day.

Steamers "Web-foot," "Spray," "Tenino," "Nes Perces Chief,"
"Yakima" and "Owyhee,"
WILL LEAVE CELILO DAILY, during business season, and TRI-WEEKLY there-
after, for UMATILLA, WALLULA and WHITE BLUFFS, (and to points on Snake
River and Lewiston while Snake River is navigable.)

A PASSENGER TRAIN ON THE

DALLES AND CELILO RAILROAD
Will be dispatched from the Dalles in time to connect with boats leaving Celilo.

STAGES will leave Umatilla and Wallula and connect with the boat on Snake River for Owyhee, Boise City, Idaho City, South Boise and Salt Lake.
Stages will also connect with the Boat on Pen de Oreille Lake for Montana Territory.

Stages will also connect with the
Steamer "FORTY-NINE," - Capt. Len. White,
At WHITE'S LANDING, for the
Mining regions of the Upper Columbia River in British Columbia.
J. C. AINSWORTH, Pres.
S. G. REED, Vice Pres.

An advertisement for the Oregon Steam Navigation Company in 1866 described the transportation network that it extended across the Pacific Northwest at the time. Only the Shoshone and a full description of the company's steamer service on the Clark Fork River and Lake Pend Oreille are missing. Courtesy Oregon Historical Society, 91757.

in the upper country. We did not get to the 'Rapids of the Dead.' The boat, this time, did not complete her ordinary trip. Some of the passengers came to the conclusion that the river was never intended to be navigated in places she attempted to run through."[4]

Leighton called the *Forty-Nine* "a very adventurous boat," the first to cross the parallel separating Washington Territory from British Columbia. "I was surprised, when we came to the first of what was called the 'bad water,' to see the boat aim directly for it. It was much better, the captain said, to go 'head on,' than to run the

risk of being carried in by an eddy. I never saw any river with such a tendency to whirl and fling itself about as the Upper Columbia has. It is all eddies, in places where there is the least shadow of a reason for it, and even where there is not; influenced, I suppose, by the adjoining waters. Some of the whirl-pits are ten or fifteen feet deep, measured by the trees that are sucked down into them." Leighton emphasized that most of the Columbia's remote tributaries were similar to the waters braved by the *Forty-Nine*, "wild, unnavigable rivers, flowing through deep cañon and full of torrents and rapids." White would eventually work the *Forty-Nine* up the Columbia almost as far north as present Revelstoke, British Columbia, but the stress of pushing the limits of steamboat navigation apparently took a severe toll on his health. He retired to the Oregon coast, where little more than a year later, the veteran steamboatman died.

In 1866, the same year it launched the *Shoshone* at Olds Ferry, the Oregon Steam Navigation Company also built the *Mary Moody* on Lake Pend Oreille in far northern Idaho to extend its reach up the Clark Fork River toward the mines of Montana. No lake or river seemed too remote to attract the attention of the Portland monopoly when pressed by competition from Saint Louis–based steamboats on the Missouri River or from the California Steam Navigation Company to the south.

During the latter half of the 1860s, merchants from several cities competed for the lucrative mining trade of Montana and Idaho. San Franciscans tested every imaginable combination of routes to gain an advantage over their Portland rivals, reaching inland via the Sacramento River and various overland trails, up the Colorado River, and finally along the Central Pacific Railroad into Nevada, where stage and freight lines extended north to Idaho. Saint Louis merchants, using a combination of Missouri River and overland routes emerged the temporary victors in the contest for Montana trade, although the Missouri entrepôt itself rapidly lost ground to upstart Chicago after 1869. The Oregon Steam Navigation Company battled valiantly for Portland from 1865 to 1867 to retain the Idaho trade and capture that of Montana and the Kootenay mining region of southern British Columbia.

It was this intense rivalry that resulted in oddities such as the *Shoshone* steaming through the sagebrush of southern Idaho.

Gateways to a Golden West

During the 1860s rush to the northern Rocky Mountains, freight and passengers reached the mining centers of Idaho and Montana mainly from three directions: up the Columbia River from Portland, up the Missouri River and overland from gateways in Kansas or Nebraska or farther north from Fort Benton, and overland from San Francisco. Salt Lake City funneled traffic north from both Saint Louis and San Francisco. One alternative to traveling west via Salt Lake City—and the trail most menacing to the Sioux, who resented its intrusion into their favorite hunting grounds—branched off the central overland route at Fort Laramie and extended northwest from there, skirting the eastern slopes of the Big Horn Mountains to reach the valley of the Yellowstone River. The federal government established several military outposts to keep the Bozeman Trail open, including Fort Phil Kearney in Wyoming, the scene of vicious Indian attacks. It was here in 1866 that the Sioux ambushed Colonel William Fetterman and eighty soldiers and left no survivors. Although used only briefly, from 1863 until 1866 (and never by overland stagecoaches), this troubled shortcut to the Montana mines was long remembered as the Bloody Bozeman.

A fourth route, mainly an emigrant trail known as the northern overland route, stretched west across the prairies of Dakota from Saint Paul. It was primarily the Salmon River excitement of the early 1860s that encouraged two large parties of emigrants to trek across the Great Plains from the Red River of the North. In command of one group was Captain James Liberty Fisk, to whom the secretary of war had assigned the duty of providing protection and "at the same time test[ing] the practicability of this northern route for future emigration." A federal mail contract subsidized a triweekly pony express across a thousand miles of open prairie from Fort Abercrombie (on the Red River near present Fargo) and Helena, but this service carried too many

empty pouches and collapsed in 1868 after only eight months of operation because of a combination of severe weather and Indian depredations. The northern overland route seemed to have no future for emigration or anything else.[5]

Ironically, the route that seemed the least promising during the 1860s became the favored thoroughfare two decades later after completion of the Northern Pacific Railroad. Then the big winners would be Saint Paul and Seattle, a city not even in contention in the 1860s. Few people could have anticipated such a thing, especially the boosters of Portland. When General James Rusling visited the Oregon entrepôt in the late 1860s he described it as "full of energy and vigor," believing thoroughly in her future. "The great Oregon Steam Navigation Company had their headquarters here, and poured into her lap all the rich trade of the Columbia and its far-reaching tributaries, that tap Idaho, Montana, and even British America itself. So, also, the coastwise steamers, from San Francisco up, all made Portland their terminus, and added largely to her commerce."[6]

Saint Louis was far older than Portland but no less vigorous a competitor. The federal census reported that Saint Louis in 1860 was by far the largest city of the Midwest with a population of 160,773. At the same time Portland had only 2,874 residents; and, in fact, all of Oregon and Washington combined (which then included Idaho) had a population of only 64,059. As early as 1832, and well before Portland existed, 532 steamboats stopped annually at Saint Louis; by 1845 that number topped 2,000 and would soon exceed 3,000 annually. The amount of freight carried by steamboats docking there jumped from 174,000 tons in 1834 to 716,000 tons a decade later and reached approximately 1.5 million tons in the mid-1850s, when Portland was still little more than an outpost in the wilderness.

Steamboats from Saint Louis transported tons of supplies up the Missouri River to Indian agencies and provided logistical support to western troops. Many an overland journey to the promised lands of Utah and Oregon actually began as a steamboat trip to Westport Landing, Independence, Saint Joseph, or another of the popular river gateways to the West. Some pioneers loaded their wagons aboard steamboats as far east as Pittsburgh, and Missouri River boats usually carried at least some westbound settlers. Because most of these emigrants were poor, boatmen allowed them special low fares: some lived in their wagons on deck and brought along food that they were permitted to prepare in the galley.

Twenty packets set out from Saint Louis for Fort Benton in 1865, and the following year almost sixty boats departed for the goldfields, although not all of them reached their intended destination. Steamboat owners nonetheless discovered gold mines of their own: the *Peter Balen* hauled almost 400 tons of freight to Fort Benton in 1866 at an average of twelve cents per pound. Add to that sum the usual fare of $150 per passenger, and it was not uncommon for steamers to pay for themselves in one trip to the mountains despite the risks that greatly increased their insurance rates. Captain Joseph La Barge

was reported to have cleared $40,000 on a single trip of the *Octavia* in 1867, and profits earned by other vessels during the previous year reportedly ranged from $16,000 to $65,000 each. During 1866 alone, slightly more than eight thousand tons of freight reached Fort Benton and some five thousand passengers (or more than a million dollars in passenger revenues). Of all the freight carried, about one-quarter belonged to the federal government, the remainder being provisions, dry goods, and mining machinery owned by private parties.

The southern gateway to Montana and Idaho was Salt Lake City, by far the most important inland transportation center between the Missouri Valley and California for three decades, 1850–1870. It was also the largest population center in the intermountain West, containing about twenty thousand inhabitants at a time when Helena had only four thousand, and Virginia City and Boise City fewer than two thousand each. After the discovery of gold in Grasshopper Gulch in the early 1860s, the Montana

One of the big Concord coaches of the central overland route pauses in Salt Lake City during the 1860s. When Samuel Bowles reached the City of the Saints in 1865, he wrote enthusiastically, "No internal city of the Continent lies in such a field of beauty, unites such rich and rare elements of nature's formations, holds such guarantees of greatness, material and social, in the good time coming of our Pacific development." Courtesy Utah State Historical Society, 382/p.14, #467.

trail rapidly evolved into the main overland link between the booming mining centers of Bannack, Virginia City, and Helena and the Salt Lake Valley (first Salt Lake City and then Corinne after completion of the transcontinental railroad). From settlements in northern Utah the freighters, stage drivers, and emigrants journeyed north across the arid Snake River plain to distant camps in Montana and Idaho, some of them located nearly five hundred miles away. Produce raised by Utah farmers trundled north in the big Diamond R wagons to feed Montana miners.[7]

Further boosting Salt Lake City's ambition to be the "natural metropolis of all Utah and portions of Nevada, Idaho, Montana, and Colorado," was the overland telegraph line connecting the Atlantic and Pacific oceans, and the daily mail coaches heading east to Nebraska and Kansas, west to California, north to Montana, and northwest to Idaho and the Columbia River. To the south there was the possibility of Colorado River trade, for boosters claimed that the Colorado was navigable all year to Callville in southern Utah, about six hundred miles from its mouth at the Gulf of California. "If the Colorado river is navigated as proposed, freight from San Francisco to Virginia City should not exceed twelve cents per pound."[8]

A Chain of Steam Communications

Though seemingly at a severe geographic disadvantage in competing with Saint Louis and Salt Lake City, the entrepreneurs of Portland labored to improve their river portal to the northern Rocky Mountain mining country. "The importance of securing the Idaho and Montana trade, by the way of Oregon, is of so grave a nature, as to make it necessary that I should dwell for a moment on the subject. The people of Oregon have now a perfect knowledge of the importance of this trade, and actively aided by the O.S.N. Company, are establishing speedy and direct communication to those Territories. But there are other sections of the country using Herculean powers to control this trade. Missouri has hitherto monopolized, and is still striving to retain it," warned C. Aubrey Angelo.[9]

He calculated that Saint Louis, "although far away, and separated from the mining districts by deserts, mountains and long and crooked rivers, difficult to navigate at any season, and impossible in some seasons, has enjoyed a large proportion of the trade, and is striving energetically to engross the whole, or lion's share of it. San Francisco, the legitimate source of supply for that country, may

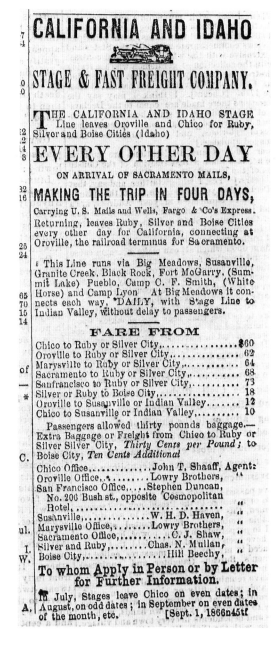

An advertisement for the California and Idaho Stage and Fast Freight Company in 1866. That year, on July 1, Captain John Mullan's first mail coach left Chico for Idaho, but the service soon proved too expensive to maintain. Mail then went by horseback for a time before the route was finally discontinued in March 1867. The Great Basin terrain and the Native Americans who lived there were both so hostile that it was impossible to maintain direct ties between Idaho and California even with a federal mail subsidy. Courtesy Idaho State Historical Society, 83–2.14.

secure the whole or the greater portion of that trade if she will exert herself. The distance from San Francisco, or California, is shorter than from any other mart from whence the required supplies may be obtained."

The possibility that traffic between San Francisco and the northern Rocky Mountain mines might continue along the Columbia River without detouring up the Willamette to be transshipped also worried Portland's pioneer merchants. "Our greatest fear is that the influx of population will be so great, that we shall be unable to keep a great portion of the trade here, and that the trade will go direct to San Francisco," Henry Failing worried in the fall of 1861. In fact, early the following year, the California Steam Navigation Company, which operated one of the two ocean steamship lines serving the lower Columbia River, threatened to run its vessels up the river from Astoria and bypass Portland. Should the Oregon Steam Navigation Company not buy them out, fretted Failing, "and should they succeed in thus diverting the trade from here it would be very disastrous to Portland." But he also believed that Portland had sufficient capital to prevent any disastrous diversion "unless the Emigration to the new mines should be very large." [10]

Later in the 1860s what most worried Portland merchants was that their San Francisco competitors would bypass the Columbia River system entirely by extending wagon routes inland to the Idaho diggings from steamboat landings in the upper Sacramento Valley. Portland had early supplied both the Boise Basin and the booming silver mines of the Owyhee Mountains in southeastern Idaho via the Columbia River–Blue Mountains route, but by 1865 the trails direct from California were hauling the major portion of traffic to the Owyhee camps. By means of desert roads extending across Nevada from Chico and Red Bluff, the California Steam Navigation Company supplied both the Owyhee and Boise Basin mines at prices ruinous to shippers from Portland over the Umatilla trail. It was to intercept this competing traffic that a desperate Oregon Steam Navigation Company launched the steamboat *Shoshone* in southern Idaho.

During the years 1865–1867 stage lines attempted with-

out success to forge a direct link between southern Idaho mining camps and the Sacramento Valley. One of the men most determined to establish an overland route was Captain Elias Davidson Pierce, who nursed a grudge against Oregon Steam because it gave him only a free pass after he discovered the bonanza that made it rich, and now he wished to ruin the Portland company. Another was William (Hill) Beachey, the resolute pursuer of the murderers of Lloyd Magruder. The first saddle train of Beachey's Idaho Stage Company left Chico, California, for the Idaho mines on April 3, 1865, under Pierce's command. It reached Ruby City twenty-seven days later, having covered about 360 miles, mostly of Great Basin desert. The lengthy mule ride cost forty-seven passengers $66 each for fare and provisions along the way. A second and third train completed the journey in less time, but the Idaho Stage Company still failed. The following year Captain John Mullan, the road builder, sought to resurrect stage service between California and Idaho. [11]

The two failed experiments forced the Oregon Steam Navigation Company to trim its rates to Idaho mining camps temporarily. But residents of Silver City still resented the Portland company's power over their daily lives, especially when ice on the Columbia River blocked its boats from delivering vital supplies. The *Owyhee Avalanche* bitterly protested in early 1866 that the "navigation vampire" wanted to kill the direct overland route between southern Idaho and California: "Like snakes, their boats run and bite everything in their way during summer and hole up in winter." [12]

Captain J. C. Ainsworth observed to two of his associates in mid-1866 that, though the *Shoshone* was running "very successfully," the steamboat "will not make any money for us this season *if she ever does,* but I think she will enable us to compete *successfully* with the Chico route for supplying the 'Owyhee District.' If she does this she is a success." He emphasized that the company must leave "no stone unturned" to divert the trade of the Boise Basin and Owyhee mines through Portland. If the cost of shipping freight from Portland to Ruby City dropped to eight cents per pound, that rate would undercut the

Chico route. Others enthusiastically viewed the *Shoshone* as "the first link in the chain of steam communications to be made continuous at no distant day," a chain that utilized a combination of steamboats, wagon roads, and railroads to facilitate trade between Portland and Salt Lake City.[13]

Once the *Shoshone* had been in operation for a few months, it became possible to assess more realistically how a steamboat in southern Idaho might link Portland and Salt Lake City. As Ainsworth now warned his colleagues, "Our Snake River boat will not assist us much in the Salt Lake trade, we cannot run successfully much higher up than the Owyhee Crossing . . . much of the river is through canyons and over Rapids, that at a low stage of water would be difficult and unsafe to navigate."

Apart from the *Shoshone*, stagecoaches subsidized by federal mail contracts ran triweekly between Salt Lake City and steamboat landings on the Columbia River. In fact, Walla Walla residents noticed in 1866 that more news than before was coming direct from Salt Lake City, not via San Francisco and Portland. This was true all through the winter when the Columbia River was frozen over. "The difficulties in making the communication through from Salt Lake are vastly greater than on the other route, and yet by the exercise of energy and enterprise, the line has been kept open. Our friends of the Columbia River would do well to take a lesson from the energy exhibited by the management of the overland mail."[14]

Territorial Ambitions

Even as it battled San Francisco for control of transportation to the Idaho mines, the Oregon Steam Navigation Company challenged Saint Louis for command of the Montana mining camp trade. The competitive position of the Missouri city was seemingly unassailable, for even heavy or bulky freight could travel through by steamboat from there to Fort Benton without requiring portage, as it did on the Columbia River. Nonetheless, Portland newspapers publicly calculated how their city could compete successfully with Saint Louis for Montana commerce, stressing the uncertainty and dangers of Missouri River navigation, plus the high cost of insurance.

Actually, when all the various charges were added

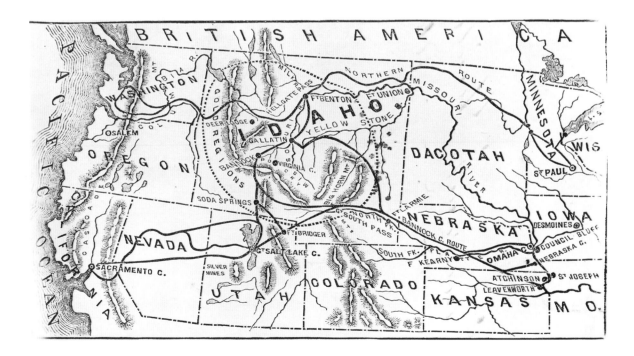

Illustrating the various ways to reach greater Idaho Territory was a map from J. C. Campbell's Idaho: Six Months in the Gold Fields *(1864). In June 1866 the* Montana Radiator *of Helena observed, "Eastern and Pacific merchants are now doing business here side by side, and this season will decide which will carry the key to the miners pocket—cheap goods. Both boast that they can sell the cheapest." Courtesy Montana Historical Society, C-61.*

together, it cost nearly the same in 1865 to ship goods from Portland to Montana as it did from Saint Louis or San Francisco. The Bitterroot Mountains and the primitive Mullan Road jeopardized the ability of Portland to compete successfully with Saint Louis; nonetheless, the number of packtrains using the Mullan Road from Walla Walla to Montana had increased steadily after 1862. These ranged from small outfits of five or six animals to large trains of more than a hundred, though the typical size was about twenty-five animals. For a brief time in 1865, camels plodded along on short stretches of the Mullan Road, but this experiment proved no more successful there than elsewhere. The camels were either turned loose or relocated to Utah and Arizona.

During the 1865 season, one hundred packtrains averaging fifty animals per train, each animal carrying about 300 pounds, hauled 750 tons of freight from the Columbia River to Montana. The total value of these goods in Helena was $1,440,000, of which freight costs amounted to $240,000. Portland merchants boldly came within 125 miles of Fort Benton for the Montana trade. Even so, the *Oregonian* still reported at the end of the year that the "goods now in the Montana market, have for the most part been brought from St. Louis."[15]

Portland merchants simply would not give up on Montana. They found a workable and possibly cheaper alternative to the Mullan Road in the Clark Fork route, which the Oregon Steam Navigation Company was determined to use to extend its reach another five hundred miles inland to Helena. In the fall of 1865, at about the same time as it laid plans for the *Shoshone,* Oregon Steam formed a subsidiary, the Oregon and Montana Transportation Company, and proposed to operate a new steamboat, the *Mary Moody,* across Idaho's largest body of water, Lake Pend Oreille. Constructed during the winter of 1865–1866, the *Mary Moody* employed machinery removed from the old *Colonel Wright* after that pioneer steamer had outlived its usefulness. Oregon Steam transported all this heavy equipment from its shops in The Dalles to Umatilla and thence overland to the southern end of Lake Pend Oreille; the lumber required to construct the *Mary Moody* and two sister steamboats far-

ther up the Clark Fork River was sawed in place. Four months after the first tree was felled for her, the new steamboat was afloat; fifteen days later her steam whistle echoed through the mountains, "the lonesomeness and mysteriousness of which she has forever banished."[16]

The Clark Fork route involved using steamboats between Portland and White Bluffs, a landing on the Columbia River north of its confluence with the Snake and about fifty miles from Wallula. From White Bluffs a wagon road ran northeast across the sparsely settled Columbia Plateau nearly two hundred miles to the southern shores of Lake Pend Oreille. Here passengers and packtrains continued aboard the *Mary Moody* another eighty-five miles to Cabinet Rapids, where a short portage connected to the steamer *Cabinet,* which ran fifty-six miles on the upper Clark Fork River to Thompson Falls. After yet one more portage, the fifth along the way from Portland, the steamboat *Missoula* churned along a stretch of the Clark Fork to reach the mouth of the Jocko River, about 125 miles from Fort Benton but still a considerable distance from the main Montana diggings. None of these difficulties seemed to temper the optimism of the Oregon Steam Navigation Company.

With these three steamboats, noted the *Montana Post,* "a continuous line of water travel, nearly two hundred miles in length, and avoiding the very worse and only bad portions of the old trail, will thus be offered." The paper predicted that within two years it would be possible for a traveler to leave Portland on the first of the month, reach Helena by the evening of the eighth, Fort Benton on the ninth, and Saint Louis by the twenty-fourth. "Stage and water travel will be so combined that neither will be irksome, and a great passenger traffic must thus spring up."[17]

Oregon Steam commenced service with the *Mary Moody* in early May 1866 and recorded that on her first day of operation she carried eighty-five pack animals, ten thousand pounds of freight, and fifty passengers. A traveler who made a westbound trip on the *Mary Moody* that same year was pleased to find a saloon aboard. The hundred-ton vessel also provided dinner and a panoramic vista of scenic Lake Pend Oreille. At the southwestern end of the immense wilderness lake was Pend Oreille City, which offered weary travelers the amenities of two grocery stores, a billiard saloon, hotel, and stable; at the eastern approach to the route was Missoula, a village that consisted of little more than a few dozen houses, some stores, and a sawmill.

In June 1866 the *Oregonian* proudly announced that the *Mary Moody* was making daily trips to Cabinet Rapids with freight priced at one cent per pound and passage at $5. But the *Montana Radiator,* a Helena newspaper favoring the Missouri River route, remained unimpressed: "The Pen d'Oreille route is the greatest humbug of all the bilks of which the country is so prolific, and which its father, the Oregon steam navigation has begotten for purposes vile as the prostitution of its offspring." The *Radiator* did admit that "the navigation of the Lake would relieve packers from having to drive their mules through about fifty miles of mud, quick sand and water, along the shore where for miles together even in the driest season of the year, it would mire a saddle blanket and no living creature can venture with any degree of safety, unless it be web-footed." [18]

Proponents of the new route claimed that "there can be no question that Portland will be a formidable rival to St. Louis for the whole trade of the Territory, but it lies in the power of the latter city to confine her to the Western slope, and it must be remembered that the goods which will be sent from Portland, for the most part, originally came from the East; but on the other hand, many articles will be imported direct from Asia, which previously traversed a distance nearly equal to the circumference of the Globe ere they arrived in Oregon by way of New York and round the Horn." [19]

Indeed, the year 1866 did bring a noticeable rise in freight traffic to Montana, but steamboats from Saint Louis accounted for much of it, to the consternation of Portland backers. During all six years prior to 1865, little more than five thousand tons of freight had reached Fort Benton via the Missouri River route, only four boats having arrived in 1862, three in 1863, and four in 1864. With the rise of Helena in the mid-1860s, steamboat traffic on the Missouri River from Saint Louis expanded rapidly: in 1866, thirty-one steamboats reached Fort Benton, and a year later, thirty-nine.

Before the Clark Fork route was in operation, it was estimated that "about one-fifth of the supplies come overland from California and Oregon; one-fifth overland from Kansas and Nebraska; and three-fifths up the Missouri from St. Louis and Fort Benton." The harsh truth was that Portland gained little in the contest for Montana trade even after the *Mary Moody* was regularly steaming across Idaho's largest lake. Gloom enveloped the Portland business community as merchants viewed with apprehension their withering prospects for inland trade. "They consider it extremely doubtful whether their sales for the markets of Montana will ever be on a large scale." When Portland merchants learned that the goods sold in March had reached the Helena market via the Lake Pend Oreille route before the arrival of Missouri River boats, their confidence was temporarily buoyed. Several Montana merchants visited Portland during the summer and fall, and the *Oregonian* reported in August that a greater amount of freight was going to Montana than ever before. While this trade increased somewhat during the summer and fall of 1866, Portland's negative forebodings were essentially justified as far as subsequent years were concerned. [20]

During 1867 the coaches of the Columbia and Montana Stage Line left Wallula each Wednesday traveling via Spokane Bridge (near the Idaho border) to Lake Pend Oreille. The 170-mile trip cost thirty dollars. For a time the *Mary Moody* had more business than it could handle. With renewed optimism the Oregon Steam Navigation Company made major improvements to its two Columbia River portages, where C. Aubrey Angelo found two beautiful new locomotives—the Ainsworth and the Bradford—in daily use hauling first-class passenger cars and covered baggage and freight cars.

Ironically, the year 1866, which witnessed the dramatic rise in the number of steamboats reaching Fort Benton, also witnessed the peak of Montana service from Portland, which after several years of decline collapsed in 1869. Operation of the *Cabinet* and *Missoula* ceased;

enough local traffic remained to keep the *Mary Moody* steaming across Lake Pend Oreille for several more years, but eventually she too made a last trip and was finally dismantled in 1876. When the Clark Fork route effectively ended in 1869, it was noted that trade between the Pacific coast and Montana, "which was quite extensive three years ago," had dwindled to "insignificant proportions, and in place of the long trains of pack animals, loaded with clothing, saddlery, and merchandise of every description which once reached the Territory from the 'other side,' there is now received almost nothing save a few sacks of flour and boxes of apples."[21]

Promoting this change was Chicago, a new contender for the Montana trade, which extended a rail line from Lake Michigan to intersect the Missouri River at Sioux City. Thus the Illinois upstart triumphed over both Saint Louis and Portland to win at least temporary control of the trade worth ten million dollars a year. "This change has been produced by the very rapid and extraordinary reduction of freights on the Missouri River—the rates from Chicago to Helena being now only seven and eight cents per pound in lieu of the twenty and twenty-five cents of three years ago. This has effectually put an end to the occupation of the packer, who cannot deliver goods from Walla Walla to Helena for less than twelve cents."[22]

Nothing was firmly settled, however, because no one could accurately predict how a new transcontinental railroad might affect the Montana market. "It is true that San Francisco will be, on the completion of the Pacific Railroad, nearly twice as near Montana as Chicago, and it is probable that California may do a fair business with this Territory in fruits, wines, teas, and other light articles of Asiatic production. After the close of navigation on the Missouri it may also do a light fall trade in flour, blankets, saddlery, and such other articles as may be found to be scarce in the market. The great bulk of goods which find their way to the Territory will, however, avail themselves of the low freights attendant on river navigation." Only after the final spike ceremony in 1869 was it obvious that the near future belonged to the trail extending north from the railhead at Corinne, Utah, but whether the primary beneficiary would be Chicago or San Francisco was not so clear at first. Only this much was certain: during the remarkable decade of the 1860s, gold had irrevocably altered the northern West, and not just in terms of patterns of transportation and communication.[23]

Gold Redefines the Northern West

Even before Walla Walla emerged as the largest population center in Washington Territory in 1870 (with 1,394 residents) and the transportation hub of the interior, Olympia residents regarded the inland settlement as a potentially dangerous rival that might replace their Puget Sound community as capital. Many people living east of the Cascades would have cheered if it had: John H. Scranton complained in his Lewiston newspaper, the

An 1881 illustration, "The Great West," suggests how transportation created a prosperous new landscape. Courtesy Library of Congress, 485.

THE GREAT WEST

The Miles, Washington, ferry across the Spokane River, 1924. This type of relatively cheap technology facilitated local transportation in many rural parts of the northern West. Courtesy Eastern Washington Historical Society, MA-2.p.76.

Golden Age, in late 1862, "Of what use to us is a capitol of Washington Territory located at Olympia on the forty-ninth parallel?" During four months of last year "no communication could be had with the place at all," he lamented. An often repeated story told of the editor of the *Washington Statesman* whom Walla Walla voters elected to the territorial legislature: before he left for Olympia to serve his constituents, he made his will, settled all of his worldly accounts, and bid his friends adieu until next summer, and perhaps forever.[24]

Supporters of Olympia were only too glad to have Congress combine Washington's remote mining regions into a new territory called Idaho (despite a last-minute attempt to name it Montana), on March 4, 1863. Idaho Territory originally sprawled across an area one-quarter larger than Texas and seemed little more than a temporary holding facility for land no other state or territory wanted or knew how to govern. "Has anybody ever figured up the size of this Territory—how many square miles it contains, how wide and how long it is, and how long it would take a man to travel 'round it, &c?" asked one Idaho journalist. Within boundaries that straddled the Continental Divide and encompassed not only present-day Idaho but all of Montana and all but the

southwestern corner of Wyoming lived a non-Indian population of 30,559 men and 1,089 women scattered among a hodgepodge of mining camps and farm villages so remote that scarcely a trail connected them. Even after Congress reconfigured Idaho to create Montana Territory on May 26, 1864, and Wyoming (a portion of which was also from Dakota) in 1868, the transportation problem remained acute.[25]

Who could ignore the dramatic changes that occurred during the golden decade? "What a contrast in so short a space of time!" Montana, "which was, but three years ago, known and marked on the maps of the West as only unexplored Indian territory—supposed to be comprised of rugged mountains and desert wastes—to-day stands unrivaled either in agricultural or mineral wealth." As for Walla Walla, it further evolved during the 1870s and 1880s into a prosperous agricultural center; its mining-derived wealth served as a source of investment capital throughout the inland Northwest. Only after the building of two more transcontinental railroads in the early 1880s, both of which relegated Walla Walla to feeder lines, did its population fall behind that of the cities of Spokane and Seattle.[26]

You ask me for our leader, I'll soon inform you then;
It is Holladay, they call him, and often only Ben;
If you can read the papers, it's easy work to scan
He beats the world on staging now, "or any other man."
  Chorus:
Statesmen and warriors, traders and the rest,
May boast of their profession, and think it is the best;
Their state I'll never envy, I'll have you understand,
Long as I can be a driver on the jolly Overland.
—*"Song of the Overland Stage-Driver," Montana Post (April 8, 1865)*

Ben Holladay Builds a Stagecoach Empire

Nat Stein composed the "Song of the Overland Stage-Driver" in the middle 1860s. At that time he worked in Virginia City, Montana Territory, as the local agent for Ben Holladay's expanding stagecoach empire, and although Stein later entered banking, he was always best known as the Poet of the Stage Line. His driver's song was popular with employees who took uncommon pride in the larger-than-life qualities of their boss, Old Ben.[1]

A commanding figure—tall, large-framed, with piercing dark eyes and a dark mustache, Holladay was a man of prodigious energy and drive who time and again shaped the course of transportation history in the northern West. John Hailey recalled that in "common conversation he could be heard clear across the street." Though fiery and irascible when crossed, Holladay was early known as "one of the boys," and nearly all the overland drivers considered him their personal friend. "Some of them fairly worshipped him," recalled Frank Root, who

regularly rode the stagecoaches as an express agent. The men of the Overland Stage Line clearly recognized that Holladay was the person in charge, and they were his employees. Once it was reported that Governor Alexander Cummings of Colorado Territory tried to bribe one of them to drive faster; the man responded emphatically that he had been hired by Holladay, and he was driving to please Holladay.[2]

Holladay himself made twice-yearly inspection trips of the Overland line in his private coach, a mansion on wheels drawn by six horses and reputed to have cost several thousand dollars, a sum that in the 1860s underscored the owner's status as the nation's Stagecoach King. His special vehicle featured cushioned seats and was mounted on spiral springs to soften the ride so that his invalid wife could accompany him across the West without much personal discomfort. The interior was equipped with expensive side curtains, beautiful silver lamps, and a writing table. Accompanying Holladay's special carriage during one of these whirlwind tours was a second coach that carried a cook and servants as well as supplies of necessities and luxuries for the trip, such as special mattresses, brandy, and cigars.

Holladay—a skilled businessman who mastered the details of a vast transportation system employing hundreds of men and coaches and thousands of mules and horses to send mails and passengers flying across half a continent—was the consummate showman. He dressed the drivers of his special coach in broad-brimmed sombreros and corduroys trimmed with velvet. A dramatic entrance into a station was calculated to impress bystanders with Holladay's power. In an enterprise where so much depended on the vagaries of weather and the goodwill of Indians, bravado was important.

However, to Holladay's many critics these cross-country spectaculars only underscored his ruthless and brutal personality. They accused him of demanding that each trip be made at breakneck speed without regard for the number of horses and mules he killed or ruined in the process, a claim that was not true in every instance. In Salt Lake City in 1862 Holladay made a large wager that on his return to Atchison (1,250 miles distant) he would cut several hours from the fastest time ever made by stagecoach. His superintendent Bob Spotswood, who by that time had replaced practically all the mules in his division with horses, personally drove the boss from Denver to Julesburg (a distance of 225 miles) in seventeen and a half hours without killing or breaking down a single animal. The performance so impressed Holladay that, except on a few extremely sandy or rough stretches, he replaced mules with horses along the entire line.

So famous did Holladay's speeding horses become that travelers regarded them with awe even in the land of the Pharaohs. Mark Twain told of an American lad journeying through Palestine who, when told that it took forty

years to lead the tribes of Israel three hundred miles from Egypt to the Promised Land, was not impressed. He himself had crossed the western deserts to California in one of Holladay's coaches. "Forty years?" he snorted. "Only three hundred miles? Humph! Ben Holladay would have fetched them through in thirty-six hours." Such was the legendary status of the Stagecoach King.[3]

The war with Mexico in 1846 first sparked Holladay's interest in transportation, and for the next three decades he maintained a passion for freight wagons, stagecoaches, river steamboats and coastal steamships, and eventually railroads. During the steamboat and stagecoach era it could safely be claimed that no individual had a hand in running more modes of transportation than Ben Holladay. In the northern West perhaps only the Oregon Steam Navigation Company exercised comparable power and aroused such public admiration or hate. But Holladay's transportation empire was only one part of a remarkable life story.

The Rise of Ben Holladay

Holladay's rise was a true rags-to-riches saga. Born in Kentucky in 1824, Benjamin Holladay was said to have run away from his parent's hardscrabble farm twelve years later and headed to the frontier, where he became a clerk at a trading post at Weston, on the east bank of the Missouri River nearly opposite Leavenworth, Kansas. At the age of seventeen he was hired as a civilian courier by Brigadier General Alexander Doniphan of Missouri's state militia, whose assignment it was to drive Mormons out of the state in 1838. Doniphan refused point-blank to carry out an order to execute Joseph Smith, founder of the Mormon religion, and he saved the lives of many other Mormons by secretly notifying Brigham Young of impending attacks by mobs. Young Holladay relayed Doniphan's messages and won Young's lasting friendship. Several years later this connection proved financially rewarding to Holladay.

After the ouster of Mormons from Missouri, Holladay returned to his clerking job in Weston but soon afterward started a trading post of his own there. Soldiers from nearby Fort Leavenworth were his principal customers, and whiskey was his most popular merchandise. By the early 1840s he was one of Weston's more prominent businessmen. Along the way he proved himself to be astute, farsighted, shrewd, and unscrupulous, so his enemies would claim, but also a man of indomitable courage, irresistible drive, and ruthless determination.

Holladay extended his reach beyond Weston during the Mexican War when he obtained contracts to supply troops headed to Santa Fe. His promptness made him an army favorite, and with its blessing he was able to accumulate unusually large profits. At the close of the war he bought a substantial amount of government surplus material—oxen, wagons, and other equipment—at low cost, and the following year he took charge of a train of freight wagons headed to Salt Lake City with goods worth $70,000. Holladay's good relations with Brigham Young and the Mormons enabled him to dispose of his merchandise at a very favorable price. In the early 1850s Holladay drove a herd of cattle west to California, fattened them on the lush grasses near Sacramento, and sold them to the Pacific Mail Steamship Company at a profit. Holladay quickly grasped another business opportunity in the goldfields, where prices were extraordinarily high, and soon he was doing an enormous freighting business from the Missouri River to California. In this way he accumulated the beginnings of a real fortune.

Following the "Mormon War" of 1857, Holladay became associated with the freighting firm of Russell, Majors and Waddell, and through this connection he capitalized on the Pike's Peak gold rush at the close of the decade. With the outbreak of the Civil War and the resultant disruption of the Butterfield Overland Mail, it was Ben Holladay who was in a prime position, from the standpoint of both financial resources and personal experience, to gain control of stagecoaching along the central overland route.

After the legislature of Kansas Territory granted a charter to Russell, Majors and Waddell in 1860 to create a commercial passenger operation called the Central Overland California and Pike's Peak Express Company, Holladay lent money to the poorly managed and always financially troubled firm, receiving in return a mortgage on the stage line and its equipment. Holladay continued to advance funds to the Central Overland when its revenues failed to cover expenses, as they often did. And when a note he held came due in December 1861, the Central Overland California and Pike's Peak Express, together with its parent firm of Russell, Majors and Waddell, failed to meet the financial obligation and sank into bankruptcy early the next year.

In mid-March 1862, with few people present except curious bystanders, the trustee sold the entire assets of the Central Overland California and Pike's Peak Express Company at public auction in Atchison to the sole bidder, Ben Holladay, for $100,000. The company at that time owed him $208,000. With this brief transaction the irrepressible Holladay gained control of over twelve hundred miles of stage lines—albeit unprofitable ones—and the once great firm of Russell, Majors and Waddell passed into history as pioneer freighter, merchant, stagecoach proprietor, and mail contractor. In reality, Holla-

day's new possession amounted to little more than the amalgamation of a Salt Lake route that was nearly penniless and a Denver route that had failed. The public nonetheless anticipated improved service from the flamboyant new owner.

The Stagecoach King's long and successful career on the frontier proved a great advantage in his newest business venture. Having crossed the plains numerous times with oxen and mules long before the first stage line turned a wheel there, he knew the terrain well. He understood what was required for success in long-distance staging in such forbidding country. Holladay thus spared no expense in purchasing the best horses and mules from all over the country to haul the many new Concord coaches he acquired from Abbot, Downing and Company of New Hampshire. He employed only the most capable and experienced stage men to be found; built many new way stations, so that the distance between any two of them was no greater than ten to fifteen miles; and relocated the main route where necessary to respond to rapid population shifts. Most important of all, he secured favorable contracts from the federal government to carry the United States mail.

His main line extended from the steamboat landing at Atchison to Salt Lake City, where Holladay coaches met those of the Overland Mail Company to provide public transportation between Kansas and California. Maintaining scheduled service across so great a distance through such sparsely settled country required an unprecedented feat of organization, but Holladay thrived on the many challenges the transportation frontier posed. At its peak in 1866, his stage empire extended along 2,760 miles of dusty western roads and required about six thousand horses and mules to maintain regular service. Just to feed the animals, which were distributed at relay stations along the system (often where seemingly nothing grew but sagebrush), Holladay's teamsters hauled hay from ranches a hundred or more miles away and corn west from the Missouri Valley. Wood for heating and cooking frequently came from fifty to one hundred miles away.

Although Holladay improved service on the line eastward from Denver as soon as he took over the Central

Passengers aboard coaches on the central overland route braved many hazards to cross the Great Plains during the 1860s. The support structure necessary for successful operation required thousands of men and wagons to haul supplies, yet the entire enterprise was at risk from both weather and Indian attackers who resented the intrusion of the stagecoach into their domain. In one year alone Indians reportedly destroyed or stole half a million dollars' worth of Holladay's property—stagecoaches, harnesses, barns, houses, animals, and feed. Courtesy Wyoming State Museum.

Overland California and Pike's Peak Express Company, stagecoach service between Denver and Salt Lake City shuddered to a halt during the spring of 1862 because of a combination of bad weather and Indian hostilities. The winter of 1861–1862 was unusually severe in the Rockies as one blizzard after another piled snow deep across the road. Following each new snowfall, stage men drove loose stock through the passes in a valiant effort to keep them open. In the high mountains they replaced heavy stagecoaches with light sleighs. Even so, by the end of January the San Francisco *Alta California* complained that a week had passed since mail of any kind had arrived

overland from the East. When the snow finally did melt, rivers overflowed their banks and roads through mountain valleys became quagmires that sucked coach wheels down to their hubs in mud.

Compounding Holladay's annual weather woes was ongoing conflict with Native Americans. Overland staging had experienced Indian trouble almost from its beginnings in the late 1850s, but not until the following decade did it become serious or chronic. During 1862 smoldering resentments erupted in active rebellion when Indians accused emigrants of invading their lands and endangering prime hunting grounds. They also charged

Lake City establishing stage stations for the company's projected Montana service. The superintendent Bob Spotswood brought 290 mules, thirty coaches, and ten lumber wagons. With these he soon made the Montana line one of the best managed of Holladay's far-flung stage routes. The four-horse coaches, drawn by good livestock, averaged 160 miles a day traveling between Salt Lake City and Virginia City. The route led north to Bear River Junction, through the Cache Valley to Franklin, then crossed the Snake River by way of the Eagle Rock ferry (now the site of Idaho Falls). In this way, the central overland route through Salt Lake City competed for the Montana trade with steamboats on the Missouri River.

At the time Holladay's Overland Stage Line commenced service to Virginia City, Jack Oliver responded to the challenge by improving the frequency of his own

service. But the Montana outfit simply did not have resources great enough to compete with the Stagecoach King, who soon slashed his fares to undercut Oliver. Holladay then boasted that several dozen new Concord coaches were en route for his line and that he intended to offer daily service to Virginia City by the following spring. The result was inevitable. On November 19, 1864, the *Montana Post* announced that Jack Oliver intended to withdraw from the Salt Lake route the following day but would continue local service to Bannack City. Soon the struggling transportation pioneer halted all service for the winter and headed east—presumably aboard Holladay's Overland Stage Line—to purchase new coaches of his own.

By the following May, Oliver and Company was once again in the stage business. With the best horses he could

A. J. Russell photographed the main street of Salt Lake City in the late 1860s. Holladay's four-year mail contract, which commenced July 1, 1864, bound his company to transport mail between Salt Lake City and Virginia City, Montana, almost five hundred miles north, three times a week for eight months of the year and once a week for the four winter months. During each of the next two years the firm received a $53,084 federal subsidy to maintain this vital service. Courtesy Utah State Historical Society, 979.21/p. 106, #17139.

purchase locally, Jack Oliver established daily passenger, mail, and express service between Virginia City and Helena. Probably in hopes of avoiding head-to-head competition with Holladay, he made the 125-mile run in the amazingly fast time of fourteen hours and charged passengers only fifteen dollars for a one-way trip, or twenty-five dollars for a round-trip, two dollars for extra suitcases, and five dollars for trunks. Not long thereafter, when the post office decided to establish a mail route between the two cities, Oliver and Company bid low and won the contract.

With federal money subsidizing his stagecoaches, Jack Oliver struggled through the winter of 1865; but the rigors of travel over mountain roads badly damaged his new coaches and forced him nearly to double his passenger and express rates in order to meet expenses. But with the coming of spring, "the Napoleon of the West," as the local press had sarcastically dubbed Holladay, moved seventeen Concord coaches and several of his fastest six-horse teams from the main line to compete once again with Oliver and Company. The Overland Stage's first daily coach from Virginia City to Helena left on June 30 with a load of fourteen passengers plus express at the same time that Oliver's coaches pulled out.

Unlike Oliver, Holladay had no mail subsidy between Virginia City and Helena, yet in another display of the bravado that had won him his exalted title, he dropped the passenger fare to $2.50, added no charge for excess baggage, carried express at the same low rates that freighters were charging for flour, and reduced the running time to ten hours. This feat required an average speed of 12.5 miles per hour including all stops for meals and a change of horses every 10 miles over the 125-mile route. The breakneck pace required more frequent team changes, and driving at a fast gallop every minute; before the hostilities ended, Holladay had lost more than a hundred horses to the killing speed. The Overland Stage had the best stock and made the best time, much to the enjoyment of backers who would bet as much as five hundred dollars each on a single race.

Cutthroat competition from Holladay was not the least of Jack Oliver's troubles: he soon faced yet another outfit that offered daily stagecoach service. Thus each morning three rival coaches departed Helena and another three left Virginia City. The result was predictable: on July 14, 1866, the newcomer withdrew, followed a month later by Jack Oliver, who assigned his mail contract to Holladay and moved his worse-for-wear coaches and horses onto feeder lines between Helena and outlying mining camps. He thus became the first of many Montana entrepreneurs crushed by a powerful out-of-state competitor.

Equally predictable was that as soon as Holladay defeated his two competitors, he doubled the running time between Virginia City and Helena, replaced his resplendent Concord coaches with an assortment of hand-me-down vehicles from other parts of his vast system, and upped the one-way fare from $2.50 to ten times that amount in gold dust, or $37.50 in "Lincoln skins," as depreciated paper money was often called. The name Ben Holladay became synonymous with stagecoaching in Montana: travelers paid him $350 for a one-way ticket to Atchison and then regretted all twenty days of their lengthy journey.

In early August 1864, about a month after Holladay extended service north from Salt Lake City across eastern Idaho to Virginia City, he inaugurated mail and passenger service from Fort Hall (on his Montana route a few miles north of present Pocatello, Idaho) west across the arid Snake River plain to Boise and Walla Walla. Eventually the new service extended all the way to The Dalles, where boats of the Oregon Steam Navigation Company connected to Portland. To operate this shortcut to the far Northwest, Holladay received an annual mail subsidy of $186,000. His own Overland coaches covered the distance between Salt Lake City and Boise. A subcontractor, George F. Thomas and Company, ran triweekly coaches between there and Walla Walla (and later The Dalles). In this way the Holladay line reduced the time of commercial travel between The Dalles and Atchison to three weeks.

"We saw with pleasure the departure of the first U. S. Mail yesterday from this city connecting directly several hundred thousand citizens in Idaho, Washington,

Oregon, and Montana with the Atlantic States and the seat of national government," reported the *Daily Telegraph* of Salt Lake City in late July 1864. "There was no display, no hurrah; everything was quiet as the neat little stage and splendid mule outfit traveled from the contractor's office; but no one accustomed to peer into the future could gaze upon that start without hearing in the first crack of the whip the announcement of a new epoch in mountain life." Indeed, not only were Holladay's branch lines to Montana and the far Northwest profitable, but by means of improved mail service they brought settlers in remote sections of the nation into closer contact with the East at a time when the unity of the nation was in doubt. Considerable gold from Idaho and Montana mines went east on Holladay coaches to aid the Union cause during the Civil War.[8]

Napoleon of the West

Holladay continued to improve, extend, and enlarge his stage empire "until it is now, perhaps, the greatest enterprise owned and controlled by one man, which exists in the country, if not in the world," wrote the newspaper publisher Samuel Bowles in 1865. The Napoleon of the West accumulated wealth faster than most Americans imagined possible, but he also spent his fortune freely. He squandered vast sums of money indulging his fondness for pretentious mansions. Ophir Place in Westchester County, sixty miles from New York City, was a magnificent edifice supported in part by Holladay's income from the famed Ophir Mine of the Comstock Lode. Its original cost was reputed to have been about a million dollars, the landscaping alone estimated at ten thousand dollars. A buffalo herd fed on the thousand-acre grounds, and a narrow-gauge railroad ran to the mansion.[9]

After receiving several lucrative mail contracts, Holladay built another elegant mansion in Washington near the residence of Senator John Sherman. This showplace contained fine furniture, a large classical library of handsomely bound volumes, oil paintings by celebrated masters in Europe and America, and elegant bronzes and marble statuary. Two bronze lions cost the then scandalous sum of six thousand dollars each. It should not be surprising that Holladay, his western transportation empire subsidized by more than one million federal dollars a year, wanted to cultivate the friendship of influential members of Congress and President Lincoln.

This long-abandoned stage station was located south of City of Rocks, Idaho. Though Holladay was technically supposed to haul mail west from Fort Hall, his Overland stages actually used a cutoff that extended from northern Utah (near future Tremonton) via City of Rocks to Rock Creek Station (between later Twin Falls and Burley). In this way they could reach Boise in only four days, rather than the allotted seven. Holladay retained the line between Boise and Fort Hall in order to speed passengers between Boise and Virginia City. Courtesy Idaho State Historical Society, 73–66.1.

After Holladay won a four-year contract to carry the overland mails in 1864, one hothead protested in a Denver newspaper, "Colorado, Utah, and Nevada belong to Ben Holladay for a footstool, and may the Lord have mercy on them." Others complained that first-class mail was left behind whenever a large load of express and passengers had to be crammed into a single coach, that schedules were disregarded, equipment was allowed to run down, and passenger fares and express rates were raised to the maximum the traffic would bear. It is true that during the rush to the northern Rocky Mountain mines, Holladay more than tripled passenger fares between Atchison and Salt Lake City to five hundred dollars. Travelers complained that meals alone on a twenty-day trip between Atchison and Helena cost two hundred dollars and were often of such poor quality as to be inedible.[10]

Passengers complained, too, about accidents, which became frequent on mountain routes. Sometimes these were the fault of drivers trying to keep up with unrealistically fast schedules on poorly maintained roads, and sometimes they were, in the words of Frank Root, the result of horses fresh from the oat box being unskillfully driven by a driver fresh from the saloon. Holladay was, of course, personally blamed for all these failings.

Bad as this was, overland mail service before Holladay had occasionally been far worse. Root recalled that "when a stage went to Salt Lake only once a week, some of the boys on the line used to despise a coach almost wholly loaded up with public documents from Washington, but such mail matter came quite handy at times. Occasionally the drivers, as they themselves said, in rough weather, would get stalled going through a bad slough, and be unable to move. In that case they were obliged to take out sack after sack of the 'Pub. Docs.,' open the bags, and pile the massive books from the Government printing office in the slough, and, by building a solid foundation with them, were thus enabled to pull the coach out of the mire."[11]

Holladay remained at the head of the great Overland Stage Line for nearly five years. From 1862 through 1866 he held nine United States mail contracts that earned him nearly two million dollars. During those same years he honed his reputation as a ruthless monopolist, and not just in Montana where he crushed Jack Oliver. In another widely cited example of his method of striking hard when he had an advantage, during the fall of 1865 his Overland coaches suddenly refused to accept con-

This advertisement for the Overland Stage Line appeared in Denver's Rocky Mountain News *in 1864. Courtesy Denver Public Library, F12440.*

placed Wells Fargo in a difficult position if it still wished to extend its own line east from Salt Lake City. The supremely confident Stagecoach King was reported to have bellowed to his personal secretary, "Answer those express companies, and tell them to stock and be damned." Holladay was certain that with all hope gone of connecting with Butterfield's Overland Despatch at Denver, Wells Fargo would abandon any further attempts to break his monopoly.[13]

Yet, Wells Fargo held one trump card, and Holladay knew it. From his own Concord coaches he could see plainly the hundreds of Irish laborers who methodically extended Union Pacific tracks westward across the Great Plains from Omaha. He knew too that, out in California and across the sagebrush plains of Nevada's Great Basin desert, their Chinese counterparts pushed the Central Pacific line east. There was also the Kansas Pacific building west toward the Rocky Mountains and a connection with the Union Pacific.

Just before the onset of another winter and the annual headaches it brought to stagecoaching on the central overland route, President Louis McLane, late of the Pioneer Line and now of Wells Fargo, made Ben Holladay a generous offer for his stagecoach empire. Details of the bargaining process are unknown, but on the first of November 1866, Wells Fargo acquired all assets of the Holladay Overland Mail and Express Company. Holladay received a sum vastly greater than the $100,000 he had paid for the Central Overland California and Pike's Peak Express only five years earlier: he gained $1.5 million in cash, plus the market value as of the sale date of all hay, grain, and supplies in his numerous warehouses, stables, and stations, $300,000 in Wells Fargo stock, and a seat on the company's board of directors.

Six months after the sale, Holladay saw his prophecy of quick decline for overland stagecoaching come true. He was fortunate that Wells Fargo had disagreed with him. Its directors optimistically estimated that staging would remain the main mode of transportation between the Missouri River and Salt Lake City for at least six more years. Had Holladay waited until 1869, when the Union Pacific and Central Pacific railroads joined to form a continuous rail route between Omaha and Sacramento, his equipment and operations would have sold for a much lower price. As it was, he retired a winner. A few months later he sold his Wells Fargo stock to raise money for yet another pioneering transportation venture, this time in Oregon.

Wells Fargo's Grand Consolidation

Prior to 1864, Wells Fargo had engaged exclusively in the express and banking business, exercising only indirect control over the Pioneer Stage Line and the Overland Mail Company line, on which it relied to transport its precious cargoes. But Wells Fargo purchased the Pioneer Stage Line from Charles and Louis McLane in 1864 and two years later began to operate stagecoaches under its own name east to Salt Lake City. In the "Grand Consolidation" of November 1866, Wells Fargo's president, Louis McLane, combined all major overland stage lines west of the Missouri River—notably the Pioneer Stage Line and Overland Mail Company routes—under the charter that Colorado granted to Ben Holladay in February 1866. In this way the name of Wells, Fargo and Company became synonymous with a vast network of stagecoach routes between the Missouri River and California.

In contrast to Holladay's usual method of operating a monopoly, McLane reduced passenger fares sharply and quickly replaced worn-out equipment. Backed by a positive reputation nationally and the vast wealth it had accumulated through various banking, express, and coaching enterprises on the Pacific Slope, Wells Fargo bought thirty new Concord coaches to improve service on its more than three thousand miles of stage routes across the West. This was among the largest orders that Abbot, Downing and Company ever filled. During Holladay's half decade as Stagecoach King, he was reported to have purchased only forty-three new stagecoaches, a majority of them for the purpose of driving competitors off the roads of Idaho and Montana.

Wells Fargo now operated through stages between Sacramento and Omaha, each covering the nineteen hundred miles in an average of eighteen days. The carrier advertised that "First class conveyances, careful and experienced drivers and attentive agents are employed, and every possible arrangement has been made for the comfort and safety of passengers." Even so, service on the overland route could still be erratic at times because of Indian troubles. As a result, the Salt Lake coach sometimes pulled into Denver two or three days late.

Wells Fargo express and stagecoaches became an institution on the western frontier. And under this name, overland stagecoaching reached its peak of efficiency, service, and glory, but the glory years were short-lived. On October 1, 1868, Wells Fargo lost the mail contract between Salt Lake City and The Dalles to C. M. Lockwood and was forced to remove its employees and equipment from the line serving the far Northwest. Even more portentous of trouble ahead was the accelerating rate at which tracks of the Union Pacific and Central Pacific railroads rushed toward one another. As soon as a fifty- to one-

hundred-mile segment of additional line was in service, stagecoaches and stock relocated to a new terminus. From there they shuttled mail, express packages, and passengers across a steadily shrinking gap.

Not long before the "iron wedding" at Promontory, directors of Wells, Fargo and Company voted to dispose of the firm's extensive stagecoach holdings, except for a short but profitable connection between Reno and Virginia City, Nevada, and concentrate fully on its express business. The company soon sold this final segment to Hill Beachey. His last stagecoach venture remained in business a scant two years; the Virginia and Truckee Railroad opened from Carson City to Virginia City in late January 1870 and finally completed a connection to Central Pacific tracks at Reno in 1872.

When it shed its stagecoach operations in 1869, Wells Fargo wisely abandoned what remained of the Central Overland route between Sacramento and Omaha because

A pass issued by Gilmer, Salisbury and Company in 1883. Staging on the central overland route died in 1869, but because of entrepreneurs like Jack Gilmer and Monroe Salisbury it continued in other parts of the American West for at least another four decades. Courtesy Wells Fargo.

it had no hope of competing with the new transcontinental railroad. It disposed of various branch lines and all surplus coaches, horses, harnesses, and diverse equipment and supplies to former division superintendents or other employees of the company and to small competing operators at prices that averaged about one-third of the original cost. Though every contract stipulated that for at least one year the buyer must transport express and treasure chests exclusively for Wells Fargo, the terms were so generous that it was possible for buyers to pay off their investments rapidly from profits.

In this way the surplus Utah assets and the Idaho and Montana branches passed into the capable hands of Jack Gilmer and Monroe Salisbury in August 1869. As for Ben Holladay, two years after he sold out to Wells Fargo in 1866, he relocated from California to Oregon where he used his bulging financial muscle to wrest control of Willamette Valley railroads from local businessmen. By gaining control of a company that operated steamships along the Pacific coast from Alaska to Mexico, he was able to extend his influence over railroad and steamboat properties in Oregon. During the 1870s, Holladay maintained mansions in Washington, D.C.; New York City and White Plains, New York; and Portland and Seaside, Oregon. All told, his many mansions no less than his far-flung transportation empire were a remarkable achievement for a man born in a log cabin in Kentucky and who got his start in western transportation as a lowly freighter.

And it seems to be the case that there are few things more comparable to the old-time seafaring pride, as it obtained especially in the handling and maintenance of the clipper ship, than the scrupulous stagefaring attitude of all stagemen toward the arts and crafts of their calling.

—William Banning and George Banning, Six Horses (1930)

Stagecoaching Adapts to the Frontier West

Steamboating and stagecoaching had common needs: to recruit and organize a work force, to erect a support structure making commercial transportation through an undeveloped region both possible and reasonably regular, and to adapt existing technologies to western conditions. Like the mountain steamboats that plied the upper Missouri River, the Concord coach represented the adaptation of existing technology to a harsh new environment. Until made obsolete by a spreading network of railroad tracks and motorized transportation in the early twentieth century, Concord coaches sped along the primitive roads of the West, drawn by four- or six-horse teams, and driven by skillful reinsmen.

Though the word *stage* was commonly used to describe any coach, wagon, or sleigh used as a public conveyance, the Concord coach emerged as the quintessential icon of commercial transportation across the frontier West, surpassing even the steamboat, which was more often seen as an icon of the antebellum South. No other vehicle became more closely identified with the West of the 1850s and 1860s, yet as the name implied, the Concord coach embodied the craftsmanship of New England Yankees.

The Wooden Machine

The first Concord coach reached California and the West Coast aboard a clipper ship that sailed from New England around Cape Horn. On June 25, 1850, it inaugurated service out of San Francisco, exactly five days before another coach, probably of Concord make, was reported to have left Independence, Missouri, on the first trip to Santa Fe. Scores of other Concord coaches soon rounded Cape Horn to replace the odd assortment of vehicles initially used by stage lines on the West Coast.

Experience taught the Concord, New Hampshire, firm of Abbot, Downing and Company to construct a special type of coach body to resist the wear, tear, and shock caused by bumpy western roads. For instance, the body was so strong that in addition to accommodating nine passengers inside, it provided room for at least half a dozen more on top. The builders also cut door openings several inches above the bottom so that the coach could be floated across a flood-swollen stream if necessary. Because rough roads combined with loads that routinely exceeded the planned maximum of fifteen passengers stressed even the strongest of coach bodies and caused glass windows to shatter, Abbot Downing instead used a

new and stronger suspension and frame and substituted adjustable leather curtains designed to keep out wind, rain, snow, and dust, but descriptions by stage passengers suggest that window covers were never very efficient.

The oval-shaped body weighing a ton or more was suspended upon two immensely thick thoroughbraces—stout six- or eight-ply belts of bull hide—slung between the front and the rear axles. The thoroughbraces functioned as a combination of springs and shock absorbers to cushion the coach body from the jolts and bounces of wheels on rutted roads. The thoroughbraces made the graceful Concord coach superior to the common spring wagons, which tended to bounce passengers skyward when a wheel hit a rut, and far surpassed the mud wagon, which had no springs at all to cushion the bumps.

When one of the big wooden wheels of a Concord coach dropped suddenly into a hole, the thoroughbraces tended to swing the body forward and maintain momentum, thus cushioning the ride for passengers and lessening the strain on horses. The sensation of a swinging and swaying Concord coach was reminiscent of that of a rocking chair, albeit an often cramped and dusty one. Some passengers complained that if the coach was heavy in front or rear, "or if the thoroughbraces be not properly 'fixed,' the bumping will likely cause nasal hemorrhage." Others suffered motion sickness. Mark Twain

aptly characterized the effect as that of a "cradle on wheels." By locating the center of gravity squarely between the wheels, the builders also minimized the chance of an upset on sharp curves or when crossing unbridged streams. Heavy-duty running gear, built of well-seasoned oak and ash or black cherry wood, was designed to endure a severe beating. Carriage makers, realizing that a thin shell had tremendous strength if properly curved, learned to shape the coach body somewhat like a hen's egg. Little iron was used in a Concord coach, although the ones Ben Holladay bought in 1864 still weighed about a ton apiece.[1]

The driver's seat was located forward atop the coach to command a panoramic view of the road and the horses. Beneath it was a large leather compartment, or boot, designed to carry mail, expressmen's gold dust boxes, and other especially valuable cargo. A large triangular rear boot carried additional express, merchandise of all kinds, and passengers' baggage (of which twenty-five pounds per person usually traveled free). If there were an exceptionally large number of mail sacks, the excess ones were simply thrown on the floor of the coach to slide about, much to the discomfiture of the passengers. A railing about a foot high enclosed the top of the coach to afford a convenient handhold for any passenger who rode there, while in inclement weather, a leather apron snapped on to cover the legs of driver's-seat passengers.

F. Jay Haynes photographed six horses pulling this Concord stage through Jefferson County, Montana Territory, on December 1, 1887. Courtesy Montana Historical Society, H-1834.

Mark Twain's Trouble with a Thoroughbrace

About an hour and a half before daylight we were bowling along smoothly over the road—so smoothly that our cradle only rocked in a gentle, lulling way, that was gradually soothing us to sleep and dulling our consciousness—when something gave way under us! We were dimly aware of it, but indifferent to it. The coach stopped. We heard the driver and conductor talking together outside, and rummaging for a lantern, and swearing because they could not find it—but we had no interest in whatever had happened, and it only added to our comfort to think of those people out there at work in the murky night; and we snug in our nest with the curtains drawn. But presently, by the sounds, there seemed to be an examination going on, and then the driver's voice said:

"By George, the thoroughbrace is broke!"

This startled me broad awake—as an undefined sense of calamity is always apt to do. I said to myself: "Now, a thoroughbrace is probably part of a horse; and doubtless a vital part, too, from the dismay in the driver's voice. Leg, maybe— and yet how could he break his leg waltzing along such as road as this? No, it can't be his leg. That is impossible, unless he was reaching for the driver. Now, what can be the thoroughbrace of a horse, I wonder? Well, whatever comes, I shall not air my ignorance in this crowd, anyway."

Just then the conductor's face appeared at a lifted curtain, and his lantern glared in on us and our wall of mail matter. He said: "Gents, you'll have to turn out a spell. Thoroughbrace is broke."

We climbed out into a chill drizzle, and felt ever so homeless and dreary. When I found that the thing they called a "thoroughbrace" was the massive combination of belts and springs which the coach rocks itself in, I said to the driver:

"I never saw a thoroughbrace used up like that, before, that I can remember. How did it happen?"

"Why, it happened by trying to make one coach carry three days' mail—that's how it happened," said he.
—Mark Twain, *Roughing It* (1872)

The standard Concord coach seated nine passengers on three leather-cushioned inside seats, and, if the coach carried an extra seat behind the driver, from five to seven on top. Passengers usually preferred the inside back seat with its large headrest. Latecomers drew the middle seat, which had no real back, only a broad leather belt suspended on straps from the ceiling, its ends attached by hooks to the door frame. Passengers on this seat enjoyed a bit more hip room than the others, but if one of them faced a long-legged traveler on the front seat they had to interlock knees. Some of the Holladay coaches were built to carry seventeen passengers, with an extra seat over the rear boot and one behind the driver. If need be, as many as sixteen to twenty passengers could be packed into or atop a standard Concord coach.

The Abbot Downing firm built about three thousand Concord coaches for customers all over the world, the price for such vehicles in the 1840s being approximately $1,200. During the 1850s and 1860s hundreds of coaches were constructed in Concord and shipped around Cape Horn to West Coast destinations. The firm also built vehicles called celerity and mud wagons, far less elegant and expensive than a Concord coach, but equal to it in durability and workmanship. Mud wagons were designed, as the name suggests, for use over extremely muddy or rough roads; celerity wagons were for fast runs with mail and express on lines where passengers were few.

When a Concord coach left Abbot Downing (a complex covering four acres in 1858, which the firm claimed was "the largest factory in the United States"), it was unsurpassed for durability and craftsmanship. A new one was the pride of every stage driver. Multiple coats of paint had been applied, rubbed down with pumice, and covered with two coats of varnish, making every surface as smooth, hard, and highly polished as a mirror. The body was usually red, with an exquisite landscape hand-painted on each door and most of the interior paneling decorated with the ornate scrollwork of the era. It was an impressive sight as it pulled into a frontier stage station, drawn by its lively animals and carrying mail and packages from distant places.

The Concord coach was transportation technology never fully duplicated by other builders—including two more giants of the trade, the James Goold Coach Company of Albany, New York, and Eaton, Gilbert and Company of Troy, New York—although some West Coast manufacturers claimed to have constructed "Concord" coaches of their own. The five coaches constructed in Walla Walla for Thomas and Company's Boise stage line were called Concord coaches and described as "fine in appearance." A local newspaper was "glad to chronicle the fact that the system of sending to Portland and San Francisco for coaches and wagons is being done away with."[2]

Structures: From Boundlessness to Organization

Acquisition of Concord coaches or other wheeled conveyances was only one part of launching a successful stage line across the West. It required nerve as well as capital to operate such a line during the 1850s and 1860s, especially in the vast country stretching from the Missouri River to the Pacific coast where so many challenges awaited transportation pioneers. Besides inclement weather there was always the possibility of an Indian attack, although writers often exaggerated this danger into "thrilling accounts of heroic resistance and wonderful escapes" and ignored the mundane details of everyday operation.[3]

What dime novels and Hollywood epics failed to mention was the support structure, the elaborate organization that made it possible for Concord coaches to traverse seemingly boundless western space. The basics of western staging owed a great deal to John Butterfield and his southern overland route of the late 1850s, but on the central overland route Hockaday and Chorpenning actually offered transcontinental mail service several months ahead of Butterfield. To enable their coaches to traverse the open country between Saint Joseph and Salt Lake City, they borrowed from railroad organization by establishing at intervals some thirty-six stage stations and a system of freight wagons to supply them. Each station purchased hay, horses, and grain from nearby farmers and ranchers, when possible, and the income of drivers,

blacksmith, hostlers, and station keepers put money into local circulation.

During the glory days of the central overland route, tons of grain had to be shipped regularly from farms in the Missouri Valley to dozens of isolated stage stations where it was used to feed horses and mules. When there was a shortage or crop failure, as occasionally happened on the high plains, the supply of grain had to come by boat from Saint Louis. David Street, general manager of the Overland line in the later 1860s, once chartered seven Missouri River steamboats at Saint Louis to haul enough corn west to maintain stage operations. Hay could usually be obtained along the route, although in some arid localities it had to be hauled fifty miles or more.

Likewise, along hundreds of miles of trail where sagebrush was the largest plant, every log needed to build a station had to be hauled by wagon, sometimes from as far away as two hundred miles. Given the difficulty of obtaining logs, many a desert station consisted of little more than the rudest kind of a shanty or sod house. All across the West, stations were typically positioned every ten to fifteen miles, depending on the availability of

water and grass. The distance between each outpost was called a stage, and each driver's run would cover from two to three stages for a total of forty to sixty miles in all. But on occasion, perhaps if a colleague became sick, a driver might have to cover four or five stages. Depending upon the difficulty of the terrain, horses were changed several times en route, but coaches usually went through to the end, where they were inspected for repairs.

Stage stations were of two types. Most substantial were the home stations, their primary purpose being to supply fresh teams for the coaches and food for the passengers. Swing stations, where only stock tenders lived, were for purposes of relay only and often consisted of a single room. Although Holladay's company owned about half of the home stations, there was no consistency among them. A few lacked even chairs, and rough board benches were substituted instead; others utilized soapboxes and cracker boxes; some embellished nail kegs with pieces of buckskin or buffalo robe tacked over the head to furnish what were apparently comfortable seats.

Except for isolated stage stations, across the plains of southern Idaho there were no real settlements in the

Rankin Stage Station, on the road between Rawlins and Grand Encampment, Wyoming, in 1897. In the days of the central overland route the most substantial outposts were the home stations, which often included the quarters of the stationmaster and his family, stock tenders, and stage drivers and other off-duty operating employees. The partitions between rooms were almost invariably made of thin muslin. Sometimes there would be a small kitchen at the rear, enabling home stations to supply hot meals to passengers. Courtesy Woodward Collection, Arizona Historical Society.

1860s apart from Boise, and there was little travel apart from the triweekly stages. As a rule these stations were dreary and dismal habitations; often their only fuel consisted of sagebrush and greasewood, "about the last apology for fuel on the earth." Elsewhere, many a desert station in hostile Indian country resembled a substantial stone fortress, with gunports in the walls and shining rifles and well-polished revolvers hanging ready to be grasped at any moment.[4]

At Atchison, Denver, and Salt Lake City—division headquarters of Ben Holladay's Overland Stage Line—were located sizable coach and repair shops, each employing blacksmiths, wheelwrights, and harness makers. Using original parts and material from Abbot Downing, they could rebuild an entire Concord coach in an emergency. Company farriers and harness repairers used

separate teams and outfits to travel from station to station on a continuous round of horseshoeing and repairing: horses had to be shod at least once a month, and sometimes more often.

Holladay's central overland organization included a general superintendent, an attorney, and a paymaster. At one time the general superintendent was George K. Otis, who resided in New York but traveled over the line about once every three months. When Holladay made one of his inspection trips, once and sometimes twice a year, in his special coach, Otis usually accompanied him. There were also division superintendents, each in charge of about six hundred miles of road. Next in rank were division agents, who supervised operations along about two hundred miles of road. This position was an especially important one and usually went only to a man who had risen from the ranks of drivers. Each division agent was responsible for all property belonging to the company in his particular territory; he looked after the stock, the running of the stages, and the stations and their keepers. He bought the hay and grain, which were distributed at the stations on his orders, and he hired the drivers, stock tenders, blacksmiths, harness makers, carpenters, and veterinarians.

Everyday management of the Overland Stage Line was always a difficult task. In addition to Indian hostilities during the early and middle 1860s, there was the problem of obtaining supplies on a route so remote from civilization; it was also hard to respond to the perils of floods, snows, and tornadoes. Adding to the problems of operating the line successfully were small bands of desperadoes, mainly coming from Texas and Arkansas, who ostensibly hunted buffalo and other animals for their hides but whose real purpose was to steal stock, to rob express coaches and their passengers, and at times even to commit murder.

The Platte River route of the Central Overland California and Pike's Peak Express Company suffered more than its share of crime until the spring of 1860, when Benjamin F. Ficklin became general superintendent. To this courtly Virginian it appeared as though "all the thieves in creation had congregated along the route and were systematically preying upon the company's property." One of Ficklin's first important moves was to relocate Joseph Albert Slade from Fort Kearny farther west to Julesburg, Colorado, to serve as superintendent of the notorious Sweetwater division.[5]

Slade, who had moved north from Texas to work as a teamster hauling supplies for the Hockaday operation in 1858, proved to be an untiring worker. He devoted most of his waking hours to company business and gave special attention to ensuring the comfort and safety of his passengers. Thus he did not postpone dealing with delinquent employees on his section of the Overland Stage Line. Slade took particular interest in the station at Julesburg, where for some time company horses had mysteriously disappeared and coaches been delayed in a way that suggested that outlaw gangs were operating nearby.

It was difficult for the company to know how to remedy the trouble, and the thieves simply laughed at the idea of anyone preventing their depredations. But Slade determined to change things, and quickly. The outlaws soon learned that he feared nothing. When there was trouble on his division, Slade personally meted out punishment. Becoming something of a one-man vigilance committee, he ensured himself a lasting reputation by killing a half dozen of the worst characters, often single-handedly. After Slade thinned the outlaw gangs, company property remained unmolested and coaches ran with more regularity.

Slade, the loyal company employee whose violent methods brought organization to a boundless landscape, evolved into a frontier character of mythic proportions. Some observers claimed that he carried both buckshot and bullets in various parts of his body; he was known to have worn the ears of "the other fellow" on his watch chain. Separating fact from fiction became more difficult with each retelling of his exploits. But Slade, valuable as his services were, seemed unable to measure up to his mythic image and finally went the wrong way. He commenced drinking heavily, becoming a terror to the very people to whom, in earlier days, he had been a most trusted friend, and fell into the ways of the outlaws he had so long fought as an employee of the Overland Stage Line.

Holladay himself came out from New York to fire him, and that, so the legend goes, he did with a Colt .44 in his hand. Slade slouched around Colorado for a few months, drinking, brawling, cursing Holladay and the Overland line, and killing at will; he was even suspected of taking part in a $60,000 government payroll robbery. Soon afterward he drifted north to Virginia City, Montana, where some of the toughest outlaws on the continent had congregated after the discovery of gold. "Well armed and well mounted the road agents stopped coaches carrying passengers and valuable freight, with cheerful and regular alacrity, and in a manner throve on booty wrung from passengers by persuasion of arms." The murder of Lloyd Magruder encouraged citizens of Bannack and Virginia City to organize a vigilance committee that by late January 1864 had broken the power of the outlaws. Virginia City was where the "notorious" Jack Slade, having shot up the town once too often, died a coward's death, whimpering and begging for mercy as vigilantes dragged him to the scaffold.[6]

Knights of the Reins

The Overland Stage Line in the 1860s was operated with the precision and punctuality of a railroad line, and in all seasons, night and day, coaches ran with nearly the same regularity as trains, or so its backers claimed. A gentleman living in Denver in those days, whose place of business was near the stage office, used to say, jokingly, that he could set his watch by the arrival and departure of the Overland. The men doing most to keep coaches running smoothly, and invariably the most visible representatives of their employers, were the drivers. Some of them had drifted west after railroads displaced them from the roads of New England; some had been driving for several years in Mexico before the discovery of gold lured them north to California. Several had held the reins of four- and six-horse stage teams in the West long before a railroad reached the Mississippi River. "Now and then there was one to be found whose locks and beard were silvered from having sat on the box and weathered the wintry blasts of a third of a century or more, driving on various lines between the Alleghenies and the Rockies."[7]

Some stage drivers were recruited from the ranks of farmers and ranchmen, others had some experience as mechanics and clerks, and a few had been formerly employed by railroads. At least one had been a canal boatman; another was the pilot of a western river steamboat. Most were by nature jacks-of-all-trades and showmen. When a driver came to a frontier outpost he intended his entry to be spectacular: "Before arriving at the end of the journey, which was the Overland Hotel at Boise, he would start his horses on a run when about six blocks away and bring them to a grand standstill in front of the hotel."[8]

Drivers played up to the fact that they and their coaches were in the public limelight in prerailroad days. Their usual attire included a white Stetson hat, a wide

decorated belt, and stylish clothes. Virtually every driver "went around with a revolver in a belt at his side, and some of them also carried in their belts or had safely secreted in their boot-legs big, ugly-looking knives." Each driver had individual preference in such accessories, but all of them cherished the whip as their prized possession. Whips would vary in length and design, including some that had hickory stocks five to six feet long, glossed down and wrapped with saddler's silk, and lashes nearly twenty feet long. Nearly every driver worshiped his whip, considering it so valuable that he hated to lend it even to a best friend and companion driver. Remarkable as it may appear, some drivers were such experts in handling their favorite whips that they could sit on the box and knock a fly off the back of the lead horses or mules with the lash, while going at a lively trot, and bring the whip back without getting it entangled with the harness or the wheels.[9]

Some drivers were also fine singers. "Often, riding over the trail in the 'stilly hour of night,' while sitting by

A group of stage drivers from southern Oregon posed for a formal portrait in 1875. As a rule, passengers idolized their drivers; the seat of greatest honor was atop the coach alongside the driver. A traveler got it by special invitation, not by being the first to hop up on the left front wheel rim and mount the box. William and George Banning noted that a driver, "though he could tolerate the affectionate or poetic expressions of 'Jehu,' 'whip,' 'whipster,' 'Charlie,' 'knight of the ribbons,' etc., could accept the appellation of coachman no more than he could accept a 'tip.'" Courtesy Southern Oregon Historical Society, 6768.

them, have I listened to their sweet songs. Quite a number could play different musical instruments. The violin was the favorite with the most of them. Some were quite expert in picking the banjo; some enjoyed the guitar; others blew the clarinet, flute, fife, or piccolo, and one good-natured chap could 'rattle the bones' to perfection. One was a good tambourine player; one was lightning on 'chin music'; while another declared he could 'rip a five-octave jew's-harp all to pieces.'" [10]

On the road, however, the driver needed to be less a showman than a man of iron, willing to endure summer heat, pelting hailstones and cloudbursts, and blinding blizzards from his exposed seat high atop the coach. A stage driver in southern Idaho once wandered around all night after snow obliterated the trail and blinded him and his horses; he eventually ended up back where he had started. Despite such hardships, nearly every driver was more or less wedded to his occupation, and it seemed that most never could retire from it. Older drivers told Frank Root that there was some sort of a charm about stage driving that they could not resist. "Some were good for nothing else." [11]

Apparently there was nothing that delighted drivers so much as handling a wild, dashing team over a rough and crooked mountain road on a down grade. The rougher the trail, the more skill it required, and thus the more some drivers seemed to like it. In rounding short curves and maintaining a breakneck speed along the edge of a dangerous-looking ledge of rocks, with a yawning abyss into which passengers could look hundreds of feet below, a fearless driver was at the height of his glory. The brake was an integral part of his driving, and a real reinsman could perform on the brake with the skill of a musician manipulating pipe-organ pedals. In handling their vehicles and horses, "they were experts and knew it and were the envy of all." [12]

Hostlers and Shotgun Messengers

The main duty of a "knight of the ribbons" was to sit on the box and drive. Proud drivers on the central overland route considered it beneath their dignity to feed or harness up their horses. That was the job of the lowly stock tender or hostler: after he had everything connected and the coach loaded, the driver would step out leisurely and climb to his lofty seat. The hostler would then hand him the reins. Every driver was a hero to the hostler, whose greatest desire was to please his superiors by keeping the animals well groomed and in excellent health. Hostlers were employed at all stations, but those assigned to swing stations endured especially lonely lives, the reading of old magazines and newspapers often being their sole entertainment. Their lives centered on the brief moment when the stage arrived for a change of mules or horses. Once in a while the hostlers at remote swing stations had other visitors, such as the division blacksmith or the harness maker and repairer.

In the early days of overland staging in the late 1840s and early 1850s, a conductor was selected from among the drivers to accompany each vehicle and be responsible for the welfare of passengers and any mail and express, or for an entire train of vehicles traveling together over long, empty stretches of the West. By the late 1850s this position evolved into that of the "shotgun messenger," who, though not so respected as the driver, was fully as important an employee to the stage or express company. His job was to guard valuable shipments, especially the gold, with the short-barreled shotgun (sometimes two) that lay across his lap. He must constantly survey the surrounding landscape for outlaws or road agents. Some messengers did this while remaining inside with the passengers, but most preferred to be aloft with the driver. The shotgun messenger rested for nine days out of every three weeks so that he might be alert for his run. Then for six days and nights he kept his nerve-wracking vigil. As mining operations increased in the West, so did the value of express shipment by stage—and also the number of desperadoes lying in wait.

Frank Root complained that shotgun messengers "were the poorest-paid men in the employ of the stage company. They were obliged to ride outside on the box with the driver six days and nights without undressing, and exposed to all kinds of weather." They received $62.50 a month and free meals on the road, but they had a lay-over of nine days out of every three weeks, so that

This stagecoach paused on an Idaho road long enough to permit horses to refresh themselves from a stream. Good drivers seemed to understand their animals well. For instance, they believed that horses had better night vision than humans and an instinct that enabled them even in pitch blackness or a blinding blizzard to follow a trail or road with which they were familiar. Drivers feared that by reining around every mudhole they would accustom their horses to depend too much upon humans for guidance, and such a team would likely wander off the road some stormy night when the driver could not see through the snow or fog to guide it properly. Courtesy Idaho State Historical Society, 73–221.55/A.

THE FORD.
BISBEE 576.

their actual working time was somewhat reduced and their exposure to the elements that much lessened.[13]

A division blacksmith on the central overland route in the 1860s earned from $100 to $125 a month; harness makers and repairers drew the same salary; carpenters earned about $75. Hostlers drew salaries of $40 to $50 a month, while drivers received from $150 to $250, depending on length of employment and ability as a reinsman, though wages and job descriptions varied widely through the West. In the early 1870s, Gilmer and Salisbury drivers earned only $40 a month and board for driving four horses, $60 a month and board for driving six horses. On shorter routes a driver usually cared for his own horses.

Staging was considered a man's business, but at many home stations lived women fully as hardworking as their husbands. Because of the isolation, most of them had little opportunity for social life of any kind, but on the first Saturday night after payday there was always a dance at one or more of the home stations on each division. Where neighbors were scarce, dances frequently took place at one of the more important home stations, and it was not unusual for women living at other stations to ride the distance on horseback or to board the coach and ride from ten to thirty-five miles, dance perhaps the greater part of the night, and return home on the next coach. These were the big social events, and no frontier woman missed one if she could possibly get there. Frank Root recalled that strangers who stopped at a station on the central overland route during a dance "would often be puzzled—simply amazed—and naturally wonder where all the women came from in such a sparsely settled country."[14]

Between Man and Beast

Teams of four or six spirited horses (sometimes mules) were required to pull each coach, trotting along at eight miles an hour, sometimes ten or twelve. "The animals themselves were our standing wonder; no broken-down nags, or half-starved Rosinantes [Don Quixote's bony horse], like our typical stage-horses east; but as a rule, they were fat and fiery, and would have done credit to a horseman anywhere. Wiry, gamey, as if feeling their oats thoroughly, they often went off from the stations at a full gallop; at the end of a mile or so would settle down to a square steady trot; and this they would usually keep up right along until they reached the next station." Many of these horses had been driven west from stock farms in Ohio, Pennsylvania, Kentucky, and Virginia, generally by emigrants but sometimes by special agents of the stage lines. Ben Holladay wanted only the fastest livestock. He expected his teams to be able to outrun Indian ponies if attacked, and expensive live horses were less costly in the long run than cheap ones shot full of arrows. It was good publicity, too, when his coaches wheeled into town at a spirited gallop.[15]

To keep the stock healthy, several veterinarians regularly patrolled the route. They inspected and treated each animal. Even so, highly contagious diseases always posed a threat to stage operations. The flu-like epizootic occasionally ran rampant on the Pacific Coast, and late in January 1873 it overwhelmed the horses of the Gilmer and Salisbury line that linked Utah with Montana. While enervating, this disease was not generally fatal, but it did reduce the available horsepower and threaten stage service. An infected horse would cough for days, have a runny nose and watery eyes, and occasionally show the secondary symptoms of dropsy. The best treatment seemed to be complete rest, adequate time for recuperation, a diet of moist, warm bran mash, and moderate medication. One supposed remedy consisted of a solution of one or two grains of sulfate of copper in four ounces of distilled water, to be injected into the horse's nostrils two or three times a day; another was an inhalation of carbolic acid that was supposed to relieve the bronchial tubes and lungs. It is no wonder that stock owners were advised that "more horses have been killed in the east by medicine than by the disease."[16]

Even if hostlers had primary responsibility for feeding and harnessing horses, every good driver knew the names and personalities of the animals pulling his coach. He checked carefully to see that his horses looked sleek and were properly harnessed. A loosely hitched six-horse team would permit the driver to have free play with the reins, which provided the best pulling power with the least amount of strain on the animals. Good horse sense might also help when the driver was drunk, although most seemed to hold their liquor well. "Frequently I saw drivers while sitting on the box and riding with them when they were so drunk that the wonder to me was how they ever kept from tumbling off the seat," recalled Frank Root. "Many times I have been anxious for them, thinking every minute they certainly would fall to the ground dead, and that it would devolve on me to drive with the corpse to the next station. But of all the drunkenness I saw on the stage line, I never yet saw a driver so 'full' that he could not, while on the box, hold the reins and his whip and go around a curve or turn a short corner as handsomely as any one who never imbibed a drop."[17]

The Episcopal bishop Daniel Tuttle, whose many miles of stage travel took him all over Idaho and Montana, agreed that a driver, "even when drunk, would be quite as skillful in handling lines as would the best of us lubberly outsiders." He recalled the time when he and his son were the only passengers and the driver was drunk. "I mounted the box, tied my boy on and sat close beside the driver for steadiness and support, never, however, venturing to take the lines. That would have been an insult to him."[18]

Eventually, however, Ben Holladay found it necessary to emphasize that any employee working for him "who shall become intoxicated, and thereby neglect the business for which he is employed, or shall maltreat any of the other employees or any person on the line of the road, shall, for every such offense, forfeit one month's wages, which will positively be deducted on proof of the same. Wages to be settled by the paymaster only, at such

Main Street, Boise, Idaho, as it looked about 1889. The city of brick and stone offered quite a contrast to the wooden village of the 1860s, when it was a major hub for stage lines across southern Idaho. Courtesy Idaho State Historical Society, 2127.

times as the regular quarterly payments of the line are made." Although no driver ever had his wages docked ("they took their 'firewater' after that in more moderate doses until the excitement finally died away"), it became necessary to prepare a secret blacklist of the most incorrigible drivers. Division agents were forbidden to employ these men again.[19]

All the dedicated employees and an organizational structure that was quite elaborate for the frontier could not mitigate the fact that stagecoach travel across the American West was ever an ordeal. Even though the trip was often exciting and always picturesque, it remained a long day's journey nonetheless. A generation of passengers endured travail by stage.

At Redding, where is the terminus at present of the California and Oregon railroad, we found the stage in waiting. The talk, half-joke and half-earnest, was as to hiding or not hiding our money. We all knew that there was a chance of being stopped and robbed; but, till we mounted the stage, we did not know that it had been stopped five times in the last eighteen months, or we should have been more inclined to take the advice of friends who insisted that the only safe place for our money was in our socks.
—*Wallis Nash*, Oregon: There and Back in 1877 *(1878)*

Travail by Stagecoach

Hollywood and popular fiction have romanticized stagecoach travel across the frontier West. True, when the daily or triweekly stagecoach reached a settlement in the sagebrush, a crowd of townspeople invariably awaited it. Stage time was often the biggest event of the day. Drivers played up to this public attention and enjoyed making a dramatic entry. They took great pride in the appearance of their outfit, especially their fine-looking horses. But passengers themselves seldom found much that was romantic or glamorous about stage travel, except in hindsight: rarely was a trip of any length without its trials and discomforts. "One of the most tedious journeys that can be made is that in a stagecoach, if one is compelled to be a cramped denizen of its hard seats for several days and nights at a time."[1]

Conquered by a Concord

A journey from Portland to San Francisco meant continuous day and night travel for seven days. To undertake it a second time required unusual determination. Offering a vivid recollection of the assorted travails of stagecoach travelers on this or any other route across the northern West was the keen-eyed German, Theodor Kirchhoff, who made the trip from Oregon to California in 1865.

"On October 27 at 6:00 A.M. I took a seat on the box of the four-horse stage and said good-bye to Portland. The city was quickly behind us. Merrily we trotted south, up the valley of the Willamette, headed toward the distant Golden Gate."[2]

Kirchhoff described his driver as a "gray-haired Webfoot" who considered it cruel to "urge his team to a trot even on the best of roads. Sharp remarks on my part did nothing to produce speed on his. When I told how California drivers go always at a gallop, he observed that life was not worth much there." Among the several miners aboard the coach were two from Montana, carrying between them a sixty-pound cantina, a kind of saddlebag used for transporting gold dust, which they never let out of their sight. "They brought it with them to meals and set it at their feet under the table. Indeed, one would plant his foot on top of it. Wise precautions, these, for travelers here are often and in mysterious ways relieved of burdens of metal. It goes without saying, every [male] passenger kept a loaded revolver at the belt, against madcap violence in these regions that respect so superficially the right to property. Besides revolvers, our Montanans each carried a Henry rifle richly ornamented with an inlay of gold."

By early afternoon Kirchhoff's stagecoach had reached
Oregon City. "Alternately riding and walking, in the best
of weather, we forged ahead: now through shady forests,
now over sunny meadows, now around well-cultivated
farms, nicely tended orchards, and pleasant settlements.
We tried to pass the time as best we could by telling stories of all sorts of adventures. Exciting ones made time
fly. Before we knew it, lengthening shadows announced
the end of the day, just as we saw before us the friendly
town of Salem, capital of the young state of Oregon,
fifty miles south of Portland. After a short stop we were
going again, this time for the night, in disagreeably cold
weather accompanied by a true Webfoot rain."

Kirchhoff described an overnight journey by stagecoach as one of the "necessary evils for the traveler in the
American West. He can be happy if a few 200-pounders
do not hog space where six and (when necessary) nine
slim passengers crowd three seats. In that miserable

event, the slim ones constrict to shadows of their former selves. (Astounding!)" As night fell Kirchhoff exchanged his outside seat on the box beside the driver for a rear one inside. "I chose the rear because experience had taught me that, due to swaying reminiscent of a ship in a storm, most passengers would avoid the rear and leave me a bigger place. Thus I hoped to catch forty winks there now and then."

Presently the driver opened the door and curtly told his passengers to make room for three women. "Already a crowd of eight, we protested unanimously and hotly such an increase. Meanwhile we glared through the downpour at those daughters of Eve and their load of giant hatboxes and unmentionable bundles. How massive those women looked in their crinoline, and how wet! But, as is well known, men in American have no rights against women and certainly none in a stagecoach. My two Montana friends awakened from a refreshing snooze. (They had curled up in the back seat.) The three women, perhaps comfortable without umbrellas, like mermaids in disguise, stood in pouring rain and demanded of the Montanans that they move aside because they, the women, could not ride backwards."

The Montanans "gave up their seats with heavy hearts. The three rainy ladies took over at once, without even a thank-you to our two gentlemen who had been so obliging. Since three Webfeet had the uncomfortable middle seats, and all others were also occupied, the Montanans could find none inside. So they picked up their heavy bag of gold and climbed outside to the roof, where sleep was unthinkable in the cold rain. Moreover, anyone camping aloft would be well-advised to keep an eye out for tree-limbs that oppose the stage—a most interesting situation when an aggressive one slashes within inches of the roof and seems to want to clip everything before it."

Kirchhoff was overjoyed when the first light of a new day peeped through the window. "It illuminated a sorry sight: bleary eyes and the waterfalls of the Three Graces, which had been dripping prosaically all night. Pity anybody Cupid could hit in these circumstances; love and a stage-coach journey are incompatible. We were ecstatic when our tender creatures and their hatboxes and their

unmentionable bundles and their crinolines and their waterfalls left us as soon as the next change of horses." When the Montanans reclaimed their seats inside to catch a little morning sleep, Kirchhoff used the opportunity to remount the box and enjoy a panoramic view of the Oregon countryside.

Bishop Daniel Tuttle reminisced that stagecoaching was "a vivid part of my Rocky Mountain memories. I have traveled more than forty thousand miles in that way. Most times I enjoyed that mode of traveling, many times I grimly endured it, a few times I was rendered miserable by it." Once only did he remember being "quite unnerved" by the experience. That was on a trip from Salt Lake to Boise City, which required about three

An advertisement for the Pioneer Hotel in Portland in 1863. From here passengers departed for southern Oregon and California aboard coaches of the California Stage Company. Courtesy Oregon Historical Society, 91755.

Overland Stagecoach Etiquette

Never ride in cold weather with tight boots or shoes, nor close-fitting gloves. Bathe your feet before starting in cold water, and wear loose overshoes and gloves two or three sizes too large. When the driver asks you to get off and walk, do it without grumbling. He will not request it unless absolutely necessary. If a team runs away, sit still and take your chances; if you jump, nine times out of ten you will be hurt. In very cold weather abstain entirely from liquor while on the road; a man will freeze twice as quick while under its influence. Don't growl at food at stations: stage companies generally provide the best they can. Don't keep the stage waiting; many a virtuous man has lost his character by so doing. Don't smoke a strong pipe inside especially early in the morning, spit on the leeward side of the coach. If you have anything to take in a bottle, pass it around; a man who drinks by himself in such a case is lost to all human feeling. Provide stimulants before starting; ranch whisky is not always nectar. Be sure and take two heavy blankets with you; you will need them. Don't swear, nor lop over on your

days and nights of travel. "Near all the way I was alone and in a 'jerker' instead of a stagecoach. The latter, of Concord make, drawn by four, often six horses, and carrying nine passengers within and five on the outside, was the Pullman car of early times. But the former was a small canvas-covered affair, seating four inside and one outside with the driver, and drawn usually by only two horses. This, when the wheels struck obstacles, did not have the easy roll and swing of the coach, but, as the name imports, jerked the passenger unmercifully on, or oftener off, his seat. To be alone in a jerker was to be in the extreme of discomfort. The vehicle not being steadied by a good load, and the passenger not being supported by contact with other passengers, the careless unsteadiness drove away sleep, and wore one out in frantic efforts to secure some tolerable sort of bodily equilibrium."[3]

Tuttle claimed that during the last fifty miles of his trip to Boise "I was more used up physically than at any other time I can think of in my life. I was past the point of grinning and bearing, or shutting the teeth and enduring. All the forces of resistance seemed to be beaten down and disintegrated. I was ready to groan and cry, and would have offered not a jot of opposition if the driver had dumped me down upon the roadside and left me behind under a sage brush. That experience made me understand the stories I had heard of the stage passengers who could not sleep, coming in after long journeys downright sick and even actually demented." The jerky described by Tuttle was commonly substituted for Concord coaches in Montana and elsewhere during times of bad weather and light business, and travelers who endured such a trip considered it the most appropriate name ever applied to any kind of vehicle.[4]

Though Concord coaches provided far more comfort than lesser conveyances, there was often the problem of overcrowding, which made even a Concord seem "to be full of feet and bony knees." Travelers claimed that this coach was designed to carry "more passengers and baggage than any other vehicle of twice its apparent capacity." Trunks, valises, and bundles packed the rear boot, while packages and sacks of mail filled the front one, with the driver occasionally pitching in an extra box or basket and an oath. A few extra sacks of oats for the horses might be hoisted on top. "At first sight, it looked as though four slim persons might ride inside and two on the box seat with the driver. But we were 10 who had paid our fares, with feelings of murder and charitableness, we looked at each other."[5]

Besides the crowding and the intense jolting that caused passengers to complain of aching bones and bruised flesh, there were the rain and dust that seeped inside through the ill-fitting curtains. Not surprisingly, it was said that many a seasoned veteran of stagecoach travel preferred to carry his twenty-five-pound allotment of personal luggage in demijohns of whiskey in order to anesthetize him against the miseries of the journey. One traveler from the East wrote that until he went by stage to California, "I had always considered the physical essentials to be food and drink, but soon I learned they were drink and food."[6]

Get Behind and Push!

No matter how much a ticket might cost, stagecoach passengers could never be certain of reaching their destinations on time. Even if the trip were free from attack by Indians or road agents, bad weather often delayed travelers. Teams might have to swim across streams swollen by sudden rains and spring thaws, with the coaches, built in such a way as to maintain an even keel, floating along behind. A traveler on C. C. Huntley's coach from Helena to Fort Benton to catch a steamboat for Saint Louis in the spring of 1867 experienced an unusual delay: "At 5 o'clock we were drummed out of our comfortable beds in the mud by the ranchman in order to take the coach. We accordingly took our places but alas for anticipations and hopes we were doomed to remain there all day. The stock, being lost during the night, did not arrive until noon, and then in very bad and exhausted condition and unable to proceed until the next morning."[7]

Early western roads were often little more than dirt paths, and a rain could turn long stretches of them into knee-deep quagmires. Passengers might then be required to trudge through the mud to lighten the load or get behind to help push. Kirchhoff recalled his 1865 stage-coach journey through the Calapooya Mountains of southern Oregon "where, for a change, the driver bade us walk in pouring rain, to spare the horses. This being our second sleepless night, you can imagine that the order met something less than enthusiasm. We protested—in vain! Soporific, we staggered through puddles and in gushing rain, across the mountains, cursing from the depths of our souls every Webfoot stagecoach driver. In truth, however, we could not justifiably damn as unfair the command that we plod a few miles; on any journey by stagecoach in America, passengers routinely help the horses by walking when the going gets tough. He errs profoundly who presumes, when he buys a ticket, that he can enjoy the coach the entire time. On a journey of 100 miles, let him consider himself lucky to walk no more than 20, and only in the worst places." Another traveler remembered a driver ordering, "First class passengers, keep your seats. Second class passengers, get out and walk. Third class passengers, get behind and push."[8]

Granville Stuart had the misfortune to travel through Idaho's Snake River country near Blackfoot Butte during a thaw late in 1866. The stage company loaded its passengers into a large freight wagon "with four little rats of mules to draw it, and as a natural consequence they 'stalled' in every low place or hollow, and we were compelled to get out in snow and water up to our hips and dig the 'outfit' out." Farther south at the Portneuf River they switched to a sleigh, "but the snow having lately all melted off, we had to walk eight or ten miles up the canyon, while the horses could hardly drag the sleigh and baggage." Stuart complained that "everything goes by contraries on the Overland; the climate changes so rapidly that where the sleds and sleighs are, there is no snow, and where the snow is, there you had to ride in coaches, steamboat wagons, carts, and anything else that's convenient—generally without seats, compelling you to sit on the mail and baggage."[9]

Winter weather so increased their operating difficulties that some stage lines simply quit running. Others struggled through: "All night long we rode, slapping our hands and stomping our feet to keep the blood circulat-ing, gradually ascending the mountains [Siskiyous], and keeping the great dipper always before us." In summer a coach might be constantly traveling through a cloud of dust raised by the horses' hooves, and the searing heat inside might rise as high as a hundred and ten degrees. The drivers and their horses were generally sheathed in a mantle of gray dust from the sagebrush plains, and after little more than an hour's ride on a dry, hot day, "passengers looked like soft-coal miners coming off shift. From head to foot they were covered with grime, their faces streaked with rivulets of mud from trickling sweat or tears from dust-inflamed eyes." Alkali made passengers' skin sore and rough and burned their eyes and noses.[10]

Rain was as much an enemy as dust or snow. Heavy downpours might cause washouts and delay stagecoaches for hours until raging streams subsided enough for the driver to ford them. At other times a heavy hailstorm might frighten the horses or mules into running away, the passengers obliged to hold on desperately during the wild ride.

Perhaps equally alarming were roads that wound down steep hillsides. West of the summit of Lemhi Pass the stagecoach from Red Rock to Salmon City descended with its wheels "double rough-locked." Seasoned passengers kept a calm silence as the coach tipped toward the cliff edge. "The narrow road would round sides of precipices, where trees grew hundreds of feet below us. Timid passengers looked not out of the windows towards the depths. The travelers on the roof of the coach were instructed to sit on the upper side, and those inside told gruesome stories of former accidents to stage coaches."[11]

"Any sensible person" who had to ride on mountain roads behind a spirited team "in the hands of an inexperienced or careless driver" would be afraid, affirmed Frank Root. "For this reason, it was the aim of the stage officials to employ none but careful, experienced men, and, when possible, only such were selected for the responsible duty of 'knight of the reins.' A prudent, level-headed driver does not fail to realize that in his hands are held the lives of a load of passengers, and, usually, he is as anxious to please all such as they are to have

This artist's grim depiction of an overland coach crossing the Rocky Mountains in 1868 did not depart far from reality. Winter travel meant windblown snow that seeped past the curtains to cover the floor, the seats, and the shivering occupants. Temperatures at night sometimes dropped below zero, causing passengers to wrap themselves in buffalo robes and huddle tightly together to conserve as much body heat as possible. At the relay posts they stumbled out of the coach, half-frozen, and by stamping their feet and thrashing their arms attempted to stir their blood circulation. Hot coffee to warm the women and children and perhaps something stronger for the men, a few rocks from the fireplace wrapped in gunnysacks to heat their feet, and they were off again to the next way station, two to four hours away. Courtesy Library of Congress, 5074.

a safe and comfortable ride to their journey's end." Even so, a frequent cause of accidents was poor judgment on the part of drivers, particularly new ones.[12]

Not unexpectedly, high speeds of ten to twelve miles per hour over rough mountain roads contributed to many stage accidents. "Crossing a low, bare divide, we leave the great basin of Utah behind, and are in Idaho, on waters of the Pacific. After dark, in the twinkling of an eye, whack! goes our coach—over upon one side. We have capsized in a mud-hole; but all escape unharmed." Bishop Tuttle was aboard a stagecoach near Echo when it tipped over. "I was the under fellow of my seat. My two neighbors, scrambling to open the coach door which was now skyward, thought not of poor me. I was constrained to shout out, 'We are safe, don't you see we have simply gone over, in the mud? Be careful of your feet, you are treading on us folk down here.'"[13]

Kirchhoff recalled that at the end of the second day of his overland journey from Portland to San Francisco in 1865, "the stage was supposed to pause four hours in Jacksonville (so we had heard) and give its dead-tired passengers a chance for a little refreshing sleep before proceeding. Toward evening, only about sixteen miles from there, the stage jolted to the rear with such force that the occupants tumbled forward together into the left-front corner. Thank the Lord the horses stopped and injuries were merely sprains and skinned faces." After the passengers clambered out of the crippled stage, they saw that one of the rear wheels was shattered. "What a mess! In order to reach Jacksonville to connect with the California stage, we had to find other transportation. But where?"

Leaving the driver alone to deal with the wreck and baggage, all eight passengers trudged ahead about two miles, looking for help. The Montanans lugged their valuable cantina with its sixty pounds of gold. "Suddenly, to our joy, we heard a violin. Its tones swelled from an inn beside the road, where locals had gathered to dance. On the porch, which also served as the dance hall, a Negro fiddler sat high on a table and emanated earsplitting melodies. The dancers moved stiffly back and forth in ornate figures of an ineffable promenade, to the

melodies and to commands given as if on a military drillfield."[14]

Only with "effort and eloquence, not to mention persuasion by gold coin," did they succeed in acquiring the use of an old farm wagon. "Its compassionate and generous owner offered to haul us and our baggage to Jacksonville at once, for the pittance of $20. But several hours passed before our express was ready. Ten hours had long since elapsed ere it and baggage returned from the wreck and our new driver bade us climb on—after he danced another Virginia reel," huffed a tired and sarcastic Kirchhoff.

Sitting on the luggage and "fitting ourselves together like a jigsaw puzzle," the hearty band of stage passengers proceeded on. "In the light of a pale moon we went toward Jacksonville, on a road as good as a German highway, and arrived at 3:00 A.M., nearly done in. Having sat on legs tucked under me (like a Yogi), I waited a while for the prickle and the pleasure of restored circulation, then ventured to walk again. Sleep was out of the question, the California stage being ready to depart, a terrible disappointment for us poor, harassed, gold-country travelers!"

Fellow Travelers and Hotels de Starvation

Like transcontinental rail passengers in a later era, all kinds of strangers found themselves stuffed together in an overland stagecoach: "The business man, the cow boy, the miner, the minister, the gambler, the teacher—all have met here on a common level, occupied these same seats and mingled together in conversation their respective views of events and conditions" to break the monotony of a long journey and divert themselves from their bodily aches. Passengers often recounted their life stories in shameless detail; and when they had exhausted the possibilities of conversation, someone might "start a song as the lazy moon came over the distant hills," and soon the whole stage would join in singing hymns or other familiar songs. As strains of "Georgia," "John Brown," and "Rally Round the Flag" floated across the prairie, they served to remind passengers that on the battlefields of the Civil War, Americans were enduring

A large crowd poses for the photographer at an elegant stage station, probably in southern Oregon. Like many of the images that survive from the steamboat and stagecoach era, this one provides no information about the place, date, or occasion for the picture. Courtesy Southern Oregon Historical Society, 2719.

discomforts far worse than anything they experienced at the moment. "If congeniality was slow in obtaining, a friendly rut into which the four wheels of the old Concord stage would suddenly fall, while the string of good stock on a smart gallop, might toss the prim old maid school teacher into the lap of the crusty old minister and serve to help them get acquainted." [15]

On occasion a passenger might become suddenly ill or, as happened in March 1866 on the Overland stage, violently insane. The crazed traveler stabbed one man several times, killed another with a pistol, and injured a third before he himself was finally shot and mortally wounded. Other passengers used whiskey freely to clear

throats clogged with alkaline dust and eventually became drunk enough to create excitement among their fellow travelers. No wonder overland passengers relished the opportunity every ten or twelve miles to get out and stretch a minute or two while the horses were changed. [16]

At home stations, stages paused long enough to change horses, and often drivers, and give passengers a chance to eat. Carrie Strahorn recalled one such place on the Snake River plain where over the door hung this sign: "Hotel de Starvation, 1,000 miles from hay and grain, seventy miles from wood, fifteen miles from water, but only twelve inches from hell." A meal of bread, beans, bacon, and black coffee cost one dollar. Meal stops also gave passengers time to exercise their legs and perhaps listen to a chorus of coyotes, but then after an hour the driver called "All aboard!" to set the stage in motion again.[17]

Few travelers had a kind word for stagecoach food and lodging. "Each meal was the same; breakfast, dinner and supper were indistinguishable save by the hour; and the price was one dollar or one dollar and a half each." Perhaps to amuse themselves, passengers circulated stories about a station kept by a Mrs. Corbet, who was a terror to all travelers. It was said to be a common thing for her to force passengers at the point of a pistol to eat meals at her table, charging them one dollar per, without any comment. Another station on the road linking Utah and Montana was commonly known as the Dirty Woman's Ranch.[18]

John Mortimer Murphy described a meal stop at Rattlesnake Station east of Boise: "I employed this interval to visit some hot springs close by, as I could not eat the half-cooked pork and watery potatoes which formed the stage dinner, and for which the sum of 1 dollar was

charged. The greatest annoyance one meets on this route is the station-houses where meals are served, as it is almost impossible to get a decent repast at one of them. The usual meal is fat ham and eggs, or boiled pork, potatoes, and bread that looks as if it were baked in black ashes, while the coffee is the very vilest stuff. One place at which I stopped did not furnish any fresh meat, although hundreds of cattle were grouped around the house; and no milk, although several cows with calves were within twenty yards. The fact is that they never again expect to see the passengers, so they give them as little as they can and charge as much as possible."[19]

Travelers often carried their own food with them, including smelly cheese, herring, bologna, or something else offensive to their fellow passengers. Others preferred to depend upon what the home stations might provide. Kirchhoff noticed a difference in the quality of food as he left frontier Oregon and entered California. "A glance merely at the coffee and sugar indicated we had reached civilization. No longer the brown grit of the dear Web-

In the sheep country of eastern Oregon, the stagecoach linking Shaniko and Madras provided a vital connection to the outside world before the coming of a railroad. Courtesy Oregon Historical Society, 23070.

feet, sugar was now the best: refined and white. Instead of murky, boiled coffee full of half-ground, burned beans, we were served the best of filtered java." [20]

Not all meal stops across the northern West elicited dyspeptic comments from travelers. There was a remote station high atop Oregon's Blue Mountains where the food never failed to delight stagecoach travelers. This was Meacham's, a place known for its cleanliness and hearty repasts. "Toward evening, twenty-five miles from La Grande, how nice (after the chill outside) to find Meacham's Hotel and its blazing fireplace! Outdoors, everything appeared wintry but no sign of high country could be seen. Hard to believe," recalled Kirchhoff, "we were 4,000 feet above sea level and on the crest of the Blue Mountains!"

This high-country lodge met his every expectation. "We were happy with nocturnal rest in this hospitable caravansary under the clouds. As night neared, the place livened. The Umatilla stage brought a load of travelers. Nearby a few hundred mules and horses—several pack-trains to Willow Creek, Boise, and the Blackfoot mines in distant Montana—filled the forest with the cheerful tinkle of harness-bells. Groups of Mexican mulateros reveled around crackling campfires. The wilderness echoes with shouts and songs." Inside, the passengers were "no less jolly in the common room, convened cozily about the great fireplace. Flames danced brightly as they consumed a dozen and more logs, each over ten feet long. Our driver, a jolly Irishman, belted out several stirring Irish ballads, with pathos, and drew thunderous applause."

Kirchhoff's stage driver rousted his passengers at four the next morning. "Leave," he admonished, "before the sun thaws the ground and turns it to mud." In the early morning light the stage rolled across an arctic landscape over ground frozen solid. "The first ten miles were nothing short of delightful. . . . The trees, gradually increasing in diameter, informed us that the high country's end drew near. More and more gaps among them treated us to vistas of rolling hills and densely forested slopes: spectacular."

Overnight Travel by Stage

Some travelers recalled overnight travel by stage as a romantic adventure. "It seemed to my unaccustomed eye as though we were constantly running into a solid wall of black, and yet the horses followed the road as it twisted in and out among the trees of the dense forest, skirted the edge of a canyon or wound up and down the steep hillsides, the driver cracking his long whip and admonishing his team in the choice English so eloquently handled by his craft, apparently as unconcerned as if on a broad turnpike under the noonday sun." Some travelers new to stagecoaching across the West remained wide awake during the first night because everything was so exciting. [21]

Most travelers, however, recalled few experiences more fatiguing than nighttime aboard a lumbering coach. Usually that was when after a full day of travel, nerves became frazzled, tempers flared, children cried, and the everlasting dust and jolting seemed intolerable. There was no such thing as a good night's sleep. When darkness fell, the passengers dozed in their places or, if there was room, would curl up in a seat corner like a dog on a rug. With an elbow resting in the window strap, a leg extending over a mail sack, and a shoulder supporting the head of a snoring companion, a passenger was apt to find any all-night trip an ordeal. Many a time in the dead of night a wheel would suddenly drop into a chuckhole and the coach lurch forward on its thorough-braces to tumble half a dozen drowsy travelers into a heap on the floor. "Get used to it," was the advice proffered by various stagemen. "Except while the horses were being changed at the stations, I do not believe that I slept at all," recalled Bayard Taylor. "The desperate attempt to do so produced a dim, dazed condition, wherein I heard the constant roll of the wheels, and felt every jolt of the coach." [22]

J. Mortimer Murphy noted that on the roads of the northern West every jolt and pitch "hurls the sleepy passenger from side to side, or sends him bounding towards the ceiling, and when he returns to his seat it is with an involuntary grunt of torture. If not overcome by weariness, however, a run by stage over some of the plains is delightful, owing to the novelty and expansive character of the scenery, the animating influence of the bracing mountain air, and the sensation of travelling through a country almost as primeval as it was thousands of years ago."[23]

Despite the excitement of his journey, Murphy was still glad "when at three o'clock in the morning the coach began crunching the sandy streets of Boise City, and still more so when I secured a good bed at the Overland Hotel and retired to rest for the first time in ninety-six hours. The delights of that sleep exceeded any I had ever known, so when I awoke in the morning I felt as refreshed as if I had never become acquainted with the tortures of a bounding stage and bad roads, or the inconvenience of bumping a fellow-passenger in the eye, mouth, or nose with my head, or driving my elbow into his ribs with a vigour that elicits a deep groan of pain."

Often on a long journey, a desperate, sleep-deprived passenger would borrow hay from a way station, place it on the flat top of the coach, cover it with blankets for a bed, "and then go luxuriously to sleep." General James Rusling recalled that "at first when we tried this, not understanding the philosophy of the situation, we came near rolling off when the coach would pitch into a chuck-hole, or give a lurch from heel to port; but we soon learned to boom ourselves on, with a rope or strap from railing to railing, and thus managed to secure not a little of 'tired nature's sweet restorer, balmy sleep,' while our fellow-passengers down below (nine inside), packed like sardines in a box, got seldom a wink."[24]

Few passengers had the physical and mental strength to endure the continuous jolting of a stagecoach for more than forty-eight hours at a stretch. For this reason, sleeping quarters had to be provided at intervals. J. H. Beadle reached Yreka "(only four hours behind time) at 2 A.M., and the old man, two invalids, and myself tumbled out of the coach, exhausted, and applied for a 'lay over,' unable to go further. Nine hours' sleep did me some good, though I felt as if I had been pounded from head to foot with a clapboard."[25]

A far more important question than whether such roadhouses were clean or not was whether, after a night's layover, a passenger could find space aboard the next stage. Especially at times when travel was heavy, there were no guarantees. Root recalled that during the summer of 1863, a minister traveling east from Denver decided to spend a restful Sunday at a way station. He was forced to endure six frustrating days before he could at last reclaim a seat aboard a coach. Not surprisingly, the main part of his next Sunday's sermon consisted of "denouncing, in most severe terms, the officials and nearly every one else in any manner connected with Ben Holladay's stage line."[26]

Diversions

"There were many nice things to admire on the long stage ride. Much of the scenery was picturesque beyond description," recalled Frank Root. On the Great Plains were "numerous prairie-dog towns, living in which were countless numbers of the harmless little animals; ranches and trading posts at convenient distances; Indian tepees scattered for hundreds of miles along the Platte valley; the grand old Rocky Mountains, gazing on which none would tire, their sides verdant with evergreens, their lofty summits crowned with perpetual snow. The sights were so grand that no one could fail to admire them."

Wildlife of any type offered welcome diversion to stage passengers. In the mountains west of Denver, they commonly saw large numbers of grouse, elk, deer, antelope, mountain sheep, bear, and even mountain lions. Buffalo wallows were numerous on the Great Plains. Veteran stage drivers informed Root that during the 1860s they seldom passed Plum Creek, in western Nebraska, without seeing immense herds of buffalo, and that at times it was necessary to stop the stage a while to let the animals pass. The hills became a moving mass of dark shaggy animals. "The sight was one greatly admired by all the passengers on the stage-coach. It was a genuine treat, for many of them for the first time in their lives imagined they were almost in shooting distance of the shaggy bison, and soon would be within a stone's throw of them," recalled Root. He noted that it was "genuine sport for some of the stage passengers, even while moving along at a lively gait, to pull their revolvers and shoot out of the windows of the coach at a herd of antelope perhaps a few hundred yards distant."

Often two or three passengers would be firing away at the same time, but it was a rare occurrence if any one of them brought down one of the swift-running antelopes. It was much the same with jackrabbits and coyotes. It required only one shot in their direction to send the fleet-footed animals bounding away beyond the reach of flying bullets. Half a dozen passengers might occasionally be blazing away at prairie dogs only a few yards away. Such "sport" was not limited to staging on the Great Plains. John Mortimer Murphy observed that in passing through the dense forests of the Blue Mountains "we caught glimpses occasionally of a timid deer, an inquisi-tive wolf, and coveys of the dusky or mountain grouse, which seemed to take no notice of the human foes firing at them with revolvers." [27]

The drivers themselves might be a source of diversion on a long trip. Many had personalities almost as colorful as the vehicles on which they rode. They would often amuse or alarm first-time travelers with any number of tall tales, especially if presented with a good bottle of liquor. No doubt their favorite yarns for newcomers to the West were of their encounters with road agents.

Robbed by Road Agents

Beyond any curve in the road one or more armed road agents might be waiting. In the front boot beneath

*M*ore stagecoach melodrama: drunken cowboys create trouble at Pole Creek Station near Cheyenne, and a brave woman saves the stage driver from harm. Courtesy Wyoming State Museum.

the driver was the express box, and often it contained thousands upon thousands of dollars in gold dust. Highwaymen knew this. With guns leveled at the driver they would typically shout: "Halt! Throw down your express box, quick!" There was nothing, then, for him to do but to comply or to say, "I've all I can do to attend to the team." Then one of the road agents would climb up and get the box himself. Neither the stage line nor the express company held the driver personally responsible for loss of the box, knowing that his full attention must be given to the team and that he could not offer active resistance.[28]

"In all my traveling I have not been on board a stage when it was attacked," recalled Bishop Tuttle. "Nor have I suffered any serious trouble as a passenger." The same could be said by most of his fellow stage travelers. Nonetheless, the chief terror for drivers and passengers alike was the sudden appearance of a gang of masked men crying out "Halt! Throw up your hands, you sons of bitches!"[29]

Under threat of instant death the road agents would rob travelers of their valuables, though if the treasure box were heavy and full, they often left passengers alone. However, if the box were empty, road agents would likely take the money and watches of the men. Seldom did they steal from women. Resistance from passengers, covered as they were by one or more guns of the assailant's confederates, usually meant bloodshed. Perhaps the worst such incident was the Great Portneuf Stage Robbery of July 13, 1865: when travelers resisted near present Inkom, Idaho, road agents riddled the coach with buckshot, killing four passengers instantly and mortally wounding another three. One passenger and the shotgun messenger survived, but the guard had both feet shot off. The robbers took $65,000 in gold, but most of them were later apprehended and hanged.[30]

Not many weeks after this infamous incident, a passenger on a stagecoach between Boise City and Walla Walla accidentally shot himself through the jaw, the ball passing up and into his head and killing him instantly. He apparently wanted to protect himself from road agents. "It is supposed that he was holding the pistol under his coat with the muzzle pointed upwards, when the stage in passing over a rough place in the road, caused the pistol to go off."[31]

Even Ben Holladay himself experienced a holdup. The Napoleon of the West was traveling with his wife along the main line between Denver and Salt Lake City when two robbers stopped his coach. One of them covered the driver, while the other thrust a shotgun into the vehicle before Holladay had time to draw his gun. "Throw up your hands and don't stir!" the outlaw threatened. "Give us your money." Holladay had about forty thousand dollars in a money belt, an expensive watch and chain, an eight-thousand-dollar emerald pin, and several hundred dollars in his pocket. When told to "shell out quick" he did a little bluffing himself. He handed over the loose money in his pocket along with the watch and chain, whispering, "There, there's every cent I've got. Take it and let me go." Then with a solicitous gesture toward his sleeping wife he added, "My wife is very ill, and I don't know what would happen to her if she knew what was going on." Both robbers left only after carefully searching the deluxe coach for a treasure box and other valuables, but Holladay and his still-sleeping wife drove away having saved his money belt and valuable emerald.[32]

Not so fortunate was Bummer Dan McFadden, who lost the fortune he made in Alder Gulch in a stagecoach robbery in 1863. When the coach pulled out from Virginia City, he was transporting several sacks of gold dust beneath his clothes. Two robbers armed with shotguns blocked the road near Bannack and demanded, "Throw up your hands." They ordered the driver to disarm his passengers and search each one. McFadden handed him two small purses. The road agents, who apparently knew in advance of his concealed gold dust, ordered the driver to search him again. "Get that big sack from 'Bummer Dan,' unbuckle the straps; he is the man we want to pan out." McFadden's face lengthened as he stripped and handed over his treasure.[33]

Finally, the two robbers ordered passengers to reboard, threatening that if they breathed one word about the robbery they would be killed. McFadden somehow saved one sack of dust but lost about seven

Killer Salmon?

In a story dated March 16, 1885, a Manchester, Iowa, newspaper gave a tongue-in-cheek account of the dangers attendant on stagecoach travel:

"The recent frightful accident which happened to a stage in Southern Oregon cannot fail, says the New York Times, *to call attention to the state authorities to the necessity of protecting settlers against the attacks of salmon. The stage in question was crossing Applegate Creek when it was suddenly attacked by a drove of salmon. The stage was instantly overturned and the hungry fish swarmed over it, while the stage driver, with great presence of mind, cut the traces of the horses and throwing himself across the off-wheel horse, a powerful animal, formerly the property of Doctor Goodrich of Olympia, managed to escape.*

"The dispatch which conveys to us that painful story says nothing of the fate of the stage passengers but, unfortunately, there is every reason to believe that they fell victim to the salmon."
—from Mike Hanley with Omer Stanford, *Sage Brush and Axle Grease* (1976)

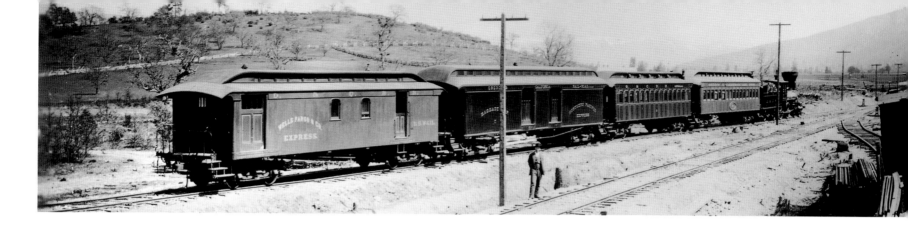

A ubiquitous presence in the far West, a Wells Fargo express car brings up the rear of the first Oregon and California passenger train through Phoenix, Oregon. Wells Fargo left the express business at the time of the First World War to concentrate on banking, with notable success. By 1996 it ranked among the ten largest banks in the United States. Courtesy MSS 1583, Oregon Historical Society, 91760.

thousand dollars' worth. He went to Colorado but never again struck it rich. The road agents, George Ives and Frank Parish, were among the troublemakers the vigilantes of Virginia City later hanged. Robber gangs maintained regular hideouts along the stage lines of Idaho and Montana, and like the more honorable fraternal organizations, many had regular initiation ceremonies and mystic signs.

Probably no routes suffered more from road agents than those that linked the mines of the Black Hills with Union Pacific tracks at Sidney, Nebraska, and Cheyenne, Wyoming, in the 1870s and 1880s. Not long after Gilmer and Salisbury opened their stage line between Cheyenne and Deadwood, the Western Stage Company established a competing route from Sidney, but the depredations of road agents nearly drove it out of business. After Gilmer and Salisbury purchased the Nebraska line to relieve heavy traffic over their Wyoming route, they rebuilt a coach to transport gold safely over their new connection. They lined its interior with bullet-proof steel plates, bolted a chilled-steel safe to the floor, and included two shuttered gunports in each door. The Iron Clad carried no passengers. One or two heavily armed shotgun messengers rode on the box beside the driver, and three or four of the West's best riflemen rode inside, making the Iron Clad as nearly bandit-proof as possible. Because more than a quarter million dollars' worth of gold was occasionally taken through from Deadwood to Sidney in a single shipment, the treasure coach remained a tempting target for road agents.

Wells Fargo recorded that between 1870 and 1884 bandits made 374 attempts to rob its stagecoach shipments of gold, but only 8 attempts to rob its train shipments. The express company spared neither effort nor money to pursue and prosecute every marauder. Its own detectives roamed the West, always working in cooperation with local lawmen. After the coming of the railroad in the 1880s there were fewer holdups and road agents turned to cattle rustling, for a time a more lucrative activity.

If the advent of railways cut short the careers of road agents, it also initially compounded the discomfort of stage travel within remote territories like Montana. The first trains steamed north from Utah and Idaho across Monida Pass to the end of the track at Red Rock, from whence stagecoaches bulged with increasingly full loads of passengers, mail bags, and express matter. The discomforts that travelers bound for Montana had once stoically endured, they now found almost intolerable. "There are those used to the luxuries and ease of older and richer civilizations who doubtless think that ice coolers and sleeping-berths could be added with greater comfort than is customarily extracted from stage travel now," observed the Helena *Weekly Herald*, "but these are bold innovations to talk about and the average Westerner would view their introduction with distrust. In their way the stages have served us to better purpose than many are willing to admit, but their speedy abdication in favor of the railroad car will cause in no quarter of the Territory suspicion of complaint or lament." The Helena *Independent* added, "All hail to the Pullman car, the successor to the jerky and the dead-ax wagon."[34]

The levee in Saint Louis was still a busy place in the mid-1890s. Courtesy Library of Congress, 40886 762 22218.

In the daylight watch the "Old Man" would leave me alone at the wheel and sit down, or, sometimes go below. That was a cub's glory, to be left in full charge of the pilot house. It was the greatest compliment the pilot could pay him. It meant one was on the road to become a real pilot, and the title of Missouri River pilot meant a great deal in those days. It brought not only glory, but substantial rewards. Salaries ran from $500 to as high as $1,000 to $1,200 a month.

—Charles Bailey, "Cub Pilot," as reprinted in Kansas City Star *(January 9, 1925)*

Navigating on a Heavy Dew

On the afternoon of May 5, 1867, the *Paragon* prepared to leave Saint Louis with a load of supplies for General Alfred Sully's army at Fort Buford on the upper Missouri River. The steamboat carried about thirty passengers, all government employees, and a crew that consisted of a captain, two pilots, two mates, two engineers, two strikers, four deckhands and about forty roustabouts. At five the captain gave three quick strokes on a big bell, the engineer blew his ready whistle, and the men sprang to the lines. As they cast off the lines, bells rang for the engines to reverse, and they maneuvered away from the crowded levee. It was a tight fit, with steamboats packed along the waterfront from one end to the other, and drays, mules, horses, wagons, thousands of tons of freight, and masses of people everywhere. Finally the *Paragon* swung into the current to begin its 2,000-mile "trip to the mountains," as it was phrased at the time.

Charles Bailey, a cub pilot on the trip, later recalled the adventure: he came "on watch" after supper with his father and mentor, Bob Bailey, "and about dusk we entered the mouth of the Missouri which was pouring a yellow streak across the clear water of the Mississippi clear to the Illinois shore. By the time we got well into

the Missouri, it was dark and the pilot's troubles commenced. My father, who was called the 'nighthawk,' could see snags at night where no one else could see anything. He kept the wheel 'hard up' and 'hard down' through the whole watch." [1]

Young Bailey recalled that "at the first streaks of daylight, a tremendous strain is taken from the pilot in the Missouri River. No trouble at all now to see a snag a mile away. The reefs and 'breaks' showed up plain and distinct and by breakfast time one feels quite refreshed." The *Paragon* made no landing "except for vegetables, butter and eggs, of which there was an abundance all along the river, and the living was about as good as any in the world: The bar, stocked with various liquid refreshments, did a lively business with the crew and male passengers." At night there was music in the main cabin; some people sang or played cards while others read or wrote. "There was plenty of fresh air and all had a good appetite. The scenery was a continuous panorama."

At Sioux City, a settlement of about two thousand people, the *Paragon* landed for fresh meat and other supplies, "and that was our last sight of civilization. From there on we laid up every night, as the pilots were not familiar enough with the river to risk running at night. This made steering almost a holiday with no night work."

Bailey remembered there being "plenty of cord wood to be had below Sioux city, which could be used without cutting, but from there on the pilot would look for a patch of timber for a night harbor, and at the first streak of daylight the mates and crew were out with axes cutting down and dragging in trees and logs, which were piled up on deck and cut during the day while underway. This kept them busy from 3 o'clock in the morning until 9 o'clock at night." From daylight to dark, the *Paragon* steadily pushed its long, sharp bow through the swift current of the Missouri.

"The pilots kept close watch on the river. George Townsend kept a book and put down the landmarks of crossings and bad spots. Bob Bailey would turn and look back over a piece of river, and it was fixed in his mind until he saw it again. It was natural instinct, coupled with long training and a high professional ambition. He had an ardent desire to be the best pilot on the river, and he came very near his goal."

The Missouri River ran high as a result of melting snow and rain in the upper country. "At Medicine Lodge Bend, in the upper stretches of the river, was the hardest fight. The water was an avalanche, the bend full of snags and for two or three hours it was a struggle. The engineer kept the fireman busy throwing dry wood into the furnace, and the noise was deafening as escaping steam roared through the smokestacks. I was steering and the boat kept dodging among snags, but not going an inch. Finally it got so hot everybody not on duty went hard aft to get out of the way of a possible explosion. At last it began to move up the river. It slid into slack water around the point and settled down to a steady gait once more."

The *Paragon* landed at Fort Buford, at the mouth of the Yellowstone, on June 28 after a trip of nearly two months. General Sully and an army of two thousand men were there fighting the Sioux. "The soldiers were glad to see us. They were a free and easy devil-may-care lot of fellows, with a good sprinkling of Scotch and Irish

among them. The officers all took their meals on the boat while we were there and the bar did a big business. We gave them the latest news from the states; about six weeks old, but news to them. The crew hustled the freight ashore and early the morning of July 1 the *Paragon* started on its wild race down the swollen, raging current. We carried no freight down and made no landings, except for wood. Nothing to do but go, and go we did! On one stretch of narrow winding channel it made one hundred and fifty miles in five hours." Crewmen "worked like tigers getting wood" because they wanted to get home.

The 1867 voyage of the *Paragon* was probably more typical than those that were memorialized because of Indian attacks, boiler explosions, or any number of melodramatic events that pulp fiction writers loved to dwell upon. Charles Bailey's recollection offers a vignette of everyday life aboard a mountain steamboat that recalls problems of supply where there were no towns and emphasizes the importance of the chain of command.

Chains of Command: Pilots and Roustabouts

At sea the captain was not only first in command but usually the most skilled member of the crew in the art of seamanship and the science of navigation. However, on the inland waters of the West, the captain was frequently less adept at handling the boat and machinery than other officers, and in practice if not in law, his authority was under some conditions subordinated to that of the pilot. Anyone with enough money to buy a majority interest in a steamboat might install himself as captain; no master's license or certificate of rating was required. The captain was essentially a business manager, although some of them had first gained skill as a pilot.

Although the captain was in theory the most important person on an antebellum steamboat, his authority and prestige were in reality of little consequence for "the truly despotic lord of the old-time river" was the pilot. It was the pilot who guided the boat along the river, and upon his skill depended the safety of vessel, passengers, and cargo. When the boat was under way, his word was the law before which everyone bowed. "The pilot is aloft

Smartly dressed officers of the steamer Hassalo, which operated out of Portland. The all-important pilot has a place of honor in the middle of the front row. Courtesy Oregon Historical Society, 9086, #1204

at the wheel, and oblivious to everything save his duty. With what skill he manages the craft! How gracefully he steers her through, and between the myriad snags—any one of which might rip her keel open—around the tortuous banks, and up again straight on her course! With what care he approaches the treacherous shoal and sandbar," wrote an admiring Henry M. Stanley.[2]

Accorded the status of king of rivermen, the pilot was for many years the most highly skilled person on the boat and the best paid as well. When business was brisk, he might receive $1,000 to $2,000 per month, though $200 to $300 was a more usual wage. Out of their wages some pilots saved enough to become captains of their own vessels. Because the pilots themselves were the only ones who could train new apprentices, they kept their ranks small in order to protect both their power and princely salaries. But the main reason for their elevated status was that their profession was a very difficult one to learn, requiring years of apprenticeship. A pilot had to be able to read the color and texture of the water's surface for

indications of what lay beneath; he must know all the clues that indicated the presence of hidden obstructions. Hundreds of islands, bars, shoals, rocks, sunken boats, and snags made steamboat navigation a kind of elaborate obstacle race in which many of the hazards were invisible while others lurked uncharted or unknown.

When the steamer *Lewiston* headed downriver to Portland for repairs in 1929, Captain James W. Troup was invited aboard as a guest. At the age of 73 he was a surviving member of the illustrious class of steamboat pioneers that included Ephriam Baughman, Leonard White, John C. Ainsworth, and Sebastian Miller. Now the general manager of Canadian Pacific steamships, Troup was traveling along a part of the Snake River he had not seen in several decades. Yet so remarkable was his memory that he was able to tell people in advance which way the channel would run.

As the *Lewiston* steamed through Palouse Rapids, crosscurrents and hidden rocks made the passage difficult. Captain Stewart V. Winslow, a veteran steamboatman, was at the wheel with Captain Troup standing behind him, peering at the foaming water. Suddenly the old man stiffened and became quite tense, but in keeping with pilothouse etiquette he said nothing. Winslow, who happened to turn and see Troup's strained expression, casually remarked, "That rock over there that used to be a foot under water the government engineers took out 15 years ago." "Oh," responded Troup, "that explains it. I thought from the course you were steering you could not miss it."[3]

Among the outstanding pilots-turned-captain on the Missouri River was Grant Marsh, who in sixty-three years lost no boat under his command excepting the *Little Eagle No. 2,* which turned over on the Mississippi River during a tornado. When he navigated a steamboat, Marsh kept a notebook beside him in the pilothouse in which he habitually recorded for his own future use the characteristics of the channel and the adjacent shores. Entries would read somewhat as follows: "Run left-hand shore up past a big bluff. Plenty of dead timber in this bend. Then cross from the dead wood in the left-hand bluff over to a short, right-hand bend. Small timber in

the head of this bend. Run to the head of this short, right-hand bend, then circle out between two islands . . . and come back to a right-hand prairie bend."[4]

Sandbars traced a faint pattern on the surface of the water, which a skilled pilot could use to follow a sinuous channel through the deepest water. Although a casual observer might not notice, weather conditions influenced the way a skilled pilot read the river. Wind was less troublesome than rain because it ruffled the deep water more than the shallow, and thus left some indication of where each was located. Rain, on the other hand, reduced everything to a uniform appearance. The sun, when below forty-five degrees of the horizon, was exceedingly troublesome because its bright light shimmered off the water's surface as a boat steamed toward it.

When the first steamboats appeared on western waters there were already men familiar with navigating the rivers. These were the hardy pioneers who guided the rafts, flatboats, barges, and keelboats of the Mike Fink era. Even so, when trade between Saint Louis and Montana first became important in the 1860s, comparatively few individuals who could qualify as Missouri River pilots. Steamboats could not be transferred indiscriminately from the Mississippi and Ohio rivers to the upper Missouri, and neither could their navigators. Experience on the Missouri itself was required before the government licensed a pilot on that river.

Every steamboat had its linesmen, often called leadsmen, who measured the depth of the river. They ascertained the river bottom by "heaving the lead," which often was a hexagonal pyramid of lead weighing five to fifteen pounds with a cavity in the base in which to press soap for the purpose of bringing up a sample of the river bottom so that its nature could be determined.

The purser functioned somewhat as prime minister to the stewards, waiters, cooks, cook's boys, deck boys, engineers, pilots, captains, and passengers who were continually asking him questions. "As he is responsible for the good name of the boat, he is expected to be invariably gracious and polite."[6]

Life in Every Phase

The typical Missouri River steamboat had two decks. The lower or main deck carried the machinery and boilers, most of the cargo, and any animals and deck passengers. The latter slept where they could and often prepared their own meals or used their own utensils to eat food supplied on board. They located themselves close to or away from the boilers depending on the weather. Deck passengers included families moving west who could not afford the cabin fare. To compensate for their low fares, all men were expected to work, such as when they helped roustabouts carry fuel aboard from woodlots along the shore.

On the second deck was a large center cabin, sometimes called the salon or saloon. The forepart of the salon was the gentlemen's cabin. Here were usually located the purser's office and a bar. The women's cabin was traditionally located at the stern end of the salon where it was farthest from the boilers and thus the safest part of any steamboat. This area usually had a rug or carpet that served to warn away the male population.

Henry M. Stanley commented upon the odd segregation of the sexes aboard a Missouri River steamboat. "During the daytime, the gaudy but commodious cabin presents a curious sight. At the after part of the saloon, which is styled the ladies' cabin, sat groups of 'muchly' crinolined farmers' wives and daughters, frowsy dowagers, and laughing maidens. Some ladies sat singly (doubtless old maids), who rocked their chairs in a very melancholy manner, or appeared absorbed in some novel. At the gentlemen's end was a motley assemblage of characters, divines, dominies, philanthropists, misanthropists, innocent youth, old sinners, ubiquitous 'drummers' or commercial travellers, which last are omnipresent agents for everything under the sun, from

F. Jay Haynes photographed the interior of the salon on the Far West, *possibly the most famous steamboat on the upper Missouri River. Located on the second deck were staterooms and a spacious center cabin, or salon, which was often furnished with the same fine carpets and gingerbread woodwork found in the lobby of a grand hotel. This public space served as a sitting room by day, a dining room at mealtimes, and place of entertainment at night. Courtesy State Historical Society of North Dakota, A-2331.*

In unknown waters the lead was kept going constantly, and especially so when crossing the dangerous bar of the Columbia River.[5]

Owners and managers were responsible for hiring a sizable work force. On a large Missouri River steamboat, that might number as many as sixty persons, including officers and men. The largest number by far (from twenty to forty men) were roustabouts, or laborers who supplied muscle to do most of the heavy and dirty work. Many roustabouts were blacks from Saint Louis or Leavenworth, but some were Irish and Scandinavian immigrants. Boat officers were ordinarily intolerant of the poorly educated "roosters," especially the blacks.

CHAS. R. SPENCER

CHAS. R. SPENCER

HOOD-RIVER OREGON
AUG. 18. 1910.

the newly invented shawl pin to the pill that cures every mortal disease in one-twentieth part of a second."[7]

To Stanley the male passengers all seemed to be "dragging a miserable existence, and constantly smoking, or indulging in agonising yawns. With their feet elevated to the level and altitude of their heads, these unfortunates contrive to pass the intervals between meals. At the first welcome sound of the bell, all unite in a grand rush to the table, gorge themselves with two dozen different viands, from fish, fowl, flesh, to pudding, cake and molasses, and in ten minutes and five seconds, they will be found around the stove, smoking away as energetically as ever. At night they stretch their dyspeptic bodies in two tiers the whole length of the cabin, and thus the passengers pass their days on board a western steamer."

A steamboat traveler on the Columbia River recalled that doors from the ladies' cabin to the dining saloon were kept closed until meals were announced, although a passenger might walk through to the forward or men's cabin if he wished. Children were not allowed to play in the dining room. Tables aboard these floating hotels, which were often set three times to accommodate all the passengers at a single meal, groaned with roasts of beef or pork and baked salmon. Bread pudding was a common dessert.

For many years sleeping arrangements often consisted of two tiers of berths along either side of the saloon from which they were separated only by curtains, which during daytime screened them from view. "On our crowded steamer every state-room is filled, and nightly the cabin floor is covered with sleepers upon mattresses. One can not promenade without endangering some unfortunate slumberer, and calling forth expostulations or curses, according to his ruling temperament," recorded Albert D. Richardson. Those passengers who paid the most might have private staterooms.[8]

Richardson observed that any male passengers who were unable to sleep congregated near the purser's office around a little table. "Upon it a gambler with hang-dog face, wearing a white hat with broad band of black crape, has arrayed two or three gold and silver watches, with money, penknives, ear-rings, breast-pins, and other cheap articles, each in one of the little numbered squares of an oil cloth. 'Gentlemen,' he begins, 'you can throw the dice for fifty cents. For every figure you turn up there is a corresponding figure on the cloth, and you draw whatever rests upon it. There are no blanks. You may get this superb gold chronometer watch worth one hundred and forty dollars, or this magnificent English lever, which cost fifty dollars at wholesale, or this elegant silver goblet, cheap at ten dollars. You are certain to get *some* article worth twice your money.'" Richardson watched as a backwoods Missouri lad in white wool hat and corduroys produced half a dollar and with nervous hand rolled the dice. The professional gamblers were invariably richer after every voyage.

It was no different on the Columbia River in the 1860s. Professional gamblers lightened many a passenger's burden of gold dust. Considerable money lay piled on rough tables in the men's cabin, often in the form of buckskin bags filled with gold dust. Games might run far into the night if the boat was tied up somewhere en route, storm-bound. During such occasions, a waiter might play an accordion to soothe the tired and nervous passengers; but once when gale force winds forced a steamboat to tie up at the lower Cascades, the only song the waiter could play was the somewhat disconcerting "I Want to Be an Angel." All Columbia River steamboats featured well-stocked and highly profitable bars, too.[9]

When travelers grew tired of conversation or pondering fellow passengers who "exhibit life in every phase," there was always the scenery outside. "Here we sit on easy chairs or walk with slippered feet on rich carpets thousand of miles from any civilization and glide our easy way through thousands of miles of unsettled wilderness." Heading downriver from Fort Benton, another traveler noted in his diary for June 7, 1867: "As usual started at daylight. The scenery still changing, flat lands & bluffs being now about evenly divided. Passed a party of Indians drawn up near a wood pile in line awaiting our approach in order to 'Swap.' Weather still delightfull, a cool breeze and warm sun—the component parts of fine weather."[10]

An entry three days later in James Knox Polk Miller's diary suggests that the lure of the passing scenery was often juxtaposed with the human spectacle aboard ship. "On each side of the river a flat bottom land, varying in width from one to three miles, is succeeded by small elevations of land covered with mountain grass and rather more gravelly soil is seen. We have on board a man and his wife, both crazy and labouring under the delusion that each night they are to be killed. A soldier, taken with delirium tremens, is howling hideously below the hurricane deck upon which I am watching the sun set."

The mix of passengers aboard a Columbia River steamboat was similar to that on a Missouri River vessel, yet travel on the two waterways differed considerably. Apart from the length of time it took to go from either Portland or Saint Louis to the head of navigation, the Missouri offered the greater frontier adventure. Nonetheless, Columbia River journeys had "singularly adventurous charm," as Theodor Kirchhoff wrote of a trip aboard the stern-wheeler *Tenino* in the summer of 1872.[11]

After the *Tenino* left Celilo, it "battles the flood, and brawls upriver—full steam ahead. In contrast to the splendidly wooded shores of the lower, the upper Columbia seems another world, so different are the surroundings. Black rocks, perhaps chunks of basalt, protrude from the riverbed into the greening torrent that rushes past. Palisades like giant, weather-beaten walls extend many miles on both shores. Beyond and above them tower bare, yellowish-gray eminences. Neither forest nor settlements nor cultivated fields trespass in this miles-long desert of mountains and crags. At the lower end, Mount Hood thrusts its colossal, snow covered pyramid into the blue. In this panorama of a primeval wilderness, the only human dwellings are occasional Indian wigwams. The sole sign of civilization is our boat, snorting in her labors against the aqua-colored currents and therewith shuddering to her last seam. Smoke belches from her stacks. Sparks rain in a downpour on her upper deck."

Hazards of Steamboat Travel

Travel aboard a steamboat was far more comfortable than aboard a jostling stagecoach. For those eating in the salon, meals were filling and served on time. Best of all, they were included in the price of passage. Another advantage of steamboat travel was that a ticket holder could ship considerably more free baggage than was usually allowed on a stagecoach. On the Columbia River, where for two decades the Oregon Steam Navigation Company maintained a fleet of seaworthy and well-staffed boats, no passenger ever lost his or her life in an accident involving one of its vessels. No such claim could ever be made for the Missouri River.

Montanans favored Missouri River steamers for sending their wives and families home to the States for a visit or for bringing them out West to settle. For all this, a steamboat trip from Saint Louis to Fort Benton was never really a pleasure cruise. E. W. Carpenter, who made a journey in 1865 aboard the *Deer Lodge,* recalled it this way: "Two months of life on a 'mountain steamer,' with cracked roofs and warped decks, especially adapted to the broiling of passengers in fair weather and drenching of them in foul; two months of life between a double wall of muddy bluffs bounding the river on either side and cutting off whatever scenery might lie beyond, was naught but tedious in the experience, and could not prove entertaining in the description." As often happened on an overland stagecoach, some boat passengers dealt with the boredom of a long journey by drinking whiskey all night and sleeping all day.[12]

Most hazards of steamboat travel on western waters were created by nature, such as when shifting currents undermined great numbers of willows and cottonwoods that grew along the banks of the Missouri River and dropped them into the stream. The trees floated along until they became anchored in the bottom, sometimes forming a cluster so dense that a boat could hardly find a way through. Always pointing downstream, snags were dangerous only to vessels moving against the current. Even so, snags (or sawyers when they slowly vibrated from the action of the current) posed the greatest peril on the river and were a pilot's worst nightmare. Between 1819 and 1898 no fewer than 295 boats sank in the Missouri River and three in the Yellowstone, and of these, snags alone wrecked 80 percent.

The worst snags remained submerged. An experienced pilot could spot one of these hazards only when it rippled the surface, and sometimes that was too late. Aboard every Missouri River steamboat was a large tarpaulin that might be used to plug a hole made by a snag until the boat could make port. However, in many cases the wound was mortal. When a steamboat running at full speed struck a snag, it often pierced through to her vitals. A few weeks after his passage up the Missouri, noted Albert Richardson, "the *Tropic,* a first-class boat, moving ten miles an hour, ran upon one of these death-dealing spears. It penetrated her hull, pierced through the deck, pantry, and two state-rooms, and came out at the hurricane roof, breaking the main pipe, deluging the cabin with hot steam, killing an engineer and leaving the wretched ship impaled like a fly upon a needle. No sagacity nor experience is proof against these unseen weapons, and one does not wonder at the wrinkled faces and premature gray hairs of pilots and captains. Even boats appear to share their terror. I could distinctly feel our steamer thrill with disgust when she ran upon a sand-bar, and shudder with horror at every snag grating against her keel."[13]

Although fog made it hard for pilots to read the water surface or find navigational landmarks along shore, it contributed to relatively few accidents on the upper Missouri River. Much the same was true of darkness, perhaps because steamboats seldom chanced the shallow water and tortuous channel by running after nightfall.

So challenging was navigation, especially above Saint Joseph, that few pilots attempted night running, except by moonlight, until the federal snag-removal program was well along in the 1870s.

Fires also posed occasional dangers to passengers. Compared to ocean vessels, river steamers seemed light and fragile as pasteboard, and if they caught fire, they burned like tinder. Passengers feared explosions even more, yet statistics suggest that snags were thirty times more likely to destroy steamboats on the Missouri River than boiler explosions. Perhaps because explosions were such horrific events, many a passenger grew alarmed when the "steamer groaned and gasped, and moaned and sighed continually. The cabin floor rose visibly at each pulsation of the engines as they drove the frail vessels," wrote Henry M. Stanley. "I fear there will be a 'fine bust-up' some of these days." [14]

During Civil War days, steamboats along the lower Missouri River encountered guerrilla bands who might ambush and attack the vessel wherever the channel ran close to wooded banks or other sheltered places. For that reason prudent captains followed the practice of anchoring for the night midstream and equipped their pilot-houses with semicylindrical shields of boiler iron that enclosed the wheel and left only a peephole for navigation. The crewmen on duty adjusted this heavy armor according to the changing course of the vessel. Similar shields also proved of value on the upper Missouri, for Indians at that time were as dangerous along that section of waterway as guerrillas were farther down.

The danger of Indian attack existed along both the Missouri and Columbia rivers, though it posed a serious problem on the Pacific Northwest waterway only for a brief time during the mid-1850s. On the upper Missouri it remained a hazard from 1860 to 1876. Though most boats steamed through safely, rivermen always feared an attack, particularly through Dakota Territory. These fears might actually cause unnecessary bloodshed, as happened on the upper Missouri in July 1863 when a frightened officer aboard the *Robert Campbell, Jr.* fired first at an Indian he thought was starting to take an arrow from his quiver. A general melee erupted, with crewmen

The Wreck of the Annie Faxon

One of the more spectacular accidents occurred on August 14, 1893, as the Annie Faxon made her regular trip down the Snake River, picking up loads of fruit and passengers at the landings along the canyon. In the pilothouse Captain Harry Baughman rang for the engines to stop for a landing below Almota. Almost at that same moment a roar pressed up from the lower deck, the boat buckled first in and then out as boilers let go. Baughman watched in horror as flying wreckage beheaded his companion in the pilothouse; the next thing the captain knew he was on the shore, dazed and lamed.

Captain Ephraim Baughman was in Pierce, inspecting some mining property, when word of the tragedy reached him. He immediately secured a horse and rode all the way to Lewiston, where he took a rowboat for the forty-mile dash downriver to check on his son, Harry. "Heads were cut open and legs and arms smashed, and scalds and blisters were plentiful," reported the Lewiston Teller. The explosion killed eight people and injured nearly every member of the crew: "To look at the wreck as it lays, the wonder is how any person escaped alive."
—Adapted from the *Lewiston Teller,* August 17, 1893

firing at the party of Indians on the shore and the Indians returning the fire. Seven died aboard the *Campbell,* and the beach was strewn with dead and wounded Sioux. In 1867, a band of Sioux fired into the *Silver Lake* forty miles above Fort Rice, wounding a son of the captain. During the same month, Sioux bullets also riddled the *Antelope.* Although the threat of Indian attack was real enough, attacks themselves were infrequent and often ineffectual.[15]

Incidents along the Way

"At about 10 o'clock the sudden reversion of the engines and sharp whistling proclaiming 'Something Up,' I dropped an abstract of mining property which I was engaged in copying in the dining room and, rushing on deck, found the entire force of the boat engaged (such as had guns) in shooting buffalo," wrote James Knox Polk Miller in his diary for June 6, 1867. Four youthful bison, attempting to cross the river, found themselves directly in front of the steamboat. "They were terribly frightened

and endeavored to reach the shore, which they did. But the banks were so steep that they were unable to ascend them. They were accordingly butchered without any difficulty although many shots were fired before the desired result was obtained. It made me pity them to see their frantic efforts to escape and the storm of bullets with which they were saluted. After they were killed, or badly wounded, the steamer's yawl was lowered and rowing to the sides of the enormous carcasses, towed them to the side of the steamer where they were hoisted aboard and duly skinned & cleaned for the table." Later as the boat tied up for the evening, Miller saw a passenger shoot at a beaver but miss.[16]

Captain Grant Marsh once observed vast herds of buffalo moving slowly across the prairie. "On arriving at the river's brink they hesitated and then, snorting and bellowing, plunged into the swift-running current and swam to the opposite shore." Everyone aboard the *Stockdale* was excited, "for the buffalo became so thick in the river that

*T*he ladies' cabin was a place of luxury aboard the Joseph Kellogg. *Courtesy Oregon Historical Society, 150.*

the boat could not move and the engines had to be stopped. In front the channel was blocked by their huge, shaggy bodies, and in their struggles they beat against the sides and stern, blowing and pawing. Many became entangled with the wheel, which for a time could not be revolved without breaking the buckets." To Captain Marsh and the others aboard the *Stockdale* it seemed almost as if the animals would overwhelm the boat. Several hours elapsed before they were able to push ahead through the migrating herds. Curiously, "no one on board cared to shoot among them, for the sight of them was too awe-inspiring a demonstration of the physical might of untamed brute creation."[17]

Such restraint was rare, however, for in common with passengers on overland stagecoaches, steamboat travelers often treated the abundant wildlife they saw along the way as convenient targets to test their marksmanship. Charles Bailey recalled the "frenzy of excitement" when passengers spotted a herd of about fifty antelope plunge

into the Missouri and swim for the other shore. "There were plenty of guns and ammunition on board, and every man of the crew and passengers was shooting into that herd. I was 'on watch,' but I grabbed the rifle and rushed forward on the hurricane deck and shot one, and by that time four had been killed and were floating down the river with the current." Bailey estimated that nearly five hundred shots were fired into the herd.[18]

Tragic incidents also befell the travelers themselves. Aboard the *Luella* were two large safes that were usually filled with gold dust, but many voyagers preferred to protect their treasure in leather belts about their waists, a fatal error in at least one instance. At the mouth of the Milk River, a tributary that enters the Missouri 460 miles below Fort Benton, the *Luella* ran aground. While the crew struggled to dislodge her, passengers stood along the sides of the boat, idly watching them work. A man named McClellan fell overboard. The water was barely two feet deep, but the swift current knocked him off his feet. So great was the weight of his treasure belt that he was dragged to the bottom and drowned before help could reach him. The boat was delayed twenty-four hours for the purpose of recovering his body, but to no avail. This was such a powerful morality tale for sentimental Americans of the Victorian era that frequent retellings of the incident became a way to pass time during a long voyage to Fort Benton.[19]

The View from the Pilothouse: Steamboat Operations

When all other diversions failed, there was always the attraction of the steamboat itself and its daily operations. A favorite haunt of passengers was the pilothouse when conditions of navigation permitted them to be there. Often a captain invited passengers into the pilothouse and let women and children steer the boat and pull the whistle rope. The pilot was always an interesting person to know because, when he was in a good mood and sailing along an easy stretch of river, he would entertain listeners with tales of his adventures. These were in reality the accumulated stories of many years, but as new to the tenderfoot as if told for the first time. One might begin,

An unidentified steamboat threads its way through the Missouri Breaks of Montana. It was in places like this that passengers anticipated a hunt. Daniel Weston wrote: "We all rushed to the hurricane roof with rifles—the cry of 'a bear in sight' being raised—but we found it was a wolf and soon many wolves appeared. The rifles cracked fast but brought none down. Pretty soon two antelopes were seen swimming the river just ahead. They were allowed to land on an open island which the boat was 'hugging' and such a fusillade is seldom heard except in war. One was shot and the other took to the river again. Where he was also shot." Courtesy State Historical Society of North Dakota, B-432.

Steamboat Talk on the Columbia River

One of the pastimes on the boat among the passengers who were "Oregon Pioneers" of at least one year's standing, was to tell the newcomer—or "tenderfoot"—about the climatic freaks of Western Oregon, where it rains so much that the inhabitants become amphibious, their feet being webbed like ducks, etc.; that the girls had to knit their socks with toes in them, like fingers of a glove, to prevent the webs from growing; all of which was exceedingly entertaining and gave great delight to the narrators.

—Randall H. Hewitt, *Across the Plains and Over the Divide: A Mule Train Journey from East to West in 1862, and Incidents Connected Therewith* (1906)

gers and crew survived for three weeks on bullberries and rosebuds that they foraged on shore.[21]

Whenever a Missouri River steamboat operated in shallow water, a deckhand took a measured pole and thrust it into the current every five seconds, at the same time calling out the depth in a drawling, singsong voice. If this method located no channel, the pilot sent the mate out in a yawl, or more generally he went himself and carefully sounded the river over the shallow portion. After finding where the deepest water lay, he would ram the boat as far along as possible. Crewmen lowered huge spars along either side and set them in the sand with the lower ends pointing downstream so that when a capstan pulled on the lines it would lift the boat and force it ahead. In this way a captain might "walk" his boat across the bar, but this slow and arduous procedure, usually called grasshoppering, might consume one or two days. When all else failed, roustabouts transferred cargo to flatboats or keelboats until they reduced the draft of the steamboat enough to free her from the bar.

Among the most serious challenges facing any Missouri River navigator was finding fuel to feed the hungry boilers. Wood alone was used. Smaller steamboats burned from twelve to twenty-four cords every twenty-four hours; larger ones consumed anywhere from fifty to seventy-five cords each day. Cottonwood gave a fierce, hot fire but one that required constant stoking; and if the wood were unseasoned, an engineer found it almost impossible to maintain steam without the aid of rosin. When buffeted by a strong headwind, many a captain preferred to tie up rather than waste precious fuel.

In early years the crew itself cut wood for fuel as the boat proceeded on her voyage. But as steamboat traffic became more regular, boat owners or resident choppers known as wood hawks established supply yards. The sight of dry cordwood stacked along a secluded stretch of water gladdened the heart of every steamboatman. Some Indians found the sale of wood to be a source of considerable revenue and attempted to bar whites from the business.

Especially during the Sioux hostilities, the wooding of a steamboat became a most perilous chore. Working by

This F. Jay Haynes photograph from 1884 illustrates how the upper deck of the steamer Coeur d'Alene *commanded a sweeping view of its namesake lake. Unlike an ocean vessel, a large part of which was buried beneath the surface of the water, the typical steamboat rode on the surface and drew at most only three or four feet of water. This created an illusion of great size compared with a boat's actual dimensions and tonnage, explained Hiram Chittenden. The successive decks, surmounted by the texas (a suite of rooms for the officers of the boat) and pilothouse, were usually painted a clear, even white, which made the vessel look like a veritable floating palace as it paddled majestically along the waters of the northern West. Courtesy Montana Historical Society, H-1391.*

"Say, did you hear about the time a man fell off the *Luella* at Milk River?"

From the pilothouse a passenger had a commanding view of how rivermen dealt with problems of low water on the upper Missouri, which always intensified the discomforts of a long trip to Fort Benton. Low water was ever a topic of conversation and concern. When in 1865 the *Deer Lodge* was unable to make the final 250 miles upriver to Fort Benton, passengers joked that the "barkeeper had taken so much water for the dilution of his whiskey" that their boat, though drawing only two feet, could proceed no farther. So much for the claim that mountain steamboats might run "on a heavy dew."[20]

The *Imperial* left Fort Benton in late summer 1867 with three hundred passengers and provisions for eight days of travel, but because of repeated groundings on sandbars the luckless steamboat required eight weeks to reach Saint Joseph. As her stock of provisions ran low, meals were reduced to two and then to one a day, and if the newspaper account of the trip is to be believed, passen-

the light of a torch or lantern, crewmen often spent the first hours of the night hurrying to gather fuel for their next day's run. To prevent an ambush, Captain Joseph La Barge equipped one of his steamboats with a small sawmill and a yoke of oxen: when he had to stop for wood he swung out a large stage, drove the team ashore, and dragged several logs aboard with utmost speed. As the boat proceeded on her way, crewmen sawed up their precious wood. During uprisings—such as occurred in 1862, 1867–1868, and 1876—steamboatmen had trouble finding fuel because Indians so often killed or drove away the nonnative woodcutters. The business of supplying fuel for steamboats on the upper Missouri was profitable, but only the bold survived. The few Euro-Americans who worked as wood choppers on the great plains of Dakota Territory or eastern Montana ranked among the most hardy and reckless types that the frontier produced.

Sometimes a boat consumed all its fuel before it reached the next wooding place. Then it was necessary to gather drift logs or anything else combustible that could be found. Especially prized in such emergencies were accumulations of driftwood, or rack heaps, which the

current piled on sandbars during seasons of high water. Whenever a trading post was abandoned, its palisades and buildings quickly found their way into steamboat furnaces. Harriet Pack Sanders, a passenger traveling from Saint Joseph to Fort Benton in April 1867, recalled that when the *Albeona* stopped in the Missouri Breaks of Montana Territory for fuel, it took thirteen hours to wood up. The boat got stuck on a sandbar the next day, prompting Sanders to write, "All got the blues. Have thrown off every stick of wood that the men cut yesterday from six A.M. to seven P.M. Required to stop for wood again the next day. All the men helped to draw in twenty loads, have all the boat will carry." No wonder it took seventy-two days to reach Fort Benton.[22]

Along the Columbia River a large-scale industry arose to supply steamboats with the hundreds of cords of wood burned each month. A single round-trip between Celilo and Lewiston might consume as much as fifty cords, some of which was driftwood but much more came from the forests of the Cascade mountains. The Oregon Steam Navigation Company transported nearly all of its fuel from the middle Columbia across the portage at The Dalles to serve its upriver fleet.

Racing

An exciting and sometimes dangerous pastime that many boatmen found irresistible was racing. On the Missouri River, racing was especially risky because of the uncertainty of the channel, the numerous snags, and the risk of a boiler explosion. Yet no captain liked to be passed: let a rival boat draw even, and the temptation to race her became overwhelming. Urging them on were settlers living along the river—all of them more or less isolated and eager for any sort of diversion—who took personal interest in the performance of individual steamboats and often wagered on their favorites and encouraged masters and crews to break speed records set by others. Among the excited passengers who crowded the railings, fights, bets, and bribes during a race were not uncommon.

Probably the longest *one-way* steamboat race in history was from Saint Louis to Fort Benton from March 27 to May 31, 1866. Officially there was no contest between

the *William J. Lewis* and the *Mollie Dozier,* yet it was tacitly understood that the two boats would be in a pitched race. Besides, the first boat to reach Fort Benton each spring always garnered business that might amount to a million or more dollars. Captain Carrol Jones Atkins piloted the new *William J. Lewis,* which was at that time the largest boat on the Missouri above the mouth of the Yellowstone River, to victory nearly thirty-four hours ahead of the *Mollie Dozier.* On June 2 the *William J. Lewis* headed back to Saint Louis, her maiden voyage having covered the entire cost of construction, about $60,000.[23]

In 1872 what was claimed to be the longest round-trip steamboat race between Sioux City and Fort Benton took place between the *Nellie Peck,* with Captain Grant Marsh in command, and the *Far West.* The *Nellie Peck* had the larger cargo, and both boats transacted much business at the various landings along the way, but Captain Marsh kept his lead for 1,370 miles. Marsh "disliked to trust the boat to another hand than his own, but at times he was forced to seek a little rest. At length one night a short distance above the point where the Bijou Hills [in present North Dakota] lie piled along the left bank, knowing that there was an easy stretch of water ahead and that everything was going smoothly on board, he surrendered the wheel to his partner at about midnight and retired to bed. But he had scarcely fallen asleep when the watchman rushed into his cabin, crying that the boat had gone hard aground."[24]

Marsh's partner, an old Missouri River pilot, thought he knew every point where the river was in the habit of changing its current, but he missed his guess. The *Nellie Peck,* two miles off her proper course, was stuck fast for the night. So tense were the emotions of the moment that Marsh had to knock a revolver out of the hands of John Belt, the cub pilot, who threatened to shoot the helmsman responsible for beaching the boat. In the end the *Far West* steamed ahead and reached Sioux City three hours ahead of the *Nellie Peck* to win the 2,800-mile race. Jubilant supporters of the winning boat gave Captain Mart Coulson and his officers watches and other gifts, and even the crew and roustabouts shared in the glory.[25]

A supply of wood stacked at Hood River, Oregon, about 1911. All along the Columbia and Snake rivers, especially in the treeless country east of the Cascade mountains, a series of wooding stations dotted the banks. John Keast Lord, who traveled upriver aboard the Colonel Wright *in the early 1860s, wrote that the boilers "are heated with wood only, which is hauled by ox-teams from the nearest forest or timbered district, often many miles; cutting, cording and hauling the wood requisite for a trip from the Deschutes to Walla Walla is a very heavy item." When steamboating began on the Snake and Clearwater rivers, the Oregon Steam Navigation Company would hire Indians "to cut wood and pay them liberally for it. We took aboard some of it above 'Reubens,' and the savages were vastly tickled at receiving money for their labor," wrote a correspondent for the* Oregonian *in mid-June 1861. Courtesy Oregon Historical Society, 47124.*

Steamboat races on the Columbia River were no less tense than in other parts of the country. When two boats ran the same route for different owners, it was a race all the way and never mind the safety value; yet no steamer blew up while racing. The two most popular racecourses were between Portland and the lower Cascades and between Portland and Astoria. But steamboat races also took place on the upper Columbia and lower Snake rivers. Henry Corbett warned one of his captains in the early 1860s that he was "inclined to think" that the rival Oregon Steam Navigation Company wanted to tempt him to blow up the *Spray* "by urging the *Wright* to run you." Whether Corbett's main concern was for safety or personal pride was not clear, however, because he added, "I do not wish to take risks in racing until we get a new boat." With the building of the really big steamboats in the 1880s, such as the *Telephone, T. J. Potter,* and *Bailey Gatzert,* came the heyday of speed in the Pacific Northwest. For some people, racing may have been a way to cope with the burdens of time and space that weighed so heavily upon residents of the northern West during the steamboat and stagecoach era.[26]

Every steamboatman dreaded running hard aground. Here the Regulator *is on the rocks on the Columbia River about 1899. Courtesy Oregon Historical Society, 79767.*

And Sundays—there were no such days in Helena! It is really the great day of the week.
Horse races are made through the streets; drunken miners lay stretched on the walk; horse
auctioneers cry horses and wagons; and gold dust is scattered as if made by a wish. To see
life in Helena of a Sunday night is worth a week's stay in the streets of New York.
—Helena *Weekly Herald (December 12, 1867)*

The Burdens of Time and Space

The Reverend Gustavus Hines arrived in Oregon from the East in 1840. He had traveled by the fastest commercial means possible at the time, leaving New York City on October 9, 1839, sailing around Cape Horn, and reaching the Columbia River on May 21 of the following year. The journey took nearly eight months. Three years later, on a lonely promontory overlooking the Columbia River near the Grand Dalles, Hines paused from his labors to reflect on the burdens of time and space that nearly overwhelmed him. The Methodist missionary lamented most of all that he was so far from home. "I thought of my beloved parents from whom I had not heard for years; of the tears they shed when last I saw them, of receiving the parting benediction, and of the anxiety they must still feel, if alive, for their wandering son." He thought too of his brothers and sisters, early schoolmates, fellow worshipers, and those "who, if they had not forgotten me, would ask, 'Where is he? and what is his employment.'"[1]

Hines fondly recalled the landscape of his native East Coast—"of bustling cities, with wheels rattling and towns, with their splendid turnpikes and McAdamized roads; of railroad cars and steamboats; of temples erected to the God in heaven; the toll of chiming bells as they informed the waiting thousands that the time of worship

had arrived"—until he actually imagined himself "amidst the scenes, the contemplation of which had produced this pleasing illusion, and starting up I found myself surrounded with the stillness of death, save the murmuring of the turbid waters of the Columbia that rolled beneath where I sat. Contrasting the land which had passed before my mental vision with that in which I felt myself a voluntary exile, I exclaimed, how changed the scene! This, thought I, is truly a land of darkness."

In the 1840s a journey from the East Coast to distant Oregon was in some ways analogous to one's own death, not just for the Reverend Hines and anyone who traveled by sailing ship, but also for emigrants who bade parents and friends good-bye and undertook the five-month-long journey west by wagon along the Oregon Trail. Any adult who survived the hazards along the way still had to overcome the overwhelming sense of isolation on the Pacific coast: during most of the 1840s the nearest post office was located in Weston, Missouri (Ben Holladay's early hometown), some two thousand miles distant. If a letter was destined for the States, the sender had first to find someone returning east who would mail it upon reaching Missouri. Incidentally, when the letter finally did reach its destination several months later, the

receiver often paid the delivery cost: many writers on the West Coast were so uncertain about transcontinental mail service that they sent their letters collect.

Oregon's provisional government urged federal officials to establish postal service as early as 1845. Among the memorials and resolutions that Washington's first territorial legislature passed in the mid-1850s was one begging Congress to establish mail service between Puget Sound points and San Francisco, New Orleans, and New York. At the very least they hoped the Pacific Northwest could connect to mail service between San Francisco and New York. A common refrain in the annual messages of territorial governors was the call for better mail service. "Nothing can possibly be more important to the inhabitants of the Territories than uninterrupted mail communication with the States."[2]

Despite the twin burdens of time and space, settlers of

the northern West during the steamboat and stagecoach era appeared to have a far more complete understanding of their region's transportation geography than most people do today. One Oregonian recalled that in 1852 "I was surprised to find that all the old settlers seemed to be well acquainted with each other, even to the most remote parts of the territory." The average resident of Portland during the 1860s knew far more about everyday economic events in distant Lewiston or Helena than most of their descendants do in the 1990s, thanks in part to the way newspapers reported Portland's attempt to enlarge its hinterland.[3]

Though the "latest news" from the East Coast might be several weeks old, its arrival in the 1850s and 1860s was a community event: Oregon settlers in the 1840s were "astonished at getting the news at all." The way it crossed the continent was both highly visible and intensely

This photograph from January 17, 1907, shows how ice on the Columbia River temporarily imprisoned the sternwheelers Capital City *and* Joseph Kellogg. *Courtesy Oregon Historical Society, 35431.*

This undated photograph shows a pioneer home near Medford, Oregon. Isolation—especially poor mail service—was a major complaint of pioneers across the northern West. Courtesy Southern Oregon Historical Society.

personal (unlike the electronic transmissions bounced off satellites today). To help residents of the far Northwest better visualize how news reached them from the East Coast, the *Oregonian* on May 10, 1861, described a Pony Express rider "splashing through mud-holes, climbing up steep hills, and sliding down the other side; fording creeks and ferrying rivers, until he reaches Fort Kearny." We pick up the story again in Sacramento: "Here he comes, panting, foaming, laden with news at $2 the half ounce, the precursor of the railroad, another link between us and the old folks at home." A few years later, when disgruntled Indians repeatedly severed the transcontinental telegraph wire across Wyoming, settlers from Virginia City to Portland were ready to do battle with "the savages" who imperiled their home ties.[4]

Home Ties

While some newcomers managed to live a self-contained existence at the fringe of society—"happy in their freedom from all wants they cannot supply and from all ambitions they cannot satisfy"—one notable thing about life in the northern West was how many Euro-American residents lacked permanent homes within the area. "Every spring hundreds of thousands of our countrymen go westward, as inevitably as wild geese fly south on the approach of winter. We are indeed 'A bivouac rather than a nation, a grand army moving from Atlantic to Pacific, and pitching tents by the way.' It is not from accident, or American restlessness, but Law fixed, inexorable as that compelling water to its level, or the magnet to its pole," emphasized the journalist Albert D. Richardson.[5]

It was estimated that in 1870 the West contained a floating population of some 250,000 hunters, trappers, traders, miners, lumberjacks, soldiers, government agents, cowmen, packers, teamsters, stage and express men, sutlers, travelers, and migrants en route from old to new locations. Further, about 100,000 persons traveled either partway or all the way across the Great Plains each year during the decade of the 1860s. Each new gold rush unleashed a fresh flood of peripatetic Americans.[6]

The *Montana Post* commonly used the headline "News From America" above stories from the eastern United States, the real home of most of the northern West's first generation of Euro-American settlers. How many newcomers to the West, both as settlers and sojourners, must have wondered, "When shall I see the old home faces and places again? This question is often on my mind. It saddens me to think it may be years—perhaps maybe never—. If I am spared to again return, whose places will be vacant? What faces have I looked my last upon?"[7]

Especially during the worrisome days of the Civil War era, any news from America was a prized commodity on the nation's western fringe. A stagecoach passenger on the central overland route recalled a brief exchange one November night in 1860 when the Pony Express rider dashed by: "What's the news?" shouted our driver. "Lincoln elected! New York gives him fifty thousand majority!" came back the cry through the darkness. "It woke up all our Republicans who sent forth cheer upon cheer, while the Democrats were sure it must be a hoax."[8]

Richardson, who penned these words, recalled that all along the way West "emigrants and ranch-men besieged us for papers. One night, when we rolled up to a lonely station, miles from any other human habitation, the stock-tender, ragged, shaggy, sunburnt and unkempt, put his lantern up to our coach window and implored: "'Gentlemen, can you spare me a newspaper? I have not seen one for a week and can't endure it much longer. I will give a dollar for any newspaper in the United States not more than ten days old.'" He was a "representative American," thought Richardson. "No other nation so subsists upon the daily journals as our own."

The same insatiable desire for news from home was noticeable along sea routes to the Pacific Slope. Frederick Billings, the Vermont-born western railroad pioneer after whom Billings, Montana, was named, recalled that on a trip around Cape Horn his ship reached Callao, Peru, in the spring of 1865 with all its passengers hungry for news. Billings asked the first Yankee he met on the shore:

"'What is the news from the United States?'

"Slowly removing his cigar, the stranger replied with genuine American nonchalance, reciting the stupendous events in a tone as monotonous as if reading a laundry-list.

"'Richmond is taken; Lee has capitulated; Johnston has surrendered; President Lincoln has been assassinated; and Jeff Davis has been caught in his wife's petticoats.'

"The listener stood speechless at the startling catalogue."[9]

Many men and women at the diggings in Montana and Idaho during the 1860s thought often of their homes back East, and distance did not diminish their loyalty to either the Union or the Confederate cause. In some mining camps and supply centers support for the South was so intense that Union supporters were afraid to admit their loyalties. When Union troops from Fort Walla Walla dared to visit nearby saloons, the town's numerous Rebel sympathizers denounced them as "Lincoln's hirelings" and drove them away. Sometimes they made a soldier drink to the health of President Jefferson Davis or General Pierre Beauregard, "and if he refused, [would] kick him or knock him down. Most of the large gambling houses were kept by Rebs or they showed Rebel sympathies and some would not let the soldiers or volunteers in either to play or drink." The greatest wonder, thought the Idaho pioneer William A. Goulder, was that brawls inspired by Civil War loyalties "were not more frequent."[10]

James Knox Polk Miller reflected on the burdens that time and distance imposed on sojourners in western mining camps when he noted in his diary for June 8, 1865, that he and some acquaintances had rented a cabin in Virginia City for ten dollars a month: "Slept in the cabin with them last night. Remington played on his guitar during the evening. I lay on the floor in a blanket. The moon cast a clear, soft light over the cabin and in the open doorway, provoking thought & reflection. The music was sad & I grew very very blue and homesick. It came so natural to think of home, friends, and all I so much loved, all lost and far away. I have 'no one to love & none to caress.' As I write this today I can not help the tears starting. I feel so much alone." So many miners experienced the same powerful emotions that columns in the *Montana Post* counseled against the "annual scourge" of homesickness when "hundreds will agitate the question, 'Are you going home this summer?'"[11]

The sense of estrangement from home was no less powerful for Bishop Daniel Tuttle, who emphasized that "next to the sense of loneliness, I was most oppressed with the sad conviction of the prayerlessness and godlessness of the people among whom I found myself." Julia Gilliss, a young army wife at The Dalles, implored her parents in December 1865: "You can write to me at *any time* as the overland mail comes every day, only you must not write (per steamer) on your letters. I am so impatient to hear from home that I can hardly contain myself. Just think, not one word have I heard since we left New York, and I have written five. I know you have written, but your letters have not caught us yet. . . ."[12]

Early the following February, Gilliss wrote to her father on the East Coast: "Your letter of the 29th December arrived yesterday being the very first communication direct or indirect which has reached us from home. I need not say that it was thankfully received, long looked for and anxiously expected; it was the brightest gleam of sunshine that the day brought forth. This morning, Jim succeeded in getting out of the mail which was passing through here on its way to Walla Walla, a letter from Annie written one month previous to yours which I was also delighted to get. I think you have not received all the letters that I have written. . . . The greatest disappointment of my life has been this Western banishment when I thought we would be so happy at home." Typical of anyone connected with a lonely military post out West, Hervey Johnson from Fort Laramie, Idaho Territory, confessed in late 1863 that "it makes me feel almost like I am at home, to read a letter from there."[13]

Any newspaper from home was likewise a treasured possession. Gilliss wrote to her parents on May 6, 1866,

from Fort Dalles: "The newspapers arrived, we are much obliged, especially Jim. I believe he reads all the advertisements. I expect next thing to see him turn the paper backwards after once reading it to see if anything escaped his notice. We get all your letters regularly."[14]

Especially before the advent of regular railroad service, the arrival of a letter or package from a distant home was an occasion for public rejoicing. "The express-company messenger delivers business correspondence. Presently I hear through the store's walls the voice of our neighbor the postmaster. Loudly every afternoon he reads the names of people who have letters addressed to them. He has trouble with names on envelopes from abroad," mused Theodor Kirchhoff. "He sounds them out slowly, to the amusement of assembled Americans. 'Mister Dthi-o-dohr ka-ei-arr—' I've heard enough. I hurry around the corner and into the post office. At once I have forgotten Oregon, The Dalles, and the postmaster who ridicules my name. The well-known penmanship of somebody dear to me speaks and I listen. A chilly autumn evening in a foreign country turns into a sunny one of great joy."[15]

Telegraph lines, like mail and express service, promised to overcome time and space. During the 1860s, the rumor of an impending telegraph connection could excite people just as much as the possibility of railroad connections did in later decades. In the spring of 1866 John A. Creighton, who together with his brother Edward had helped construct the first transcontinental telegraph, secured financial backing for a line to link Virginia City and Salt Lake City. In record time, workmen strung wires for the new branch, soon to become a segment of the expanding Western Union system, and the whole town eagerly paused to hear the clicking dots and dashes that radically redefined distance for their hitherto isolated settlement. On November 2, 1866, Edward Creighton sent the first telegram into Montana which read: "Citizens of Montana, allow me to greet you. It gives me pleasure to connect your city by lightning. Men of so much enterprise should not be forgotten. Your brave governor will send the first message free to A. Johnson, President of the United States." A week

POST OFFICE, SAN FRANCISCO, CALIFORNIA.

A FAITHFUL REPRESENTATION OF THE CROWDS DAILY APPLYING AT THAT OFFICE FOR LETTERS AND NEWSPAPERS.

*I*n early San Francisco a large black ball hoisted atop Telegraph Hill announced the mail steamer. Extra editions of local newspapers were published immediately after her arrival, while month-old eastern newspapers sold readily for a dollar apiece. The all-important mail was transferred from ship to post office, there to be sorted and delivered on the next and succeeding days. Eager for letters from relatives and friends in the States, San Franciscans began to line up for mail a full day before it was available at the post office. Courtesy Library of Congress, 3045.

The Miner's Fourth Commandment

Thou shalt not remember what thy friends do at home of the Sabbath day, lest the remembrance may not compare favorably with what thou doest here.— Six days thou mayest dig or pick all that thy body can stand under; but the other day is Sunday; yet thou washest all thy dirty shirts, darnest all thy stockings, tappest thy boots, mendest thy clothing, choppest thy whole week's firewood, makest up and bakest thy bread, and boilest thy pork and beans, that thou wait not when thou returnest from thy long-tom weary.

—Matthew Macfie, *Vancouver Island and British Columbia* (1973 reprint of 1865 edition). 418–422. Macfie copied these words from James M. Hutchings' popular 1853 handout in California.

later the *Montana Post,* delighted that it could now print the latest news, reported: "The telegraph works beautifully."[16]

Telegraph wires soon extended into the northern Rocky Mountains from the West Coast as well. The first line was completed from Portland to The Dalles in 1868, and through to Boise the following year. The expanding network also joined Portland to Puget Sound in 1864 and to Victoria and New Westminster in 1865. Despite occasional downed poles and frequent breaks in the slender wires, the ability to communicate at the speed of lightning represented a vast improvement over the links that existed only a decade earlier: "By means of the electric cord, we can triumph over the elements and present the citizens with reliable intelligence."[17]

In 1864 a Salt Lake City newspaper defined progress in terms of visible changes wrought by the new modes of communication and transportation: "But a few years ago the country we habit, and for many hundred miles around, was an almost uninhabited desert—a wilderness. To-day we have instant relations with all parts of the Union by electric wires, daily communication with the east and west by mail stage"; and now triweekly mail coaches link to Salt Lake City "the rich mines of Montana and Idaho and the fields of industry and commerce in Washington and Oregon."[18]

As Good as Other Days

If popular consciousness of time and space took a highly visible form during the northern West's steamboat and stagecoach era, so too did something so fundamental as the rhythms of the week on the nation's far frontier. In Virginia City, John Knox Polk Miller confided to his diary on June 11, 1865: "Today showed me an entirely new phase of life. There was nothing visible to remind a person in the slightest degree that it was Sunday. Every store, saloon and dancing hall was in full blast. Hacks running, auctioneering, mining, and indeed every business, is carried on with much more zeal than on week days. It made me heartsick to see it."[19]

In most mining camps and towns little business was conducted during the week, but Sunday was different.

Across the northern West it meant that businesses, sidewalks, and streets were packed with people acquiring their supplies for the coming week. The special day began early when "from every direction, along narrow mountain paths come in long-bearded, flannel shirted miners, until the streets and saloons are crowded from a distance of several miles, to buy provisions or get a battered pick sharpened, or it may be only to borrow a short oblivion from the monotony of camp life and to lay aside even in thought the weary six days' burden." If a miner rested from his usual labor it was only to wash and patch his clothing, cook up food for the following week, and mend broken tools.[20]

Sunday in the towns was generally the liveliest day of the week. "Dance halls, saloons, and gambling houses ran full blast, and usually there was a horse-race or prizefight." An Idaho law that forbade court procedures on Sunday had to be modified so as to permit taxation of those packers who waited until Sunday to bring in their trains, and to allow issuance of attachments on that day, in order to stop absconding debtors. Daniel Weston noted in 1866 that "no games are played on Sunday, all by common consent doing this much to observe the Sabbath." However, even that small concession was not typical for all the West. A first-time visitor to the Pacific Coast noted with dismay, "On our return to the ship, we found the passengers playing cards, singing songs, drinking whiskey, etc.—a Californian sabbath."[21]

Sunday in the Oro Fino diggings was special because on that day the weekly express arrived from Walla Walla. A large crowd invariably gathered to await distribution of the mail. "During the remainder of the summer one week was like another with no local events cropping much above the general surface, only that each succeeding Sunday would bring its quota of news from the battlefields in the distant East, and its alternating tide of joys and sorrows, hopes and fears." When John Hailey first saw a throng of men "gathered on the streets and but few of them moving, I feared a big row was at hand, and got on an elevated place to watch the great crowd and listen to the conversation."[22]

The mining historian William J. Trimble believed that

Sunday observance in mining camps of the northern West was so different from that in pious New England because on the frontier "the men really had few, except reminiscent, motives for observing the day, and that in the mining season it was necessary to push all work hard." One of Hailey's contemporaries suggested that frenzied Sunday work appealed to miners because "thinking of loved ones at home, it seems no sin in this savage country to exert oneself on their behalf, on the Sabbath."[23]

The new definition of a weekly time cycle was no less noticeable to easterners who traveled on the overland stagecoach. "There are no aristocratic distinctions between the days of the week west of the Missouri," observed Samuel Bowles. "Sundays are as good as other days, and no better. Stages run, stores are open, mines are dug, and stamp mills crush. But our eastern prejudices are not yet altogether conquered by the 'spirit of the age,'" and upon reaching Virginia Dale "yesterday morning at sunrise, we commanded a twenty-four hours' halt."[24]

As different as Sunday in the West was, the region's transportation pioneers remained uneasy about operating on Sunday. The pioneer missionary Samuel Parker wrote in his 1830s journal while traveling aboard the steamer *Siam* on the Missouri River: "Two miles above us lay the steam-boat Nelson, upon a sand bar high and dry. She ran around upon the sabbath, and being left by a freshet in the river, is waiting for another to take it off. Our captain remarked at dinner to-day, that most of the accidents, which happen to steam-boats, take place on the sabbath; and that he did not believe it would be long before they would not run on that day."[25]

Alexander Majors—who urged rest on Sunday as company policy because he believed God commanded it and that his freight wagons made better time in the long run—emphasized that "in all my vast business on the plains I adhered strictly as possible to keeping the Sabbath day, and avoided traveling or doing any unnecessary work. This fact enabled me to carry out perfectly the 'iron-clad rules' with my employees. When they saw I was willing to pay them the same price as that paid for

RIP ROARING FUN.

HOW THE MERCHANTS AND THE COWBOYS OF BUTTE CITY, MONTANA, RUN THE LOCAL CONCERT HALLS AFTER THEIR OWN FASHION.

work including the Sabbath day, and let them rest on that day, it made them feel I was consistent in requiring them to conduct themselves as gentlemen."[26]

The devout Majors would have felt at home in Portland, the city that became the most conspicuous exception to the West's loosely interpreted custom of Sunday keeping. "The population of Portland is about seven thousand; they keep Sunday as we do in New England, as no other population this side of the Missouri now does," emphasized Samuel Bowles. The unusual piety of Portland even influenced operations of the Oregon Steam Navigation Company: "The steamers do not run on Sunday, and we were compelled to lay over till the following Monday, when at 5 A.M. the *Wilson G. Hunt* started down stream with our party aboard." A traveler stranded in The Dalles complained that although the Columbia River was "the great artery for transportation," pilgrims "could only await the pleasure of the steamboat managers to be

*E*ven on a Sunday: a dance hall in Butte, Montana Territory, in 1886. Courtesy Library of Congress, 408866 762 63903.

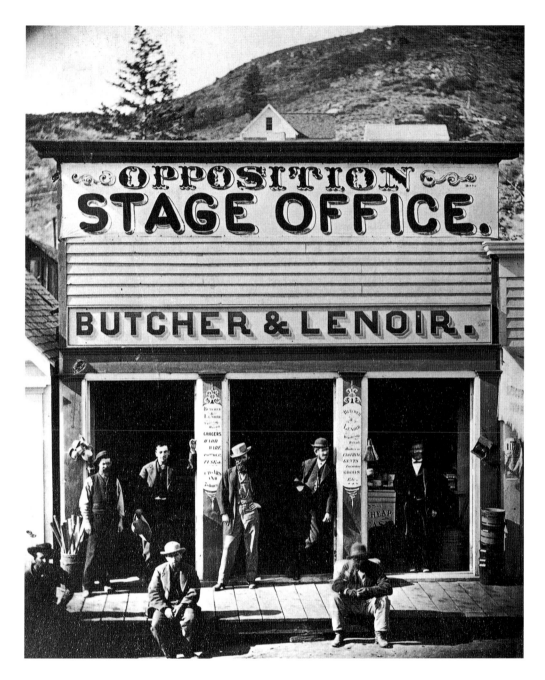

*A*re these men just loafing at the stage office in Silver City, Idaho, in 1868, or waiting for a coach to Fort McDermitt? The photographer did not say. Courtesy Idaho State Historical Society, 77–19.1.

moved from place to place. Though all other kinds of business went on unceasingly seven days in the week, recognizing no Sabbath, the river was closed to navigation, and boats and boatmen rested." Even competitors of the Oregon Steam Navigation Company adhered to the same policy of no Sunday service, if only for reasons that bordered on superstition. Henry Corbett advised his purser to start trips on Monday, giving crews of his Merchants' Transportation line a full day's rest: "You will *avoid running* on Sunday when it is possible. In my opinion there is nothing made by working on Sunday, we always lose in some other way what we gain on that day."[27]

The Four Seasons

During the steamboat and stagecoach era, mining settlements of the northern Rocky Mountains experienced distinctive seasonal rhythms as well. In summer months of the 1860s, letters from New York reached Montana in about twenty-two days; during snowy months of winter, when the Missouri River froze over and drifts closed mountain passes to stagecoaches, no one dared to predict how long the mail might take. "The Mud, the beautiful Mud" was a popular excuse in the spring when Virginia City awaited the long-postponed cry, "The coach is coming!" By late March or early April the first trains of freight were on their way north to Montana from Utah. Summer was the time of greatest bustle and prosperity for merchants, but in high mountain country, autumn followed all too soon. November concluded the hectic days of freighting for another year.[28]

"Summer now wanes and blends into autumn," wrote W. A. Goulder. "The first of October comes bright, clear, and cold, with several inches of the new white winter dress covering mountain, hillside, and creek flats. The ice now begins to check the flow of water in the creeks. The nights begin to be too long and too cold and the days too short and often too stormy to allow placer mining, except on a much diminished scale, to be either comfortable or profitable." Mining gradually ceased altogether, and many of the miners, "particularly those who have homes and families in the Walla Walla, Willamette, and

other valleys in the lower country, begin to gather their ponies from the neighboring 'horse ranches' and prepare to abandon their camp until the following spring, when they would return to their claims and their labors." By the first of November, all who wanted to leave the camp for the winter had departed.[29]

Invariably some miners chose to remain behind. "By wintering in the mines, a man can make his arrangements for the early spring; and if the gold-fields are extensive, he will be as far advanced in his objects as those who strive to overcome impossibilities." This claim, of course, presumed that a miner would survive the rigors of winter; for all who remained in camp, everyday life became a struggle. "Having to live together in board shacks was not inviting, what with temperatures 20 to 30 below zero, north winds vicious, and snow twenty-seven feet deep." The dreaded nutritional deficiency of scurvy was a real possibility. "Uncooked potatoes sliced up and soaked in vinegar were far from affording a very appetizing dish, but it proved a sovereign remedy for scurvy," recalled Goulder.[30]

Winter in a mountain mining camp was not without some charm, however, at least in hindsight. "December comes and the snow is falling, gently and steadily, and almost constantly day after day and night after night," reminisced Goulder of the winter of 1863. "The sun comes out, shining with renewed brightness, but the mercury falls rapidly. Yet there is no wind. A death-like calm, almost oppressive in its stillness, pervades the scene. The inmates of the cabins are soon abroad on various errands. Some make their way on snowshoes to the town to see if the express has been in, and to learn the news. Others force their way to the tops of the neighboring ridges to get a view of the surrounding country. The scene is one of bewildering beauty, far exceeding all powers of description, for who could paint in words the magical effects of a heavy fall of fleecy snow in the evergreen forest of the Bitterroot Mountains?"

Goulder emphasized that although "the snow lay deep on all the roads and trails from December till April, there was but little interruption to the tide of travel that went on. All winter long men were daily leaving Oro Fino on snowshoes with heavy packs on their backs for the distant mining camp, Florence in the Salmon River country being the principal point that attracted them."

Some who remained behind at the Oro Fino diggings organized a Lyceum and Debating Club and spent their winter evenings pondering such weighty matters as whether a state had the right to secede from the Union. Similar pastimes, from "bean poker" to downhill sledding made life bearable in other isolated camps. "I well remember that we were ten weeks without mail during the first winter of my residence in Virginia City. There was no moping about it, but we all set to work to make the time as pleasant as possible."[31]

Winter often inflicted real hardship. "You went from camp to camp on snowshoes or not at all. Visitors from outside were barred for months at a stretch. Mail became a long-cherished hope; none but the couriers of Wells, Fargo & Company risked life and limb to deliver sacks of letters from the Columbia then. Food frequently grew scarce, prices soared, and flour at $1.00 a pound was common. Many miners surrendered their last specks of yellow dust to the food seller to ward off starvation."[32]

During the winter of 1865 a number of freight wagons lumbered north to Virginia City from Salt Lake City bringing precious flour, but they became snowbound in Beaver Canyon and all the oxen perished. Day by day, provisions of every kind grew more scarce in the Montana mining camp. In late February the price of flour almost quadrupled in a matter of days. Most people, "especially those with families," were unable to purchase flour at so inflated a price "and as all provisions were scarce, many were reduced to a diet of meat straight. Beef was quite plentiful and sold for fifteen cents per pound. It was evident that a corner was held on flour. Groups of people collected on the streets and the all absorbing topic of conversation was the price of flour." In mid-April an armed body of almost five hundred men resolved the crisis by confiscating all available flour—searching for "sundry lots of flour concealed under coats, in boxes and barrels and under hay stacks"—and selling it to hungry citizens at the usual price. "After the flour was distributed the members of the committee returned to their homes."[33]

When Florence became snowbound during the winter of 1862, its residents suffered not just from a lack of edibles but also from the craving for "a well-appointed and well-supplied first-class saloon. To meet this crying want, several kegs of alcohol were carried over the snowy trail, accompanied by the enterprising proprietor of the contemplated liquor emporium, traveling on snowshoes and carrying in a satchel the little vials of chemicals that would convert this alcohol into the mildly-exhilarating liquids of various names and colors and flavors to suit the whims and tastes of his future customers."[34]

While some miners remained snowbound at the diggings, confined for months by deep snow and cold weather, others departed the northern Rocky Mountains each fall for Saint Louis, Walla Walla, Portland, and even San Francisco. But both Walla Walla and Portland suffered occasionally themselves when winter blocked the usual transportation and communication routes. During the 1860s it was not uncommon for the Columbia River to freeze above the Cascades for as long as eight weeks at a time. During the severe winter of 1861–1862 the mercury dropped to 36 or 37 below zero: "It kept men more quiet, and they stayed closer to shelter and fires. The people of Walla Walla ran out of wood and burnt their fences, and rails sold for $60 per cord, and those that had no money took hand sleds at night and went out to the government fence of rails and slabs and posts and brought in every thing that would make heat. Crowds of miners wintering in Walla Walla ran out of money and went to the bakeries and hotels and made them give up bread, cheese, bologna and meat to keep from starving."[35]

The following spring, when Preston W. Gillette made his way along the road between The Dalles and Walla Walla, he found the land strewn with dead cattle, "which had starved during the late unprecedented hard winter. Where Arlington [Oregon] now stands, I counted 150 dead cattle on less than one acre of land. They had come down the ravine in quest of water and food, neither of which they could get: the river was frozen over and snow was so deep that they could find no grass." An estimated one million cattle died that winter; the spring floods ran full with their bloated bodies.[36]

Julia Gilliss vividly recited the difficulties of winter travel between Portland and The Dalles in a letter she sent her parents in late December 1865. "Last Monday we made the attempt, that is we went on board the steamboat and steamed out to the confluence of the Willamette with the Columbia. We laid there for two or three hours, our progress impeded by the masses of floating ice; at last we were obliged to abandon the attempt and turn our faces Portland-ward."[37]

A wintertime trip from Montana to Salt Lake City usually involved a sleigh ride over Monida Pass, with coaches meeting sleighs along either side of the snowy mountain divide. Frequent blizzards made it easy for either conveyance to miss the road and overturn into a drift. When one "slow coach" finally did reach Virginia City, it brought nine bags of eagerly awaited "literary

matter, which were delivered into the hands of the Postmaster." These formed so large a pile needing to be sorted that the *Montana Post* advised "all impatient people, who have not been weaned from their former homes in the States, to complacently 'grin and bear it.'"[38]

For stage drivers who had to sit on the box of the coach exposed to the snow and bitter cold, winter travel meant long johns and extra layers of insulation. "Unfortunately, he could not adequately protect his driving hand from the cold, for he could not encumber the fingers that held the lines. On this hand he wore a silk glove next to the skin, covered by a buckskin glove, protection so slim that following any bad weather stagedrivers were to be seen loafing about stations, nursing frost-bitten hands." Sometimes in severe weather the drivers bundled up in such heavy clothing that they gave the impression that Saint Nick himself had arrived on the stage.[39]

To lonely dwellers in the northern Rocky Mountains the annual breakup of the ice on the Missouri and Columbia rivers was the most welcome event of the year, "for it was the knell of the long and tedious winter, and the certain harbinger of approaching spring."

> Fair spring! Fair spring! we welcome you here,
> To warm our vallies, and our hearts to cheer,
> Thy smiles and thy frowns we willingly bear,
> And Pray to kind Heav'n to lighten our care.[40]

Harvey Scott, editor of the *Oregonian,* put the rigors of winter travel across the northern West in historical perspective when he wrote in 1879: "Formerly we cared little. To the general community the inconvenience was small, for there were few travelers, and the business of the country was not so extensive as to make a little interruption serious. Portland did not care much for the occasional midwinter suspension, and the country and towns up and down the Columbia River really had little to do at this time of year, so we all got on comfortably enough and did not worry very much about it." But the pace of life on the West Coast had quickened to the point that the annual interruption of communication and transportation became "both inconvenient and irksome, as well as a serious drawback to the country. When the

"About Time" during the Steamboat and Stagecoach Era

Before the early 1880s, when railroads created four standard time zones in the United States, local time prevailed. On June 17, 1866, the Idaho World *explained to its readers how frontier communities reckoned the passing hours during the steamboat and stagecoach era, when idiosyncratic and imprecise timekeeping was a metaphor for a simpler age: "The difference in time between Idaho City and New York is about two hours and forty minutes; between San Francisco and this place about thirty-five minutes. When it is 12 o'clock at Idaho City it is about twenty minutes to 3 o'clock in New York and twenty-five minutes past 11 o'clock in San Francisco."*

The Blackford farm of Willow Springs, Oregon, seems to exude prosperity and to suggest population growth. Courtesy Southern Oregon Historical Society, 7916.

main avenues of our commerce are closed, even for a fortnight, we begin to feel more keenly how important it is that provision be made to overcome the obstacles thus interposed, and the railroad question, under this view, grows very much in importance." [41]

Nothing weighed more heavily in favor of railroads in the northern West than the promise of the new technology to redefine time and space and especially to offer freedom from seasonal interruptions due to inclement weather. Though this was not the only source of a railroad's competitive advantage, to settlers who had

endured the isolation imposed by winter it was certainly an important one.

What of the Future?

Unlike a steamboat or small stagecoach outfit, the typical western railroad was not a modest undertaking to be financed and built by two or three tradesmen. Except for the shortest and most primitive tramways, railroads were large-scale industrial enterprises that required vast amounts of capital. The price of a steamboat before 1860 might total several thousand dollars, yet that was only a fraction of the cost of constructing and equipping a railroad. Even Holladay's entire Overland Stage Line was cheap by comparison. Thus though individuals or partnerships might succeed in steamboat or stagecoach operations, the work of building and operating a railroad usually demanded corporate enterprise. The difficulty of carrying out a railroad project of any size was so great that planning, promoting, constructing, and equipping it usually extended over a period of years and required the investment of millions of dollars from outside the capital-starved West.

When people first thought seriously about railroad transportation across the West, some imagined only an extended portage across the six hundred miles of land that separated the navigable waters of the Missouri and Columbia rivers. People of still greater vision contemplated a railroad extending from the Great Lakes to the Pacific that was completely independent of the two historic waterways. Politicians and promoters cited dozens of reasons why such a railroad should be built, often claiming military necessity or noting how much money the federal government could save by freighting supplies by train to the army's remote outposts across the northern West. Their speeches contained numerous references to how railroads would enable the region to secure the trade of Asia which has been a great commercial prize since ancient times.

To people like Julia Gilliss, the promise of improved transportation links with the East assumed a personal significance. As she confided in a letter to her mother from Fort Dalles: "There is a project on foot to start a line of steam-wagons across the plains very soon, that will render the journey of only six days duration which now takes a stage between thirty & forty days. The capital in hand amounts to six millions, so I hope it will be carried out; then we can run back and forth to spend the day." Few statements have so succinctly explained how the new railroad technology would lighten the burdens that time and space imposed on westerners.[42]

*H*arbingers of the future: railroad location engineers in the Siskiyou Mountains of southern Oregon. Courtesy Southern Oregon Historical Society.

Landscapes of the Steamboat and Stagecoach Era

During the formative fifties, observers from outside the region so often misperceived the Pacific Northwest that Washington's Governor Isaac I. Stevens complained that his territory's remoteness "has operated prejudicially" to its best interests. "Our territory seems almost a *terra incognita* at home [on the East Coast], yet, it is situated on the great highway of the road of nations, and has the most magnificent and capacious harbors and roadsteads either on the Atlantic or Pacific shore." Stevens enumerated Washington's various attractions, including its "coal, its fisheries, its lumber, its gold, its extensive and rich grazing lands, its genial climate, its manufacturing advantages, and its soil," which presented a "combination of advantages second to no state or territory of our common country."[1]

Steamboat and stagecoach companies did not immediately step forward to advertise the attractions of Washington Territory or any other part of the trans-Mississippi West. Not in Stevens's day, and not later. Perhaps the greatest contrast between their era and that later defined by railroads was how different modes of transportation shaped the landscape of the northern West, both literally and perceptually. Transcontinental railroads, and even some regional carriers, funded elaborate advertising campaigns to sell the northern West to prospective tourists and settlers, but operators of stagecoach and steamboat lines did so only rarely. That was true even for large carriers like the Oregon Steam Navigation Company or Ben Holladay's Overland Stage Line.

It was difficult enough just to maintain reliable transportation and communication to frontier communities. "The Oregon Steam Navigation Company's enterprising spirit deserves recognition for putting steamboats on the Columbia. Nobody who understands the difficulties will deny praise," asserted Theodor Kirchhoff. "In a young, sparsely settled state, three steamboat lines, separated by the Cascades, operated on the regular and dependable schedules customary in the older states, up and down extended and dangerous stretches of river, deep into the interior of a continent. Railways were built and are maintained through wilderness and around two sets of falls and rapids: Cascades and Dalles. To work this miracle, machine shops had to be set up, barges constructed, warehouses erected, docks blasted out of cliffs, telegraph lines extended through untrodden mountain wastes—all with limited means."[2]

When steamboat and stagecoach lines advertised their services, they typically did so by posting notices in newspapers or in public places. In either case, they relied almost exclusively on blocks of black-and-white type. The use of illustrations or color was rare, and images seldom consisted of more than small, decorative woodcuts or engravings that profiled a generic steamboat or stagecoach. The general lack of visually arresting material was, of course, consistent with the printing technology of the nineteenth century. During the era of steamboat excursions in the early twentieth century, some companies did prepare more elaborate tourist brochures similar to those issued by railroads.

Apart from listing the settlements it served and giving the approximate length of the trip—"Through in Six Days to Sacramento!"—a stagecoach company might direct public attention to the advantages it offered. "Travelers avoid Risk of Ocean Travel," boasted an 1866 broadside for Henry Corbett's "Overland Mail Route to California." Listed almost as an afterthought and in the smallest type on the entire poster was one section that anticipated the kind of regional boosting that railroads did so well in later years: "This portion of the Pacific Slope embraces the most BEAUTIFUL and attractive as well as some of the most BOLD, GRAND and PICTURESQUE SCENERY on the Continent. The highest snow-capped mountains (Mt. HOOD, Mt. SHASTA and others) deepest ravines and most beautiful valleys." Devoting even this amount of attention to the countryside along the route would have been unthinkable only a decade earlier, when the bold landscape of the West was viewed mainly as an impediment to travel.[3]

Travel, however, was not the same as tourism, and during the pioneering phase of steamboat and stagecoach travel across the northern West, neither mode of passenger transportation advertised for tourists. These were vehicles intended mainly to haul passengers, goods, and express from one point to another. Any pleasure a traveler might derive from the scenery was incidental. Elaborate color posters advertising the West to tourists would wait until well after completion of the first transcontinental railroad. The same was true for the elaborate promotional brochures designed to draw settlers west.

Steamboats and stagecoaches provided basic transportation in exchange for payment, but provided no special inducements for people from outside the region to travel west. Precious metal was apparently lure enough.

Frontier travel was dangerous, and perhaps that was part of its romance, at least in hindsight. The Columbia bar was a well-recognized peril to travelers. Danger also lurked along the banks of the upper Missouri River in the 1860s. At Great Bend (1,280 miles above Saint Louis), where the river made a forty-mile loop that was only three miles across by land, the steamer *W. J. Lewis* hailed the crew of another boat and asked if anyone had seen its engineer and a party of travelers that had started across the neck of the bend to hunt, intending to meet the boat when it came around. "Some Indians probably got them, as they were never found."[4]

Captain Grant Marsh recalled making a trip from Saint Louis to Montana in the 1860s aboard the steamer *Luella*. Her pilothouse, "like that of every upper-river boat was sheathed with boiler iron against which the bullets of the savages might patter harmlessly. The people in the cabins below were not quite so well protected, but among them all there was only one who so completely lost his nerve that he could not bring himself to go through to Fort Benton. This was the boat's clerk, a young fellow named Mellon. So panic-stricken did he become that he was on the verge of nervous collapse when the *Luella* reached Milk River, Montana, 350 miles below her destination. Here was encountered the deep-draft steamer *Rubicon,* Captain Horace Bixby, which, finding herself unable to proceed farther upstream, was preparing to return to St. Louis. Regardless of protests and ridicule, Mellon immediately left the *Luella* and took passage on the *Rubicon* for home."[5]

Stagecoaching, especially along the central overland route during the 1860s, also entailed the possibility of an Indian attack. At most times, this was no real threat, but the fear of attack was real enough: "Wild rumors of Indian depredations continued to reach us almost daily—sometimes the reports were so thick that they came every few hours—recounting the brutalities

Stagecoach Tourism

Overland stages were strictly utilitarian vehicles. Companies did not normally advertise for or attempt to cater to tourists, and most tourists would have found several days of stagecoaching unbearable. Stagecoaches later became familiar for day trips in national parks like Yellowstone and Yosemite, and even today they continue to haul sightseers around Yellowstone. Occupying the middle ground between these two opposites were stages that operated in the mid-1880s out of Kelton, Utah, on the transcontinental railroad.

"Tourists will also bear in mind, that this is the station nearest to the great Shoshone Falls. These falls are 110 miles from Kelton. Passengers from the east will arrive at about 10 o'clock P.M., and stay all night. Passengers from the west will arrive at about two o'clock A.M. The next morning they will take the stage run by the North-western Stage Company, 100 miles to Rock Creek Station, which are made over good roads in twelve hours. Here you will stay over night, and take a team the next morning for the falls; distance ten miles over a lava plain, with stinted sage brush. No sight of the great falls is seen, until you reach a point one mile from them, when they suddenly burst upon the eye with a grandeur and magnificence truly bewildering."

—from Pacific Tourist (1884), 187

being committed by the hostiles down the Platte east of Latham. Some of the stories told almost made the blood run cold," recalled Frank Root. "From the best information to be gathered, there were hostiles north, south and east of us, but the route between Latham and Denver was open, and the overland stages between these two points, and also the line to Salt Lake and beyond, ran daily without interruption. I never before experienced such feelings, and trust I never shall again."[6]

Despite the dangers, real or perceived, the stagecoach offered travelers a relatively easy way to view the frontier West. "Our road traversed portions of Colorado, Dacotah, Montana and Utah, over endless wastes; and among the Black Hills, Wind River, Uintah and Wasatch ranges and offshoots of the Rocky Mountains. We saw clear trout-haunted brooks and little lakes; lofty peaks; terrible wastes white with alkali; dreary ashen hills of bare drab

earth, the parched ground deeply gashed and gullied, the faint streams bitter and poisonous, blinding dust filling the air; and no atom of vegetable life except the sage-brush and the cactus. This is indeed the desert—the very abomination of desolation," added Albert D. Richardson.[7]

In staging overland, "it was all-day and all-night riding over the rolling prairies, as it was across the plains and over the rugged mountain passes. But," emphasized Frank Root, "one would enjoy the long all-night rides far better when going along the Platte river, especially when there was a moon, which lighted up the surrounding country, its silvery rays being reflected in the waters of the beautiful stream, which silently flowed along the great overland pathway."[8]

Steamboats offered passengers a somewhat different view of the landscape of the northern West, portions

In the Columbia River's hinterland was Palouse Falls, portrayed here in Captain John Mullan's Report on the Construction of a Military Road from Fort Walla-Walla to Fort Benton *(1863). This spectacular landmark in eastern Washington is a state park today, but it did not become a tourist attraction during the steamboat and stagecoach era because, though it lay within five miles of the north bank of the lower Snake River, it was too difficult for passengers to reach. Courtesy Day-Northwest Collection, University of Idaho Library.*

A herd of bison near Lake Jessie,
a portion of the millions that roamed
the Great Plains during the time of the
Pacific Railroad Survey. Courtesy Day-
Northwest Collection, University of
Idaho Library.

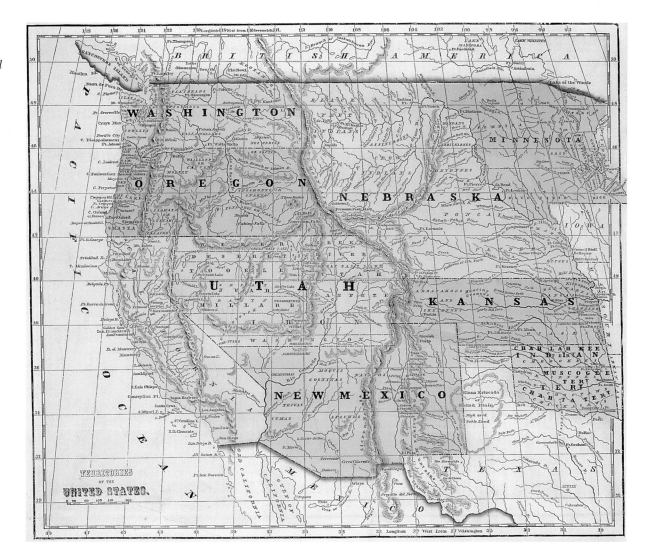

A map of the northern West during the late 1850s, when both Oregon and Washington extended to the Continental Divide, which marked the eastern boundary of the old Oregon Country. Courtesy Special Collections Division, University of Washington Libraries, N 979.5 Map #52.

of which obviously had great tourist appeal even in the early years of travel. "Clear, blue, glassy, dotted with little islands of greenest foliage, and broken by dangerous rapids which make steamers shake like rocking-chairs, the Columbia is unrivaled upon our continent, in grandeur and magnitude. The Hudson no more compares with it than does the Arkansas with the Hudson," or so Richardson claimed in the mid-1860s.[9]

But railroads promised still greater inducements to prospective tourists: "One sees, at a glance, that the Northern Pacific will at once become the favorite route

for tourists from the East," Harvey Scott predicted in the *Oregonian* during the summer of 1882. "On none of the other railroads is there anything to compare with its noble scenery. The blank and tedious sameness, presented on the other routes, gives place here to the most agreeable variety and pleasant surroundings."[10]

Railroads also had an advantage when it came to colonization. The small amount of personal baggage a stagecoach could carry discouraged companies from promoting western settlement, whereas later, railroads would offer to carry the household belongings of any

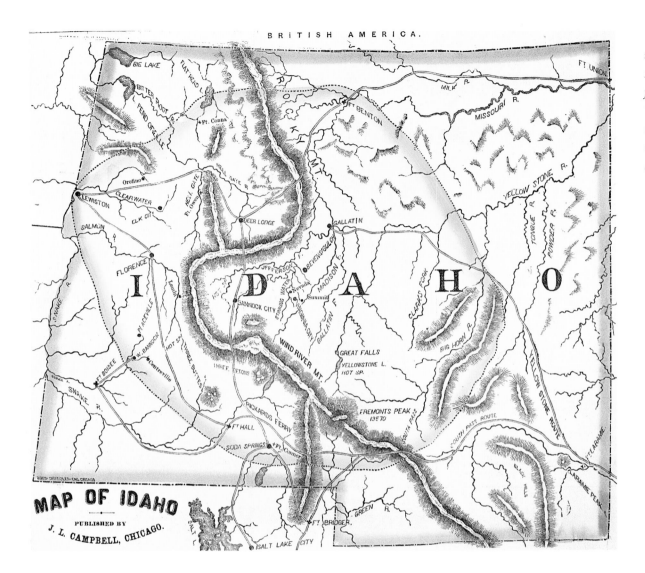

prospective settler in a boxcar, and at a very attractive "colonist" rate. Railroads with their high fixed costs and their vast land grants (in the case of several transcontinental lines) had every inducement to encourage settlement along their tracks. Even before both parts of the Northern Pacific line were finally spiked together in 1883, it occurred to many people that if they wanted to claim the best land of the northern West, they had better hurry before transcontinental trains brought crowds of homeseekers from the Midwest and East. In June, just four months before the rails met in Montana, prospective settlers crowded aboard coastal steamers between San Francisco and Portland to race ahead of people soon expected to arrive by train. The "tide of immigration" severely "tested the capacity" of the steamships and "caused the putting on of more vessels and the making of more frequent trips both to the Columbia River and Puget Sound. We now have a steamer every three days that brings a full load of passengers—probably 700 would be an average."[11]

The popular expectation was that after the Northern Pacific opened a new transcontinental line "immigrants can reach their destinations and locate themselves with half the time and expense now incurred. The thousands now arriving are aware of the advantage of having an early choice of location." It was curious to see, observed the *New York Times* in mid-1883, "thousands every week coming in and scattering through the country, absorbed and then disappearing from view as if the earth swallowed them. The process goes on very quietly. Information of a general character is well distributed and they all have some destination. Some have friends who they visit first, and perhaps leave their families with them while they prospect for a homestead."[12]

During the steamboat and stagecoach era, the representative machines and their support structures formed a small presence in an expansive landscape. Apart from the ubiquitous relay posts of the longer stage lines or the portage railroads that linked steamboats on the Columbia River, these pioneering technologies did not leave enduring evidence across the northern West, as railroads later did with their tracks, bridges, tunnels, and stations. Perhaps the single most impressive example of infrastructure building to meet the needs of steamboats was the Cascades Canal that the United States Army Corps of Engineers completed in the mid-1890s; but by that late date, railroads had already written their own bold signatures across the landscape of the northern West.

Stagecoaching left almost as faint a physical imprint on the land as steamboating did on the water. "Many a time, way out on the plains . . . one could see," Frank Root observed, "while sitting on the stage-box with the driver, a tiny cloud of dust, but could only conjecture what might have caused it. Small as it appeared at first, it would steadily grow larger and, for a few moments, invariably set one to thinking and asking himself 'What is it?' . . . No one at first could tell. The cloud was becoming larger and rapidly driving nearer. We knew that it would not be long until our curiosity would be gratified. Soon it was discovered to be the approaching stage-

coach, which could now and then be seen in spite of the dust, as it rounded a curve and gently rocked to and fro on its thoroughbraces. The two vehicles were steadily coming nearer together. Only a minute or two more and the prancing, foaming steeds hitched to the two Concords had drawn up and stopped alongside each other. After the drivers had exchanged the usual 'Howdy,' and perhaps with a laugh or a joke, or 'Give me a chaw of tobacker,' or 'Will you join me in a drink of 'tarantula juice?' each would then throw the lash into his leaders, and the two vehicles were almost instantly moving away from each other towards the rising and setting sun." Except for the light imprint of their wheels along the dusty road, they had vanished from the landscape.[13]

Yet, in the larger sense they did permanently alter the landscape of the northern West by making Euro-American settlement not only possible but also more comfortable than it would have been without mail and express service, or wagon freighting of food and a few of life's luxuries, or at least the possibility of regularly scheduled public transportation. They also had an economic impact that was perhaps most visible when they were gone. After the coming of railroads, many stagecoach and freight lines closed down, idling an army of agents, drivers, stock tenders, and station keepers. Owners often could not sell their teams or rolling stock at any price; and farmers rued the loss of valued customers for their grain and hay. Most farmers would eventually find other markets, and unemployed stagemen and teamsters would migrate to other jobs; but across the northern West there was no return to the landscape—whether physical, economic, or social—that existed before the steamboat and stagecoach era.

Where the Willamette and Columbia rivers meet: looking south from Vancouver, Washington, across to Portland and up the Willamette Valley. A portion of Sauvie Island around which the Beaver steamed in 1836 is visible in the lower right corner. Courtesy Oregon Historical Society, 91811.

A map of Portland, Oregon, in 1881, by which time the settlement had expanded along both banks of the Willamette River. The Columbia River and snow-clad peaks of the Cascade Range are visible in the background. *Courtesy Oregon Historical Society, 91805.*

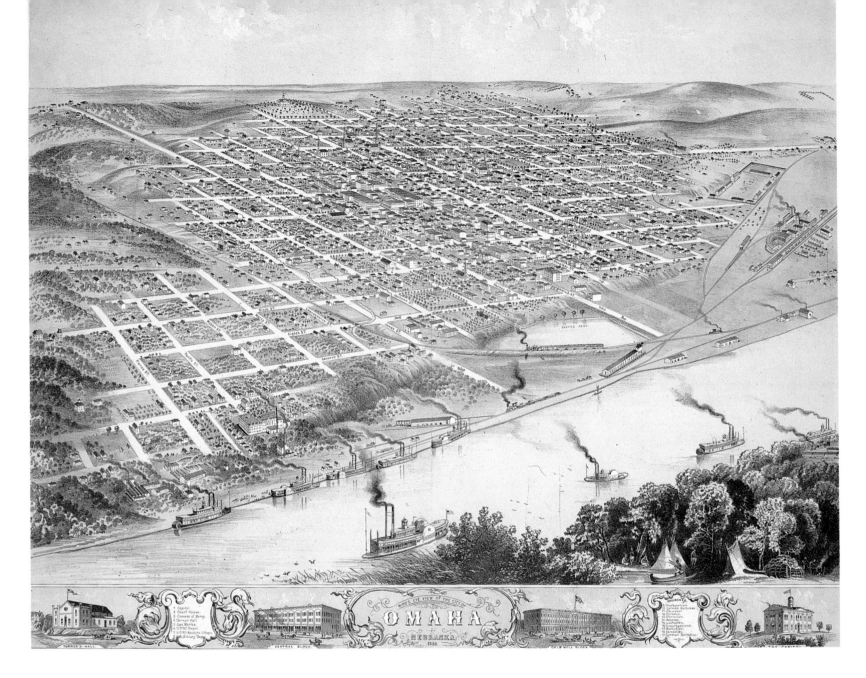

*T*he Missouri River and Omaha, Nebraska, in 1868, the Union Pacific's new gateway to the West. At this time no railroad bridge yet connected Council Bluffs and Omaha. By 1880 Crofutt's New Overland Tourist, and Pacific Coast Guide *was* able to observe, "Thus we see that the 'Far West' of to-day has become far removed from the West of thirty—or even ten— years ago, and what is now the central portion of our commonwealth was then, the Far, Far West." Eight years later the same publication recalled, "When we published our first trans-continental book, September 1, 1869, the Missouri river was the rec- ognized frontier line. It was there all travelers for the great unknown, towards the setting sun, congregated; it was there they bid good-by to many friends, or mailed their parting lines, many times with fearful misgivings for the future." Courtesy Library of Congress.

*T*he Union Pacific system across
Wyoming and north into Montana.
In this railroad portrait of the northern
West, the Missouri River and whatever
steamboat competition it offered fades
from view at the top of the map. Courtesy Oregon Historical Society, 91823.

GARFIELD BEACH.   AMERICAN NATIONAL BANK   PROGRESS BUILDING.   HOTEL ONTARIO.   TEMPLE & GROUNDS.   WASATCH BUILDING.   MIDLAND INVESTMENT CO'S   AND   GRAND VIEW ADDITION   POPPERTON

A map of Salt Lake City, the onetime hub of overland stagecoaching in the northern West, shows the prosperous metropolis in 1891. Two decades earlier, the steamboats City of Corinne *and* Kate Connor *churned across the Great Salt Lake to haul ore from mines in the Oquirrh Mountains west of Salt Lake City to the railhead at Corinne on the Bear River. Neither vessel proved profitable. Courtesy Library of Congress.*

A freighters camp in eastern Oregon. This illustration from the front cover of West Shore, *July 26, 1890, suggests the emptiness of the landscape. Courtesy Oregon Historical Society.*

MERRIMAC BRAND

BELOW U. S. STANDARD

GOOD FOOD - NOT HIGH GRADE

WATER PACK

APRICOTS

NET CONTENTS 6 LBS. 4 OZ.

PACKED BY

SEUFERT BROS. COMPANY

THE DALLES, OREGON

*A*n apricot label from the Seufert
Brothers cannery in The Dalles features
a steamboat nearly overwhelmed by the
spectacular scenery of Multnomah Falls
and the Columbia River gorge. Courtesy
Oregon Historical Society, MSS 102.

A Combined Harvester Scene.
Near Colfax, Wash.

A combine harvester near Colfax,
Washington, where grain began its long
journey to market. Courtesy Special
Collections Division, University of
Washington Libraries.

Tramway for conveying wheat from field to warehouse on Snake River, a tributary of the Columbia

High bluffs along the lower Snake River made it difficult to convey grain from farms and ranches on the plateau to steamboats below. One innovation was a wooden pipe four inches square and 3,200 feet long that ran down Knoxway Canyon and entered the roof of a warehouse. Soon pipelines made of wood, sheet iron, or tin appeared at other locations along the Snake River. These were a mixed success because in the earliest ones the grain traveled too fast and burned off the hulls, but after modification some pipelines remained in use until well after the first railroad line was extended along the river in 1907. The first bucket tram was strung in 1893 and operated for several decades. Courtesy Special Collections Division, University of Washington Libraries.

A special insert in the Oregonian *celebrated the opening of the Cascade Locks in 1896. The image on the left depicts the locks at Oregon City, with Portland in the distance. Courtesy Oregon Historical Society, 91819.*

OREGON—A Steamboat Passing Through the Locks at Oregon City.

A closer view of the locks at Oregon City, as depicted by West Shore, *August 2, 1890. This image suggests how the steamboat changed the landscape of the Willamette River. Yet when compared to the impact of railway and highway engineering in later decades, the built environment created to serve the needs of steamboats left a relatively modest physical signature. Courtesy Oregon Historical Society.*

This postcard image shows ocean shipping on the Columbia River near Astoria. Author's collection.

This turn-of-the-century postcard image highlights the working waterfront of Coeur d'Alene, Idaho. Author's collection

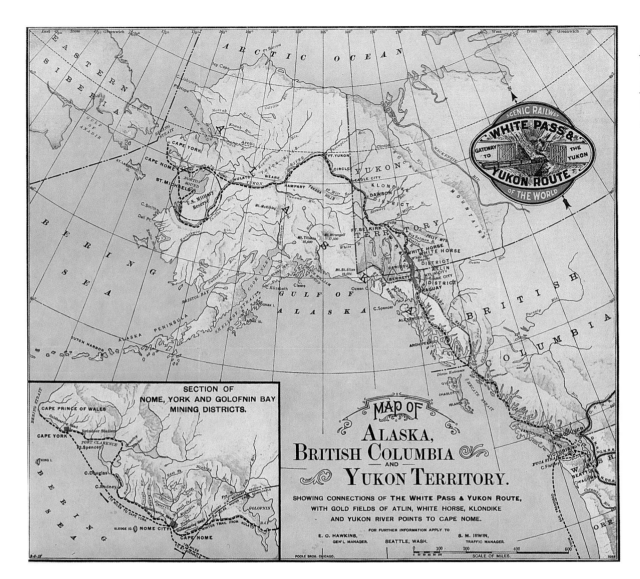

This map shows the North Pacific coast from Seattle to Alaska in the early twentieth century, the area that became a last frontier for some of the steam-powered boats and ships of the northern West. Courtesy Library of Congress.

*B*oth the company name and the imagery on this 1932 schedule depict the modern bus as the successor to the overland stagecoach. Author's collection.

Before the construction of railroads to the Pacific, the States of California and Oregon were, owing to the difficulty of reaching them, practically as remote from the Atlantic and [Mid-] Western States as though they formed part of another continent. The fame of their favored climate and great natural resources had previously attracted to them, it is true, a considerable population from the older States; but the flow of immigration remained sluggish until the completion of those artificial highways had greatly reduced the expenditure of time and money, and the hardships of a journey to the Pacific.
—Oregon . . . For the Use of Immigrants *(1876)*

Reconfiguring the West, 1869–1900

F. Jay Haynes photographed at least eight Northern Pacific locomotives testing the strength of the new railroad bridge across the Missouri River at Bismarck, Dakota Territory, on October 21, 1882. Courtesy Montana State Historical Society, H-815.

Compared with ocean vessels, these river steamers seem light and fragile as pasteboard, and if they take fire, they burn like tinder. But many run fifteen miles an hour with the current, carry enormous loads, and often pay for themselves in a single year. Still their hey-day is over. The conquering railway robs them of nearly all passengers, and much freight. Gone forever the era of universal racing, with all its attendant excitements;—its pet steamers, high wagers, and fierce rivalry!
—*Albert D. Richardson,* Beyond the Mississippi: From the Great River to the Great Ocean *(1867)*

A happy day for Union Pacific workers: the paymaster's car is recorded by A. J. Russell. Courtesy Utah State Historical Society, ƒ385/p5, 846.

Overland to Promontory and Beyond

From a distance and to the untutored eye the commemorative monument that occupies a windswept plateau between Cheyenne and Laramie, Wyoming, may resemble a large, naturally occurring pile of boulders. This two-step pyramid is actually the only structure west of Saint Louis designed by the architect Henry Hobson Richardson, who was without doubt the leading figure in his profession in the United States during the 1870s and 1880s. The style now known as Richardsonian Romanesque favored heavy and dramatic design elements; and indeed the cairn fashioned from random blocks of native red granite has a rugged appearance suitably Richardsonian.

Near the top of the sixty-foot-high monument is the artistry of yet another scion of New England, Augustus Saint-Gaudens, who sculpted the bas-relief medallions of the brothers Oakes and Oliver Ames. Richardson's contemporary, Frederick Law Olmsted, the landscape architect and designer of New York's Central Park, viewed the Ames pyramid shortly after it was completed in 1879, and the sight moved him to pen this enigmatic comment: "I never saw a monument so well befitting its situation or a situation so well befitting the special character of a particular monument."[1]

This oddly located display of American artistic talent makes sense only when the modern observer realizes that this plateau was once the highest point on the Union Pacific Railroad (some 8,247 feet above sea level), and when the company finally realized its destiny to form the eastern half of the nation's first transcontinental railroad, it was because the Ames brothers, two Massachusetts shovel magnates with connections on Wall Street and Capitol Hill, had supplied the needed financial and political muscle. But no tracks pass here now. In 1901 the Union Pacific relocated its main line about four miles south, leaving behind the Ames Monument as a singular reminder to the occasional visitor that the pattern of transportation across the West is always evolving. Another forceful reminder of that truism is the National Park Service's Golden Spike National Historical Site at Promontory Summit, Utah. It receives far more visitors than the Ames Monument, and there is actually a short section of track along which run replicas of the Union Pacific and Central Pacific locomotives that met there in 1869. Again, however, the modern railroad has relocated its tracks miles away.

Even before Union Pacific trains reached Promontory, the new railroad line fostered the rise of new towns along its right-of-way across Wyoming, among them Cheyenne, Laramie, Rawlins, and Rock Springs. At the same time, it forced out of business most of the freight wagons that once lumbered across the high plains and mountains and the brightly painted stagecoaches that once sprinted along the central overland route. Together with the Central Pacific, it offered improved transportation to settlements in the northern Rocky Mountains and created new competition for steamboats that plied the Columbia and Missouri rivers. At Corinne, Utah, north of the Great Salt Lake, passengers and freight transferred from Union Pacific trains to stagecoaches and wagons that headed north to eastern Idaho and Montana. Farther west, a variety of conveyances met Central Pacific trains at Kelton, Utah, to haul freight and passengers northwest to Boise, Walla Walla, and The Dalles; at Winnemucca, in northern Nevada, Central Pacific trains established new and shorter connections between California and southern Idaho. Today nothing remains of Kelton except for a Bureau of Land Management historical marker indicating that this was once the main gateway from the East into Idaho and the Pacific Northwest. The site is as solitary as that of the Ames Monument: for both locations it was only the passing trains that truly energized them.

Envisioning a Transcontinental Railroad

Well before freight and passenger trains could thread their way through the expansive western landscape, the idea of a transcontinental railroad had first to gain popular credibility. As early as 1838, when the missionary Samuel Parker published his *Tour Beyond the Rocky Mountains* detailing his experiences in the northern West (including his excursion aboard the *Beaver*), he predicted that a transcontinental railroad could be built easily and inexpensively. Few Americans at the time were so optimistic. First, it would be very costly to extend a transcontinental railroad across the Great American Desert, an area with few farms or towns to offer investors any prospect of a return on their money. Then there was the primitive technology itself. At the beginning of the 1830s exactly twenty-three miles of working railroad track

existed in the entire Western Hemisphere, and these consisted mainly of hardwood rails topped with a bearing surface of strap iron. By 1840 a total of 2,818 miles of track—constructed for the most part of iron rails— served the main population centers of the United States; by 1850 the nation had 9,021 miles of functioning track, and this increased during the next ten years to an imposing 30,626 miles. Each year during the formative fifties, on average, 2,160 miles of new track were spiked into place, yet only a fraction of the total was located west of the Mississippi River, mainly in Missouri and California.

Despite technological improvements and rapid evolution of a railroad network in the Northeast, travel by train was not yet a particularly safe mode of transportation. According to the *American Railroad Journal*, 903 railroad accidents occurred during the last seven years of the 1850s, and some of them were spectacular. These wrecks killed 1,109 people (mostly employees) and injured another 3,611; however, the *American Railroad Journal* seemed almost smug when it noted that during the same span of time, 2,304 people died in 203 recorded steamboat accidents. No one was immune to death in a railroad accident, not even the only son of President-elect Franklin Pierce, who was horribly mangled and killed before his parents' eyes in a train derailment outside Boston in early 1853. The death of eleven-year-old Bennie apparently unhinged his mother and cast a gloomy shadow across the White House during four critical years in American history.

To inventive minds in both the North and the South, the improvement of transportation presented intriguing challenges. Between 1820 and 1860, despite national growing pains in the form of an occasional financial panic, civil engineers (most of them self-educated) and tinkerers rearranged the landscape of the northeastern United States by building a complex network of canals and turnpikes, while a growing fleet of steamboats plied thousands of miles of rivers and lakes. The "transportation revolution" joined together communities, states, and even regions, but largely because of geographical obstacles it failed to bind together the nation as a whole.

Americans who used commercial transportation to travel from one coast to another before the Civil War still depended mainly on the circuitous sea routes.

Only during the last half of the 1840s did the dream of a transcontinental railroad gain national attention. That was, after all, the decade of expansion when Americans acquired nearly half of Mexico (if Texas is included), a flood of emigrants headed west in search of Oregon farms and California gold, Mormons trekked to Utah, and the nation agonized over the growing sectional split between North and South. Prominent among the early dreamers was Asa Whitney, a wealthy Connecticut-born New York City merchant, who in early 1845 sent Congress a memorial stressing the importance of such a project and recommending that it grant a swath of land sixty miles wide from Lake Michigan to the Pacific to subsidize construction.

A convert to railroad transportation from the time he first pondered the new technology in England a decade earlier, Whitney emphasized how a Pacific railroad could divert the rich trade of Asia, so long controlled by Europeans, into American hands. He had been in China in 1843 when the emperor opened the first five ports there to free trade; a decade later, Commodore Perry's "opening" of Japan provided an added inducement to supporters of a Pacific railroad. One of Whitney's most influential converts was the explorer John C. Fremont, who prophesied that an American railroad would form a "golden vein" to channel trade between Asia and Europe. Fremont's enthusiasm derived from his extensive personal knowledge of the West's seemingly boundless space.[2]

Congress responded in 1853 and 1854 by appropriating $340,000 for the United States Army's Corps of Topographical Engineers "to ascertain the most practicable and economical route for a railroad from the Mississippi River to the Pacific Ocean." Isaac Stevens, first territorial governor of Washington, led the team that surveyed a northern transcontinental route. The federal government published his data together with that collected on four other possible routes in thirteen lavishly illustrated volumes between 1857 and 1860 to make visible and concrete what a few years earlier had been only a matter of speculation.

Meanwhile, the Pacific Railroad Company of Missouri (later the Missouri Pacific) attained the distinction of being the first enterprise to lay rails west of the Mississippi River. This railroad obtained a charter on March 12, 1849, and the following February made a formal request for a right-of-way and donations of government land. It broke ground at Saint Louis on July 4, 1851—fourteen years before the Union Pacific commenced building west from Omaha—and the tracks reached Franklin (now Pacific), thirty-eight miles west of Saint Louis, two years later. By 1858 the trains ran another 122 miles to Tipton, from whence John Butterfield's stagecoaches rolled west across the continent to San Francisco.

On the Pacific Slope the Sacramento Valley Railroad opened in early 1856 between Sacramento and Folsom to connect steamboats of the California Steam Navigation Company with stagecoaches that sped to mining camps in the Sierra Nevada. But apart from the Sacramento Valley Railroad and a short portage line around the Cascades of the Columbia River, the railway operating farthest west on the continent was the Hannibal and Saint Joseph in northern Missouri. Not long after the final spike was driven in 1859, Saint Joseph emerged as an important shipping center on the Missouri River and the starting point for the overland mail.

The North Missouri Railroad soon offered competition, but guerrilla warfare during the Civil War caused disruptions on both lines. Saint Joseph and Atchison feared that transcontinental mail service would be relocated north to safer ground in Iowa, a move that would benefit the new town of Omaha. The Civil War further called into question the nation's dependence upon round-about sea links via Cape Horn and the Isthmus of Panama. Confederate commerce raiders such as the *Alabama* and *Florida* caused insurance rates on the Cape Horn route to inflate by some 700 percent, and when the Southern warship *Shenandoah* cruised off the West Coast in 1865 it underscored the threat that existed there also.

ACROSS THE CONTINENT,
"WESTWARD THE COURSE OF EMPIRE TAKES ITS WAY."

Despite opposition from wagon freight and stage companies in California, President Abraham Lincoln signed the Pacific Railroad Act on June 20, 1862. At this time more than half of all passengers bound for the West Coast and most freight went by sea.

Congress supported both the Central Pacific and Union Pacific railroads with generous land grants and loans. At the same time it imposed restrictions that not only delayed construction but inflated costs as well; for example, Congressman Thaddeus Stevens of Pennsylvania required that only American iron be used for tracks. British rails were two or three times cheaper, but Stevens was solicitous of his own constituents. Worse still, the military had such an enormous appetite for iron and iron products that as long as the Civil War raged, Pacific railroad builders had to compete with the federal government for scarce iron.

Congress increased construction costs in other ways as well, chiefly through the technical restrictions it imposed on the Pacific railroads: it permitted no grade in excess of 116 feet per mile (even in the mountains)—specifications for grade and curvature were based on those of the successful Baltimore and Ohio Railroad—despite the fact that grades in excess of 200 feet per mile were common on New England carriers. This mandate meant expensive cuts, fills, and tunnels; a limitation on tight curves virtually eliminated the use of switchbacks.

Months passed during which rails were unavailable at any price. Each ton of rails, moreover, cost $17.50 to ship around Cape Horn to San Francisco, and during the Civil War both the cost of shipping and insurance premiums soared. The price of common spikes—2.5 cents a pound before the war—jumped to 6.5 cents. That of blasting powder rose from $2.50 to as high as $15.00 a keg. In addition, the purchase of explosives during the Civil War required a special Presidential license. Because of wartime inflation the *Huntington,* a small locomotive the Central Pacific had shipped west via Cape Horn, cost $13,688, a sum that ballooned to almost twice an earlier estimate.

The Road to Promontory

Despite the Central Pacific's numerous start-up troubles—including a congressional mandate that forced it to re-lay the first thirty miles of track to standard gauge (4′ 8½″)—the California railroad at first made more impressive progress than the Union Pacific. To the accompaniment of brass bands, it broke ground at Sacramento in January 1863, while the Union Pacific turned its first spade of earth early the following December in Omaha. Charles Crocker of the Central Pacific early solved the problem of a chronic labor shortage by hiring gangs of Chinese workers, importing several thousand each year. At one time he commanded an army of fifteen thousand men, mainly Chinese and Irish, all working in different camps to surmount the granite mass of the Sierra.

While Crocker's tracklayers progressed slowly east from Sacramento, the Speaker of the House and future vice-president, Schuyler Colfax of Indiana, commenced a tour of the American West. His entourage, which included Samuel Bowles, editor of the *Springfield Republican,* and Albert D. Richardson, war correspondent of the *New York Tribune,* crossed the Great Plains from Omaha to Denver under the protection of the United States cavalry. Thanks to the generosity of Ben Holladay, the Speaker traveled in style aboard the Stagecoach King's own deluxe Concord with its well-stocked bar.

When the Colfax party at last reached California in mid-1865, Leland Stanford, the most politically astute of California's "Big Four" railroad builders, invited the Speaker and his entourage to ride with him into the foothills where Central Pacific tracks ended near the settlement of Illinoistown. Along the way, railroad officials lavishly wined and dined their special guests, and then as the day's grand finale they renamed the town at the end of the track for Colfax. The Central Pacific, unlike the Union Pacific, was not a creation of Congress, but it still needed friends in high places.

During an earlier stop in Omaha, Colfax had inspected the Union Pacific. Its tracklaying went forward only slowly because of Civil War labor shortages, and

even as late as the end of 1865 its workmen had spiked down only forty miles of track. But soon the pace of construction quickened, especially after the federal government provided more protection to the railroad during the protracted conflict in the mid-1860s with the Sioux, Cheyenne, Arapaho, and other hostile Indians of the Great Plains.

When Union Pacific rails reached North Platte, three hundred miles west of Omaha, stagecoaches ceased offering service parallel to the new railroad line but stepped up service beyond the end of the track, where business

increased so much that it became necessary to run three coaches a day and an express wagon every other day. By the end of 1866, the tedious stage ride between the ends of each railroad was shortened from seventeen to ten days. For another two years, until the tracks were joined at Promontory, the big Concord coaches bridged the ever shrinking gap.

On November 13, 1867, when Jack Casement and his track crews reached Cheyenne, they were met by a brass band and an assemblage of citizens bearing banners, including one that read: "Old Casement We Welcome

You." Almost immediately the new settlement by the tracks became a crossroads and melting pot of the West. Day and night its dirt streets overflowed with buffalo hunters, trappers, traders, railway workers, engineers, Indians, soldiers, mule skinners, bullwhackers, stage drivers, gamblers, actors, miners, and assorted ruffians. Less than a year after the first tracks arrived, Wyoming Territory was formally organized.

Construction crews on both railroads raced toward one another at hitherto unprecedented rates. Charlie Crocker's men once spiked down ten miles of track in a single day, and the laborers of the Union Pacific were not far behind. At times the process continued as rapidly as a man could walk. "Behind the cars follow two boys on each side, who drop the spikes, others set the ties well under the ends of the rails, then come thirty or forty men driving in the spikes and stamping the earth under the ties."[3]

Federal legislators who framed the Pacific Railroad acts of 1862 and 1864 failed to designate where the two railroads should meet to form a continuous line of track from the Missouri River to Sacramento. Because every mile of railroad increased the size of its federal subsidy, each company pushed ahead as far and as fast as possible. The 1864 legislation actually gave the two railroads until 1875 to join their tracks, but their need for return on capital compelled them to hurry toward completion. It was in anticipation of that glorious day that the Portland *Oregonian* confidently predicted that "the year 1869 will witness a most striking revolution in the course of travel and mail transportation between the Eastern and Western seaboards. It is now almost certain that during next year the great railway track across the continent will be completed, and then, fare well to the glory of the steamships." Farewell also to a decade of overland staging.[4]

Frank Root, whose life was intimately linked to the central overland route, had mixed feelings as he reflected on what the final spike meant to stagemen: "The generation then living, and for years eagerly watching the progress of the building of the road, will never forget that glorious day of May 10, 1869. The event was eagerly watched by the nation, for it comes but once in a life-

time. It will be remembered as a day of vast importance in history, for it closed the era of overland staging on the great central route." North of the Great Salt Lake at Promontory the railroad dignitaries drove a last spike to form a line of tracks extending from the Atlantic to the Pacific and spoke many flowery words about the significance of the wedding of the rails. No part of the northern West seemed too remote to remain unchanged by the new transportation technology. Even in distant Deer Lodge, Montana, located nearly five hundred miles north of the newly joined tracks, a newspaper prophesied that "its completion will be the means of settling up the Rocky mountain country in an incredibly short space of time, and rendering it the most desirable place of residence on the continent."[5]

A decade later *Crofutt's New Overland Tourist* mused that the "change wrought within the last few years have robbed the plains of its most attractive feature, to those who are far away from the scene—the emigrant train. Once, the south bank of the Platte was one broad thoroughfare, whereon the long trains of the emigrants, with their white-covered wagons, could be seen stretching away for many miles in an almost unbroken chain. Now, on the north side of the same river, in almost full view of the 'old emigrant road,' the cars are bearing the freight and passengers rapidly westward, while the oxen that used to toil so wearily along this route, has been transformed into 'western veal' to tickle the palates of those passengers, or else, like Tiny Tim, they have been compelled to 'move on' to some new fields of labor."[6]

New Gateways to the Northern West

Moving on was the lot of the western stage driver during the early years of the new age of railways. The same day that the rails met at Promontory, Sam Getts drove the last stage out of Salt Lake City on the central overland route. The following day he returned to Salt Lake and commenced driving for a feeder line that met the rails at Ogden. Getts moved to Montana the following year to work as a driver and later as superintendent for Gilmer and Salisbury until the completion of a Union Pacific branch north to Butte in the 1880s ended stage service along that route too.

This pattern was typical for the years 1869 to 1900, which saw a gradual winding down of the stagecoach and steamboat era. Although resplendent Concord coaches and steamboats no longer defined progress in the continuing contest to conquer time and space, neither did these two pioneer modes of transportation soon disappear. They simply sought to survive in an age when railroads defined the latest advances in speed and comfort. Each time a railroad superseded stage operations on one route, many of the displaced coaches moved on to link still smaller and more isolated towns and villages with the spreading network of tracks, and in this way stagecoaches served remote parts of the West as late as the 1930s. Steamboats found new jobs to do, too, such as running special excursions for Sunday school classes or hauling local freight instead of pioneering new routes to the goldfields, although the Klondike rush to Alaska in 1898 provided some of the West's veteran boatmen a sense of déjà vu.

In 1866 the directors of the Union Pacific paused at the hundredth meridian, 257 miles from Omaha and the symbolic meeting place of East and West. This is the site of Cozad, Nebraska, today. Courtesy Library of Congress, 408866 762 5447.

On August 26, 1869, the *Helena Herald* announced that Wells, Fargo and Company had sold the remaining northern branches of its once extensive overland stage system, including the mail contract between Ogden and Helena and seventy thousand dollars' worth of nearly new coaches and equipment, to two Salt Lake City entrepreneurs, Jack Thornton Gilmer and Monroe Salisbury. These two energetic men had been running stage lines in Utah and were now eager to expand their business. And expand it they did. Within a decade of their purchases from Wells Fargo, Gilmer and Salisbury coaches operated under a variety of names to serve the main mining regions of the northern West. The partners' most famous route—and the one Buffalo Bill Cody immortalized in his Wild West extravaganzas—was the Deadwood line between Cheyenne and the Black Hills. During the 1870s and 1880s these two businessmen

earned a nice profit utilizing a technology that many Americans considered passé.

Gilmer became the dominant member of the largest stagecoaching firm to succeed Wells Fargo, and he was the partner who handled the day-to-day operations. His entry into the transportation business had been as a bullwhacker and mule skinner for Russell, Majors and Waddell in the 1850s. He served an apprenticeship as one of the first stagecoach drivers on the Leavenworth and Pike's Peak Express line in 1859, later becoming a division superintendent of Ben Holladay's Consolidated Overland Mail and Express Company and briefly manager of the Idaho and Montana branches under Wells Fargo. Gilmer took great pride in claiming that he had turned the first wheels on the great central overland stage line, and the last. Before he died in 1892 he had accumulated staging and mining interests all over the West from South

Dakota to California. Salisbury, the less visible partner, eventually became a banker and moved to San Francisco.

For nearly two decades after 1869, Gilmer and Salisbury coaches sped passengers, mail, and express between Utah and Montana. The coaches of Bradley Barlow and Jared Sanderson provided the same service in parts of Colorado, Utah, Nevada, and California. John Hailey succeeded Wells Fargo in another part of the northern West by running a stage line from the railroad at Kelton via Boise and Walla Walla to The Dalles until July 1870. Pausing only briefly at stations that were spaced at twelve-mile intervals across the Snake River plain, Hailey's mail coaches daily covered the 232 miles between Kelton and Boise in forty-two hours, carrying passengers at a cost of fifty dollars each in greenbacks.

When his federal mail contract expired, Hailey sold his stock, wagons, and stations to the Northwestern Stage Company, an eastern syndicate that for another eight years held the contract for carrying mail over the southern Idaho route. At its height, the Northwestern Stage Company employed fifty drivers and owned eighty-five stations and eight hundred horses. When it lost the mail contract in 1878, this enterprise sold out to the Utah, Idaho and Oregon Stage Company. For every one of the large or middle-size firms, there were dozens of small stage outfits that provided unassuming but vital service to out-of-the-way locations, often with nothing more than a single coach or wagon.

More than a century later it is impossible to track all the stage lines that once served the northern West. There was no monthly official guide listing their schedules and services, as there was for the railroads, and the contraction of even major stage systems could be surprisingly sudden. *West Shore* reported in November 1883 that eighteen months earlier, Gilmer and Salisbury had used eight hundred horses and equipment and property worth $85,000 to provide service along an extensive network of lines in Montana. "Now their total stage lines in Montana aggregate only 175 miles, being the Helena and Dillon line, with branches to Butte and Virginia." Such was the impact of the railroads' twin ribbons of steel.[7]

Even before the first transcontinental railroad was completed, it loomed large in the transportation geography of settlers of the northern West, though few of them actually lived within easy distance of the rails. One of the first new gateways was Winnemucca, Nevada, which Central Pacific tracks reached in September 1868 and from whence a stage line ran to Silver City, shortening the distance between southern Idaho and San Francisco. But what residents of the northern West wanted even more was a better route to the East. As Harvey Scott of the *Oregonian* had editorialized in 1867, "Oregon and Washington and Idaho wish to reach this railroad by some means, or, which is better, to obtain railroad communication with the East by an independent route."[8]

Because the Northern Pacific line (the "independent route" mentioned by Scott) was not completed until 1883, most residents still had to calculate time and distance in terms of the central railroad route. "Passengers from Portland can now go through to Chicago, by the Columbia River and Idaho route, in nine days, and the fares have been reduced to moderate figures." In an 1871 editorial, Scott predicted that "a large number of people" would enter Oregon by the stagecoach and steamboat route that extended northwest from the railhead in Utah.[9]

Indeed, for a period of fifteen years the eastern gateway to southern Idaho and the Pacific Northwest remained the hamlet of Kelton, located along the Central Pacific main line about ninety miles west of Ogden. Passengers for places as distant as Boise, Walla Walla, and Portland might leave the overland train at Kelton and board a connecting stagecoach. In the early 1880s the first-class fare from Omaha to Kelton by train and continuing to Boise by stage was $96.75. For ten dollars more a traveler could go through to Walla Walla. An alternative route after 1869 was for travelers to continue all the way to San Francisco by train and proceed from there to Portland by coastal steamships. Supporters of this route boasted that it offered no disagreeable staging over dusty roads. Kelton was also where freight wagons met the trains. In 1875 alone, six million pounds of freight traveled overland from Kelton to Idaho.

Located on a sterile plain about three miles north of the Great Salt Lake, Kelton consisted of a bedraggled

During 1870 at least four different wagon companies, including the mighty Diamond R, hauled goods north to Helena from Corinne, seen here. Because so many people believed the settlement would continue to grow, there was considerable land speculation around Corinne. Courtesy Utah State Historical Society, 979.2/p.2, #15260.

cluster of about fifty frame or log houses, a hotel, three general stores, two saloons, a post office, drugstore, blacksmith shop, barbershop, two feed yards, and a restaurant—all arrayed around the depot and the large commission warehouses that handled freight for Idaho. Most travelers chose to remain in Kelton only long enough to board the next stage or train out of town.

"Kelton being notorious for its bad hotels, high prices, and uninteresting situation, I left it at the earliest opportunity, and was content with a seat in the caboose of a cattle train rather than wait there until the passenger train arrived," grumbled John Mortimer Murphy. "Moving out of the town, the long line of cars was soon winding over the great American desert, a region so barren that it yields nothing of greater utility than a coarse grass, and stunted artemisia and kindred shrubs, while its soil is so strongly alkaline in some places that it does not produce even the most useless plant."[10]

After a "tediously slow journey," Murphy's cattle train reached Corinne, "the one gentile settlement in Utah, and therefore a perfect Babylon of wickedness in the eyes of Mormons. This place was formerly unusually prosperous and enterprising, as it was the head-quarters for the numerous prairie schooners that transported goods into Montana; but since the construction of the Utah Northern Railroad it has lost its commerce and *prestige,* and is now only a sleepy village of 700 inhabitants."

Corinne was Kelton's equivalent for travelers and goods headed north from the railroad to destinations in eastern Idaho and Montana (though Corinne is still very much alive today, unlike Kelton). The chief engineer of the Union Pacific laid out the townsite in February 1869, retaining for the company the alternate town lots. At first it was just another of the hell-on-wheels settlements that sprang up alongside the advancing tracks. In one two-week period nearly five hundred houses and tents went

up in Corinne. "We reached Corinne at 6 A.M., Friday. It was a town of tents, and in one of them we spent the day and night. A new order of things had set in."[11]

Certainly it had. The route from the railhead at Corinne had a great competitive impact on the Missouri River steamboats serving Fort Benton, and freight poured north from the new gateway. A businessman in Helena could now telegraph New York City and start his teams for Corinne the same day. By the time the wagons reached the railhead, the order would have been filled and merchandise sped west by the Union Pacific. Within five days, sixteen-mule trains or ox trains would be loaded with as many as sixty thousand pounds of freight and returning north. On April 21, 1870, the mighty Diamond R shipped twenty thousand pounds of goods to Helena by a single mule train. A total of three million pounds of freight traveled north from the railhead at Corinne during the summer of 1870, much of it destined for army outposts.

The Missouri River was still able to offer cheaper transportation, but because of low water a delivery date was never certain. Bulk or heavy cargoes continued to reach Montana by boat, but items such as tools, clothing, and fresh fruit in season usually arrived aboard freight wagons from Utah. The first transcontinental railroad shifted the pattern of trade routes to boost the fortunes of Corinne and its eastern supply centers, Omaha and Chicago, but it would diminish those of both Saint Louis and Salt Lake City. Yet Corinne's own favored position in the transportation geography of the northern West was tenuous because what the rails gave, they could also take away.

About six hundred freighters were engaged in hauling goods from Corinne to Montana in 1873, with an average of eighty wagons en route day and night. Thus when a narrow-gauge railroad was completed north from the Union Pacific at Ogden to Franklin, Idaho, in 1874, Mormon journalists and even some Corinne residents predicted doom for the lively burg on the Bear River. Two factors helped postpone the inevitable: the financial panic of 1873, which delayed the extension of rails farther north, and the labor-intensive transfer of goods from

standard- to narrow-gauge railroad cars at Ogden, which added to freight charges. The slim-gauge Utah Northern Railroad originated as a Mormon project to link settlements in northern Utah with Salt Lake City. Promoters soon envisioned extending its tracks north to tap the rich Montana markets, but the panic of 1873 dried up sources of investment capital. Only when Jay Gould of the Union Pacific gained control of the line did the narrow-gauge tracks finally push through eastern Idaho and into Montana. For a time, both Corinne and Franklin engaged in competition for the Montana trade, until in 1877 the railroad was reorganized as the Utah and Northern and bypassed both settlements on its way north.

The year 1877 was one of Corinne's best; 5,700 tons of freight went north to Montana and Idaho, and 1,128 tons of valuable ore came south from there, but the advancing rails portended a major change. The *Salt Lake Tribune* foretold the end when it wrote: "The shipping season in the town is closed, and perhaps forever." A few teams and wagons pulled up to Corinne's once-bustling freight transfer houses during 1878, but most were hauling only short distances. By late 1878, the Utah and Northern Railroad opened a new northern terminus at Eagle Rock (now Idaho Falls).

The advancing rails had a similar impact on Gilmer and Salisbury stage operations. Anticipating a boost in traffic, the partners ordered a number of new coaches that could carry as many as thirty riders each. By the spring of 1880 it took Gilmer and Salisbury only thirty-six hours to reach Helena from the Utah and Northern's temporary terminus at Beaver Canyon (near present Spencer, Idaho), a time that just a few years earlier would have sent Montanans into a "delirium of joy."

On March 9, 1880, almost eleven years after Promontory, the advancing tracks finally crossed the Continental Divide at Monida Pass, giving Montana its first railroad line. The 290-mile-long Utah and Northern was only a narrow-gauge line—albeit the longest three-foot gauge line in the world—but Montanans were happy for a railroad of any width or length. A special train of three cars steamed up Beaver Canyon to celebrate the driving of the first spike in Montana, and a telegraph line was

*W*aking up the Wrong Passenger," a satirical view of travel by train. The new railroads not only redefined time and space across the West but also the meaning of comfort on a transcontinental journey: "It is impossible to tell of the pleasures and joys of the palace ride you will have—five days—it will make you so well accustomed to car life, you feel, when you drop upon the wharf of San Francisco, that you have left genuine comfort behind, and even the hotel, with its cozy parlor and cheerful fire, has not its full recompense," enthused the Pacific Tourist in 1884. The implied comparison with the rigors of overland stagecoach travel is obvious. Courtesy Library of Congress, 1377.

rigged to transmit every strike of the hammer to all connected points. Every blow, said the Deer Lodge *New Northwest*, "will be remembered as a blow for freedom— freedom from isolation and the oppression of Colonial Government." [12]

The elimination of a difficult stage ride across the Continental Divide was only one reason why more people than ever before traveled to Montana. The Union Pacific's aggressive advertising called travelers' attention to a revised schedule that connected Omaha to Helena in less than five days, and listed first-class fares at $100, second-class at $75, and emigrant-class at $45. Space was soon booked days in advance, and by late April 1880, four or five passenger cars left Ogden daily on the way north. That summer—when Gilmer and Salisbury were still operating some five thousand miles of stage line, including a new route from the end of the railroad to Yellowstone National Park—traffic was especially heavy north into Montana. By early October, passengers could detrain at Dillon and complete the 125 miles to Helena in only twenty-four hours. Soon even that gap was closed.

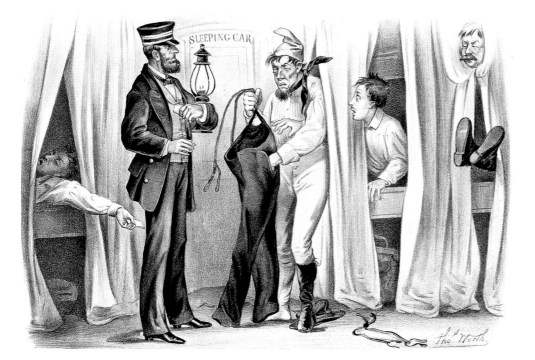

The editor of the *New Northwest* wrote a cheerful epitaph for stagecoach travel between Montana and Utah when he described his day-and-a-half train journey to Ogden. It was, he noted, "a happy contrast to the five days' time that was formerly occupied in the winter trip, with a chance to 'hoof it' through mud or snow, and emerge from the coach in Utah with all the aches that name has been given to. Now, you go flying, warm, cozy, and comfortable, except in the event of being 'snow-bound' or 'ditched,' in which case you starve respectably or are neatly and thoroughly killed." [13]

The advancing tracks of the Oregon Short Line had a similar impact on travel east from Portland along the Kelton Road through southern Idaho. At intervals, as railroad operations were extended, stagecoaches would be withdrawn from the route and moved elsewhere. At last in late 1884, the tracks extended from Granger, on the Union Pacific main line in Wyoming, across Idaho to Huntington, Oregon, to open a long-awaited shortcut to Portland. After through mail, express, and freight traffic had migrated to the trains, rail travelers soon noticed that grass had grown over the road where stagecoaches once traveled between Kelton and Boise in clouds of dust. A Portland booster magazine enthused that the railroad "pushes its way into uninhabited wilds, and the shriek of the locomotive seems endowed with the potency of the conjurer's magic wand" to call into "instant life wealth, industry, population, and all that these can produce." [14]

That Once Distant Land

When the first transcontinental railroad redrew the transportation map of the West, it transformed the mental geography of westerners. *Bancroft's Guide for Travelers* observed in mid-1869 that "the influx of transient visitors, who are now able to see the wonders of California, that once 'distant land,' and of permanent settlers, who seek homes in our fertile valleys, has already begun. The arrivals by rail far exceed those by steamer, and there is no prospect of any diminution in the number of the latter." [15]

Only two years earlier Harvey Scott had complained

that "this country has always been—speaking after the manner of the old geographers—almost literally beyond the verge of the world; and those who have made their homes on these shores have been quite as effectually shut off, from the centers of population and commerce in the East, as if they had taken their station the other side of the globe. The remoteness of our situation, the cost, danger and discomfort of travel, and the length of time required to reach the Pacific states and territories, have overbalanced the natural advantages which the country has always offered, and prevented that rapidity of growth which would have been effected had the Pacific slope been accessible to the crowding population of the Eastern states." Railroads would change everything.[16]

The fact that, although "G & S" was once among the best-known symbols in the northern Rocky Mountains, Gilmer and Salisbury have been virtually forgotten in the region's transportation history today suggests how quickly popular attention shifted from the likes of John Butterfield and Ben Holladay to the railroad barons Henry Villard and James J. Hill, who increasingly defined the new era. For long-distance stagecoaching and steamboating, the age of railroads meant operating in history's shadows.

We are blessed with one more favor, the price of freight on the Columbia River, which depreciates the value of our stock and produce, and increases the price of goods we are obliged to have. We can, when compelled, live without tea, coffee or tobacco, but we must have warm clothes, some fruit and divers other articles to live on, as well as implements to carry on farming.

—*T. W. Clark,* Portland Oregonian *(February 13, 1874), describing everyday life on the Palouse prairie*

Monopoly Rules the Empire of the Columbia

In the early 1870s a traveler bound for Walla Walla disembarked from a Columbia River steamboat at Wallula, a hamlet that claimed the distinction of "supporting neither lawyer, physician, nor minister, and only one school-teacher." To his dismay he learned that the stage had already left and that the only way to reach his destination was to hire a farm wagon or ride in a freight car of the Walla Walla and Columbia River Railroad, a narrow-gauge line that crept unsteadily thirty miles across a sandy alkaline desert on wooden rails topped with strap iron.[1]

For two dollars John Mortimer Murphy secured a seat atop iron construction materials in an open car, but a company official warned him to cling to the sides and be careful "not to stand on the wooden floor if I cared anything about my limbs. I promised a strict compliance with the instructions, and the miserable little engine gave a grunt or two, several wheezy puffs, a cat-like scream, and finally got the car attached to it under way. Once in motion, it dashed on at a headlong speed of two miles an hour, and rocked like a canoe in a cross sea. The gentleman who represented all the train officials did not get aboard, but told the engineer to go on and he would overtake them in the course of an hour."

Before the train had gone half a mile, the lone traveler saw why he had been advised not to stand on the floor of the freight car: "a piece of hoop-iron, which covered the wooden rails in some places, curled up into what is called a 'snake head,' and pushed through the wood with such force that it nearly stopped the train." After this was removed the engine resumed its course, and at the end of seven hours hauled one weary passenger, "with eyes made sore from the smoke, and coat and hat nearly burnt off by the sparks into a station composed of a rude board shanty," through the open windows and doors of which the wind howled. Here the traveler secured a seat on a farmer's wagon bound for Walla Walla in exchange for a promise to drive the team while the owner slept, "a proposition I gladly accepted; but I soon repented of my bargain, as every driver I met who had any sense of humour in him began to make fun of my 'stove-pipe' hat, and to suggest that I ought to take my first lessons in driving behind donkeys. The *badinage* was, as a rule, so original and witty that I had several good laughs at my own expense; and I found after awhile that the chaff was richly merited, as my black broadcloth coat was one mass of burnt holes in the back, and my silk hat looked like a sieve. I did not bless that railway, perhaps!"

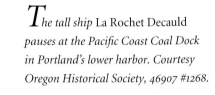

night the sea was so boisterous that Captain DeWolfe decided to turn the *Brother Jonathan* about and wait out the storm at Crescent City, but as the steamship changed course it struck a submerged rock and sank about forty-five minutes later. Only the first lifeboat containing nineteen passengers got away safely. Bodies washed ashore for the next several weeks. Many of those who drowned were prominent residents of Portland and other towns in the Pacific Northwest. The sinking of the largest side-wheeled steamer that regularly sailed to Oregon during the 1850s and early 1860s both saddened and angered the whole Pacific Coast and intensified frustration over poor steamship service. Much to the dismay of Portlanders, the *Orizaba,* another of the California Steam Navigation Company's "old hulks," replaced the ill-fated *Brother Jonathan.*

Just then the Oregon Steam Navigation Company began to contemplate offering service on the route between Portland and San Francisco. In 1865, at about the same time that the company responded to competition from overland routes between San Francisco and the mines of southern Idaho with the steamboat *Shoshone*, it recognized that the high rates and poor service on the coastal steamers run by Holladay and Flint and the California Steam Navigation Company, especially after the highly publicized sinking of the *Brother Jonathan*, were lessening the attractiveness of its Columbia River route to the interior. Repeatedly the *Oregonian* had urged Oregon businessmen to place a home-owned steamship on the coastal route. Oregon Steam believed that even if one of its own vessels had to carry freight at low or losing rates it would still function as a valuable feeder for the lucrative Columbia River boats.

In the fall of 1865 the Oregon Steam Navigation Company contracted with a New York shipbuilding firm for construction of a new, first-class steamship to be named the *Oregonian*. Built in secrecy to prevent possible retaliation from the wily Holladay, the new vessel was launched in April 1866. She sailed to San Francisco but was never placed on the coastal route for which she was originally intended because the situation had changed radically. The Anchor Line entered the competition in 1866 with its fine new steamship *Montana* and planned to add a second boat, the *Idaho,* as soon as it was completed. Ben Holladay's operations, reorganized in 1865 as the California, Oregon and Mexico Steamship Company, rose to the challenge with a new steamship of its own, the *Oriflamme.* This ship boasted such superior passenger accommodations that Holladay occasionally treated it as his private yacht, using it to host lavish parties intended, as always, to entertain and impress his influential guests.

Ironically, competition on the San Francisco-Portland route intensified just as mining-camp commerce waned and transportation facilities at long last caught up with demand. Cabin passage aboard a coastal steamship dropped to forty five dollars, which included meals and berth for four days, before plunging even lower to twenty dollars for cabin class and ten dollars for steerage. When freight rates fell to three dollars per ton, the slower sailing vessels had nothing to haul. The steamships of all three competitors raced back and forth between San Francisco and Portland, but at these low rates none made a profit. The *Montana* made eighteen trips; the ships of Holladay's company nineteen; and those of the California Steam Navigation Company, twenty-one, for an unprecedented total of fifty-eight trips by coastal steamships during 1866.

Disadvantaged by having only one ship on the route, the Anchor Line was expected to win the contest once its new *Idaho* came into service, since many shippers preferred the new carrier. But the *Idaho* made only one trip under the Anchor banner early in 1867 before Holladay decided the time had come to act. His remedy as usual was to create a monopoly, the North Pacific Transportation Company, by uniting his California, Oregon and Mexico Steamship Company with the Anchor Line and the oceangoing ships of the California Steam Navigation Company, which then retreated to the inland waters of California.

The Oregon Steam Navigation Company sold its new ship, the *Oregonian,* to the North American Steamship Company with the understanding that she would not compete against the Holladay line. Out of this shuffle, Holladay gained a fleet of sixteen or seventeen steamships and full control of coastal commerce from British Columbia to Mexico. For a time it was possible for a traveler to claim that these were "fast vessels, well officered by experienced men, and receiving the full support of the community." But in the steamship business Holladay proved as ruthless as he had been as a stagecoach entrepreneur. No one should have been surprised when, after the creation of his $5-million maritime monopoly, passenger and freight rates climbed sharply.[2]

Ben Holladay's New Empire

Ben Holladay was not content to limit his entrepreneurial talent to coastal shipping and stagecoaching. In August 1868, not quite two years after he sold his stagecoach empire to Wells Fargo, Holladay relocated to Oregon where he wrested control of Willamette Valley railroads from local businessmen. The Willamette Valley, an area the size of the state of Massachusetts, was the first

A Willamette River steamer uses the locks at Oregon City. For several years all passengers and freight portaged around the falls where Oregon City entertained dreams of becoming the chief manufacturing center of Oregon. Through navigation became possible only in 1873 when a canal and locks eliminated the need for a portage railroad. Courtesy Oregon Historical Society, 91704.

part of the northern West to be settled extensively by a non-Indian population. By the mid-1860s it had become an agricultural cornucopia and an attractive prospect for local railroad builders.

Two rival groups proposed to extend tracks along opposite sides of the Willamette River to link Portland with San Francisco. Congress in 1866 provided incentive in the form of a 3.7-million-acre land grant that included some of the world's richest stands of Douglas fir timber. Federal lawmakers stipulated that Oregon legislators would choose the recipient, and the Salem legislature in turn awarded the land and timber bonanza to backers of the Oregon Central Railroad, or west-side line. But that did not end the intense rivalry. The west-siders broke ground at Portland, April 15, 1868, and the east-siders, across the Willamette at East Portland a day later. The rival companies had essentially fought each other to a standstill before Ben Holladay swaggered onto the scene.

Perceiving an opportunity to increase his already considerable fortune by gaining control of the land grant riches, Holladay distributed money and favors lavishly, subsidized newspapers, hired lawyers, and purchased politicians in a spectacle the likes of which pioneer Oregonians had never seen. Holladay, who bragged openly of his control of the press and his influence over Oregon politics, introduced the far Northwest to an era of corruption aptly labeled "the great barbecue." During one session in Salem, he entertained regally and unblushingly corrupted Oregon lawmakers. For $35,000 he purchased legislation that enabled him and his east-side allies—backers of what soon became known as the Oregon and California Railroad—to win the land grant originally awarded to the west-siders.

Public criticism of Holladay's growing control of Willamette Valley transportation brought a reminder from Harvey Scott to his readers in the *Oregonian*: "Oregon needs railroads, and for several years has been endeavoring to enlist capital in the work of building them. It should be of little consequence who furnishes the money, so long as we get the railway communications which we need." For this reason, Scott looked "with favor on the enterprise of the Holladay company, just as we should do in the case of any other like enterprise which seemed to promise good results for Oregon. Any railroad that can be built through our state will contribute to its improvement, development and prosperity. It seems to us that it is not good policy to condemn one enterprise or another, but to speak hopefully of each. While we hope that the west side company will build its railroad we see no reason why the building of the east side railroad is not also to be desired and encouraged."[3]

Two months later, in December 1868, Scott again enthusiastically applauded the new Holladay enterprise. "The railroad era has fairly commenced in Oregon; no one can doubt it who inspects the enterprises now in progress. Much of the east side railroad is graded for a distance of seventy miles." Although rain forced Holladay's crews to discontinue grading for the winter, the work of constructing a support structure was "carried on with vigor in the company's mills and shops." The railroad erected a large sawmill two miles east of Milwaukie, "which will run during the winter cutting ties for the railroad." Another mill nearby was to be "employed exclusively in cutting timber for bridges and trestlework." A considerable force of men labored in the car shops near East Portland; "and at all these places the work will be continued without interruption. About 150 men will be employed during the winter."[4]

Holladay put down the first rail of the Oregon and California Railroad on October 28, 1869. Two weeks later, on November 10, "the first genuine locomotive that ever ran over a genuine railroad track in the Willamette Valley, left East Portland and went screaming and puffing through the forest toward Milwaukie," six miles distant. By Christmas Eve the tracks had reached New Era, twenty miles south of Portland. Not only had Holladay won the prized land grant, but he soon acquired his erstwhile rival, the Oregon Central Railroad, then creeping along the west bank of the Willamette River. He operated these two carriers as one company.[5]

The rate of progress may have impressed Harvey Scott, but not J. H. Beadle during his visit to Oregon during the early 1870s: "To one lately accustomed to the driving ways of the Union Pacific and Iowa roads, there does

not appear to be any particular stir about the Oregon and California road." What he observed of work on the unfinished southern end caused him to scoff at newspaper announcements that the connection to California would be completed by 1874. "If the 'Webfeet' don't display more enterprise in this than in other things I've noticed, I should say 1974 would be nearer the figures." Indeed, it would take eighteen years, until December 17, 1887, to complete a railroad connection to California.[6]

But why should Holladay hurry to finish a railroad that would only compete with his coastal steamships? He had his coveted land grant in hand, or nearly so, and now he preferred to take his time constructing yet another transportation monopoly. In 1871, about the time that his tracks reached Eugene, Holladay acquired the

People's Transportation Company in order to eliminate the threat of steamboat competition on the Willamette River, which paralleled his tracks. This gained Holladay a monopoly of Willamette Valley transportation between Portland and Eugene and brought nine steamboats into the fold of his North Pacific Transportation Company empire, which he reorganized the following year as the Oregon Steamship Company. Meanwhile, Holladay engaged in numerous dealings throughout the West that included land and mining speculations and the first street railway line in Portland.

When Holladay decided that the time had finally come to push the Oregon and California line toward completion, he recklessly sold bonds at 60 to 75 percent of their par value to raise the needed money. With capital thus

Coles Station at the summit of the Siskiyous lay in the shrinking gap between the northern and southern portions of the Oregon and California Railroad. Courtesy Oregon Historical Society, 91789.

secured at ruinous discount rates, he noticeably stepped up the pace of construction and spent extravagantly until 240 miles of track were in place and a portion of the valuable land grant was secured. By 1873 the Oregon and California stretched as far south as Roseburg and, together with the Oregon Central, opened new country by promoting immigration to Oregon. However, for the next ten years Roseburg remained the southern terminus of the Oregon and California Railroad for construction once again stalled.

This time the cause of the delay was the downfall of Holladay himself. He dominated Oregon politics and transportation for nearly a decade, yet his great business enterprise rested upon a surprisingly shaky foundation. He was forever rearranging his holdings by creating or merging subsidiaries. His steamship and railroad interests were interlocked in a bewildering arrangement that involved double-pledging their securities to creditors, many of whom were European investors. As Harvey Scott recalled in 1889, "Those whose memories go back to the period before the Civil War, will remember that the money for building railroads then came from abroad. There was not, up to 1860, home money at command to build railroads." By 1873, English and German capitalists had acquired some eleven million dollars' worth of Holladay's bonds.[7]

The result of Holladay's frenzied finance, observed Henry Villard, the man who finally beat him at this game, was that although Holladay's creditors were among the shrewdest and most experienced bankers in Europe they

A train on Dollarhide Trestle, where in 1887 Southern Pacific (Oregon and California) trains replaced stagecoach connections that dated back to 1860. Some astute travelers realized that increased speed offered by the railroad came with a price attached. On crossing a difficult portion of the Blue Mountains by train, where cursing teamsters once turned the air blue, a reporter for the Morning Oregonian wrote in mid-September 1884, "Old travelers, who for years past have crossed and recrossed the range in the lumbering stage coach can but wonder how the science of civil engineering even has overcome the difficulties and the dangers incidental to journeys of the past.... High mountains, grand forests, and the wonderful results of civil engineering attract your attention, and time is not afforded to enjoy it as one would wish." Courtesy Southern Oregon Historical Society, 12848.

allowed themselves to be caught in the web of his financial machinations. Holladay eventually overreached himself, and the panic of 1873 left his companies destitute. When the Oregon and California defaulted on interest due its German bondholders, they sent Henry Villard to Oregon in 1874 to untangle the financial snarl and see what they might salvage from their American misadventure. Villard and his German backers gradually tightened the financial noose around Holladay.

But this debacle was not entirely Holladay's fault, for as Harvey Scott explained, "Even at the time when Ben Holladay took hold of the Western Oregon railroads, with the intention to make himself the railroad king of the North Pacific, he was obliged to depend on German capital." These investors purchased bonds at an average of 75 percent of their face value, and the syndicate that marketed them in Europe added its sizable commission. "As Holladay had to pay one year's interest on the bonds at seven per cent, he got only forty-eight cents on the dollar out of the $11,000,000 bonds issued. That illustrates how business was managed in former times."[8]

When Villard returned to Oregon in April 1876, he removed Holladay from control of the Oregon and California and the Oregon Central railroads by purchasing his remaining interests. The erstwhile transportation king retired for a last time and lived in Portland until his death in 1887. He died at the age of sixty-eight, having lost fame and good health along with his fortune. More than one hundred lawsuits punctuated his final years.

When Holladay's influence waned on the Willamette River, the Oregon Steam Navigation Company returned to the picture. Its steamboats (and those of its successor companies, notably the Oregon Railway and Navigation Company formed in 1879) would continue to link Portland, Salem, Corvallis, Harrisburg, and Eugene until the last one withdrew in 1916. The *Columbia* and the *Oregon* became the first coastal steamships to fly the flag of the new Oregon Railway and Navigation Company. Meanwhile, Holladay's original fleet of coastal steamships gravitated to the Pacific Coast Steamship Company formed in 1877. The enormous quantities of coal consumed by

these various transportation enterprises led to formation of the Oregon Improvement Company, an early-day enterprise with large mines in the Washington Cascades which was allied with the Oregon Railway and Navigation Company and the Pacific Coast Steamship Company.

The Wheat Fleet

Holladay played little role in Columbia River transportation (apart from his coastal fleet that used the lower river to reach Portland), but the changes along the Great River of the West during the late 1860s and 1870s were no less dramatic than those that Holladay wrought in the Willamette Valley. After the Rocky Mountain gold rushes peaked in the mid-1860s, a depressing scene greeted steamboat travelers who remembered the exciting times of only a year or two earlier. For Theodor Kirchhoff the return to Umatilla was a "peculiarly painful disappointment. For if, after roaming far and ranging wide, the traveler finds the once-bustling place moribund—what a sad surprise! If where he appreciated greatness, he sees its shadow; and where he witnessed life, he sees its ghost—what a tragic shock!"[9]

Walking to the first row of houses, Kirchhoff could not believe his eyes. "Freight used to be stacked everywhere, the riverfront alive with people on the move and things in transit. Now it is deserted. Umatilla I knew had fallen on evil days but I never expected such a sorry sight. Once, in lively streets, harness bells jingled while hundreds of muleteers' whips cracked. This town of scarcely 1,000 people, the major point of transshipment for freight from California and western Oregon to Idaho's rich mining camps, had accommodated more traffic than would clog a German city ten to twenty times as big. But *that* Umatilla has vanished."

Kirchhoff blamed part of the decline on the transcontinental railroad, which opened easier routes to the northern Rocky Mountains via Winnemucca, Nevada, and Kelton, Utah, for gold seekers from California and the East: "Freight is shipped to Idaho via depots on the Central Pacific, a shorter haul than on the Columbia through Oregon." Thus, "while a lone wagon in a space

In the early twentieth century the steamer Lewiston *hauled grain from several Snake River landings between Lewiston and Riparia. During the gold rush years of the 1860s, freight traffic was almost exclusively upriver; but as the interior Northwest made the transition from mining to agriculture and stock raising, the pattern changed. As early as 1865, wool, vegetables, hides, and other items began to flow downriver, and the first shipments of flour from Walla Walla mills commenced two years later. "Stacks—mountains!—of sacked wheat, in sheds at Wallula, proved the Walla Walla valley's fertility; the valley is the Northwest's breadbasket," wrote Theodor Kirchhoff. Courtesy Idaho State Historical Society, 1269-A.*

of several days might take the dusty road toward the Blue Mountains and Grande Ronde valley, the Pacific railroad bustles with freight for Boise mines."

While Kirchhoff's journey afforded him ample opportunity to lament the lost days of the gold rush, it also gave him a glimpse into the future of Columbia River transportation, though he apparently did not recognize what he saw: "The insignificant freight upstream is only for destinations in the Grande Ronde and Walla Walla valleys. Downstream, on the other hand, boats are scarcely able to handle the wheat from the Walla Walla valley, the principal commodity transported on the upper Columbia now, 18,000 tons in 1875."

Walla Walla wheat producers began to compete with growers in the Willamette Valley as early as 1867. At first the Oregon Steam Navigation Company did not want to haul the grain, complaining that it could not make any money on the traffic. It was in response to a request from Captain James W. Troup that J. C. Ainsworth reluctantly yielded, saying, "Well, Captain Troup, you may try it, do the best you can." A year after the initial downriver shipment of grain from the Walla Walla Valley, the first British vessel hauled grain from the Pacific Northwest to Liverpool, a market sixteen thousand miles away. Within five years, a fleet of eighty-five tall ships was required to haul the golden grain to distant markets.[10]

Even as gold had once influenced the evolving transportation network centering on Portland, so too would wheat beginning in the late 1860s. As soon as wheat could travel by sailing ship direct from Portland to distant markets, the dependence of the Pacific Northwest economy on San Francisco markets and merchants lessened. Within the region, patterns of trade and commerce changed as well: the bulk of Northwest wheat exports had originally come from the Willamette Valley, where every town aspired to have a flour mill because flour was cheaper to ship than bulk wheat and the demand for it was greater. During the harvests of the 1850s, steamboats kept busy going up the Willamette light and coming down with sacks of wheat piled high on their freight decks.

But by the late 1860s the inland Northwest became a wheat producer that eventually overshadowed the Willamette Valley, and grain supplanted the cargoes of gold that once steamed down the Columbia. Wheat growing also transformed the original bunchgrass prairie landscape of the Columbia Plateau into numerous farms and ranches. Grain growing spread from the Walla Walla Valley to the fertile hills of the Palouse country north of the Snake, and from there the first wheat was hauled to Almota, a steamboat landing on the lower Snake, in 1876. The following year almost twenty-five wagonloads a day headed to Almota for shipment downriver. Other tiny river settlements evolved at Penewawa and WaWaWai, all confined to the river's edge by the steep walls of a narrow, winding canyon. Along the lower Snake River, grain warehouses sprang up.

The area's first orchards dated from the early 1870s when millions of trees were planted along the river; they would bear apples, peaches, pears, and other fruit for nearly a century until dam building in the lower Snake Valley flooded the benchlands. By the late 1870s, steamboats like the *Spokane* and *Harvest Queen* would bring settlers, agricultural implements, and soldiers upriver and return with cargoes of wheat and fruit. At one time as many as sixteen steamboats plied the lower Snake River, with Oregon Steam holding a virtual monopoly on the river's commerce.

The fact that the future prosperity of agriculture in the Palouse country and the Walla Walla Valley depended so much on freight rates set by the Oregon Steam Navigation Company irritated many of the growing number of settlers in the two areas. One warned that "when the railroad is completed through this upper country, it will be a staggering blow upon several of those distributing points along the Snake River," a blow especially to Portland monopolists. Although harvest season in August and September occurred when low water on the Snake often prevented steamboats from reaching the landings, nothing changed the region's transportation geography until a network of railroad lines was constructed during the 1880s, and especially after a direct railroad line over the

Cascades to Puget Sound made it relatively easy to ship carloads of wheat from the inland Northwest to upstart ports like Tacoma and Seattle.[11]

Unlike most wheat-producing regions of the United States, the Columbia Plateau sent its grain to market in burlap sacks. One reason for that was the number of times it had to be handled between inland farms and ranches and Portland. Another compelling reason was the fear that bulk cargoes were liable to shift dangerously in rough seas or spoil as a result of exposure to the prolonged warmth of the tropics. The Panama route was not used for wheat cargoes because of the need to transfer cargoes there, but for several decades marine underwriters simply would not insure bulk cargoes of Northwest grain traveling around Cape Horn. This situation did not end until World War Two.

Each fall for nearly forty years a fleet of tall-masted ships hauled wheat from the wharves of Portland, Tacoma, and Seattle to ports as distant as Cork, Queenstown, and Liverpool, although Portland remained preeminent for many years after the first ship sailed in 1868. Enormous saloons like Erickson's and an underworld

of crimps (men who specialized in shanghaiing sailors) did a lively business along the city's grimy waterfront. The wheat fleet lasted until World War One, when the sailing ships rapidly began to disappear until there were none left, but each year the flood of golden grain continued to flow down the Columbia River. And it still does, although today it reaches Portland mainly by barge and covered hopper cars and is shipped by bulk carriers primarily to markets in Asia.

A Northern Transcontinental Railroad

When Henry Villard and his German backers gained control of the Oregon and California Railroad and other Holladay properties in 1876, Villard also seemed to acquire his predecessor's dreams of empire. Using Holladay's rail and river monopoly in the Willamette Valley as his financial base, Villard soon gained a similar position in the Columbia Valley by acquiring the Oregon Steam Navigation Company for five million dollars in 1879. On July 12 of that year he merged this venerable enterprise with the Oregon Steamship Company, the portage railways at the Cascades and Celilo, and the "rawhide"

Getting heavy wagonloads of wheat down to the steamboats from the farms and ranches of the Palouse plateau (some two thousand feet above the Snake River) remained a problem until Major Sewell Truax, an engineer and surveyor, invented and constructed the first grain pipeline in 1879. Courtesy Washington State University, 78–005.

One of the hazards of living next to a river: the flood of June 1894 inundated the streets of Portland. Courtesy Oregon Historical Society, CN 015 477 984 0120.

railroad linking Wallula and Walla Walla to create the Oregon Railway and Navigation Company. Under this name the new firm operated a fleet of steamboats and extended a network of railway lines east from Portland along the Columbia River to tap the agricultural riches of the Walla Walla Valley and other interior points. The new Portland-based transportation giant earned huge profits serving the inland Northwest.

When Villard added to his holdings a still uncompleted northern transcontinental railroad, the Northern Pacific, he exercised more power over transportation in the northern West than did any other person before or

since. In addition to his twenty-eight steamboats on the Columbia and Willamette river systems, the locks at Oregon City, two portage railways, the Oregon and California Railroad, and the Walla Walla and Columbia River Railroad, he acquired the potential to tie all of this to the rest of the United States via the Northern Pacific. Across most of the northern West, the decade after 1875 could accurately be described as the age of Henry Villard.

Villard hoped to close the remaining gap in western Oregon to join Portland and San Francisco by rail. The popular belief was that "life and animation, population and wealth, follow in the wake of our railroads" and that

The Oregon Railway and Navigation Company car manufactory at The Dalles as depicted in West Shore *in May 1882. Courtesy Oregon Historical Society, 91785.*

"the iron horse will soon draw the commerce of these large districts to first-class markets, instead of the hard process of wagons in the intolerable sticky mud half the year," or so David Newsom wrote in the early 1880s to express his optimism that Villard would soon complete the line between Oregon and California. But Villard first needed to complete the Northern Pacific line from Lake Superior to Portland and Puget Sound, which got off to an exceedingly slow start after Isaac Stevens and John Mullan prepared the first formal surveys and reports in the 1850s. Finally, in the late 1860s, active construction of the Northern Pacific began, and by the early 1870s it was far enough along that the northern West "generally was feeling the benign effects of the anticipated railroad connection."[12]

Construction on the Pacific end of the Northern Pacific commenced in December 1870 at Kalama, on the north bank of the Columbia River, and three years later the line was finished to Tacoma, forming for the first time a convenient land bridge for steamboat traffic on both the Columbia River and Puget Sound. Initially this rail portage was seen as a way to extend Portland's reach all the way up the Inside Passage to Alaska. Meanwhile several troops of engineers remained busy during the year 1872 attempting to solve thorny problems of where to locate tracks through the northern Rocky Mountains, but the Northern Pacific had made no decision before the panic of 1873 temporarily halted construction and left a lengthy gap in the rails between Dakota and Washington.

Construction of Northern Pacific tracks through Washington Territory to join with the section completed earlier from Lake Superior as far west as Bismarck did not commence again until well after 1873, and success seemed assured only when Villard committed his considerable entrepreneurial talent to completing the northern transcontinental line. From Ainsworth, a place on the north bank of the Snake River not far from present Pasco (and the junction with Oregon Railway and Navigation tracks from Portland), tracklayers extended the rails east across the treeless Columbia Plateau. Their camp

kitchens could burn local sagebrush for fuel, but because there was no timber close at hand, ties were rafted down the Clearwater and Snake rivers from Idaho forests and down the Yakima River from the Cascade mountains. Each mile of track required ten thousand ties. Logs for trestles were also floated down the Yakima River. "If no accident befalls the vessels now afloat with iron, and the rails are shipped promptly to Ainsworth, cars will be running over the road to Spokan Falls by next Christmas," wrote the *Oregonian* in 1880.[13]

"Until the advent of the Northern Pacific Railroad, the Spokane country was a *terra incognita* to all other than the residents of Eastern Washington, and it was not an uncommon thing to meet people in Oregon, and California, even, who asserted that the terms Sahara or arid plains and Spokane were synonymous." This impression changed after the coming of a telegraph line. From Spokane Falls, August 31, 1880: "We are now in communication with the civilized world by telegraph. At present, we have a tri-weekly mail from the South, with fair prospects for daily communication soon. A recently established tri-weekly line of stages between Ainsworth and Spokan Falls carries loaded coaches each way; and daily trips will soon be made between this city and the end of the railroad track." Northern Pacific tracks reached finally reached Spokane in 1881, barely pausing before they pushed ahead toward the mountains of Idaho and Montana.[14]

For the pioneer Montanan Granville Stuart, the advancing tracks meant that "no more will the happy denizens of Bozeman and Yellowstone walk o'er the mountains behind Gilmer & Salisbury's 'palace jerkies,' while the unpleasant driver thereof regards them as did the Roman general of old when looking upon the long procession of prisoners that follow his victorious chariot. . . . At last, Oh people of Montana, the hour of your deliverance draws nigh. Job has been handed down through all the ages as the most patient man, but we all do feel and know that if it had only occurred to Satan to try him with a Montana stage line from the proprietors down to the off-wheeler, he would have sworn."[15]

F. Jay Haynes photographed Spokane, Washington, in 1890. Perhaps nowhere along the new Northern Pacific track was the transition from the age defined by stagecoaches and steamboats more dramatic than in Spokane, which until the tracklayers arrived was a mere hamlet. Not only was the proper spelling of its name uncertain, but so too were communication and transportation. In the late 1870s the usual way to reach the future metropolis of the inland Northwest was by steamboat to Almota on the Snake River, and from there by stage to the hamlet of Colfax. Any mail continued north on the backs of one or two horses. There were no settlements along the seventy-two-mile trail between Colfax and Spokane. Courtesy Montana Historical Society, H-2082.

An F. Jay Haynes photograph of Northern Pacific tracklayers near Missoula in 1883. When tracklayers from the east finally reached Helena in mid-June of that year, a throng of people turned out to greet the construction train: "The work of a hundred men or more laying ties, carrying rails, spiking down, fishplating and straightening track was witnessed by hundreds of citizens from Helena, who stood around the curious and exciting scenes," reported the Helena Weekly Herald. *Nearly every resident hailed "the great civilizer" with "enthusiasm and zeal." Courtesy Montana Historical Society, H-1064.*

Finally the long-anticipated day arrived in September 1883 when both ends of the Northern Pacific were joined at Gold Creek, Montana. Many of the "potentates and money kings" of England, Germany, and the United States arrived on special trains to participate in what one Montana newspaper called "a three-ring circus—too much to take in all at one time." During the lengthy ceremonies the crowd repeatedly called for former President Ulysses S. Grant to speak, a popular demand that he could not deny; and "as he came forward and squarely faced the thousands on the platform, the voices of all burst forth in prolonged cheers, the wild, irrepressible acclaim that he had heard on a hundred battlefields, and that greets him wherever he goes throughout the land." Grant spoke "not long but well," recalling how as a young quartermaster and commissary officer at Fort Vancouver he had provided supplies to Isaac Stevens's surveying expedition thirty years earlier.[16]

After a tracklaying contest, Villard stepped up to the rails where a nicely polished tie had been placed to receive the final spike, the same one that had been the first driven years earlier in Wisconsin. A telegraph line was attached to it and the sledge hammer to transmit the sound of the final blows to Northern Pacific officials waiting at distant points. Villard struck the spike a heavy blow. He was followed by his wife and their baby boy ("Henry the Second"), and then former President Grant. A somewhat unruly crowd of onlookers cried out, "Drive it home, Grant." And home it went while the guns thundered, the band played "Yankee Doodle," and the crowd cheered "till the roof wasn't safe on the pavilion." Also included among the honored guests was Captain John Mullan.[17]

A traveler by train from Helena to the final spike ceremonies observed: "While I looked down the steep mountain into the old Mullan wagon road, my own thoughts

F. Jay Haynes photographed the triumphal arch that stretched across Bismarck's Main Street and welcomed in German the final spike excursion led by Henry Villard in 1883. Courtesy Montana Historical Society, H-916.

went back to a sultry day in August 1866, when I acted as brakeman and engineer of the then fashionable [wagon] trains. Our trains, consisting of three cars, with twelve yoke of bovines to each train, pulled and reeled a full half day to reach the summit. The hip-ha-hoy and loud popping of the whips echoed from hill to hill and back again, lending an enchantment to the scene, which in those days the carrier of goods and wares loved dearly to hear."

He continued: "It was pleasant to look back over the seventeen years and note the change. Then the oxen pulled our trains and we were content. Now steam draws us. Grant has been promoted and rides in the car ahead of us. The oxen go to market on the steam-propelled trains, and the engineers have exchanged their rawhide whips for iron levers, lead pencils, etc." [18]

The *New Northwest* of Deer Lodge complained that the

Pursuit of game animals lost none of its popularity after the coming of the railroad. Wallis Nash wrote that when he crossed western Nebraska by train in 1877 the antelope seemed "too tame for their own comfort. Often they were within range of the train and there was a perfect fusillade from the rifles and revolvers with which a good many of the passengers were armed." For more civilized hunters the Worcester Excursion Car Company operated this special car on the Northern Pacific line, and F. Jay Haynes photographed it in Fargo, Dakota Territory, in 1884. Later in the decade the Northern Pacific Railroad ended special carload rates on wild animal meat traveling to eastern markets. After hauling tons of buffalo hides and meat from the Great Plains, the railroad became a convert to conservation when it realized that tourism was a much more profitable and enduring business than the wholesale slaughter and ultimate extinction of the West's game animals. A general passenger agent, Charles S. Fee, noted in Forest and Stream *in 1888 that "to a very considerable portion of the traveling public, the game and fish of the region traversed by the Northern Pacific Railroad constitute its chief attraction. This large and ever increasing class of travelers are well-to-do people who have money to spend, and are thus desirable patrons of the road. Any course which will decrease the supply of the game which they seek will tend to reduce the travel over the road by this class, who will go where they believe game to be most abundant." Courtesy Montana Historical Society, H-1324.*

last spike ceremony was an advertising gimmick for the Northern Pacific that will "sound pretty loud throughout the length of the land." Of the approximately 150 Montanans invited to the ceremony, some had decidedly negative feelings about the enterprise that Granville Stuart hailed as the territory's deliverer. Some of the egalitarian frontiersmen complained of "exhibitions of aristocratic exclusiveness and small discourtesies" of the occasion. Another grumbled, "During the driving of the last spike, the band played, one hundred guns were fired, and a general squabble prevailed. I have not as yet been able to find a Montanan who saw the golden spike, but presume it was there and was driven. I stood only six feet away when the driving took place, but the crowd was so thick and strong that I could not see the work performed. I heard the speaking, but was unable to understand what was said. Villard entertained his guests from the East in high style, but our Montana guests did not fare so well.

They took a lunch along and ate at their own 'bidding.' Many of them expecting to return soon, took but little lunch, and the result was they had to fast most of the time."[19]

Indeed, Villard wanted most to impress his investors because at this time (and unbeknownst to most people) his financial future was tenuous because of massive cost overruns on construction of both the Northern Pacific and Oregon and California railroads. By the end of 1883, Villard was out, but the empire of the Columbia was about to experience a massive transformation as a result of the Northern Pacific that he had been so instrumental in completing. This railroad would reconfigure the northern West in a way that the Columbia and Missouri rivers never could. Especially dramatic were the changes that this and other railroads brought to steamboat traffic on the Missouri River.

a Victorian settlement of substantial business blocks where merchants demanded propriety and stability.

During Fort Benton's heyday as the link between river commerce and the prairies of Montana and Canada, the focal point of everyday life was the Grand Union Hotel, which boosters now claim featured the finest accommodations between Minneapolis and Seattle. That may be true. However, Fort Benton was never really part of a meaningful connection between Minneapolis and Seattle until long after railroads had supplanted Missouri River steamboats. When in the 1860s Fort Benton formed the busy hub of a network of steamboat, stagecoach, and freight lines, Seattle was scarcely more than a sawmill outpost that clung precariously to the eastern shore of Puget Sound. Fort Benton's ties were with the river, and the coming of railroads to the plains of Montana in the 1880s devastated the would-be metropolis of the northern West. It is not a ghost town today, but it is a ghost of its former self. As river commerce went, so went Fort Benton.

Mackinaw Fleet

Among the many frustrations experienced by steamboaters, merchants, and travelers on the upper Missouri River from the 1860s through the 1880s was the lack of reliable river transportation to and from Fort Benton apart from the high-water seasons of spring and early summer. That was why during the early spring, newspapers of the Midwest were flooded with advertisements that announced the sailing dates of Montana-bound steamboats. One issue of the *Missouri Republican* in 1865 carried eleven such items; the following year the *Saint Louis Dispatch* recorded seventy-five steamers that announced April sailing dates. The boats usually reached Fort Benton by late May, June, or even early July and remained in port just long enough to take aboard outbound cargo and passengers. The last steamer of the year ordinarily departed from Fort Benton by the first part of July, and then except for the fall mackinaw fleet, the levee was virtually deserted until the annual cycle began again. This schedule presented a problem for the typical placer miner, who wanted to return to the States only at the end of the season in August or September, for that was when water was low and steamboats could not possibly reach Fort Benton. Fall was the time, too, when businessmen left for the large cities to bank their profits and when all those who dreaded another Montana winter headed for a warmer climate.

Most people who went east before winter arrived had little choice but to travel overland on the stagecoaches of Ben Holladay or Wells Fargo to Salt Lake City, and thence to the Missouri Valley. Some private wagons also made the trip, their passengers enduring two months of hard travel and the danger of an early blizzard. For the adventuresome few there was the alternative of the mackinaw fleet that every fall during the 1860s floated slowly down the Missouri River to Omaha or Saint Louis. "At all seasons of the year, when the river was open, mackinaws were to be found descending it," recalled Lieutenant James Bradley, "but it was in September that the great rush commenced." [3]

A mackinaw was a flat-bottomed boat that was sometimes as large as fifty feet long and twelve feet wide. It was constructed of timber boards that, if nails were not available, were held together with wooden pins. The center of the mackinaw was partitioned off from the ends by watertight bulkheads between which the cargo, weighing perhaps as much as fifteen tons, was piled to a height of three or four feet above the gunwales. Skins drawn tight over the payload and fastened with cleats at the sides made the freight compartment nearly waterproof. Mackinaws could also accommodate as many as fifty passengers. Invariably, some of these were returning miners who carried their gold in strongboxes to which they attached buoys with heavy rope, so that in the event of a wreck, they could still locate their treasure.

Mackinaws were supplied with oars and sometimes sails, but mainly they relied on the current of the Missouri River. An oarsman sat in the bow and a steersman in the stern on an elevated perch, from which he would see over the cargo and direct the crew, which normally consisted of four men. These were usually French Canadians who might work from fifteen to eighteen hours a day to travel down 75 to 150 miles of water, some of it very shallow.

Mackinaws, however, required only ten inches of water and offered a journey that many passengers considered infinitely more pleasant than one aboard a bouncing, dusty stagecoach.

Thus in the fall, the Fort Benton levee was again briefly the scene of a whirl of activity reminiscent of the spring steamboat rush. Most of the mackinaw fleet was constructed here, and curious townspeople often crowded around before departure. Lieutenant Bradley described the annual excitement: "Scores of rough boats sprang into existence and day after day they would push off with a crew of from half a dozen to thirty and forty souls—sometimes singly—sometimes in flotillas, and drop down the river to various points from Sioux City to St. Louis. In the neighborhood of 200 boats and 1200 passengers would thus sail from Benton annually." At the end of the voyage, their owners would sell these boats as lumber for four or five dollars apiece (about the value of the lumber in them) or simply abandon them.[4]

Boats also left from landings along the Yellowstone River that flowed through southern Montana. To publicize the 1867 departure of thirty mackinaws, outfitters advertised in the *Montana Post* of Virginia City under the heading "HO! FOR AMERICA!" The fare to Omaha was twenty-five dollars. Outfitters promised that covered mackinaws would be available to accommodate women and children, and all passengers would be allowed one hundred pounds of baggage free.[5]

outside world first news of the Custer massacre. It was probably this race more than any other achievement that made Marsh a legend among steamboaters and the *Far West* the best-known name on the Missouri and Yellowstone rivers.

After the Rush

Steamboat traffic on the upper river recorded two distinct peaks of activity during the years from 1860 to 1890. The first was during the second half of the 1860s, when gold rush traffic was at its highest volume and miners imported most of what they needed from outside the territory. River commerce would fall off sharply after 1869 for lack of new gold discoveries and because the transcontinental railroad through Utah was completed. The second peak occurred during the 1880s when freight to western Canada and a growing number of agricultural settlements in Montana again stimulated steamboat traffic. The second and final decline followed completion of the Northern Pacific line between the Great Lakes and Puget Sound in 1883 and the Great Northern from Saint Paul to Butte, Montana, in 1887.

Traffic up the Missouri River first became significant in 1866 when thirty-one steamers discharged approximately ten thousand tons of freight at the Fort Benton landing. Of this total, the *Mollie Dozier* and *Peter Balen* carried nearly 350 tons each. With the river running high, steamboat traffic remained heavy until late in the season. Freight from the steamer *Deer Lodge,* which left Saint Louis on June 6, was delivered in Helena on July 26, a remarkable achievement considering the date and distance. At the end of the season the *Montana Post* estimated that approximately half of all Montana-bound freight arrived by way of the river. The year 1866 was also the first for regular stagecoach service between Fort Benton and Helena.

In 1868, when thirty-five boats landed five thousand tons of merchandise at Fort Benton, it was reported that 725 wagons shuttled between Fort Benton and Helena carrying the merchandise to its destination. These were prosperous years for the little river port, the self-described Queen City of the Northern Plains. From an unimpressive frontier village of only twenty-seven log or adobe huts in 1866 it had rapidly evolved into a bustling town of warehouses, business firms, hotels, and public buildings.

The *Montana Post* boasted in mid-January 1869 that there was "achieved last year a success that is a sure guarantee of future importance in the commercial history of Montana." In fact, the end of an era was at hand when the last spike at Promontory opened the new railroad link between East and West. Montana was not on the direct route, but with railroad service available only five hundred miles away at Corinne, the distance was not great, especially when measured against Missouri River steamers and plodding bull trains. The new route through Utah received a good deal of the Montana business that would in previous years have gone to Missouri River steamboats.[9]

In 1869 the river port saw forty-two arrivals, but the following year, with the end of the gold rush and freight trains steaming across northern Utah, only eight boats carrying about sixteen hundred tons of freight reached Montana's inland port. For the next several years Fort Benton and steamboat traffic on the upper Missouri River languished. Only seven steamboats arrived in 1873, and just six more the following year. Several Fort Benton businessmen went bankrupt, and their settlement's former importance seemed only a distant memory. Yet by middecade the number of arrivals began to climb once again. Fifty-four steamboats reached Fort Benton in 1878, and forty-two a year later.

This increase resulted from a number of causes. Some shippers to Montana still found it more convenient to transport goods by way of the Missouri River than by the Union Pacific and the overland wagon route. Even more significant, Fort Benton's persistent merchants replaced markets in southwestern Montana lost to the railroad after 1869 with new ones in the great hinterland that extended hundreds of miles north from the Missouri River into Canada, where the first North West Mounted Police arrived in 1874. The Canadian constabulary created a demand for provisions and supplies that could not be met by distant Winnipeg. Another reason for the increase in Fort Benton trade was the settlement of northern Montana, an area not effectively supplied by the Union Pacific and freight wagons from Corinne. In addition, some of Montana's miners and fur traders who remained active through the 1870s continued to rely on steamboats to transport their goods.

Finally, there was the shipment of goods to Indians as required by treaties signed by the United States government, and to army personnel stationed on the northern Great Plains. During the twelve years that followed the end of the Civil War in 1865, the federal government utilized numerous steamboats to transport troops and supplies along the upper Missouri River. Forts and cantonments dotted the prairie all the way from Fort Randall to Fort Benton, and all of them, as well as troops in the field, depended upon steamboats for their logistical support. A fleet of steamboats from Fort Abraham Lincoln—notably the *Far West* under Captain Grant Marsh—played a prominent part in the Sioux campaign of 1876. These vessels not only carried military supplies but also assisted in relocating troops quickly and patrolled the river to prevent Indians from crossing. Although military traffic on the upper river diminished rapidly after 1880, freight shipments by steamboat from Bismarck, the temporary end of the Northern Pacific, increased because of the settlers who moved into western Canada, northern Montana, and regions near the Missouri in Dakota.

So striking was Fort Benton's recovery in the mid-1870s that a local newspaper compared the period to the boom times of the 1860s gold rush. By 1877 the Fort Benton *Record*'s editor claimed that he knew of no business failures in Montana that year. Fort Benton's newfound prosperity was mirrored in the rising fortunes of its two foremost merchants, Isaac Gilbert Baker and Thomas C. Power. First to arrive was Baker, twenty-eight years old when he reached the river port in 1865 with a stock of merchandise brought up the Missouri by steamboat from Saint Louis to use in the fur trade among tribes of the northern plains. Soon he founded the firm of I. G. Baker and Brother. Baker secured profitable government contracts to supply and transport goods, in one instance

two million pounds of beef for the Indians. Branch posts at Fort Macleod, Fort Calgary, and Fort Walsh extended his firm's reach into Canada. One January his mule train sped thirty thousand pounds of oats from Fort Benton across the frozen plains to Fort Macleod to meet an urgent order from the North West Mounted Police. Baker's main competitor, Thomas C. Power, was also in his twenties when he came to Fort Benton in 1867 to launch a mercantile business destined to grow and serve a vast hinterland.[10]

With the increase in the population on the Great Plains and the rise of new markets north of the Missouri River, Fort Benton's two greatest merchants joined forces in the steamboat business to reduce their transportation costs and thereby increase their profits. Forming the Fort Benton Transportation Company, Power and Baker purchased the steamer *Benton* in 1875, the first of eight vessels to carry the Block P insignia, the most famous hallmark on the upper Missouri. The company's *Helena, Butte, Black Hills,* and other steamboats became familiar names in the hinterland of Dakota and Montana (operating under the name Benton Transportation Company from 1885 to 1904).

The I. G. Baker firm withdrew from Block P in 1877 when Baker purchased the *Red Cloud* and inaugurated the Baker Line. He subsequently added three more steamboats before ceasing operations with the conclusion of the shipping season of 1882 and the wreck of the *Red Cloud.* Meanwhile, C. K. Peck, who had helped form the Coulson Packet Line—which maintained near-monopoly status on river traffic from 1872 until the formation of the Block P line in 1875—established the Peck Line and commenced operations on the upper Missouri two years later. Overland transportation from Fort Benton evolved too. Along a dozen trails reaching out from Fort Benton, wagon trains carried the commerce of the plains. In the lowly business of wagon freighting, I. G. Baker, T. C. Power, Murphy, Neel and Company, and, of course, Diamond R became great enterprises. Each dispatched hundreds of wagons every spring and owned several thousand oxen and mules to keep the freight moving. The region between the upper Missouri

and North Saskatchewan rivers became a land criss-crossed by carts, wagons, buckboards, prairie schooners, and stagecoaches. As Paul Sharp aptly phrased it, in the Whoop-up Country, "the wheel ruled supreme."[11]

The year 1882 proved to be Fort Benton's greatest river season. For the eighth consecutive year, the I. G. Baker firm received the lucrative contract to supply the North West Mounted Police outposts at Fort Macleod, Fort Walsh, Lethbridge, Medicine Hat, and Calgary. And with the increase in steamboating and freighting to

northern Montana and the Canadian prairies, Fort Benton acquired an air of respectability. For many years no trees had softened its bleak landscape, and careless citizens added to the ugliness by tossing garbage and trash into the streets or over the riverbank along the levee. Numerous saloons and hurdy-gurdy houses also sullied the town's reputation. The golden years of the late 1870s and early 1880s, on the other hand, brought prosperity, families, law and order, and Fort Benton's first brick buildings.

T. C. Power and Company established a branch at Front Street and Higgins Avenue in Missoula, one of Montana's growing population centers. This photograph dates from about 1887. Courtesy University of Montana Library, 70–32.

F. Jay Haynes photographed the steamers Far West, Nellie Pick, Western, *and* Benton *loading cargoes at the levee in Bismarck in 1877. Courtesy Montana Historical Society, H-56.*

But the would-be metropolis could never afford to become too smug, especially when railroad tracks defined the limits of its hinterland: the Northern Pacific reached Helena in June 1883, and two months later the Canadian Pacific reached Calgary. Northern Pacific freight and passenger trains ended the long reign of the Mullan or Benton Road to Helena as one of the territory's most important highways; that same summer the last major freight shipments left Fort Benton for Fort Macleod and the Canadian prairies. The wounds these two railroads inflicted on Fort Benton's commerce that summer, though not immediately fatal, eventually proved mortal. So rapidly was northern Montana's cattle industry growing, providing numerous new customers to

steamboats, that Fort Benton lasted another half decade as a major port. Yet isolated as it was in a 400-mile-wide but steadily shrinking gap between Northern Pacific and Canadian Pacific tracks, the little village with big aspirations slowly withered. Once again, the twin ribbons of iron and steel doomed a commercial empire built upon river traffic.

During the three decades of upper Missouri navigation after 1860, steamboats hauled more than 160,000 tons of freight into Montana, took down about 35,000 tons, and transported more than 40,000 passengers, nearly all of them through Fort Benton. Down cargoes included three-quarters of a million buffalo robes, half that many wolf skins, valuable furs, and perhaps as many as 150 tons of gold worth more than one billion dollars at today's prices, as well as heavy shipments of silver ore concentrates, even some copper ore sent to Swansea, Wales, for processing, as well as horses, cattle, and millions of pounds of wool. As late as 1882, Fort Benton still shipped out buffalo hides worth $112,000 a year; but by 1885 almost none of the shaggy beasts remained alive, and wolves were reported to be a greater nuisance than ever as a result of the disappearance of the buffalo on which they had once depended for food.

For a time there was a profitable business shipping out buffalo bones that littered the prairie to make fertilizer. One observer who contemplated a pile of bones being loaded aboard the *Helena* for a trip down the Missouri to Bismarck, mused: "Here's a skull. From the high cheek bones, broad, low forehead . . . you know that it is the skull of an Indian." Another skull apparently belonged to a Euro-American. "He little thought while on the fertile empire of Dakota that his bones would some day be ground into powder to fertilize some barren garden patch in the New England states." There seemed to be a moral lesson there.[12]

Regional Hierarchy: Saint Louis Blues

During the 1860s most of Montana's steamboat traffic funneled through Saint Louis. But the tracks that had such a dramatic impact on the later fortunes of Fort Benton would first jolt the Missouri metropolis. The greatest threat to Missouri River steamboat traffic was always the railroad. During the span of nearly thirty years—from 1859 when the Hannibal and Saint Joseph Railroad reached Saint Joseph, to 1887 when the Great Northern reached Helena—railroads periodically altered the pattern of steamboat traffic between Saint Louis and Fort Benton. The pattern of winners and losers was complex. When a railroad line opened between Saint Louis and Jefferson City in 1856, it had little immediate impact on steamboat business serving the two ports. Most steamers ran along the Missouri River and served isolated settlements well beyond the reach of the tracks.

However, when the Hannibal and Saint Joseph Railroad reached the Missouri River three years later, Saint Joseph was ready to intercept water commerce bound for Saint Louis. Steamboat traffic below Saint Joseph by no means disappeared immediately—many travelers could not afford the rail rates, and there were still numerous settlements and army posts not yet located close to the tracks—but the new railroad demonstrated how commerce could be directed into new channels. During the decade of the 1860s additional east-to-west railroad lines intercepted the Missouri north of Saint Joseph and redirected still more of the river commerce away from Saint Louis to benefit Chicago, the rapidly growing metropolis on Lake Michigan. Tracks of the Chicago and North Western line reached Council Bluffs in mid-March 1867. Five years later a bridge opened from there to Union Pacific tracks across the Missouri River in Omaha, eliminating a ferry crossing and creating for the first time a through railroad line from Chicago to the Pacific Coast. Omaha now largely supplanted Saint Joseph in the upper river trade and further restricted the business of Saint Louis.

In 1868 the Sioux City and Pacific Railroad was completed to Sioux City, adding yet another link to the network of Chicago and North Western rails extending west from Chicago across Illinois and Iowa. When the first train arrived on March 9, the *Sioux City Journal* greeted it with exuberant headlines proclaiming "Saved at Last" and "All hail Chicago." Although Sioux City had only 1,030 inhabitants at the time, it was there at Iowa's new river and rail gateway to the northern West that the veteran steamboatman Joab Lawrence based his recently formed Northwest Transportation Company and five steamboats. A port at Sioux City enabled him to eliminate about a thousand miles of lower river travel to Saint Louis and instead make two Fort Benton trips per season with each boat. Operations commenced in the spring of 1868 and were so successful that Lawrence doubled the size of the Northwest fleet the following year.[13]

Using their new Missouri River gateway, Chicago merchants avoided a thousand miles of dangerous river navigation and saved about twenty days time by going north to Fort Benton from Sioux City instead of from Saint Louis. Consequently they could deliver goods at Sioux

A birds'-eye depiction of Sioux City in 1888. Chicago merchants and the Chicago and North Western Railroad supplied much of the capital for the Northwest Transportation Company because they intended to use the Sioux City–based steamboat line to gain control of Missouri River commerce with Montana. Courtesy Library of Congress, GM 1404/412 070.

PERSPECTIVE MAP OF.

SIOUX CITY, IOWA.

1888 POPULATION 35000

THE PEAVEY GRAND OPERA HOUSE,
CHAMBER OF COMMERCE
BUILDING.

CORN PALACE.

City for little more than the cost of insurance alone on merchandise shipped by boat from Saint Louis. Sioux City navigation interests presented even greater competition to Saint Louis steamboatmen after the federal government channeled its considerable business on the upper Missouri River through the Iowa port. All during the Indian wars of the 1870s, Sioux City remained the great shipping point for the army on the upper river.

When the upstart community on Lake Michigan was incorporated, Saint Louis had dominated trade along the Missouri River for nearly three-quarters of a century. The advent of steamboat transportation had promised the first truly new way to master space since the invention of the wheel, and nature had endowed Saint Louis with a perfect location to benefit from it. During the 1850s, Saint Louis had symbolized Missouri's importance to the commercial growth of the United States by receiving annually more than three thousand steamboats laden with nearly a million tons of freight.

The new railroad technology shifted the commercial advantage from Saint Louis to Chicago, and from Missouri to Illinois, during an amazingly short span of time. Captain Grant Marsh noticed the difference early in the summer of 1870 when he was aboard the *Kate Kearney* engaged in commerce between Saint Louis and lower Missouri River points: "But the trade between St. Louis and the Northwest, which had so long flourished, was now waning, owing to the arrival of the railroad at Sioux City. That point was beginning to reap the reward of enterprise and becoming the distributing center for Dakota and eastern Montana, while the merchants of Chicago, who shipped to Sioux City, were wresting from their rivals in St. Louis a market which was rapidly increasing in value and which in later years the metropolis of the Mississippi Valley was to miss sorely."[14]

Railroad lines radiating from Chicago would not only intercept the Missouri River at Saint Joseph, Council Bluffs, Sioux City, and Yankton but also connect through Saint Paul and Minneapolis to reach the river at Bismarck, Dakota Territory. In 1872 when Northern Pacific tracks finally reached Bismarck, they immediately diminished upper river trade from Sioux City. That same year the steamboat commerce above Bismarck was controlled by William J. Kountz, who worked in cooperation with the Northern Pacific Railroad. By 1885 there was little upper river business for steamboats based in Sioux City.

End of an Era

When railroad tracks first entered Montana in 1880, the new connection provided a rare opportunity for head-to-head competition between steamboats and railroads of the northern West. Oddly, for a year or two the Union Pacific and the Block P Line battled one another for freight and passenger traffic to central Montana. "Beware of Missouri River Navigation and the Awful Benton Road!" warned a railroad brochure in 1880. The Union Pacific urged settlers bound for Montana to take its trains from Omaha to Ogden, continue three hundred miles north from there aboard the Utah and Northern Railroad to the end of its tracks at Red Rock, and thence by stagecoach to Virginia City, Bozeman, Helena, and Butte.[15]

The Omaha-based railroad advertised that major population centers of Montana were "now easily reached via the Union Pacific and Utah & Northern Railways and the Gilmer and Salisbury Stages." There were still other inducements to train travel: "No country in the world offers such a wide, sure field for the profitable employment of labor as Montana. Having until quite recently been far distant from the railroad, few seekers of work of any kind could afford the journey thither. Now, as the iron horse is just on the eve of entering the Territory, is the time above all others, to take advantage of this state of affairs." Another headline in the railroad brochure warned, "Avoid the Dangers and Delays of River Navigation. Save Time, Interest and Insurance."[16]

The Block P Line retaliated with advertising folders of its own. The steamboat company claimed a clear advantage for passengers going from Bismarck to western points "because you avoid a tedious ride" over the narrow-gauge Utah and Northern. "Because you know when you start just what your expenses will be, as our rates are published open, and that is the limit of your expense. Not so by other routes, where only a portion of your expense is published, and before you reach your destination you find your outlay doubled, and expenses for extra baggage more than passage." The folder urged immigrants to take the river route because "it is more comfortable for families and children to travel on a steamer than to be cooped up in emigrant cars for 6 days. Meals and berth are included in a first-class ticket via Benton Line. Three square meals a day. A good bed at night. The best attention, the finest scenery and the healthiest climate in the world" were the inducements offered by the Benton Line. These were brave words, but it was a hopeless contest for steamboatmen.[17]

What river traffic the Union Pacific failed to win, the Northern Pacific claimed. By 1883 the only business left to steamboats on the upper Missouri River was a limited amount of local commerce between Fort Benton and Bismarck. Trade above Bismarck actually increased briefly in 1887 because steamers hauled construction materials for the Great Falls and Helena extension of the Saint Paul, Minneapolis and Manitoba Railroad (later

In 1889 West Shore depicted the new wagon bridge across the Missouri River at Fort Benton, but the days when steamboats sailed beneath it were numbered. When James J. Hill's Saint Paul–based railroad reached the river port on September 28, 1887, it took away the need for the mountain steamboats that had been so much a part of Montana's transportation landscape for three decades. Courtesy Oregon Historical Society, 91795.

known as the Great Northern). Thirty steamboats reached Fort Benton that year, but this was a statistical aberration.

The Great Northern fostered the growth of a new town called Great Falls, which absorbed most of the former trade of Fort Benton and eventually became one of the largest cities in Montana. Fort Benton meanwhile declined, and all but one of the regular steamboat owners ceased service to the river port. The lone hold-out was Isaac Post Baker and the Benton Transportation Company, which after 1885 controlled nearly all the commercial steamboating that remained on the upper river. For all practical purposes, the final year for both

Montana steamboating and Fort Benton's commercial importance was 1887. The following year only four steamboats arrived at Fort Benton, and in 1890 the *F. Y. Batchelor* delivered the last sizable commercial cargo to the onetime river gateway. There was no long-haul business to Fort Benton after that date, though in 1907 the little, fifty-nine-ton steam packet *O. K.* arrived mainly as a publicity stunt. The year 1910, incidentally, was the last for steamboats on the Yellowstone River.

The Block P boats made at least 158 trips to the Fort Benton vicinity between 1875 and 1889, the most for any of the steamer lines, but after that era ended, the company maintained a only a small fleet at Bismarck. Baker and the Benton Packet Company operated eight boats as of 1911, all but one of them gasoline powered, in the grain trade between the North Dakota capital and nearby river points that still depended on steamboats. From 1924 until 1936, shortly before operations ceased, two of Baker's sons primarily controlled the business. When Benton Transportation finally quit, commercial boating on the upper Missouri ceased, too. None of the several giant dams later erected across the waterway above Sioux City had navigation locks that would permit tourist travel by boat from South Dakota to Montana, whereas on the Columbia River, week-long sightseeing voyages became common in the 1990s.[18]

As the network of rails expanded and steamboats disappeared from the upper Missouri River, some Montanans voiced reservations about the new compe-tition, or lack thereof. The *Montanian* took the railroad to task for imposing a rate of only $1.60 per hundred pounds during the summer season but immediately advancing charges to $3.93 per hundred pounds as soon as the last steamboat departed downstream. "We are at the mercy of the U. P. road. . . . Railroads are all robbers; this is an established fact." The coming of railroads to Montana during the 1880s not only ruined Fort Benton's river-based economy but also shifted the main axis of trade north from Sioux City and Yankton to Saint Paul and Minneapolis. Chicago and its tributary gateways in Iowa and Minnesota used the new transportation tech-nology to win the prize of western commerce from long-established Saint Louis. Farther west, another upstart city, Seattle, did something equally unthinkable by challenging Portland's hegemony over commerce and trade in the Pacific Northwest.[19]

When the steamer Benton *sank near Sioux City on July 18, 1890, it seemed to symbolize the end of an era on the upper Missouri River. The photograph is by L. C. Cooper. Courtesy State Historical Society of North Dakota, C-1361.*

But great as is the sum of the commerce already reached here, it sinks into insignificance
compared with the prospective transcontinental and oceanic business that is heading for Puget
Sound. Note the position that this body of water occupies with respect to the world. It sounds
extravagant now, but sober and cool-headed businessmen, familiar with the facts, believe that
Washington holds the key to the future commerce of the world. She stands at the cross roads
of the nations, at the confluence of the commodities of the four quarters of the globe.
—W. D. Lyman, "The State of Washington," Atlantic Monthly *(April 1901)*

Sail, Steam, and the Rise of Seattle

In 1880, at the start of the decade that brought rails and ruin to Fort Benton, the Montana river settlement had a population of 1,618. Seattle that same year had a population of 3,533 and was just beginning its dramatic rise to prominence, not just on Puget Sound but within the northern West. For three previous decades Seattle had depended mainly on water connections, and until the 1880s, Puget Sound itself had remained somewhat outside the main currents of transportation history, which until then almost always seemed to flow along the Columbia River valley to the benefit of Portland, or north from California. With a population of 17,577 in 1880, Oregon's largest city was still the region's main center for trade and commerce. Seattle, like Fort Benton earlier, would benefit from a major gold rush—the one to Alaska and the Yukon in 1898—but unlike the river-dependent Montana community, Seattle was able to utilize *both* rail and water connections to boost its growth.

Early Sail and Steam on Puget Sound

Puget Sound, the arm of the Pacific Ocean that linked together most early settlements in western Washington, seldom failed to elicit effusive comments from those who saw it. After Charles Nordhoff observed its blue-green waters and forest-fringed shores juxtaposed with high, snow-covered mountain ranges, he pronounced it "one of the most picturesque and remarkable sheets of water in the world." Other enthusiasts compared it favorably to the Mediterranean Sea, and a promotional booklet issued by the Northern Pacific Railway in the early twentieth century claimed that Puget Sound "comes close to the perfection of natural beauty and scenic grandeur." [1]

Port Blakely, Port Orchard, Port Madison, and half a dozen other sawmill villages arose on its shores, "and the present entire export of the Sound, in prepared lumber and masts and spars, reaches nearly to one hundred millions of feet yearly, and yields at the average price of ten dollars a thousand about one million dollars." San Francisco was the largest customer, but the Hawaiian Islands, China, and even Argentina obtained building materials from Puget Sound, "and France finds here her cheapest and best spars and masts." [2]

Seattle was originally no larger than any of the other tiny clearings in the big woods. The town's founders reached Alki Point on November 13, 1851, from Portland aboard the schooner *Exact.* Soon, however, blustery winter weather caused them to abandon their rough cabins

New beginnings on Puget Sound: launching the schooner Minnie A. Caine *on October 6, 1900. Courtesy Washington State Historical Society.*

of fir logs and split cedar boards in favor of a less exposed site along the east shore of Elliott Bay, where there was also an excellent deepwater anchorage. Here Henry L. Yesler built a small sawmill in October 1852. Other businesses soon followed, and a small settlement called Seattle emerged at the foot of the steep hills that rose abruptly to four hundred feet at the crest of the ridge separating Puget Sound from Lake Washington, a large body of fresh water.

Yesler's mill was the first example of steam power on Puget Sound, except for the *Beaver,* which had arrived in 1836. The *Beaver* remained the only steam-powered vessel on the waterway for half a generation, until a second Hudson's Bay Company ship, the propeller steamer *Otter,* joined her in 1853. Local common-carrier steam navigation on Puget Sound dated from 1853 when the

Fairy, a small side-wheeler, commenced service between Olympia and Seattle. Mainly, though, it was billowing sails and not steam that dominated the waterway during the first half of the 1850s. Furnaces, boilers, and steam power gradually gained supremacy as a growing fleet of small vessels connected outposts along Puget Sound.

By 1854 four lines docked regularly at Seattle's wharves, which extended into the deep water of Elliott Bay. Steam navigation on Puget Sound did suffer setbacks, however. Shortly after the *Fairy* relocated to the Olympia-Steilacoom route in 1857, she exploded and sank. To this vessel belonged the distinction of being the first American steamer to sail the waters of Puget Sound, the first to carry United States mails there, and the first to rupture her boiler. More successful was the *Traveler,* which alternated directions each week on a run between

Olympia and Seattle and stopped at all intermediate points. The *Traveler* was also the first steamboat to navigate the White, Snohomish, Nooksack, and other rivers that flowed into Puget Sound. Late in August 1857, the *Constitution,* a small oceangoing steamer, arrived to run between Olympia and Victoria. Mail for the tiny Puget Sound communities traveled aboard coastal steamers from San Francisco and Portland. When the local mail contract went to Captain James M. Hunt and John M. Scranton in 1854, they brought the *Major Tompkins* north from the Golden Gate to shuttle mail, passengers, and freight among Olympia, Seattle, Victoria, and intermediate ports.[3]

The number of steamboats plying Puget Sound waters increased noticeably after news of gold on the Fraser River sparked a major rush of miners during the spring and summer of 1858. Almost overnight a population explosion transformed the quiet fur-trading post of Victoria into a bustling city. When Wells Fargo opened an office there it seemed to validate the importance of the new bonanza. From Victoria, miners scrambled for passage aboard the few steamers destined for Fort Hope or Fort Yale; some argonauts even crossed the broad Georgia Strait to the Fraser River by canoe, small boat, and raft. By the summer of 1858, the American stern-wheelers *Umatilla* and *Enterprise,* both built for service on the Columbia River, transported eager miners and their supplies up the Fraser and made enormous profits.

Thousands of people clamored for passage aboard the steamships departing San Francisco. The Pacific Mail Steamship Company dispatched any old hulk it could spare and loaded it to the gunwales with passengers. In June the *Panama* carried 1,070 passengers on one trip from San Francisco to Victoria, and the *Republic, Commodore,* and *Sierra Nevada* hauled more than nine hundred passengers each on trips in June and July. At the height of the rush, a total of 7,149 passengers left San Francisco in June and another 6,278 in July. Sailing vessels also benefited from the Fraser River rush, but they carried far fewer people. Many argonauts, unable to obtain deck passage aboard coastal steamers, headed north from California on inland routes via The Dalles or the Willamette Valley. Here they crowded aboard river steamers out of Portland and made the overland portage from the Cowlitz River to Olympia, where they reboarded steamboats. An estimated twenty thousand people traveled by sea, and probably another ten thousand trudged north by land during the spring and summer of 1858.

Hoping to tap into the new riches, Puget Sound promoters advertised a projected road from Bellingham Bay to the Fraser River diggings. Gold finds north of the border also encouraged the construction of the first locally built steamboat, the *Julia Barclay,* a fast stern-wheeler. But almost as suddenly as it began, the rush to the Fraser River subsided. Miners quickly collected any surface gold and moved on, leaving the camps deserted. Thousands of gold seekers returned to the United States; most steamboats lured north dispersed to other locations in search of work.

Illustrative of the peregrinations of pioneer steam vessels on Puget Sound was the *Wilson G. Hunt.* Built in New York as a Coney Island excursion steamer in 1849, the big ship instead joined the rush to California where she plied the Sacramento River between San Francisco and Sacramento and reportedly earned a million dollars in a single year. In 1858 the *Wilson G. Hunt* steamed north to British Columbia where she shuttled between Victoria and New Westminster in search of another fortune. Not long after the Fraser River rush, the newly formed Oregon Steam Navigation Company acquired the steamer and assigned her to the Columbia River between Portland and the lower Cascades. Rebuilt in 1865, the *Wilson G. Hunt* returned to Puget Sound four years later. Finally, about 1877, the big steamboat sailed back to San Francisco, where she ran until 1890.

Even more beloved by a generation of Puget Sound residents was the side-wheeler *Eliza Anderson.* Built in Portland and launched on November 27, 1858, she was originally intended for service between Portland and Astoria. Instead, she splashed up the Washington coast during the Fraser River rush. After that excitement, the *Eliza Anderson* settled into forty years of steady service on Puget Sound that would bring more celebrity to her

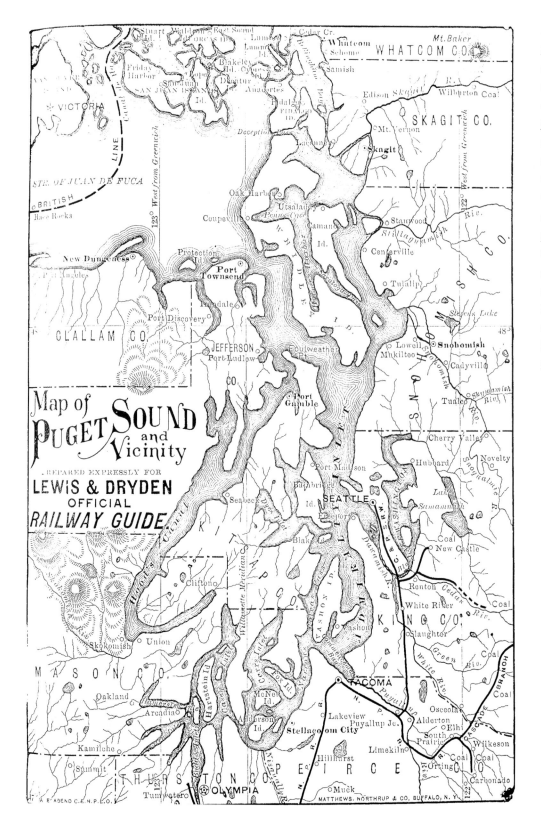

Map of PUGET SOUND and Vicinity

PREPARED EXPRESSLY FOR

LEWIS & DRYDEN

OFFICIAL

RAILWAY GUIDE

It was mainly in response to the California gold rush that the number of sailing ships on Puget Sound waters increased in the early 1850s. When the brig Leonesa returned to San Francisco from a trip to Puget Sound in search of ice, the captain reported back to the ship's owners that the waters of the sound did not freeze and consoled them with a valuable cargo of wooden pilings instead. Puget Sound soon became a prime source of lumber for the Pacific Coast. Extending all along the shores of its many islands and estuaries was a dense forest that lured woodsmen from New England, Michigan, and Minnesota. Courtesy Special Collections Division, University of Washington Libraries, 5144.

*S*eattle as seen from Beacon Hill in 1881. Olympia and Steilacoom being the only two settlements on Puget Sound easily accessible by road, pioneers substituted canoes, sailboats, and small steamboats for the wagons and stagecoaches commonly used in other parts of the northern West. In fact, early Seattle was practically without roads, and outlying parts of the Puget Sound lowlands were difficult to reach except on foot or by horseback. For this reason a mosquito fleet consisting of several small steamers shuttled passengers and freight from one tiny port to another and distributed goods and an occasional bit of news to isolated stump farmers. Courtesy Spokane Public Library.

than to any other steamer in western Washington except the *Beaver.* The Old *Anderson,* as she was familiarly known, touched at Steilacoom, Seattle, Port Madison, Port Gamble, Port Ludlow, and Port Townsend during her weekly round-trip mail run between Olympia and Victoria. For years the entire week's mail to Seattle consisted of little more than a small locked pouch and a sack of newspapers that any able-bodied man could carry on his shoulders.

At all of these settlements the arrival of the steamer, bringing letters and weekly news from the outside world, was a major event, and a crowd was always on hand to greet the *Eliza Anderson* even when she was delayed until late at night. D. B. Finch, purser and later master and managing owner, was credited with installing the ship's famous calliope: its steam-energized music carried for several miles across the calm waters of Puget Sound and not only helped drum up business but also gladdened the lives of lonely settlers along the shore. The *Eliza Anderson* had competitors, but her owners made so much money that their floating gold mine attracted the attention of John C. Ainsworth and his ever vigilant Oregon Steam Navigation Company.

After that enterprise had its operations well organized

Port Blakely and Hall Brothers Shipyard in 1902. Courtesy San Francisco Maritime National Historical Park, F11.7, 494n.

The schooner Nokomis *nears completion at Hall Brothers Shipyard. Courtesy San Francisco Maritime National Historical Park, F4.7, 489n.*

on the Columbia River, it began to envy the growing Puget Sound trade that the *Eliza Anderson* had long dominated. Thus in 1869 Oregon Steam sent its furbished *Wilson G. Hunt* to Puget Sound waters to challenge the *Eliza Anderson.* To the delight of shippers and passengers, the vigorous competition soon dropped rates almost to nothing. The owners of the *Eliza Anderson* had already ordered an elegant new steamer to replace their aging vessel, but in the interim they paid a handsome price for the *Wilson G. Hunt* to eliminate rivalry from Oregon Steam. The Portland company withdrew to its river stronghold, although surplus Columbia and

Willamette steamers occasionally ventured north to the sound to handle the growing volume of local freight and passengers or to excite settlers with another rate war.

The *Eliza Anderson* ambled from port to port until 1870 when her owners replaced her with their fine new steamboat *Olympia.* Taking over and expanding this business the following year was the Puget Sound Steam Navigation Company, which proposed to operate steamboats on the sound, the Strait of Juan de Fuca, and adjoining waters. So successful was this new enterprise that by the mid-1870s it controlled nearly all available steam craft on Puget Sound. Among the few exceptions were the several small steamers that Captain J. C. Brittain acquired from the Oregon Steam Navigation Company and operated on the lower reaches of the sound, to San Juan Island ports, and along the Skagit and Snohomish rivers.

Although the mill villages along Puget Sound lacked railroads and thus easy access to markets in the Midwest and East, cargoes of top-quality lumber from western Washington sailed aboard windjammers to far-off markets accessible by sea. By the mid-1870s, before Puget Sound ports began to export wheat, the oceangoing lumber fleet had already grown as big as the Columbia River grain fleet. In addition, a large number of sailing ships hauled coal from Puget Sound to San Francisco buyers. The shipment of coal from mines in the Cascade foothills was vital to Seattle's early economic health.

Tall ships that hauled coal and lumber did not operate on regular schedules and so were unsuited to the needs of most Puget Sound passengers. In 1875, however, regular passenger steamship service commenced between San Francisco and Tacoma, Seattle, and Victoria; and among the pioneers was the *Pacific,* commanded by Captain Jefferson Davis Howell, an Annapolis graduate whose nautical experience included service aboard the Confederate privateer *Alabama.* The *Pacific* completed only a handful of voyages before she collided with the sailing ship *Orpheus* on November 4, 1875, and sank in one of the more notable marine disasters of the Pacific coast. The *Pacific* left Victoria with perhaps as many as 275 passengers aboard, but after the collision she went under so quickly that there was time enough to lower only a single boat filled with women and children. The Pacific Mail Steamship Company put on a new steamship, *City of Panama,* making two trips per month from San Francisco to Olympia, with intermediate stops at Seattle, Port Townsend, and Victoria.[4]

Terminus Fever

As magnificent as Seattle's water connections were, the Puget Sound settlement still yearned for railroads and the municipal greatness they could confer. It was Seattle's desire to become the main meeting place on the North

Pacific coast between the network of rails building across North America and trans-Pacific commerce. That was quite a dream because when Seattle was incorporated in 1869 it still was a mere village; yet its pioneer settlers boldly claimed that Seattle would be chosen as the Pacific terminus of the northern transcontinental railroad chartered by Congress chartered in 1864.

Well before it selected its Pacific entrepôt, the Northern Pacific extended its westernmost line of tracks across the neck of land separating steamboat navigation on Puget Sound and the Columbia River. The California State Telegraph Company had stretched a telegraph line north from Portland to Seattle as early as 1864, but commercial transport between the two great waterways continued to vary from poor to nonexistent. No one could take a boat at Portland and be certain of getting from the Cowlitz River to Puget Sound without traveling on foot along a trail often muddy and always obstructed by logs and overhung with dense branches. Even travelers who had money to pay for a canoe to the head of navigation on the Cowlitz, about thirty miles inland from the Columbia, were not guaranteed a seat, for the canoes were apt to be overloaded or to have no load at all, which meant that would-be passengers had to wait for days or push ahead on foot.

The situation had improved somewhat by the early 1870s when Charles Horetzky traveled from Tenino by train south. Because of the unfinished state of the right-of-way it still took him five hours to reach Kalama, sixty miles distant on the Columbia River. "The road was not ballasted, and extreme caution was necessary in some places. The country through which this piece of road passed was heavily timbered, and for the greater distance passably level; some rather shaky trestle bridges were also crossed." After an overnight stay in Kalama, Horetzky continued by stern-wheel steamer to Portland.[5]

At the time Horetzky made his railroad portage, the question on everyone's mind was where the Northern Pacific would finally locate its Pacific coast terminus. Public opinion pointed to Bellingham Bay or a similar port, but Seattle residents remained confident that, by whatever route the rails finally reached Puget Sound,

The Portland booster magazine West Shore *depicted the popular coastal steamship* Queen of the Pacific *in October 1882. Courtesy Oregon Historical Society, 91786.*

their community was the only logical terminus. But so too did the residents of every other settlement of consequence. In the summer of 1869, Thomas H. Canfield, president of the Northern Pacific, traveled to Seattle and held out hope that it would be chosen. As if to confirm this, Ben Holladay soon arrived on board his steamship *Oriflamme* with a party of investors eager to appraise things for themselves. The flurry of attention sparked a building boom in Seattle and caused one observer to emphasize that "terminal fever rages at Puget Sound with more violence than ever." But the company refused to reveal its intent. "Meanwhile the suspense is terrible."[6]

During the summer of 1872 a committee of Northern Pacific directors visited Puget Sound with the announced intention of making their final selection. For a week they cruised aboard the steamer *North Pacific* and pondered offers from rival communities. Tiny Seattle generously pledged 7,500 town lots, 3,000 acres of land, $50,000 in cash, $200,000 in bonds, and much of its valuable waterfront for tracks and a depot. The railroad's list of finalists included only Seattle, Tacoma, and Mukilteo. With Olympia eliminated, which Seattle residents thought was their strongest opponent, they smugly considered the fight over because neither Tacoma or Mukilteo could come anywhere near matching the offer Seattle had made. Discovery of coal nearby and development of some of the deposits to a point that proved their value further strengthened their conviction that Seattle was the only logical terminus.

Nearly a year dragged by while Seattle residents waited for word from the railroad. Finally, Arthur A. Denny received a telegram. It read:

Kalama, July 14, 1873

A. A. Denny, Seattle:
We have located the terminus on Commencement Bay.
R. D. Rice,
J . C . Ainsworth,
Commissioners.

The terse announcement dealt a stunning blow to the village that had grown up around the site of Yesler's sawmill. Some residents, firmly convinced that Seattle would never amount to anything other than another small milltown, closed their shops and relocated to Tacoma in anticipation of a brighter future on Commencement Bay. Among those who remained behind was born a stubborn self-confidence known as the "Seattle Spirit."[7]

Seattle's loyal citizens resolved that what they believed was the best harbor in the world should not be without a railroad to funnel freight traffic from the farms and ranches of eastern Washington. Wheat production in the Walla Walla area had supported construction of the famous and highly profitable "rawhide" railroad to Wallula on the Columbia River, but grain growers still complained that it cost half the value of their product to transport it by steamboat to Portland. Might not Seattle prosper by furnishing them a railroad alternative? The true believers promptly organized the Seattle and Walla Walla Railroad and Transportation Company to extend narrow-gauge tracks east across the Cascade mountains through Snoqualmie Pass to the prosperous wheat country.

This railroad was a true grass-roots effort. Monetary contributions were not large, but many Seattle residents donated land and waterfront property that was eventually worth millions of dollars; and citizens turned out en masse on May 1, 1874, to donate the labor needed to launch their narrow-gauge carrier. A railroad construction engineer directed the day's work. Starting near the south shore of Elliott Bay, an energetic army of men and boys cleared the right-of-way and leveled the roadbed for a distance of about three miles, while the women of Seattle helped by serving workers a picnic lunch. The men resolved to continue work by voluntary labor, each giving one day a week until the railroad topped the Cascade Range and dropped down to the fertile valleys on the other side. However, this ambitious objective proved far more difficult to reach than they had thought. Voluntary work continued in a desultory manner, but any hope of having fifteen miles in operation by winter vanished, although twelve miles of line had been graded by October.

Directors of the railroad faced a formidable task. After

Tacoma's harbor as it appeared in West Shore *in June 1885. Courtesy Oregon Historical Society, 91788.*

the panic of 1873, money for construction was extremely hard to obtain, and their homegrown enterprise lagged. Fifteen miles of track finally opened to Renton by 1875 and operated at a profit, but construction again halted before the line reached the coal mines at Newcastle in the Cascade foothills. Given their troubles, it was easy for Seattle partisans to believe that the Northern Pacific was somehow responsible for thwarting their best efforts.

In fact, the Northern Pacific was mired in troubles of its own. The failure of Jay Cooke and Company in 1873

forced the would-be transcontinental railroad to suspend construction. Because at this time the valuable land grant within Washington Territory, except for the portion from Kalama to Tacoma, remained unearned, Seattle partisans sought revenge by urging Congress to open the Northern Pacific's vast landholdings to settlement. The railroad appeared to retaliate against the upstart village by making it difficult for anyone to travel to Seattle by train. "If I had it in my power a locomotive would never turn a wheel into Seattle," a president of the Northern Pacific was supposed to have complained. It seemed certain to Seattle residents that the railroad refused to recognize the existence of their community and did all in its power to force citizens to abandon their homes and relocate to Tacoma, where the Northern Pacific owned considerable land and hoped to build the great metropolis of Puget Sound. It even rearranged its train and boat schedules so that anyone traveling between Seattle and Portland had to remain overnight in Tacoma.[8]

Through engineering skill, public commitment, and strict economy, Seattle backers finally extended their narrow-gauge railroad from coal bunkers at the foot of King Street to the Newcastle mines before the end of 1877. After adding extensions to the Black Diamond and Franklin coal mines, the tiny carrier became a major wealth producer, though its tracks never did reach the Walla Walla Valley granary or even ascend the west side of the Cascade Range. Despite this, the little railroad became too rich a prize for the Northern Pacific to ignore.

Not long after the transcontinental railroad resumed limited construction, Henry Villard gained control of it in 1881. His sudden rise to power gave Seattle residents renewed hope, for they believed that he was a friend of their aspiring city and would remedy the railroad blockade. When Villard visited Puget Sound in 1883, Seattle offered to contribute $150,000 to build a standard-gauge railroad up the Cedar River valley to provide their community a direct connection with coal deposits along the Green River and the Cascade Division that the Northern Pacific planned to extend from eastern Washington to Puget Sound. Villard's response was noncommittal but comforting. When his new subsidiary for coal production, the Oregon Improvement Company, acquired the Seattle and Walla Walla Railroad and its real estate and fleet of coal ships, hope soared in Seattle but sank in Tacoma. Even this purchase, however, did not immediately gain Seattle its coveted access to suppliers and markets east of the Cascades. For another decade and more, the rivalry with Tacoma seethed. Villard, meanwhile, was clearly up to something in Pacific coast maritime transportation.

Over the Water Like a Cannon

During the decades that Seattle lusted for railroad connections, the Puget Sound fleet continued to increase in size and scope. As early as 1880 the Northern Pacific Railroad built its first steamer, the *Frederick K. Billings*, although it was originally intended for use as a train ferry on the Columbia River and not Puget Sound. When Villard became head of the Northern Pacific the following year, the Pacific Coast Steamship Company (successor in 1877 to the line of coastal steamers operated by Charles Goodall and George C. Perkins) sold the Villard syndicate ten coastal steamships, including the *Idaho, Ancon,* and *Queen of the Pacific.* Also in 1881, two years after the Oregon Steam Navigation Company became the Oregon Railway and Navigation Company with Villard as its head, the transportation colossus of the Columbia River reached north to Puget Sound once again. Well aware of the Oregon company's reputation for sweeping all opposition before it, most local operators bowed out gracefully. Without a struggle, the Puget Sound Steam Navigation Company sold all its steamers to Villard's rapidly expanding transportation empire.

In this way the Oregon Railway and Navigation Company transferred its flag to the *George E. Starr, Isabel, Alida, Otter,* and *Annie Stewart.* The latter was an old Columbia River stern-wheeler that the Puget Sound Steam Navigation Company purchased in 1879 and now sold to Villard along with the rest of its fleet. Several more Columbia River steamers soon entered service on Puget Sound waters. As the Oregon Railway and Navigation Company extended a line of tracks up the Columbia River valley to tap the wheat country of eastern Oregon and Washington, it transferred several more of its out-of-work steamboats to Puget Sound routes. The large and luxurious *Emma Hayward* left the Portland-Astoria trade to run between Seattle, Tacoma, and Olympia.

The Oregon Railway and Navigation Company had not been flexing its muscle on Puget Sound even a year before opponents formed the Washington Steamboat Company. But rather than fight a money-losing competitive duel, the two firms worked out a kind of armed truce by 1884. The Oregon company controlled the Tacoma-

Seattle in 1878. To observers from Portland, the "growth of the inland commerce of Puget Sound has certainly been remarkable," or so West Shore *commented in 1884. "A few years ago half a dozen small steamers and a few schooners did all the passenger and freight traffic of the whole Sound, while now 78 steamers are profitably employed in the local traffic of its harbors, bays, and rivers." Ironically, when steamboats were in decline on the waters of the East and Midwest, they had just entered their golden era on Puget Sound. Courtesy Library of Congress, GM 2965/412070.*

Seattle and Tacoma-Olympia trade. In addition, the *Idaho,* an old side-wheeler built for Columbia River service in 1860, would fly the corporate flag to Sehome, on Bellingham Bay, while the *Olympian* did likewise between Seattle and Victoria. The Washington Steamboat Company retained a virtual monopoly on the Skagit River, controlled the Bellingham Bay trade, and operated its stern-wheeler *Nellie* along the Snohomish River.

The half decade between 1889 and the 1894 brought still more major adjustments to steamboat operations on Puget Sound. In 1889, Captain D. B. Jackson dissolved his Washington Steamboat Company and organized the Puget Sound and Alaska Steamship Company. The new

enterprise brought two fine, modern steamers to Puget Sound, the first of a fleet of fast propeller-driven ships that plied the major routes during the closing decades of the steamboat era. Of even greater consequence, the Oregon Railway and Navigation Company withdrew from Puget Sound steamboat operations a final time in 1892. The following year the Alaska Steamship Company was formed, which later established the Puget Sound Navigation Company to operate Puget Sound service. The two firms eventually separated, but for years the Alaska Steamship Company dominated shipping between Seattle and Alaska, while the Black Ball Line held a virtual monopoly of ferry routes on Puget Sound.

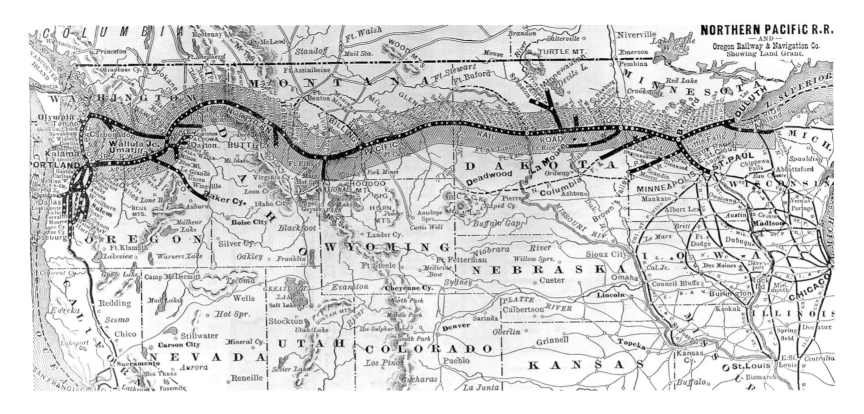

These same years witnessed the best that steam technology could offer travelers on Puget Sound waters. A steamboat called the *Flyer* "is the most admirable vessel of its kind that I have ever seen. It is of the build of a fish, and is almost as swift. Its two saloons, one above the other, are carpeted, and provided with soft plush-covered reclining-chairs. The walls are, to all intents and purposes, plate-glass. The machinery is exhibited like jewelry, in a glass case. By day the panorama of nature is uninterrupted in the view of the passengers; by night the little *Flyer* is all aflame with electric light, like a glass boat or a lantern shot over the water from a cannon."[9]

North to Alaska

Seattle eventually won its long struggle for transcontinental railroad connections. The Northern Pacific grudgingly offered through service by 1893, the same year that James J. Hill's Great Northern Railway was completed between Saint Paul and Seattle. But Seattle residents now asked why they should be content with railroad service merely to the Midwest and East. The seas of China and Japan and even Alaska beckoned, whereas water links forged with the northern West during the 1880s and 1890s would only enlarge the basic pattern of service already established on Puget Sound and the Columbia River. Travel to Alaska involved many of the same ships and people making history in Oregon and Washington and some of the same navigational challenges and opportunities encountered earlier on Puget Sound. It was the existence of a sheltered Inside Passage that did most to link the maritime histories of the Pacific Northwest and Alaska. Threading its way between islands and mainland from Puget Sound to Glacier Bay, the "inside passage" offered panoramic views of a magnificent landscape and protection from storms brewed farther north in the Gulf of Alaska.[10]

In mid-1869, two years after the United States acquired Alaska from Russia, the steamer *Wilson G. Hunt* docked at Seattle with Secretary of State William H. Seward and a party of federal officials who were headed north to Sitka.

*T*his map of the Northern Pacific Railroad circa 1885 appeared in A Description of Lands and Country Along the Line of the Northern Pacific Railroad. *Note its emphasis on Tacoma. Courtesy Day-Northwest Collection, University of Idaho Library, HC108 A19 N52.*

In a brief talk, Seward bedazzled a cheering crowd when he described the unbounded possibilities of the North and predicted that Washington Territory would eventually rival many older states in wealth and population. Such words intoxicated every Seattle booster, although the outpost was not without formidable rivals for the Alaska trade.

Foremost was San Francisco, from whence steam whalers pioneered American trade with Alaska. Another rival was Portland, which, beginning in the late 1860s, inaugurated service to Puget Sound and British Columbia (and later Alaska) with the *George S. Wright,* the first steamship to engage regularly in the trade, although San Francisco–based steamers had previous handled cargoes for northern ports, calling at Portland along the way. As late as 1876 the bulk of trade between Oregon and Alaska still traveled aboard the *George S. Wright,* which completed one trip a month hauling mainly freight, mail, and military personnel between Portland and Sitka, with intermediate stops at various Puget Sound ports.

Discovery of gold in 1879 near what is now Juneau encouraged the first regular passenger steamship service in southeastern Alaska. Tourist voyages probably dated from 1881 when Henry Villard took the first large excursion party north and excited growing popular interest in the Great Land. His eighty guests included General Nelson Miles, then in command of the army on the Pacific Coast, and a military band. They cruised aboard the well-equipped steamer *Idaho.* The Alaska excursion offered an example of how much Villard loved to impress the public. Just a year earlier his new steamer *Columbia* had fascinated Portland citizens when it brought the first of Thomas Edison's new incandescent bulbs to the Pacific Northwest and cast a warm glow across the Willamette River. It was perhaps fitting that the impresario of light would leave transportation in the northern West to head the Edison General Electric Company.

Villard's 1881 excursion was the result of rising American fascination with Alaska since its purchase fourteen years earlier, a fascination roused by a growing number of writers, including the naturalist John Muir, who inspired would-be travelers with glowing descriptions of Alaska sights and dispelled the notion that it was a "Polar Bear Garden" festooned with icicles. From the comfort of deck chairs, tourists could enjoy an ever-changing panorama of snow-capped mountains, glaciers, verdant forests, and native villages, and along these sheltered waters none need suffer the discomfort of seasickness. As Muir summed it up, "No excursions that I know of may be made into any other American wilderness where so marvelous an abundance of noble, newborn scenery is so charmingly brought to view as on the trip through the Alexander Archipelago to Fort Wrangell and Sitka. Gazing from the deck of the steamer, one is borne smoothly over calm blue waters, through the midst of countless forest-clad islands." [11]

Dominating the Alaska tourist trade in the 1880s were the *Queen, George W. Elder, Idaho, Ancon,* and *Corona* of the Pacific Coast Steamship Company. Each vessel offered accommodations that were clean and reasonably comfortable for $130 round-trip from San Francisco, meals included. Word of Alaska tours spread throughout the United States, and after a through railway line was completed from the East to Portland and Puget Sound in the fall of 1883, the number of Alaska tourists increased rapidly. Of paramount importance, the Inside Passage excursion kept thousands of Americans in touch with events in Alaska. Nothing, though, had as much impact on transportation between the northern West and Alaska as the excitement known as the Klondike rush.

The Klondike Rush

After nearly a month's voyage from Saint Michael (on the Bering Sea near the mouth of the Yukon River), the North American Trading and Transportation Company's steamship *Portland* neared Seattle on the morning of July 17, 1897. Wild rumors circulated that the ship was filled with gold. The *Post-Intelligencer* chartered a tug, loaded it with reporters, and sent it to intercept the *Portland* as she entered Puget Sound. Newsmen clambered over the rails and into an excited crowd of miners as eager for news from outside Alaska as reporters were for news of the Klondike. The tug soon raced back to

Seattle, and the first of the *Post-Intelligencer*'s three extras hit the streets almost at the same moment as the *Portland* nosed into Elliott Bay. Headlines screamed:

Gold! Gold! Gold! Gold!

68 Rich Men on the Steamer Portland

Stacks of Yellow Metal!

Some Have $5,000, Many Have More, and

a Few Bring Out $100,000 Each

The Steamer Carries $700,000.[12]

Though it was not yet six o'clock, five thousand early risers jammed Schwabacher's Dock as several dozen bewhiskered passengers held up sacks stuffed tight with thousands of dollars' worth of the yellow metal. This sight disarmed even the most stubborn skeptics. The arrival of the *Portland* provided the confirmation that cities and hamlets across the United States were looking for since rumors of gold first flashed over the wires after the steamship *Excelsior* reached San Francisco three days earlier. One *Post-Intelligencer* story was written by Beriah Brown, who coined the phrase "A Ton of Gold," calculating that the weight of the treasure would be more impressive than its value. Newspapers around the world repeated the phrase. In fact, there were at least two tons of gold aboard the *Portland.* It required Seattle police and Wells Fargo guards armed with rifles to clear a path for miners through the crowd.

The events of July 17 were like the sunburst that follows a violent storm. In a single day, or so it seemed to many Americans, the gloom and pessimism produced by four long years of economic depression and social and political turmoil vanished. "Prosperity is Here" cried the *Post-Intelligencer* just four days after the *Portland* docked. So far as Seattle was concerned the depression was at an end. Merely thinking about finding fortunes in Canada's fabulous Klondike diggings revived hopes and dreams battered by years of monetary crises, widespread unemployment, and popular unrest.

Within just ten days of the *Portland*'s arrival, fifteen hundred people left Seattle for Alaska and the Yukon. Around the docks the streets were so packed with merchandise that people and animals had to thread their way between supplies stacked ten feet high. Goats, dogs, sheep, oxen, mules, and ponies—all headed north to pull Klondike packing outfits—were tied to hitching posts or to great piles of lumber. A steady stream of bony and worn-out horses kept arriving from Montana, worth only three to five dollars each a week earlier but now priced at twenty-five dollars or more. Mules came from Colorado, and some observers even claimed that reindeer with their horns removed were sold as pack animals. No household's pet dog was safe. All over the United States, people jammed transportation company offices to seek information and tickets. Nearly every passenger train traveled across the northern West with its special gold rush car, its walls lined with glass jars full of nuggets and dust and photographs of the mining areas and its tables strewn with books and maps, pamphlets, picks, pans, and shovels. The streets of Seattle remained crowded all night long. Men without lodging slept in stables and washed at fire hydrants.

Merchants of the Pacific coast, eager to capitalize on the Klondike trade by mining the miners' pocketbooks, intensified their long-standing commercial and urban rivalries. Only days after receiving news of the fabulous Klondike bonanza, the Seattle Chamber of Commerce organized a special committee to boost the city as the chief gateway to Alaska. The committee secretary was a veteran journalist, Erastus Brainerd, a Harvard graduate who had once been the curator of an art gallery. It was Brainerd who made certain that a special Klondike edition of the *Post-Intelligencer* reached all corners of the nation. More than seventy thousand copies went to every postmaster in the United States, fifteen thousand to the Great Northern and Northern Pacific railroads, six thousand to public libraries, and four thousand to mayors.

This public relations feat not only fostered a boom that effectively doubled the city's population shortly before the turn of the century but also helped link Seattle and

The Klondike *and* Willamette *ready to leave Seattle for the Klondike. "Seattle," a* New York Herald *reporter wrote, "has gone stark, staring mad on gold." Within three hours of the* Portland's *arrival on July 17, 1897, downtown streets were jammed with so many people that some streetcars had to stop running, which was fortunate since motormen and conductors had already begun to resign in order to head for the Klondike. Theirs was the first of the mass resignations (among them, that of Seattle's mayor W. D. Wood) that became a feature of the early rush. Courtesy Washington State Historical Society, Curtis 26440.*

Alaska in the public mind for decades to come. One million people, or so it was claimed, made plans to go to the Klondike; about a hundred thousand of them actually set out for the diggings. Most of the gold seekers of 1897–1898 chose Seattle as their jumping-off point because of Brainerd's vigorous boosting and the city's obvious geographical advantages. Vancouver, Portland, San Francisco, and Tacoma soon became also-rans in the contest to capture the trade of Alaska. Klondike gold boosted Seattle fortunes in the late 1890s much as Idaho gold did Portland's in the early 1860s.

When the main horde of gold seekers reached Seattle they learned that regular Alaska steamers were booked solid for months ahead. But this did not present an insurmountable problem: during the depressed times of the 1890s, both seamen and ships were idled in ports all along the Pacific coast. Any would-be steamship magnate had only to comb the mudflats and boneyards in search of anything that resembled a ship and gave promise of remaining afloat long enough to reach "golden Alaska." Sharp operators hastily patched up even condemned ships and put them to work in northern waters; they obtained crewmen to run the motley flotilla just as easily.

The little Al-ki was the first ship to head north from Seattle, on July 19. The forty-five-foot steam launch Rustler with a former San Francisco milk wagon driver in command reached Skagway with seventy passengers, though she was licensed for twenty-five on the calm waters of San Francisco Bay. When the Willamette left Tacoma on August 7, 1897, more than seven thousand people pressed together on the dock and waited for hours to watch her sail. This ship was an old coal carrier that the Pacific Coast Steamship Company hastily converted to passenger service. Coal dust still layered the decks, and passengers—some eight hundred men, women, and children—and three hundred horses were soon black with it. The Willamette had eating facilities for sixty-five; thus meal service required nine or ten seatings.

Even the ancient side-wheeler Eliza Anderson, perhaps the oldest steam vessel on the Pacific coast, was hauled from the boneyard and dispatched on a three-thousand-mile misadventure to distant Saint Michael on the Bering Sea. The "Old Anderson" had plenty of passengers but lacked up-to-date boilers, electric power, refrigeration, and even a compass. She nonetheless became the flagship of an odd flotilla that sailed from Seattle on August 10, cheered on by as many as five thousand onlookers. The Richard Holyoke towed the little river steamboat W. K. Merwyn with a bulging load of passengers sealed in the Merwyn's enclosed cabin. The plan was for the Eliza Anderson to be abandoned at Saint Michael and her passengers transferred to the W. K. Merwyn for a river voyage to the Klondike.

With her decks loaded with all the paraphernalia of the gold rush, from tents to mining equipment, the Eliza Anderson limped north, plagued by one mishap after another. The steamboat ran out of fuel because lazy crewmen hid half the coal sacks at Kodiak so nobody would notice. Shipboard furniture, stateroom partitions, and wooden bunkers were then burned for fuel, until little more than a hollow shell remained. The situation grew so precarious that some travelers reportedly wrote farewell notes, stuffed them into bottles, and threw these overboard before the truly old Anderson finally blundered into Unalaska (Dutch Harbor), smashing part of the dock in the process. A broken pipe in the boiler room vented plumes of steam into the arctic air; the captain vowed to sail on to Saint Michael, but passengers hastily abandoned ship to seek other transportation. Some returned to Seattle; others chartered the whaler Baranof to take them the final 750 miles across the Bering Sea to Saint Michael. From there they struggled up the Yukon River to Dawson, though the W. K. Merwyn got only to Nome. Most ships went to Dyea or Skagway instead, at the head of the Inside Passage, but from either port the argonauts faced a long and arduous overland journey to the goldfields.

Although the mad rush to the Klondike was fairly well over by the end of 1898, many argonauts continued to sail to Alaska in search of gold. For the northern West, the Klondike excitement was but a prelude to a renewal of dramatic growth. Astute land speculators, industrialists, financiers, railroad barons, and others realized that

*F.*Jay Haynes photographed Seattle's Madison Street from the city's waterfront coal bunkers in 1890. Visitors to Seattle sometime shook their heads in wonder as they surveyed its landscape. "Seattle clings to a steep hillside; a little shake, it seems, would send it sliding down into the sea," wrote Ray Stannard Baker in 1903. "Loaded teams go tacking zigzag up these hills like a sailing-ship in the wind, and pedestrians are given cleats and railings on some of the sidewalks to help them make the climb. But in the face of these difficulties, Seattle has built a fine city, a great harbor and docks, a ship-building plant, a coaling-depot, a navy-yard and manufacturing industries. No other American city that I know of gives such an impression of boundless activity, such a stir of enterprise and noise, as Seattle, such a determination to grow and be big." Courtesy Montana Historical Society, H-2260.

Loading apples at Seattle's Hanford Dock on October 20, 1921. Courtesy Washington State Historical Society.

economic revival made the vast natural resources of the northern West every bit as attractive as those of the remote Klondike.

The Seattle Spirit

If anything, the Klondike excitement only amplified the Seattle Spirit, that city's relentless recitation of its attractions and its commitment to growth. "Seattle's matchless harbor may be said to have produced its own business; its location made it impossible for any other city on the Sound in the days before the railway to wrest from it its supremacy in the local trade, and it was from this trade that Seattle derived its first nourishment," or so claimed

the city's boosters. By the early twentieth century, Seattle's reach extended not only to Alaska but also across the Pacific Ocean to Asia, encouraging one enthusiast to assert that, while "the development of the United States began at the back door" of the Atlantic coast, "you shall see one day what the front door is like." By the end of the 1880s, the Canadian Pacific Railroad had already established a steamship route across the North Pacific from its new terminus at Vancouver, British Columbia, and ships returned from Asia with substantial cargoes of silk and tea. A steamer line was established between Portland and Japan and China in 1890, causing one local booster to proclaim that this "means that the time when

San Francisco was commercial autocrat of the Pacific coast has passed away."[13]

The possibilities of trade with Asia were not lost on James J. Hill. Three years after his Great Northern Railway was completed from the Great Lakes to Seattle in 1893, he negotiated a deal with the Japanese Nippon Yusen Kaisha (NYK) line to provide steamship service between Hong Kong, Japan, and his trains at Puget Sound. The Great Northern's main competitor, the Northern Pacific, over which Hill and his allies were to gain control in 1901, had established shipping connections across the North Pacific as early as 1892.

Hill saw such enormous potential in shipping freight, particularly grain, to Asia that in 1900 the Empire Builder ordered two giant cargo vessels, the *Minnesota* and *Dakota,* to offer six-week service linking Great Northern trains in Seattle with Japan, China, and the Philippines. Hill's leviathans had the distinction of being the largest vessels then afloat, nonetheless they were plagued by trouble, particularly by spontaneous fires in their coal bunkers. After the *Dakota* was wrecked near Yokohama

in 1907, the *Minnesota* alone toiled slowly across the Pacific, making four voyages a year. The *Minnesota,* an unprofitable white elephant, was sold in 1916. All this, of course, proved to be only a rough beginning for Seattle's trade with Asia.

At the time of the Alaska-Yukon-Pacific Exposition in 1909—Seattle's combination of world's fair and self-congratulatory coming-of-age party—Harvey Scott of the *Oregonian* pondered the city's unthinkable rise. Most Portland residents tended to dismiss Seattle as a brash upstart, but the usually acerbic Scott was magnanimous on this occasion. He cited three reasons why Washington had so rapidly forged ahead of Oregon. First, there was the completion of four transcontinental railroads to Puget Sound; next there was the transformation from pioneer and agricultural conditions to commercial activity ("the more rapid submergence of the early settler in Washington than in Oregon"); and finally there was the bonanza that Alaska provided to Seattle. Good transportation and the Seattle Spirit had triumphed over early adversity.[14]

The making of a icon of the old West: this stagecoach, which made its final trip between Julesburg and Cheyenne in December 1866, later advertised Cheyenne's Frontier Days. Courtesy Wyoming State Museum.

Many notable American writers, in poetry and prose, have recorded the activities of the
conventional stage coach of the Great West and the characteristics and social amenities of
its driver. Today no wild west show is thought complete without the old-time lumbering
vehicle with its leather springs and driver's seat, perched high in front over the boot, and with
from four to six spirited horses attached. The part played by these ships of the plains in the
development of the states west of the Mississippi River has been perpetuated in fiction and
in history.
—*Clarence B. Bagley,* History of Seattle *(1916)*

Symbols of an Era

The last overland stagecoach rolled out of Deadwood on Sunday afternoon, December 28, 1890, like an actor taking a final curtain call. The Knights of Pythias, dressed in plain clothes and carrying canes instead of their usual swords, escorted it out of town. A band played "Fare Thee Well for I Must Leave Thee." The next morning the first train from Chicago on the Chicago and North Western line whistled to a stop before a large crowd that greeted it with mixed emotions of joy and sadness. Flags waved from every building, and welcoming banners fluttered above Deadwood's main street. The Knights of Pythias drill corps strutted about in colorful uniforms. The hills echoed with staccato blasts of dynamite to herald this new phase of civilization. By this date the term *stagecoach town* had become popularly equated with municipal lethargy and sleepiness. But there were tradeoffs, for as a Deadwood judge huffed as he surveyed the motley crowd of railroad passengers from distant points, "Now we'll have to lock our doors."[1]

An older generation of westerners had "many a sweet recollection" of travel aboard stagecoaches, but they were nonetheless "a poor substitute in the faster time and more comfortable accommodations of railway trains."

The old Concord coaches, "so tastefully constructed and so useful and important in their day," became "too slow for the steady advance of civilization. The iron sinews of commerce that were rapidly stretching out over the rolling prairies from the great western bend of the Missouri were forcing the Concords to the rear."[2]

The need for fast, uninterrupted transportation and communication was one reason why the northern transcontinental railroad was such a tantalizing prospect: "Montana has the advantage of river communication during a few months in each year, but her rapidly developing mineral resources require something more than the uncertain river facilities and the slow progress of wagon transportation," observed the *Montana Post* in 1867. When the northern West was an isolated region, its settlers tolerated a leisurely pace of life; but once residents saw the possibilities that railroads offered elsewhere, their expectations rose, a point emphasized by Harvey Scott of the *Oregonian.* He noted that in the early 1850s the residents of Portland "had a steamer from San Francisco once or twice a month, and we felt, in fact, quite as near to the world as we wished to be." It was not until California obtained a railway connection with the

East that Oregonians "began to feel so remote and to long so much for nearer and closer" communication and transportation links for their state.[3]

"This is the age of speed," Uncle Frank emphasized to his steamboatman nephew, Louis Rosché. "A telegraph operator taps a key and flashes a message instantly across the country where a few years ago it would have required weeks, even months, for that message to have been carried on horseback." Even after information could speed over a telegraph wire and passengers and freight could travel swiftly aboard railroad trains, people invested stagecoach and steamboat travel across the West with romantic qualities, for these technologies represented a familiar and comforting presence in an expansive and hostile land. In the early days of travel, on the trip overland from the Columbia River to Puget Sound, "there was not a house, much less a settlement to break the monotony of the long ride through heavy timber, which shut one in like high walls. But, strange though it may seem," the journey "was far more interesting than it has been since the era of the railroad, which, in spite of its manifold changes, brings in its wake conventional customs and seems to banish all romance from the scene."[4]

Symbols: Selling the Romance of the Frontier West

After Gilmer and Salisbury acquired the Montana and Idaho lines of Wells Fargo in 1869, the firm continued to expand its stagecoach operations until it maintained a far-flung transportation network across the northern West. But no longer did most newspapers and popular magazines send reporters out to write stories about this mode of travel; if anything, most western communities now viewed staging as only an interim phase until the coming of a railroad. Perhaps the most notable exception to waning public interest in this early mode of travel occurred after the discovery of gold in the Black Hills, when the 1876 rush actually fostered an expansion of staging along the high plains routes to Deadwood and for a time seemed to turn back the clock to the glory days of the California rush. Deadwood's nearest transportation

gateways were Sidney, on the Union Pacific tracks in Nebraska; Bismarck, on the Northern Pacific in Dakota Territory; and Yankton, a Missouri River steamboat landing at the southeastern edge of Dakota Territory. Each of these places was located more than two hundred miles from Deadwood and, at the time of the gold discovery, had no established trails or roads to the Black Hills over which a stagecoach might operate.

The lack of public transportation to the Black Hills offered an unusual opportunity to Gilmer and Salisbury. A link with the Black Hills enabled this ambitious outfit to round out an expanding stagecoach network that specialized in serving most major mining camps of the northern West. The new route, acquired by purchase of the Cheyenne and Black Hills Stage Company, took shape under the guidance of their superintendent, Luke Voorhees, who located the most practical route, established the necessary relay stations, and equipped the line with thirty new yellow-and-red Concord coaches. On April 3, 1876, three loaded coaches—each bearing a distinctive name, such as the Deadwood—rolled north out of Cheyenne and up the Black Hills trail to make through service on the new route a reality. Jack Gilmer himself handled the reigns on the lead coach.[5]

Stages left Cheyenne at two o'clock every Monday and Thursday afternoon and returned on Tuesday and Saturday. But dust from the first through stages had scarcely settled before Indians attacked a party of gold seekers near the Cheyenne River. Native Americans complained that the Black Hills had not been opened legally to prospecting and settlement by outsiders. Gilmer and Salisbury persisted in the face of Indian opposition. In addition to numerous army officers and soldiers who rode the stagecoaches, a frequent passenger in the fall of 1876 was Buffalo Bill Cody, a personal friend of Luke Voorhees's. Cody later immortalized these tense times on the Great Plains in his Wild West extravaganzas, which featured a Deadwood coach chased by Indians. For many Americans this contrived excitement formed the enduring image of a frontier mode of travel.[6]

While Superintendent Voorhees was busy running the Cheyenne and Black Hills route, Gilmer and Salisbury

established a four-horse Concord stage line to run
between the end of Northern Pacific tracks and Helena
via Bozeman, thus enabling the railway to form a
through connection from Saint Paul and Minneapolis to
Helena, where connections were made with stage lines
for Fort Benton, Butte, Deer Lodge, and Virginia City.
But stage service from the end of the tracks was only
temporary, the beginning of the end for staging in

another part of the northern West. In 1883 Gilmer and
Salisbury sold the Cheyenne and Black Hills line, which
operated a few more years until railroads reached the
mining towns of the Black Hills. The partners meanwhile
devoted more attention to their extensive mining and
banking interests.

Besides Gilmer and Salisbury, there were numerous
local stage outfits that continued to operate during the

early railway era. Ernest Ingersoll wrote about the Palouse country of eastern Washington and northern Idaho in September 1884; "Stages traverse it, carrying the mail in several directions, and I chose the route from Lewiston to Cheney, a station on the Northern Pacific Railway." Ingersoll described his lengthy ride aboard an "open two-seated and badly used-up buckboard" in the pages of *Harper's New Monthly Magazine.* Even after the Northern Pacific extended its tracks across Montana, stage lines continued to serve as feeders for the railway. As late as the 1890s there were still hundreds of small stage lines serving remote settlements across the northern West. Thus horse-drawn coaches disappeared only gradually, in some places yielding to the new "automobile stages" only in the early twentieth century. Connections were often listed as "Stage and Auto Routes" in railroad timetables, with little distinction made between horse-drawn and motorized vehicles.[7]

However, one by one, like autumn leaves, the old stagecoach lines fell, usually without much fanfare or mourning. The eighty-mile stagecoach ride from Redrock, Montana, to Salmon, Idaho, over the Continental Divide at Lemhi Pass, "was picturesque," a local newspaper affirmed shortly before the trains of the Gilmore and Pittsburgh Railway put the stage line out of business in 1910. "Its drivers were artists at their business. Its officials were little czars. Its passing will be mourned by the keepers of eating houses along its route, but by few other people."[8]

It was true that few travelers missed the many discomforts of a long stagecoach journey, but as a romantic symbol of the frontier West, this mode of transportation remained unrivaled even by the steamboat. Not long after Gilmer and Salisbury shut down most of its Montana operations, nostalgia moved a Deer Lodge newspaper to write: "The stage horse out to grass, har-

The Crescent City–Grants Pass stage pauses for its portrait, probably in the early twentieth century. Courtesy Southern Oregon Historical Society, 11130.

The Marysville train, photographed by F. Jay Haynes in April 1889, was typical of the locals that replaced stagecoaches serving some of the small towns of Montana and other parts of the northern West. The Haynes Palace Studio Car, a darkroom on wheels, sits on the trestle. Courtesy Montana Historical Society, H-2045.

ness hung in the stables and the coaches parked in the yards and sheds. It reminds us that the days of stage coaching are over in this part of Montana, and nearly everywhere. We haven't seen a coach and six on the street for a fortnight, and miss them not altogether without regret. If there is a prettier picture of animation than a red Concord coach, with six spirited horses in bright harness and a good reinsman on the box, we haven't seen it. But it was not always clean Concords and six prancing horses. There are jerkeys and mud wagons, with two and four horses, and passengers packed in like sardines, or footing it through the mud at the rate of two miles an

hour, in the dark background of memory on which the brighter picture is painted."[9]

Only two decades earlier, in the 1860s, the stagecoach had been widely heralded as a symbol of progress, an agency to develop and civilize the Wild West, and an important way to redefine its time and space. As the *Montana Post* of Virginia City phrased it in 1865: "Quartz mills, crushers, and a great many machines of different kinds, are arriving constantly. Daily lines of communication are opened by stage companies, and we think that there never was a place so far from a settled country, or the ocean, where so much has been done in so short a time." In anticipation of the first through stage from Boise to Walla Walla in 1864, arrangements were made to celebrate the arrival with a torchlight parade. Walla Walla merchants illuminated their buildings, agreeing that "when ever" the expected stage got to town, "a new era will have dawned upon this country." The first stage finally rolled in on Friday evening, March 25, 1864. The festive occasion included speeches by Captain John Mullan and other notables. The following July, the first regular delivery of mail from the East Coast began, and it was universally hailed as one of the many signs that Walla Walla was evolving from a mining supply town into a more cosmopolitan and diverse city and that civilization had arrived.[10]

The stagecoach as a symbol of civilization in a hostile wilderness was employed in one of Bishop Daniel Tuttle's reminiscences. He was aboard the early morning stage from Boise to Silver City in the Owyhee Mountains: "Generally the country through which we passed was a monotonous, sage brush plain; towards the end of our journey, however, we began to wind in and out of the cañons of this Owyhee range. We came through a hostile Indian country, and again had loaded revolvers at our sides. In the driver's seat we saw three loaded rifles. But we had no trouble and we arrived safely here about 4 P.M." Some travelers could well ponder, however, exactly what kind of civilization the new transportation technologies brought in their wake. Many Americans who crossed Panama carried firearms and used them to shoot at wildlife—alligators and monkeys that frequently presented themselves as unwitting targets—much as travelers did on steamboats and stagecoaches crossing the northern West. For Native Americans too, the new transportation and communication technology was a symbol, not of civilization or a link with home, but of intrusion into their homelands.[11]

During the 1850s and 1860s, local newspapers usually chronicled the arrival of every stage. The best drivers were well known to all. Their showmanship when arriving with the overland coach and their manner of dress, with buckskin gloves, Stetson hat, and ever-present vest, contributed to their larger-than-life image. A stage driver was always a proud man who "might accept a cigar, a box of cigars, a new hat (or, if over-tempted, even a ten dollar bill!), but the typical tip was as far beneath him as any coachman. Similarly the word coaching was not in his professional vocabulary; the operation was one of staging."[12]

Some drivers had picturesque names like Rattlesnake Pete, Fiddler Jim, Happy Jack, Smiling Tom, One-eyed Tom, Cross-eye John, Red Horse, Rowdy Pete, Fish-Creek Bill, and Long Slim. "All of these men were skilled drivers, as was Bob Hedges who developed a reputation for playing, 'Get out of the Wilderness' on his copper bugle as the coach rolled into the station. He liked fast driving and was reported to have driven a stage forty-eight miles in one day." Youngsters at isolated ranches or stations and in the towns adored these drivers, "not only because they were colorful figures, but because often there were packages of firecrackers, candy, or gum in their pockets for the small fry."[13]

Townsfolk eagerly greeted each stage for the news and personal messages it carried. Mail seemed far more important than passengers, both to stagecoach companies and the general citizenry of the northern West. Relatively few people traveled aboard the stages, but every settler welcomed the United States mails they carried. Perhaps more than anything else it was the close relationship between stagecoaches and the arrival of mail from distant locations that made these vehicles symbols of modernity and their drivers important persons in any community. "As bearers of the U. S. Mail, they felt themselves kings of the road, and were seldom loathe to show it," observed James Rusling. "'Clar the road! Git out of the way thar with your bull-teams!' was a frequent salutation, when overtaking or meeting wagon-trains; and if this was not complied with quickly, they made little hesitation in running into the oxen, and swearing till all was blue. I have a vivid recollection of one instance of this kind, when we ran into an ox-team, and the justly exasperated teamster sent us his compliments, in the shape of a bullet whizzing through the air, as we whirled away again."[14]

It was Colonel William F. Cody who recognized what a

*O*n the Stage Coach," a color lithograph poster from the late 1880s. William
F. Cody's Deadwood coach attracted
crowds everywhere, and during a tour
of Europe it was examined and admired
even by the president of France, the king
of Spain, the emperor of Germany, and
Pope Leo XIII. On one occasion in London, by special invitation, it happened
that four European kings were seated
inside the old coach for a ride, while the
Prince of Wales sat on the box alongside
Buffalo Bill, the driver. In one often-
repeated story, the prince jokingly
remarked to the renowned showman that
"this coach now holds a big poker hand."
"Yes," responded Cody; "four kings
inside and the 'joker' on the box."
Courtesy Buffalo Bill Historical Center,
1.69.107.

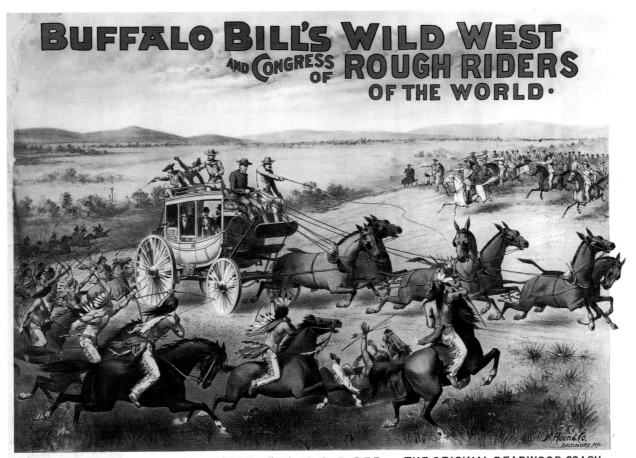

potent symbol of the frontier West the stagecoach had
become when he acquired one for his Wild West show.
Cody obtained his soon-to-be-famous Deadwood coach
in 1883 from his friend Luke Voorhees, who sent the
showman a battered hulk that had cost $1,800 when it
was fresh from the Abbot Downing factory in 1863. It
was one of several similar Concord coaches that Louis
McLane had ordered for the Pioneer Stage Company of
California. It had once traveled from Boston around
Cape Horn aboard the clipper ship *General Grant*, a distance of nineteen thousand miles, to reach the Golden
Gate sometime in 1864. It later migrated across the Sierra
on the overland line, subsequently reaching the Rockies
and Great Plains, where it rolled across eastern Wyoming

during the exciting days of early Gilmer and Salisbury
staging between Cheyenne and Deadwood.

Cody shipped his worse-for-wear coach back to
Abbot, Downing and Company in New Hampshire and
had it overhauled completely. Thereafter the Deadwood
mail coach was a feature of Buffalo Bill's Wild West
shows and parades throughout the United States and
Europe, its owner always regarding it as one of his prime
attractions. "And well he might," noted a Concord newspaper of the vehicle in its prerestoration condition: "its
battered sides, its paintless panels, its missing boot, its
rusty iron, are eloquent of hard knocks. The vicissitudes
of its career are marvelous. In the days of its prosperity,
glistening with new paint and varnish, bedecked with

gold leaf, every strap new and shining, it traversed the most deadly mail route in the West, from Cheyenne to Deadwood *via* Laramie, and through a country alive with the banditti of the plains."[15]

Buffalo Bill played up the idea that he was "the most far-famed" of all of Ben Holladay's drivers. It was true that for a time he drove between Plum Creek, Nebraska Territory, and Fort Kearny and also in a portion of Dakota Territory that later became Wyoming. On one trip in the latter region his coach was suddenly attacked by several hundred Sioux. There were seven passengers inside, among them the division agent of the line, and all were well armed. A long chase ensued until soldiers arrived and drove off the Indians. In after years Buffalo Bill reenacted this dramatic scene in his Wild West show. On another occasion, Buffalo Bill's stage was attacked by Indians who killed two passengers and wounded another before the driver reached the safety of the nearest relay station.[16]

It was with this dramatic narrative (some of which was true) of Indian attacks, narrow escapes, and lengthy chases with bullets and arrows flying that Cody cloaked his Deadwood coach, and in this way the big Concord became the artifact equivalent to the dime novels of the era. It was a prominent and popular attraction at the great Columbian Exposition in Chicago in 1893, along with a coach exhibited by Wells Fargo. Two years later, on Independence Day 1895, Cody exhibited his famous old coach in a Wild West show at Concord, New Hampshire. Though the Deadwood coach attracted much attention and drew crowds of enthusiastic admirers, none of them enjoyed it more than the employees connected with the great manufactory where it was built, including the artisans who had crafted it thirty years earlier. For this special occasion, six mules were hitched up and a photograph taken of the vehicle, with its veteran builders seated inside and no less a personage than the renowned Buffalo Bill himself sitting on the box holding the lines. On the side of the coach was placed this inscription: "1863. HOME AGAIN. 1895." The Deadwood coach is now preserved in the nation's capital at the Smithsonian Institution, and Cody's grave on Look-out Mountain west of Denver still attracts hundreds of visitors each day to pay homage to the showman who invented a popular version of the West.[17]

Cody's last Wild West show was in 1916, but the Concord coach as a romantic symbol of a bygone era lived on in John Ford's 1939 classic movie *Stagecoach.* More recently, Yellowstone's new "tally ho" stagecoaches were based on models that from 1875 until 1915 transported visitors from Gardner to Mammoth Hot Springs and provided the main form of mass transportation within the national park. With the advent of motor transport the first generation of stagecoaches retired, but new coaches built in 1980 continue to carry thousands of tourists each year. Wells Fargo, which still uses the Abbot Downing Concord coach as its corporate symbol, maintains a fleet of twenty of them (ten parade coaches plus ten historic ones, including two it ordered back in 1867). In 1995 some seven million people saw the Wells Fargo parade coaches in three hundred civic and promotional events.

Although steamboats today are less conspicuously identified with the frontier West, they too earned a special place in the hearts of a generation or two of westerners. Each Puget Sound steamboat, like its counterparts on the Columbia and Missouri rivers, had a distinct personality. Each also had its hated rivals: when the crew sighted one, the engineer hung his cap over the steam gauge, the fireman tossed carefully hoarded pitch slabs into the firebox, and a race began. Along all the navigable waterways of the northern West, the steamers formed an integral part of the towns they served. When one settlement staged a major celebration, people from other towns and villages chartered 'their' steamboats and traveled to the festivities as proudly and almost as comfortably as if they were aboard private yachts. When steamboats emptied the warehouses of the last of the annual wheat harvest, then rivermen and settlers would use the empty floor to hold a country dance. The arrival and departure of boats was always an exciting occasion for waterfront towns, and so too were the periodic rate wars.

Steamboat design, amenities, and speeds of up to

Transfiguration on the Pacific Slope

Steamboating, like stagecoaching, died the death of a thousand cuts, though the pace and nature of the industry's demise varied according to location. Even as steamboats disappeared from the upper Missouri River, their numbers actually increased along other waterways of the northern West, especially those west of the Continental Divide, during the 1890s. Commercial navigation of Montana's 33-mile-long Flathead Lake did not even begin until the early 1880s when the Northern Pacific trains brought an increasing number of settlers to this rugged and hitherto remote location. Steam navigation on Flathead Lake rose and declined several times. Opening the Flathead reservation to non-Native settlement in 1910 brought another boom to the three small boats then operating, the *Eva B.,* the *Queen,* and the *Mary 5.* The *New Klondyke,* built by the Hodge Navigation Company, had the largest capacity of any boat ever to sail Flathead Lake: it could carry 110 tons of freight and 425 passengers.

Farther west on the Kootenai River (Kootenay in Canada), a small fleet of steamboats cut through shoals and rapids beginning in 1892 to haul ore from mines near Fort Steele, British Columbia, to Jennings, Montana, on the Great Northern Railway. Old-timers long recalled May 1896 when the British boat *Gwendoline* and the American boat *Ruth* smashed on the rocks in a narrow, twisting canyon within an hour of each other. The two steamers were racing through high and dangerous waters when the *Ruth,* then ahead in the contest, lost power because a log jammed her paddle wheel; the *Gwendoline* swept unsuspectingly around the bend and piled into the helpless vessel. Fortunately, no lives were lost. The last big boat on the river in Montana was the elegant *J. D. Farrell,* financed by the Great Northern and launched in the late 1890s by a railroad subsidiary, the Kootenai River Transportation Company (of which Farrell was then president). The decline of mining and the improvement of nearby highways soon made steamboating in far northwestern Montana both unnecessary and unprofitable.

Farther west, steam returned to the Clark Fork River

*T*he crew of the Harvest Queen *and* Mrs. Minnie Ashley Burkholder, wife of Captain Nathan Burkholder. Even steamboat names were once a part of community life, and later the mere mention of a popular boat like the Bailey Gatzert *could evoke fond memories. Courtesy Oregon Historical Society, 089110OPS.*

fifteen miles an hour connoted the modern age in isolated frontier settlements. Many structural embellishments were purposefully evocative, such as chimneys that rose higher and higher until on the larger boats their tops towered seventy-five, eight-five, and even ninety feet above the surface of the water. It appears that some boat owners wanted tall chimneys as much for looks as for raising steam. Nonetheless, the era of steamboats as developers of the frontier West was largely over by the end of the 1880s, though in the Pacific Northwest they continued to provide basic transportation for several more decades. At the height of their era, steamboat captains were always counted among the most distinguished citizens of their home communities. "Their dignity was enhanced by impressive side-whiskers, handlebar mustaches, at the very least, blue serge, brass buttons, and, when ashore, high silk hats." To youngsters, they took the place of the modern jet pilots, locomotive engineers, and racing car drivers. Small boys could reel off the names of their favorite boats; they could recognize their distinctive whistles too.[18]

EXCURSION DAY ON THE SCENIC FLATHEAD LAKE
SOMERS (LANDING) MONT.

F.A.V.S
1911
COPYRIGHT
F.F.F.F

A. GUTHRIE

*S*omers Landing on Montana's Flathead Lake in 1911. Steamboating peaked on the lake in 1915 during the rush of settlers to claim land made available on the Flathead reservation. At that time twenty boats were in service. The number dropped rapidly after 1915 when automobile roads were built to serve the growing population around the lake. The last steamer left Flathead Lake in 1954. Courtesy Montana Historical Society, 955–085.

in 1882 with the *Katie Hallett,* built to facilitate Northern Pacific construction work nearby. On Lake Pend Oreille, where Northern Pacific tracks skirted the north shore for several miles, the railroad steamed up to the elegant *Henry Villard* in an effort to turn the lake into a tourist attraction. "The company has a steam-boat on the lake, and if someone will put up a good hotel and the boat make excursions, it would be a delightful recreation to spend a few days there in the proper season. A sportsman would go wild there, with elk, deer, and bear and game birds in abundance." In command of the *Henry Villard* was George A. Pease, a veteran of the lower Columbia and Willamette rivers, "under whose genial influence the pleasures of a trip around the lake are much enhanced." One of the first large steamboats to appear on Lake Pend Oreille in the twentieth century was the *Northern,* with a capacity of 250 passengers. It maintained a mail route between Hope and Bayview and later operated from Sandpoint to Bayview. This big steamer burned in 1928.[19]

The 1884 stampede to Idaho's Coeur d'Alene gold and silver mines once more popularized travel by snowshoes and toboggans. When the winter snow melted, a pack-mule trail and wagon road extended from Thompson Falls over a portion of the Bitterroot range. During the height of the 1880s boom, steamboats sped across the cold, clear waters of Lake Coeur d'Alene and up the river of the same name to a landing near the old Cataldo mission. From there the trains of the Coeur d'Alene Railway and Navigation Company continued east another twenty-eight miles to Wallace, center of the mining excitement. During the first two decades of the twentieth century, steamboat traffic on Lake Coeur d'Alene boomed again as a result of growing tourist traffic from Spokane and other nearby settlements.

On few stretches of inland waters was steamboating more extensive or longer lasting than along the lower Snake River. Here in the 1860s the Oregon Steam Navigation Company had made considerable money hauling miners and supplies to Lewiston and the Clearwater and Salmon mines. This traffic barely survived the decade, but grain, fruit, and cattle traveled aboard steamboats during the 1870s and 1880s. Between Lewiston and the mouth of the Snake, several tiny river settlements served to transfer the products of fields and orchards to stern-wheelers. The steamboats that plied the lower Snake were numerous and stylish, and many of them ran special excursions in addition to carrying local passengers and freight. With the expansion of wheat-growing in the inland Northwest came the *Lewiston* in 1894 and the *Spokane* in 1899, two big boats that hauled the valuable grain crop to Riparia and other rail shipping points downstream. Steamboating continued to thrive in this remote location because no railroad ran along the lower Snake River canyon to Lewiston until the early twentieth century.

Periodic attempts were made to extend steamboating up the Snake River from Lewiston into the heart of Hells Canyon, especially after a copper boom promised rich rewards to brave boatmen. One of the most notable steamers was the *Imnaha,* built in Lewiston in 1903 with the most powerful boiler on the Columbia system; it was needed to climb through numerous rapids to a point fifty-three miles south of Lewiston, where the Eureka mine was located. Harry Baughman commanded the vessel on her first run to the diggings. When not hauling ore, the *Imnaha* was supposed to carry grain between Lewiston and Riparia. The steamer made thirteen successful trips to Eureka Bar, battlng upstream through lengthy stretches of white water, including the boiling Mountain Sheep Rapid. This final obstacle the *Imnaha* surmounted with the aid of a line and a capstan winch powered by her own great boiler. According to the practice of the day, one end of the line was anchored above the rapids and the other was floated downstream by a keg buoy so that the upbound vessel could take the line aboard. After having successfully winched themselves through the rapids, steamboatmen were supposed to send the line back downstream for other users. Like so many technologies, this system produced unforeseen consequences; the line fouled the paddle wheel of the *Imnaha* and caused the vessel to sink after only four months of service.

Steamboat Tourism

During the early railway age, tourism played a major role in steamboating on the rivers and lakes of the Pacific Northwest: the last two decades of the nineteenth century were probably the heyday of special-occasion excursions. Two routes, in particular, became popular as excursion runs and attracted boats and services that catered primarily to pleasure-seekers. From Portland up to the Cascades went tourists who wanted to spend a leisurely day touring the Columbia Gorge; downriver to Astoria steamed people who wanted to spend a few days, or the entire season, at the seashore. Both routes attracted pleasure riders almost from the beginning of steamboating on the Columbia River, but the Astoria run was the first to evolve into a popular excursion trip, since more vacationers used it.[20]

Randall V. Mills in his *Stern-Wheelers up Columbia*

The steamer Ione *plies the lonely waters of the Pend Oreille River in northeastern Washington. Courtesy San Francisco Maritime National Historical Park, F11.4.739n.*

provided an evocative account of steamboat tourism in the Pacific Northwest. He recalled that every summer a growing number of tourists from the Willamette Valley traveled to Astoria and the ocean beaches of Oregon and Washington. The mills and canneries of Astoria itself offered little to the excursionist, but south from the Columbia River stretch the Clatsop Plains, fronted by the ocean and wide, clean beaches, and backed by quiet woods and the wandering Lewis and Clark River that paralleled the coast for miles, sometimes coming within the sound of the breakers just two or three miles to the west. Disembarking near the remains of Lewis and Clark's Fort Clatsop, passengers could hire horses or carriages for the short trip through the forest to the beach or

walk the distance themselves. The area became popular with campers as early as the 1860s when some Portland families took their summer holiday at the coast.

The Oregon Steam Navigation Company, ever alert to new business opportunities, ran special boats for vacationers as early as July 1862, when the *Jennie Clark* started once-a-week service between Portland and Seaside. The few beach-bound passengers became hundreds by the 1870s, and no longer did they need to pack their own tents to the beach. Ben Holladay built the Seaside House in 1873, where in addition to serving tourists, he entertained lavishly to impress prospective investors and Oregon's most influential citizens. The Seaside community aspired to become the Pacific Northwest equivalent of an

In the early twentieth century, interurban trains of the Spokane and Inland Empire Railway sped excursionists to waiting steamboats at the Electric Dock in Coeur d'Alene, Idaho. Courtesy Eastern Washington Historical Society, L86–219.155.

T*he steamboat* Almota *is stopped at Fort Lapwai. In mid-May 1897 a writer from the Grangeville, Idaho,* Free Press *described a typical excursion party that left Lewiston on a day trip aboard the handsome new* Lewiston. *Chartered by the local Presbyterian church to make a leisurely voyage up the Clearwater River, the boat had a band aboard to play music, sometimes to the accompaniment of the steamer's immense chime whistle. "Everybody had been filled with the good things to eat and drink when they arrived at Big Eddy." With Captain Ephraim Baughman at the wheel "we all felt safe," unless in enthusiasm to see the scenery a passenger ventured onto the bow of the upper deck and obstructed Baughman's view of the narrow channel. "Then a man was liable to have an ear shot off" (verbally) by the captain. "He crossed the famous eddy and tied up and allowed everybody to go ashore and gather flowers and stroll in the woods until the whistle called them to return." The day "was perfect and everybody returned happy and well pleased with the trip." Courtesy Oregon Historical Society, 12392, #1196.*

Corps of Engineers completed The Dalles–Celilo Canal and opened it to navigation on April 28, 1915, when the *J. N. Teal* and the *Inland Empire* passed through it upriver. Extending eight and a half miles and commanding a total ascent of eighty-one feet by means of five locks, it replaced a cumbersome portage railway. The new facility—some would call it the Panama Canal of the Northwest—made the Columbia River navigable year-round from the Pacific Ocean to Priest Rapids, a distance of about 415 miles. The Snake River was navigable for light boats for eight months of the year nearly 200 miles from its mouth, or about 450 miles from the Pacific. The

early part of May 1915 witnessed a week-long celebration that began at Lewiston and ended at Astoria. Nearly all the senators, representatives, and governors of the Pacific Northwest states participated. On May 5, trains brought more people up from The Dalles, and the steamers of the Open River Navigation Company arrived, also with delegations. A vital part of the river was finally free of impediments to navigation.[23]

Ironically, The Dalles–Celilo Canal had hardly opened to traffic before steamboating on the Columbia River seemed to collapse; excursion runs between Portland and The Dalles remained popular for a time, but above

Carleton Watkins photographed the still-unfinished Cascades Canal in 1882. When it was completed a decade later, the canal was nearly 3,000 feet long and passed around the upper Cascades where the river was practically unnavigable. At the lower end was a lock of two chambers, each a little over 460 feet long, which gave a lift ranging from 24 feet at low water to 14 feet at high water. Courtesy Oregon Historical Society, 21617, #1100-B.

The steamer Lewiston *eases through the Celilo Canal. Steamboating struggled to survive on this part of the Columbia River, but after 1919 the new locks of The Dalles–Celilo Canal lay virtually idle until barge traffic began to develop two decades later. Courtesy Oregon Historical Society, 45969, #1207.*

Celilo, service rapidly withered and died. The Open River Navigation Company quietly sold its fleet to another company. Below The Dalles, steamers one by one halted service after the opening of all-weather highways lured tourists from excursion boats and the completion of James J. Hill's Spokane, Portland and Seattle Railway along the north bank took the traffic from the formerly isolated steamboat landings. Even efforts to coordinate river and highway freight service failed. In 1923 the last stern-wheel packet gave up the run between Portland and The Dalles.

End of the Line?

Just as steamboat and stagecoach transportation evolved in inland portions of the northern West in response to a spreading network of railroads (and later highways), so too did the coastal steamship service that operated between North Pacific ports and California since the 1850s. As late as 1914, eleven companies competed for coastal passenger and freight traffic, although the Pacific Coast Steamship Company did more business than all the rest combined. Its spacious and luxurious fleet of coastal liners operated from 1877 until September 1916, when Captain H. F. Alexander bought the company and

reorganized it as the Admiral Line. But by the 1920s and 1930s, coastal steamships were no more successful than the steamboats on the Willamette and Columbia rivers. On the Willamette River, the last stern-wheeler left Eugene in 1905. Ten years later the Oregon-Washington Railroad and Navigation Company quit the Willamette altogether, but steamboats of the Oregon City Transportation Company made daily runs as far upriver as Independence awhile longer. Seven decades of freight and passenger transportation on the Willamette River ended when the last stern-wheeler halted service between Salem and Portland.

The pattern of decline was much the same elsewhere. The lower Snake River valley, so long neglected by railroads, finally saw tracks extended from Riparia (on the Union Pacific line between Portland and Spokane) to Lewiston in 1908. Travel by train caused scheduled passenger service to disappear from the river a short time later. The two big steamers *Spokane* and *Lewiston* were henceforth used exclusively as freight boats, transferring sacks of wheat from landings to railroad tracks along the Snake River. The stern-wheelers worked together until on the morning of July 12, 1922, they both burned in a raging fire while they were tied up side by side at the docks in Lewiston. The Union Pacific Railroad built a smaller but more powerful *Lewiston* at Linnton, Oregon, to be used solely as a freight hauler, but Snake River traffic continued to decline as a result of competition from trains and a growing number of trucks. The new *Lewiston* had little work to do after 1930, and spent most of her time at the dock until the railroad, abandoning its last river service, sold her. Like so many steamboats before, she went north to Alaska in 1943; having metamorphosed into the towboat *Barry K*, she joined the fleet of stern-wheelers the Alaska Railroad operated on the Yukon and Tanana rivers.[24]

The ending of scheduled steamboat service by no means eliminated all river traffic between Portland and Lewiston, nor did it diminish the call for improved waterways, though demands for hydropower and irrigation water replaced the old cry for an open river. Bonneville, the first of the great dams, was completed in 1937.

Ten years later, work began on another major Columbia dam, McNary, which blocked the river at Umatilla Rapids and created slack water all the way to Pasco to form a river highway for tugs and barges. Nonetheless, river transportation remained in the shadow of the railroads until the Corps of Engineers completed a total of eight dams and locks on the Columbia and Snake rivers in the 1960s and 1970s that rejuvenated the water highway. After the last one opened in 1975, railroads actually found themselves at a rate disadvantage with barge lines for grain traffic from the interior Northwest as far east as Montana, where grain traveled by truck across the Bitterroot Mountains to Snake River ports.

Portland today remains the hub of the Columbia, Snake, and Willamette river transportation system, 534 miles of certified navigable waterways. In Oregon's largest city, barges meet the oceangoing ships that still transport grain from the inland Northwest to distant markets. About 60 percent of the grain reaches Portland by train, the rest arrives by barges and towboats, some of which have threaded the 364-mile-long, 14-foot-deep channel that reaches to Lewiston, Idaho (a total of 465 miles from the sea). Whereas Mississippi River locks typically provide 10 to 25 feet of lift, the John Day Lock lifts 113 feet and is thought to be the highest lift lock in the world. The locks at both Ice Harbor and Lower Monumental dams on the Snake River lift a hundred feet.

As of the mid-1990s about six hundred people were employed aboard the Snake and Columbia rivers' 40 towboats and 175 barges. They moved nearly 5 million tons of grain, 3.7 million tons of forest products, plus sizable quantities of petroleum products, fertilizer, and intermodal containers. The Snake and Columbia rivers are bargeable twelve months a year. In 1995 a large diesel-powered paddle-boat, *Queen of the West*, began carrying as many as 149 overnight passengers on the Columbia and Snake. Like the several smaller motor vessels operated by other companies, the *Queen of the West* is part of the revival of tourism between Lewiston and the sea that occurred during the 1990s.[25]

In some sense the Columbia River is more fortunate than the upper Missouri River, where barge lines are able to travel only as far north as Sioux City. The romance and adventure of Missouri River steamboats still remain a part of the American consciousness, but a series of massive earthen dams—all without locks—prevent a revival of steamboat navigation on the upper Missouri. No less dead is stagecoaching in all but a handful of tourist centers, notably Jackson, Wyoming; Columbia, California; and Yellowstone National Park.

When the history of the northern West was told from the perspective of the railway era, everything that went before was slow or sleepy. The "old settler watched through the long years the gradual unfolding of these resources, the slow increases in population. At last the railroads came, linking us with the populous centers of civilization. A change came over the sleepy old Territory," observed Governor Miles C. Moore of Washington in 1889. But the steamboat and stagecoach era of the northern West deserves recognition as a distinctive age all its own, with its peculiar definitions of time and distance and the odd juxtaposition of the romance of frontier travel with the travail of a long day's journey.[26]

A. Brown photo of the steamer Bailey Gatzert *approaching the Cascade Locks. Courtesy Oregon Historical Society, 49059.*

*C*hildren play on an old stagecoach in
City Park in Blackfoot, Idaho. Courtesy
Oregon Historical Society, 32261.

*A*board the Pommeran, *one of the many tall-masted ships that once sailed the West Coast. Probably the last cargo to leave the Columbia River on a merchant sailing vessel was three million board feet of timber that on May 2, 1942, headed for Cape Town, South Africa, aboard the six-masted schooner* Tango. *Courtesy San Francisco Maritime National Historical Park, J9.26,747.*

Notes

Preface

1. Carlos A. Schwantes, "Promoting America's Canals: Popularizing the Hopes and Fears of the New Nation," *Journal of American Culture* 1 (Winter 1978): 700–712; and "The Joy of Timetables [Timetables and Guides as Library Resources]," *Journal of Popular Culture* 9 (Winter 1975): 604–617.

Introduction

1. Frederic Trautmann, ed. and trans., *Oregon East, Oregon West: Travels and Memoirs by Theodor Kirchhoff, 1863–1872* (Portland: Oregon Historical Society Press, 1987), 62.

2. Boise *Idaho Daily Statesman,* November 16, 1924.

3. As quoted in *An Illustrated History of North Idaho* (Chicago: Western Historical Publishing, 1903), 21.

4. Portland *Oregon Weekly Times,* May 11, 1861.

5. As quoted in *An Illustrated History of North Idaho,* 21.

6. "Jefferson's Instructions to Lewis [June 20, 1803]," in *Letters of the Lewis and Clark Expedition,* 2 vols., ed. Donald Jackson (Urbana: University of Illinois Press, 1978), I, 61.

7. Gary Moulton, ed., *The Journals of the Lewis and Clark Expedition,* 11 vols. (Lincoln: University of Nebraska Press, 1988–), V, 74.

8. *The Storied Northwest* (Saint Paul: Northern Pacific Railway, ca. 1925).

Soft Gold Defines a Distant Land

1. Samuel Parker, *Journal of an Exploring Tour Beyond the Rocky Mountains* (Minneapolis: Ross and Haines, 1967 reprint of 1838 edition), 310–11, 343.

2. Joseph Drayton's description of his 1841 journey up the Columbia comes from Charles Wilkes, *Narrative of the United States Exploring Expedition During the Years 1838, 1839, 1840, 1841, and 1842,* 5 vols. (Philadelphia: Lea and Blanchard, 1845), IV, 293, 305, 378–91 *passim.*

3. William E. Lass, *A History of Steamboating on the Upper Missouri* (Lincoln: University of Nebraska Press, 1962), 1–2; Joel Overholser, *Fort Benton: World's Innermost Port* (Fort Benton: J. Overholser, 1987), 33. Although in the 1890s several small steamers navigated the 130-mile stretch of river between Stubbs Ferry (near Helena) and the town of Cascade, navigation on the river above the Great Falls was the exception rather than the rule.

4. Samuel L. Clemens, *Life on the Mississippi* (New York: Dodd, Mead, n.d., reprint of the 1883 edition), 129–130.

5. James G. Swift, "Steamboating and Transshipment on the Missouri River," *Gone West* 1 (ca. 1980s): 10; Louis C. Hunter, *Steamboats on the Western Rivers: An Economic and Technological History* (Cambridge: Harvard University Press, 1949), 228; Albert D. Richardson, *Beyond the Mississippi: From the Great River to the Great Ocean* (Hartford, Conn.: American Publishing, 1867), 20. Much of my description of the nature

of the Missouri River comes from Hiram Martin Chittenden, *History of Early Steamboat Navigation on the Missouri River: Life and Adventures of Joseph La Barge,* 2 vols. (New York: Francis P. Harper, 1903).

6. Bayard Taylor, *Colorado: A Summer Trip* (Niwot: University Press of Colorado, 1989 reprint of 1867 edition), 2; Horace Greeley, *An Overland Journey from New York to San Francisco, in the Summer of 1859,* ed. Charles T. Duncan (New York: Alfred A. Knopf, 1969 reprint of 1860 edition), 13.

7. Chittenden, *Steamboat Navigation on the Missouri,* I, 84; Lass, *Steamboating on the Upper Missouri,* 4.

8. Chittenden, *Steamboat Navigation on the Missouri,* I, 85.

The Way West by Land and Sea

1. As quoted in Harvey W. Scott, *History of the Oregon Country,* 6 vols. (Cambridge, Mass.: The Riverside Press, 1924), II, 309.

2. Dorothy O. Johansen, "A Working Hypothesis for the Study of Migrations," in *Experiences in a Promised Land: Essays in Pacific Northwest History,* ed. G. Thomas Edwards and Carlos A. Schwantes (Seattle: University of Washington Press, 1986), 46. Also see David Alan Johnson, *Founding the Far West: California, Oregon, and Nevada, 1840–1890* (Berkeley: University of California Press, 1992).

3. Samuel Bowles, *Across the Continent: A Summer's Journey to the Rocky Mountains, the Mormons, and the Pacific States* (Readex Microprint, 1966 reprint of 1865 edition), 370; Oscar Lewis, *Sea Routes to the Gold Fields: The Migration by Water to California in 1849–1852* (Sausalito, Calif.: Comstock Editions, 1987 reprint of 1949 edition), 16.

4. Jean-Nicolas Perlot, *Gold Seeker: Adventures of a Belgian Argonaut during the Gold Rush Years,* ed. Howard Lamar (New Haven: Yale University Press, 1985), 24–25. A good summary of the Cape Horn route to Oregon is Paul G. Merriam, "Riding the Wind: Cape Horn Passage to Oregon, 1840s-1850s," *Oregon Historical Quarterly* 77 (March 1976): 37–60.

5. James K. Polk, "Fourth Annual Message, December 5, 1848," in *A Compilation of the Messages and Papers of the Presidents,* 20 vols. (New York: Bureau of National Literature, 1897), VI, 2486.

6. Jay Monaghan, *Chile, Peru, and the California Gold Rush of 1849* (Berkeley: University of California Press, 1973), 112–113. Also see Ernest A. Wiltsee, *Gold Rush Steamers of the Pacific* (San Francisco: Grabhorn Press, 1938).

7. As quoted in Duncan S. Somerville, *The Aspinwall Empire* (Mystic, Conn.: Mystic Seaport Museum, 1983), 40, 41.

8. Bayard Taylor, *Eldorado; Or, Adventures in the Path of Empire* (Lincoln: University of Nebraska Press, 1988 reprint of 1850 edition), 12–13.

9. Albert D. Richardson, *Beyond the Mississippi: From the Great River to the Great Ocean* (Hartford, Conn.: American Publishing, 1867), 541.

10. Taylor, *Eldorado,* 17–18, 25.

11. Taylor, *Eldorado,* 26–27, 30, 39, 41.

12. Bowles, *Across the Continent,* 370, 385–386.

13. Frederic Trautmann, ed. and trans., *Oregon East, Oregon West: Travels and Memoirs by Theodor Kirchhoff, 1863–1872* (Portland: Oregon Historical Society Press, 1987), 107–109.

Oregon Unbound, or the Formative Fifties

1. Charles Wilkes, *Narrative of the United States Exploring Expedition During the Years 1838, 1839, 1840, 1841, and 1842,* 5 vols. (Philadelphia: Lea and Blanchard, 1845), IV, 293, 305, 378ff.

2. Frederic Trautmann, ed. and trans., *Oregon East, Oregon West: Travels and Memoirs by Theodor Kirchhoff, 1863–1872* (Portland: Oregon Historical Society Press, 1987), 5.

3. P. W. Gillette, December 7, 1900, in George H. Himes Scrapbook #21, Oregon Historical Society, Portland (first quotation); Jesse A. Applegate, *Recollections of My Boyhood* (Roseburg, Oreg.: Press of Review, 1914), 155–160 (second quotation).

4. Randall H. Hewitt, *Across the Plains and Over the Divide: A Mule Train Journey from East to West in 1862, and Incidents Connected Therewith* (New York: Argosy Antiquarian, 1964 reprint of 1906 edition), 490.

5. Arthur L. Throckmorton, *Oregon Argonauts: Merchant Adventurers on the Western Frontier* (Portland: Oregon Historical Society, 1961), 177–178.

6. Throckmorton, *Oregon Argonauts,* 126.

7. Portland *Democratic Standard,* August 2, 1855 (first quotation); Throckmorton, *Oregon Argonauts,* 197 (second quotation).

8. A. H. Sale to H. S. Lyman, in *Oregon Native Son* 1 (August 1889): 212–214.

9. *Hood River Glacier,* November 27, 1896.

10. *Hood River Glacier,* November 27, 1896.

11. As quoted in G. Thomas Edwards, "The Oregon Trail in the Columbia Gorge, 1843–1855: The Final Ordeal," *Oregon Historical Quarterly* 97 (Summer 1996): 160–161.

12. The Oregon Steam Navigation Company was originally organized under the laws of Washington Territory.

13. Oscar Osburn Winther, "The Place of Transportation in the Early History of the Pacific Northwest," *Pacific Historical Review* 11 (December 1942): 383.

14. As quoted in Ralph Moody, *Stagecoach West* (New York: Thomas Y. Crowell, 1967), 29.

An Ingersoll photograph of the Saint Paul riverfront about 1900. By this time the Minnesota capital had become a major railroad gateway to the northern West and headquarters city for both the Northern Pacific and Great Northern railroads. Courtesy Minnesota Historical Society, M R2.9 Sp4.3/p11.

15. Oscar Osburn Winther, *The Old Oregon Country: A History of Frontier Trade, Transportation, and Travel* (New York: Kraus Reprint, 1969 reprint of 1950 edition), 140.

16. As quoted in Winther, *Old Oregon Country*, 141.

17. As quoted in *Vancouver Register*, November 18, 1865.

18. Oscar Osburn Winther, *Via Western Express and Stagecoach: California's Transportation Links with the Nation, 1848–1869* (Lincoln: University of Nebraska Press, 1979 reprint of 1945 edition), 9.

19. William Banning and George Hugh Banning, *Six Horses* (New York: Century, 1930), 47.

20. As quoted in Oscar Winther, "California Stage Company in Oregon," *Oregon Historical Quarterly* 35 (June 1934): 135–136.

21. As quoted in Winther, *Via Western Express and Stagecoach*, 102.

The Pulse of a Continent

1. Portland *Weekly Oregonian*, March 19, 1859.

2. On March 5 the California State Telegraph Company opened a line between Portland and Yreka, California, where it connected with Marysville and transcontinental service.

3. James F. Rusling, *Across America; Or, The Great West and The Pacific Coast* (New York: Sheldon and Company, 1874), 474; Albert D. Richardson, *Beyond the Mississippi: From the Great River to the Great Ocean* (Hartford, Conn.: American Publishing, 1867), 539–542.

4. John Haskell Kemble, *The Panama Route, 1848–1869* (Berkeley: University of California Press, 1943), 194; Oscar Lewis, *Sea Routes to the Gold Fields: The Migration by Water to California in 1849–1852* (Sausalito, Calif.: Comstock Editions, 1987 reprint of 1949 edition), 151–153.

5. Richardson, *Beyond the Mississippi*, 542; Normand E. Klare, *The Final Voyage of the "Central America," 1857* (Spokane, Wash.: Arthur H. Clark, 1992), 58; Bancroft quoted in Lewis, *Sea Routes to the Gold Fields*, 150; Samuel Bowles, *Across the Continent: A Summer's Journey to the Rocky Mountains, the Mormons, and the Pacific States* (Readex Microprint, 1966 reprint of 1865 edition), 384.

6. William Banning and George Hugh Banning, *Six Horses* (New York: Century, 1930), 96.

7. As quoted in Ralph Moody, *Stagecoach West* (New York: Thomas Y. Crowell, 1967), 81.

8. A copy of the advertisement appears in Seymour Dunbar, *A History of Travel in America,* 4 vols. (Indianapolis: Bobbs-Merrill, 1915), IV, 1303.

9. As quoted in Moody, *Stagecoach West,* 97.

10. "Overland Mail Company Through Time Schedule," September 16, 1858, copy in Denver Public Library.

11. Frank Root and William Elsey Connelley, *The Overland Stage to California* (Topeka, Kans.: F. Root and W. Connelley, 1901), 43. Until overtaken by the Civil War, the nation's first overland stage line, the San Antonio and San Diego Mail Line, continued to supplement the Butterfield operation with weekly connections from San Antonio to El Paso and from Fort Yuma to San Diego. Although on December 1, 1860, the post-master general had described the line as "entirely useless," it did not cease operation until August 1861, a few months after the Butterfield line left the southern route. Le Roy R. Hafen, *The Overland Mail, 1849–1869: Promoter of Settlement, Precursor of Railroads* (Cleveland: Arthur H. Clark, 1926), 108; Albert Shumate, *The Notorious I. C. Woods of the Adams Express* (Glendale, Calif.: Arthur H. Clark, 1986), 90, 100.

12. As quoted in E. D. Smith, Jr., "Communication Pioneers in Oregon," *Oregon Historical Quarterly* 39 (December 1938): 356.

Rocky Mountain Gold Fever

1. *Butte Miner,* May 15, 1877; Boise *Idaho Daily Statesman,* September 8, 1929; *Anaconda Standard,* December 24, 1899 (quotation); W. Turrentine Jackson, *Wagon Roads West: A Study of Federal Road Surveys and Construction in the Trans-Mississippi West, 1846–1869* (Lincoln: University of Nebraska Press, 1979 reprint of 1964 edition), 273.

2. Olympia *Pioneer and Democrat,* August 27, 1858 (first quotation); *New North-West* 14 (April 27, 1883): 3 (second quotation); Portland *Oregonian,* June 27, 1861 (third quotation).

3. Frederic Trautmann, ed. and trans., *Oregon East, Oregon West: Travels and Memoirs by Theodor Kirchhoff, 1863–1872* (Portland: Oregon Historical Society Press, 1987), 57.

4. As quoted in Arthur L. Throckmorton, *Oregon Argonauts: Merchant Adventurers on the Western Frontier* (Portland: Oregon Historical Society, 1961), 226.

5. David Newsom, *David Newsom, the Western Observer, 1805–1882* (Portland: Oregon Historical Society, 1972), 120.

6. J. Gary Williams and Ronald W. Stark, eds., *The Pierce Chronicle* (Moscow: Idaho Research Foundation, [ca. 1974]), 81.

7. William Armistead Goulder, *Reminiscences: Incidents in the Life of a Pioneer in Oregon and Idaho* (Moscow: University of Idaho Press, 1989 reprint of 1909 edition), 203.

8. Throckmorton, *Oregon Argonauts,* 226 (first quotation); Harvey W. Scott, *History of the Oregon Country,* 6 vols. (Cambridge, Mass.: Riverside Press, 1924), III, 78 (second quotation).

9. As quoted in the Portland *Morning Oregonian,* February 5, 1883.

10. Trautmann, *Oregon East, Oregon West: Travels and Memoirs by Theodor Kirchhoff,* 61.

11. Philip Ritz in *Oregon Sentinel* (Jacksonville), February 22, 1862.

12. P. W. Gillette in *An Illustrated History of North Idaho* (Chicago: Western Historical Publishing, 1903): 1222–1224.

13. Portland *Oregon Argus,* August 23, 1862; Gillette in *An Illustrated History of North Idaho,* 1222–1224.

14. John Hailey, *The History of Idaho* (Boise: Syms-York, 1910), 31.

15. *Walla Walla Statesman,* December 6, 1862.

16. Granville Stuart, *Forty Years on the Frontier as Seen in the Journals and Reminiscences of Granville Stuart, Gold-Miner, Trader, Merchant, Rancher and Politician,* 2 vols. (Cleveland: Arthur H. Clark, 1925), I, 270.

17. Virginia City *Montana Post,* July 24, 1866.

18. Trautmann, *Oregon East, Oregon West: Travels and Memoirs by Theodor Kirchhoff,* 61.

19. As quoted in Portland *Oregon Argus,* August 16, 1862.

20. *Helena Herald,* March 21, 1867; Windham Thomas Wyndham-Quin, Earl of Dunraven, *The Great Divide; Travels in the Upper Yellowstone in the Summer of 1874* (Lincoln: University of Nebraska Press, 1967 reprint of 1876 edition), 46–51; Walla Walla *Washington Statesman,* April 19, 1863.

21. *Walla Walla Statesman,* May 30, 1862.

22. *Helena Weekly Herald,* January 1, 1880; Goulder, *Reminiscences of a Pioneer,* 206–207; [Edward B. Nealley], "A Year in Montana," *Atlantic Monthly* 18 (August 1866): 236–250; Julian Ralph, *Our Great West: A Study of the Present Conditions and Future Possibilities of the New Commonwealths and Capitals of the United States* (Freeport, N.Y.: Books for Libraries Press, 1970 reprint of 1893 edition), 261–263, 270–271 (quotation).

23. Ralph, *Our Great West,* 263–264 (first quotation); *Oregon Argus,* August 23, 1862; *Oregonian,* June 22, 1861; *Helena Weekly Herald,* January 1, 1880; *Olympia Transcript,* November 13, 1869.

24. Ralph, *Our Great West,* 265.

25. P. W. Gillette in *An Illustrated History of North Idaho,* 1222–1224; John S. Collins, *Across the Plains in '64, Incidents of Early Days West of the Missouri River. . . .* (Omaha: National Printing, 1904), 33–35; Portland *Oregon Argus,* August 23, 1862; Boise *Idaho Daily Statesman,* September 7, 1941.

26. Newsom, *David Newsom, The Western Observer*, 122; Portland *Oregonian*, June 27, 1861.

27. Hailey, *History of Idaho*, 32.

Ho for Idaho! Steamboats to the Gold Country

1. *An Illustrated History of North Idaho* (Chicago: Western Historical Publishing, 1903), 21.

2. Henry Miller, "Letters from the Upper Columbia," *Idaho Yesterdays* 4 (Winter 1960–61): 17; William J. Trimble, *The Mining Advance into the Inland Empire*, University of Wisconsin Bulletin No. 638 (Madison: University of Wisconsin, 1914), 124–125.

3. Portland *Oregonian*, June 8, 1861 (first quotation); Fitz-Hugh Ludlow, "On the Columbia River," *Atlantic Monthly* 14 (December 1864): 703–705 (second quotation).

4. The summary description of the extension of steamboating up the Missouri River comes from Hiram Martin Chittenden, *History of Early Steamboat Navigation on the Missouri River: Life and Adventures of Joseph La Barge*, 2 vols. (New York: Francis P. Harper, 1903).

5. Robert Hereford, *Old Man River: The Memories of Captain Louis Rosché, Pioneer Steamboatman* (Caldwell, Idaho: Caxton Printers, 1943), 107.

6. Arthur L. Throckmorton, *Oregon Argonauts: Merchant Adventurers on the Western Frontier* (Portland: Oregon Historical Society, 1961), 248–249, 252; Portland *Daily Oregonian*, June 11, 1861.

7. W. D. Lyman, *Lyman's History of Old Walla Walla County*, 2 vols. (Chicago: S. J. Clarke, 1918), I, 158.

8. As quoted in the *Vancouver Register*, November 11, 1865.

9. As quoted in the *Vancouver Register*, November 11, 1865.

10. Frederic Trautmann, ed. and trans., *Oregon East, Oregon West: Travels and Memoirs by Theodor Kirchhoff, 1863–1872* (Portland: Oregon Historical Society Press, 1987), 14–15.

11. C. Aubrey Angelo, *Sketches of Travel in Oregon and Idaho* (Fairfield, Wash.: Ye Galleon Press, 1988 reprint of 1866 edition), 24.

12. Trautmann, *Oregon East, Oregon West: Travels and Memoirs by Theodor Kirchhoff*, 16, 19.

13. Samuel Bowles, *Across the Continent: A Summer's Journey to the Rocky Mountains, the Mormons, and the Pacific States* (Readex Microprint, 1966 reprint of 1865 edition), 188; Trautmann, *Oregon East, Oregon West: Travels and Memoirs by Theodor Kirchhoff*, 30–32.

14. James F. Rusling, *Across America; Or, The Great West and The Pacific Coast* (New York: Sheldon and Company, 1874), 253 (first quotation); Albert D. Richardson, *Beyond the Mississippi: From the Great River to the Great Ocean* (Hartford, Conn.: American Publishing, 1867), 403 (second quotation).

15. Bowles, *Across the Continent*, 189.

16. Richardson, *Beyond the Mississippi*, 405.

Via Shank's Mare and Stagecoach

1. Frank Root and William Elsey Connelley, *The Overland Stage to California* (Topeka, Kans.: F. Root and W. Connelley, 1901), 305–307.

2. C. Aubrey Angelo, *Sketches of Travel in Oregon and Idaho* (Fairfield, Wash.: Ye Galleon Press, 1988 reprint of 1866 edition), 29; Fitz-Hugh Ludlow, "On the Columbia River," *Atlantic Monthly* 14 (December 1864), 703–715.

3. Randall H. Hewitt, *Across the Plains and Over the Divide: A Mule Train Journey from East to West in 1862, and Incidents Connected Therewith* (New York: Argosy Antiquarian, 1964 reprint of 1906 edition), 477–481.

4. Frederic Trautmann, ed. and trans., *Oregon East, Oregon West: Travels and Memoirs by Theodor Kirchhoff, 1863–1872* (Portland: Oregon Historical Society Press, 1987), 26–27, 29–30.

5. Angelo, *Sketches of Travel in Oregon and Idaho*, 25, 30.

6. As quoted in *An Illustrated History of North Idaho* (Chicago: Western Historical Publishing, 1903), 1222–1224.

7. Jacksonville *Oregon Reporter*, July 22, 1865; Angelo, *Sketches of Travel in Oregon and Idaho*, 37–38.

8. Virginia City *Montana Post*, February 2, 1867.

9. Angelo, *Sketches of Travel in Oregon and Idaho*, 38.

10. Salem *Pacific Christian Advocate*, April 9, 1859.

11. Hewitt, *Across the Plains and Over the Divide*, 463; *Walla Walla Statesman*, February 9, 1866.

12. As quoted in *An Illustrated History of North Idaho*, 1222–1224.

13. *Overland Monthly* 2 (April 1869): 378–386 (quotation); Alton B. Oviatt, "Fort Benton, River Capital," in *A History of Montana*, 3 vols., ed. Merrill G. Burlingame and K. Ross Toole (New York: Lewis Historical Publishing, 1957), I, 141.

14. Betty M. Madsen and Brigham D. Madsen, *North to Montana! Jehus, Bullwhackers, and Mule Skinners on the Montana Trail* (Salt Lake City: University of Utah Press, 1980), 33; William J. Trimble, *The Mining Advance into the Inland Empire*, University of Wisconsin Bulletin No. 638 (Madison: University of Wisconsin, 1914), 121.

15. *Idaho State Historical Society Bulletin* 1 (April 1, 1908): 23.

16. John Hailey, *The History of Idaho* (Boise: Syms-York, 1910), 61–64, 116–117.

17. Hailey, *History of Idaho*, 62 (first quotation); *Idaho State Historical Society Bulletin*, 22–28.

18. Hailey, *History of Idaho,* 95.

19. Root and Connelley, *The Overland Stage to California,* 219–220, 324.

20. Hailey, *History of Idaho,* 96–98.

Long Hauls Overland: The Freighters

1. "The Magruder Corridor: A Drive on the Wild Side," pamphlet issued by the United States Forest Service.

2. Samuel Parker, *Journal of an Exploring Tour Beyond the Rocky Mountains* (Minneapolis: Ross and Haines, 1967 reprint of 1838 edition), 73.

3. Thomas J. Dimsdale, *The Vigilantes of Montana* (Norman: University of Oklahoma Press, 1953 reprint of 1866 edition), 123.

4. As quoted in Oscar Osburn Winther, "Pack Animals for Transportation in the Pacific Northwest," *Pacific Northwest Quarterly* 34 (April 1943): 146.

5. Frederic Trautmann, ed. and trans., *Oregon East, Oregon West: Travels and Memoirs by Theodor Kirchhoff, 1863–1872* (Portland: Oregon Historical Society Press, 1987), 21; Spokane *Spokesman-Review,* April 15, 1928; *Lewiston Morning Tribune,* February 28, 1937.

6. Portland *Oregonian,* June 12, 1861; Portland *Oregon Argus,* April 5, 1862.

7. As quoted in William J. Trimble, *The Mining Advance into the Inland Empire,* University of Wisconsin Bulletin No. 638 (Madison: University of Wisconsin, 1914), 115.

8. Boise *Idaho Daily Statesman,* February 19, 1911; John Hailey, *The History of Idaho* (Boise: Syms-York, 1910), 62–63.

9. Boise *Idaho Daily Statesman,* June 26, 1921.

10. *Lewiston Morning Tribune,* August 23, 1936.

11. As quoted in Trimble, *The Mining Advance into the Inland Empire,* 120n.

12. Granville Stuart, *Forty Years on the Frontier as Seen in the Journals and Reminiscences of Granville Stuart, Gold-Miner, Trader, Merchant, Rancher and Politician,* 2 vols. (Cleveland: Arthur H. Clark, 1925), II, 22.

13. C. Aubrey Angelo, *Sketches of Travel in Oregon and Idaho* (Fairfield, Wash.: Ye Galleon Press, 1988 reprint of 1866 edition), 46–47.

14. Hailey, *History of Idaho,* 96, 184.

15. Frank Root and William Elsey Connelley, *The Overland Stage to California* (Topeka, Kans.: F. Root and W. Connelley, 1901), 303–304.

16. Agnes Wright Spring, *The Cheyenne and Black Hills Stage and Express Routes* (Glendale, Calif.: Arthur H. Clark, 1949), 172.

17. Samuel Bowles, *Across the Continent: A Summer's Journey to the Rocky Mountains, the Mormons, and the Pacific States* (Readex Microprint, 1966 reprint of 1865 edition), 5.

18. Alexander Majors, *Seventy Years on the Frontier* (Minneapolis: Ross and Haines, 1965 reprint of 1893 edition), 77.

19. As quoted in Betty M. Madsen and Brigham D. Madsen, *North to Montana! Jehus, Bullwhackers, and Mule Skinners on the Montana Trail* (Salt Lake City: University of Utah Press, 1980), 83.

20. Richard F. Burton, *The City of the Saints, and Across the Rocky Mountains to California* (New York: Harper and Brothers, 1862), 22.

21. James F. Rusling, *Across America; Or, The Great West and The Pacific Coast* (New York: Sheldon and Company, 1874), 236.

22. Charles S. Walgamott, *Six Decades Back* (Moscow: University of Idaho Press, 1990 reprint of 1936 edition), 255–256.

23. William Francis Hooker, *The Bullwhacker: Adventures of a Frontier Freighter* (Lincoln: University of Nebraska Press, 1988 reprint of 1924 edition), 25.

24. Root and Connelley, *The Overland Stage to California,* 304.

25. As quoted in Walgamott, *Six Decades Back,* 256.

26. Burton, *City of the Saints,* 23–24; Spring, *The Cheyenne and Black Hills Stage and Express Routes,* 177.

27. Herman Francis Reinhart, *The Golden Frontier: The Recollections of Herman Francis Reinhart, 1851–1869,* edited by Doyce B. Nunis, Jr. (Austin: University of Texas Press, 1962), 218–219.

28. Rusling, *Across America,* 237–238.

29. Majors, *Seventy Years on the Frontier,* 72–73.

Contested Terrain

1. *Walla Walla Statesman,* March 2, 1866; The Dalles *Daily Mountaineer,* May 26, 1866; J. C. Ainsworth as quoted in Frank B. Gill and Dorothy Johansen, eds., "A Chapter in the History of the Oregon Steam Navigation Company: The Steamship *Oregonian,*" *Oregon Historical Quarterly* 38 (December 1937): 398.

2. As quoted in the Boise *Idaho Daily Statesman,* March 31, 1929.

3. The Dalles *Daily Mountaineer,* January 19, 1866; Ainsworth as quoted in Gill and Johansen, "A Chapter in the History of the Oregon Steam Navigation Company," 322.

4. Caroline C. Leighton, *Life at Puget Sound: With Sketches of Travel in Washington Territory, British Columbia, Oregon and California, 1865–1881* (Boston: Lee and Shepard, 1883), 63–65.

5. William J. Trimble, *The Mining Advance into the Inland Empire,* University of Wisconsin Bulletin No. 638 (Madison: University of Wisconsin, 1914), 131.

6. James F. Rusling, *Across America, Or, The Great West and The Pacific Coast* (New York: Sheldon and Company, 1874), 265.

*T*his photograph dates from the early twentieth century when Washington became the lumber capital of the nation. Even after transcontinental railroads reached the Pacific Northwest, much lumber still traveled to distant markets by ship. Courtesy Washington State University, Pratsch# 469.

7. Betty M. Madsen and Brigham D. Madsen, *North to Montana! Jehus, Bullwhackers, and Mule Skinners on the Montana Trail* (Salt Lake City: University of Utah Press, 1980), xiii; Brigham D. Madsen, "The Montana Trail: Salt Lake City–Corinne to Fort Benton," *Overland Journal* 13 (Spring 1995): 19–34.

8. Albert D. Richardson, *Beyond the Mississippi: From the Great River to the Great Ocean* (Hartford, Conn.: American Publishing, 1867), 351 (first quotation); Virginia City *Montana Post*, October 19, 1867.

9. C. Aubrey Angelo, *Sketches of Travel in Oregon and Idaho* (Fairfield, Wash.: Ye Galleon Press, 1988 reprint of 1866 edition), 11.

10. As quoted in Arthur L. Throckmorton, *Oregon Argonauts: Merchant Adventurers on the Western Frontier* (Portland: Oregon Historical Society, 1961), 253.

11. In June 1865 Hill Beachey opened a short-lived stage line from Unionville and Star City to Ruby City and Silver City in Idaho. The following year his Railroad Stage Line linked the advancing Central Pacific tracks with mining camps in southern Idaho. By the winter of 1867–68, Beachey had four hundred horses in service on the line. Service by 1870 switched from Winnemucca to Elko.

12. Silver City *Owyhee Avalanche*, April 7, 1866. When the *Shoshone* inaugurated service on the Snake River to interdict the California trade, B. M. Durell and Company inaugurated a "fast freight" and passenger line to join the steamboat landings at Umatilla and Olds Ferry, ninety miles west of Boise City. The plan was for freight from Olds Ferry to continue by boat up the Snake River to the Owyhee ferry on the main road linking Silver City and the Boise Basin. From the *Shoshone* at the Owyhee ferry, Durell and Company arranged to run a line of stagecoaches and freight wagons to Boise City, thirty-three miles north.

13. As quoted in Frank B. Gill and Dorothy Johansen, eds, "A Chapter in the History of the Oregon Steam Navigation Company," 321; *Walla Walla Statesman*, April 26, 1866.

14. *Walla Walla Statesman*, February 9, 1866.

15. Throckmorton, *Oregon Argonauts*, 269.

16. As quoted in E. W. Wright, ed., *Lewis and Dryden's Marine History of the Pacific Northwest* (Portland: Lewis and Dryden Printing, 1895), 145.

17. As quoted in Virginia City *Montana Post*, February 2, 1867.

18. Helena *Montana Radiator*, March 17, 1866.

19. Angelo, *Sketches of Travel in Oregon and Idaho*, 43; Virginia City *Montana Post*, February 17, 1866.

20. Richardson, *Beyond the Mississippi*, 482; Throckmorton, *Oregon Argonauts*, 272 (second quotation).

21. "A Glimpse of Montana," *Overland Monthly* 2 (April 1869): 383.

22. "A Glimpse of Montana," *Overland Monthly* 2 (April 1869): 383.

23. "A Glimpse of Montana," *Overland Monthly* 2 (April 1869): 383–384.

24. As quoted in Portland *Oregonian*, December 10, 1862; Merle W. Wells, "The Creation of the Territory of Idaho," *Pacific Northwest Quarterly* 40 (April 1949): 113.

25. *Boise News*, November 3, 1863.

26. Virginia City *Montana Post*, August 25, 1866.

Ben Holladay Builds a Stagecoach Empire

1. One of the best sources of information on Holladay and his stagecoach operations is J. V. Frederick, *Ben Holladay, the Stagecoach King: A Chapter in the Development of Transcontinental Transportation* (Lincoln: University of Nebraska Press, 1989 reprint of 1940 edition).

2. *Idaho State Historical Society Bulletin* 1 (April 1, 1908): 27; (quotation) *Idaho Scimitar* (July 25, 1908): 9; Frank Root and William Elsey Connelley, *The Overland Stage to California* (Topeka, Kans.: F. Root and W. Connelley, 1901), 439.

3. Mark Twain, *Roughing It* (Cutchogue, N.Y.: Buccaneer Books, 1976 reprint of 1872 edition), 19.

4. Ralph Moody, *Stagecoach West* (New York: Thomas Y. Crowell, 1967), 223.

5. Samuel Bowles, *Across the Continent: A Summer's Journey to the Rocky Mountains, the Mormons, and the Pacific States* (Readex Microprint, 1966 reprint of 1865 edition), 6–7; Moody, *Stagecoach West*, 226.

6. Root and Connelley, *The Overland Stage to California*, 360, 439 (quotation); Moody, *Stagecoach West*, 249.

7. Larry Barsness, *Gold Camp* (New York: Hastings House, 1962), 188.

8. Salt Lake City *Daily Telegraph*, July 28, 1864.

9. Bowles, *Across the Continent*, 51.

10. As quoted in Frederick, *Ben Holladay*, 119.

11. Root and Connelley, *The Overland Stage to California*, 73.

12. As quoted in Moody, *Stagecoach West*, 268.

13. As quoted in Frederick, *Ben Holladay*, 159ff.

Stagecoaching Adapts to the Frontier West

1. Richard F. Burton, *The City of the Saints, and Across the Rocky Mountains to California* (New York: Harper and Brothers, 1862), 13.

2. Ralph Moody, *Stagecoach West* (New York: Thomas Y. Crowell, 1967), 18, 40; Agnes Wright Spring, *The Cheyenne and*

Black Hills Stage and Express Routes (Glendale, Calif.: Arthur H. Clark, 1949), 89; C. Aubrey Angelo, *Sketches of Travel in Oregon and Idaho* (Fairfield, Wash.: Ye Galleon Press, 1988 reprint of 1866 edition), 152; Walla Walla *Washington Statesman*, May 5, 1865.

3. Frank Root and William Elsey Connelley, *The Overland Stage to California* (Topeka, Kans.: F. Root and W. Connelley, 1901), 77.

4. James F. Rusling, *Across America; Or, The Great West and The Pacific Coast* (New York: Sheldon and Company, 1874), 214, 340; Root and Connelley, *The Overland Stage to California*, 607.

5. Root and Connelley, *The Overland Stage to California*, 157, 159.

6. Root and Connelley, *The Overland Stage to California*, 218, 479; William Banning and George Hugh Banning, *Six Horses* (New York: Century, 1930), 257; Idaho City *Idaho World*, May 26, 1866; *Helena Weekly Herald*, July 25, 1878; Moody, *Stagecoach West*, 236.

7. Root and Connelley, *The Overland Stage to California*, 268.

8. Fred T. DuBois, *The Making of a State*, ed. Louis J. Clements (Rexburg: Eastern Idaho Publishing, 1971), 99.

9. R. L. Potter as told to Rozetta Bailey Sylten, *Saco Independent*, August 1, 1936. Potter worked in the Stafford harness shop in Lewistown, Montana.

10. Root and Connelley, *The Overland Stage to California*, 268.

11. Root and Connelley, *The Overland Stage to California*, 271.

12. DuBois, *The Making of a State*, 99.

13. Root and Connelley, *The Overland Stage to California*, 73.

14. Root and Connelley, *The Overland Stage to California*, 67.

15. Rusling, *Across America*, 41.

16. As quoted in Betty M. Madsen and Brigham D. Madsen, *North to Montana! Jehus, Bullwhackers, and Mule Skinners on the Montana Trail* (Salt Lake City: University of Utah Press, 1980), 116, 183.

17. Root and Connelley, *The Overland Stage to California*, 275.

18. D. S. Tuttle, *Reminiscences of a Missionary Bishop* (New York: Thomas Whittaker, 1906), 94.

19. Root and Connelley, *The Overland Stage to California*, 275.

Travail by Stagecoach

1. John Mortimer Murphy, *Rambles in North-Western America from the Pacific Ocean to the Rocky Mountains* (London: Chapman and Hall, 1879), 173.

2. Frederic Trautmann, ed. and trans., *Oregon East, Oregon West: Travels and Memoirs by Theodor Kirchhoff, 1863–1872* (Portland: Oregon Historical Society Press, 1987), 44–52 *passim.*

3. D. S. Tuttle, *Reminiscences of a Missionary Bishop* (New York: Thomas Whittaker, 1906), 91.

4. Tuttle, *Reminiscences of a Missionary Bishop*, 91–92; *Helena Weekly Independent*, January 16, 1890.

5. *Lemhi Herald*, June 9, 1910.

6. Henry L. Wells, "Staging at Night," *West Shore* 10 (January 1884): 5.

7. Andrew Rolle, ed., *The Road to Virginia City: The Diary of James Knox Polk Miller* (Norman: University of Oklahoma Press, 1960), 116.

8. Trautmann, *Oregon East, Oregon West: Travels and Memoirs by Theodor Kirchhoff*, 50; F. E. Smith, "Evolution of Traveling Comforts," *Union Pacific Magazine* 1 (August 1922): 5.

9. As quoted in Virginia City *Montana Post*, January 5, 1867.

10. Wells, "Staging at Night," 6 (first quotation); Ralph Moody, *Stagecoach West* (New York: Thomas Y. Crowell, 1967), 244 (second quotation).

11. *Lemhi Herald*, June 9, 1910.

12. Frank Root and William Elsey Connelley, *The Overland Stage to California* (Topeka, Kans.: F. Root and W. Connelley, 1901), 66.

13. Albert D. Richardson, *Beyond the Mississippi: From the Great River to the Great Ocean* (Hartford, Conn.: American Publishing, 1867), 476; Tuttle, *Reminiscences of a Missionary Bishop*, 94–95.

14. Trautmann, *Oregon East, Oregon West: Travels and Memoirs by Theodor Kirchhoff*, 51–52.

15. As quoted in *Idaho Scimitar* 1 (May 2, 1908): 2.

16. Idaho City *Idaho World*, January 19, 1867.

17. Carrie Adell Strahorn, *Fifteen Thousand Miles by Stage*, 2 vols. (Lincoln: University of Nebraska Press, 1988 reprint of 1911 edition), I, 79; Boise *Idaho Daily Statesman*, April 5, 1936.

18. Samuel Bowles, *Across the Continent: A Summer's Journey to the Rocky Mountains, the Mormons, and the Pacific States* (Readex Microprint, 1966 reprint of 1865 edition), 21.

19. Murphy, *Rambles in North-Western America*, 177.

20. Trautmann, *Oregon East, Oregon West: Travels and Memoirs by Theodor Kirchhoff*, 51, 99–100.

21. Wells, "Staging at Night," 6.

22. William Banning and George Hugh Banning, *Six Horses* (New York: Century, 1930), 118; Bayard Taylor, *Colorado: A Summer Trip* (Niwot: University Press of Colorado, 1989 reprint of 1867 edition), 172.

23. Murphy, *Rambles in North-Western America*, 173–174.

24. James F. Rusling, *Across America; Or, The Great West and The Pacific Coast* (New York: Sheldon and Company, 1874), 44.

25. J. H. Beadle, *The Undeveloped West; Or, Five Years in the Territories* (Philadelphia: National Publishing, 1873), 756.

26. Root and Connelley, *The Overland Stage to California,* 250, 252, 255, 512, 513.

27. Root and Connelley, *The Overland Stage to California,* 250; Murphy, *Rambles in North-Western America,* 166.

28. Tuttle, *Reminiscences of a Missionary Bishop,* 95.

29. Tuttle, *Reminiscences of a Missionary Bishop,* 96–97; Betty M. Madsen and Brigham D. Madsen, *North to Montana! Jehus, Bullwhackers, and Mule Skinners on the Montana Trail* (Salt Lake City: University of Utah Press, 1980), 123–124.

30. J. V. Frederick, *Ben Holladay, the Stagecoach King: A Chapter in the Development of Transcontinental Transportation* (Lincoln: University of Nebraska Press, 1989 reprint of 1940 edition), 159; Tuttle, *Reminiscences of a Missionary Bishop,* 96; Brigham D. Madsen, "The Montana Trail: Salt Lake City–Corinne to Fort Benton," *Overland Journal* 13 (1995): 19–34.

31. Walla Walla *Washington Statesman,* September 15, 1865.

32. Frederick, *Ben Holladay,* 164.

33. Michael A. Leeson, *History of Montana, 1739–1935* (Chicago: Warner, Beers, 1885), 270–271.

34. *Helena Weekly Herald,* July 29, 1880; *Helena Weekly Independent,* January 16, 1890.

Navigating on a Heavy Dew

1. The Bailey account is from *Waterways Journal* as reported in *Kansas City Star,* January 9, 1925; Louis C. Hunter, *Steamboats on the Western Rivers: An Economic and Technological History* (Cambridge: Harvard University Press, 1949), 237.

2. Henry M. Stanley, *The Autobiography of Henry M. Stanley,* ed. Dorothy Stanley (Boston: Houghton Mifflin, 1909), 101.

3. Fred W. Wilson, "The Lure of the River," *Oregon Historical Quarterly* 34 (June 1933): 132.

4. Joseph Mills Hanson, *The Conquest of the Missouri: Being the Story of the Life and Exploits of Captain Grant Marsh* (New York: Murray Hill Books, 1946 reprint of 1909 edition), 207.

5. *West Shore* 16 (August 9, 1890): 988.

6. Stanley, *Autobiography,* 101.

7. Stanley, *Autobiography,* 102–103.

8. Albert D. Richardson, *Beyond the Mississippi: From the Great River to the Great Ocean* (Hartford, Conn.: American Publishing, 1867), 24, 25.

9. *Lewiston Morning Tribune,* March 29, 1936.

10. Lee Silliman, "'Up the Great River': Daniel Weston's Missouri Steamboat Diary," *Montana, the Magazine of Western History* 30 (July 1980): 37 (first quotation); Andrew Rolle, ed., *The Road to Virginia City: The Diary of James Knox Polk Miller*

(Norman: University of Oklahoma Press, 1960), 126 (second quotation).

11. Frederic Trautmann, ed. and trans., *Oregon East, Oregon West: Travels and Memoirs by Theodor Kirchhoff, 1863–1872* (Portland: Oregon Historical Society Press, 1987), 153, 154.

12. *Overland Monthly* 2 (April 1869), 378–386.

13. Richardson, *Beyond the Mississippi,* 21.

14. Stanley, *Autobiography,* 100–101.

15. *Billings Gazette,* April 20, 1935; William E. Lass, *A History of Steamboating on the Upper Missouri* (Lincoln: University of Nebraska Press, 1962), 48.

16. Rolle, *The Road to Virginia City,* 121–122.

17. Hanson, *Conquest of the Missouri,* 97–98.

18. Virginia City *Montana Post,* January 26, 1867 (second quotation), regarding a trip made in 1866; Bailey as quoted in *Kansas City Star,* January 9, 1925.

19. Virginia City *Montana Post,* November 3, 1866; Hanson, *Conquest of the Missouri,* 81.

20. *Overland Monthly* 2 (April 1869): 379.

21. Hunter, *Steamboats on the Western Rivers,* 416.

22. As quoted in Dorothy M. Johnson, "Slow Boat to Benton," *Montana, the Magazine of Western History* 11 (Winter 1961): 8.

23. *Billings Gazette,* March 27, 1966; Robert Hereford, *Old Man River: The Memories of Captain Louis Rosché, Pioneer Steamboatman* (Caldwell, Idaho: Caxton Printers, 1943), 117, 118.

24. Hanson, *Conquest of the Missouri,* 140–141.

25. Boise *Idaho Daily Statesman,* October 15, 1922; *Fort Benton River Press,* June 16, 1932; Hanson, *Conquest of the Missouri,* 140–141.

26. H. W. Corbett to J. W. Gates, November 5, 1862, in H. W. Corbett Letterbooks, Whitman College.

The Burdens of Time and Space

1. Gustavus Hines, *Oregon: Its History, Condition and Prospects* (New York: C. M. Saxton, 1859), 151–152.

2. Governor William Pickering, December 17, 1862, in *Messages of the Governors of the Territory of Washington to the Legislative Assembly, 1854–1889,* ed. Charles M. Gates (Seattle: University of Washington Press, 1940), 104.

3. P. W. Gillette, December 7, 1900, in George H. Himes Scrapbook #21, Oregon Historical Society, Portland.

4. Portland *Daily Oregonian,* May 10, 1861. By the time this story appeared it was already out of date: extension of the telegraph wires meant that pony express riders sped the news only between Fort Kearny, Nebraska, and Fort Churchill, Nevada.

5. Wallis Nash, *Oregon: There and Back in 1877* (Corvallis: Oregon State University Press, 1976 reprint of 1878 edition), 104 (first quotation); Albert D. Richardson, *Beyond the Mississippi: From the Great River to the Great Ocean* (Hartford, Conn.: American Publishing, 1867), 23.

6. Oscar Osburn Winther, *The Transportation Frontier: Trans-Mississippi West, 1865–1890* (New York: Holt, Rinehart and Winston, 1964), 8.

7. Lee Silliman, "'Up the Great River': Daniel Weston's Missouri Steamboat Diary," *Montana, the Magazine of Western History* 30 (July 1980): 37.

8. Richardson, *Beyond the Mississippi*, 326, 331.

9. Richardson, *Beyond the Mississippi*, 387.

10. Herman Francis Reinhart, *The Golden Frontier: The Recollections of Herman Francis Reinhart, 1851–1869*, ed. Doyce B. Nunis, Jr. (Austin: University of Texas Press, [1962]), 204–205; William Armistead Goulder, *Reminiscences: Incidents in the Life of a Pioneer in Oregon and Idaho* (Moscow: University of Idaho Press, 1989 reprint of 1909 edition), 207.

11. Andrew Rolle, ed., *The Road to Virginia City: The Diary of James Knox Polk Miller* (Norman: University of Oklahoma Press, 1960), 75; Virginia City *Montana Post*, June 29, 1867.

12. D. S. Tuttle, *Reminiscences of a Missionary Bishop* (New York: Thomas Whittaker, 1906), 172; Julia Gilliss, *So Far from Home: An Army Bride on the Western Frontier, 1865–1869*, ed. Priscilla Knuth (Portland: Oregon Historical Society Press, 1993), 18–19.

13. Gilliss, *So Far from Home*, 34–35; William E. Unrau, ed., *Tending the Talking Wire: A Buck Soldier's View of Indian Country, 1863–1866* (Salt Lake City: University of Utah Press, 1979), 75.

14. Gilliss, *So Far from Home*, 61.

15. Frederic Trautmann, ed. and trans., *Oregon East, Oregon West: Travels and Memoirs by Theodor Kirchhoff, 1863–1872* (Portland: Oregon Historical Society Press, 1987), 32.

16. Merrill G. Burlingame and K. Ross Toole, *A History of Montana*, 3 vols. (New York: Lewis Historical Publishing, 1957), II, 66 (first quotation); Larry Barsness, *Gold Camp* (New York: Hastings House, 1962), 195–196 (second quotation).

17. Virginia City *Montana Post*, September 29, 1866.

18. *Salt Lake City Daily Telegraph*, July 28, 1864.

19. Rolle, *The Road to Virginia City*, 77.

20. As quoted in "We're Off to the Mines," *Idaho Yesterdays* 5 (Summer 1961): 14.

21. William J. Trimble, *The Mining Advance into the Inland Empire*, University of Wisconsin Bulletin No. 638 (Madison: University of Wisconsin, 1914), 159 (first quotation); Silliman, "'Up the Great River,'" 37 (second quotation); Francis P. Farquhar, ed., *Up and Down California in 1860–1864: The Journal of William H. Brewer* (Berkeley: University of California Press, 1974 reprint of 1966 edition), 12.

22. Goulder, *Reminiscences*, 216; John Hailey, *The History of Idaho* (Boise: Syms-York, 1990), 107.

23. Trimble, *Mining Advance into the Inland Empire*, 159; Hailey, *History of Idaho*, 107.

24. Samuel Bowles, *Across the Continent: A Summer's Journey to the Rocky Mountains, the Mormons, and the Pacific States* (Readex Microprint, 1966 reprint of 1865 edition), 56.

25. Samuel Parker, *Journal of an Exploring Tour Beyond the Rocky Mountains* (Minneapolis: Ross and Haines, 1967 reprint of 1838 edition), 30.

26. Alexander Majors, *Seventy Years on the Frontier* (Minneapolis: Ross and Haines, 1965 reprint of 1893 edition), 74.

27. Bowles, *Across the Continent*, 183; Virginia City *Montana Post*, November 3, 1866 (second quotation); Randall H. Hewitt, *Across the Plains and Over the Divide: A Mule Train Journey from East to West in 1862, and Incidents Connected Therewith* (New York: Argosy Antiquarian, 1964 reprint of 1906 edition), 477–481; H. W. Corbett, to J. W. Gates, August 29, 1862, in H. W. Corbett Letterbooks, Whitman College.

28. As quoted in Barsness, *Gold Camp*, 194.

29. Goulder, *Reminiscences*, 217–218.

30. C. Aubrey Angelo, *Sketches of Travel in Oregon and Idaho* (Fairfield, Wash.: Ye Galleon Press, 1988 reprint of 1866 edition), 48 (first quotation); Trautmann, *Oregon East, Oregon West: Travels and Memoirs by Theodor Kirchhoff*, 63 (second quotation); Goulder, *Reminiscences*, 218–220, 233.

31. As quoted in *Helena Weekly Herald*, January 1, 1880; Virginia City *Montana Post*, December 3, 1864; *Walla Walla Statesman*, February 10, 1865.

32. Trautmann, *Oregon East, Oregon West: Travels and Memoirs by Theodor Kirchhoff*, 63.

33. Granville Stuart, *Forty Years on the Frontier as Seen in the Journals and Reminiscences of Granville Stuart, Gold-Miner, Trader, Merchant, Rancher and Politician*, 2 vols. (Cleveland: Arthur H. Clark, 1925), II, 28–30.

34. Goulder, *Reminiscences*, 240.

35. Reinhart, *The Golden Frontier*, 200.

36. *An Illustrated History of North Idaho* (Chicago: Western Historical Publishing, 1903), 1222–1224.

37. Gilliss, *So Far from Home*, 20–21.

38. Virginia City *Montana Post*, December 29, 1866.

39. Boise *Idaho Daily Statesman*, April 5, 1936.

40. Deer Lodge *Weekly Independent*, March 29, 1868.

41. Harvey W. Scott, *History of the Oregon Country*, 6 vols. (Cambridge, Mass.: Riverside Press, 1924), V, 126.

42. Gilliss, *So Far from Home*, 39.

Landscapes of the Steamboat and Stagecoach Era

1. As quoted in *Messages of the Governors of the Territory of Washington to the Legislative Assembly, 1854–1889,* ed. Charles M. Gates (Seattle: University of Washington Press, 1940), 44–45.

2. Frederic Trautmann, ed. and trans., *Oregon East, Oregon West: Travels and Memoirs by Theodor Kirchhoff, 1863–1872* (Portland: Oregon Historical Society Press, 1987), 16.

3. Advertisement for "Overland Mail Route to California," issued in Portland, July 19, 1866. Copy in the Bancroft Library, University of California, Berkeley. After its grand consolidation, Wells Fargo on April 1, 1867, promoted overland coaches between Omaha and Sacramento with these words: "The route passes through the celebrated silver regions of Nevada, the valley of Great Salt Lake, the beautiful scenery of the Rocky Mountains and the GREAT PLAINS, and is the cheapest and most expeditious route to the Atlantic States."

4. As quoted in *Kansas City Star,* January 9, 1925.

5. Joseph Mills Hanson, *The Conquest of the Missouri: Being the Story of the Life and Exploits of Captain Grant Marsh* (New York: Murray Hill Books, 1946 reprint of 1909 edition), 71.

6. Frank Root and William Elsey Connelley, *The Overland Stage to California* (Topeka, Kans.: F. Root and W. Connelley, 1901), 331.

7. Albert D. Richardson, *Beyond the Mississippi: From the Great River to the Great Ocean* (Hartford, Conn.: American Publishing, 1867), 340.

8. Root and Connelley, *The Overland Stage to California,* 74.

9. Richardson, *Beyond the Mississippi,* 401.

10. Harvey W. Scott, *History of the Oregon Country,* 6 vols. (Cambridge, Mass.: Riverside Press, 1924), IV, 147.

11. *New York Times,* June 11, 1883

12. *New York Times,* June 11, 1883.

13. Root and Connelley, *The Overland Stage to California,* 513.

Overland to Promontory and Beyond

1. H. R. Dieterich, Jr., "The Architecture of H. H. Richardson in Wyoming," *Annals of Wyoming* 38 (April 1966): 53.

2. John Hoyt Williams, *A Great and Shining Road: The Epic Story of the Transcontinental Railroad* (New York: Times Books, 1988), 17–18. An excellent account of the project.

3. Henry M. Stanley, *The Autobiography of Henry M. Stanley,* ed. Dorothy Stanley (Boston: Houghton Mifflin, 1909), 195.

4. Robert M. Utley, "The Dash to Promontory," *Utah Historical Quarterly* 29 (April 1961): 99; Frank B. Gill and Dorothy O. Johansen, eds., "A Chapter in the History of the Oregon Steam Navigation Company: The Steamship *Oregonian,*" *Oregon*

Historical Quarterly 39 (March 1938): 61 (quotation).

5. Frank Root and William Elsey Connelley, *The Overland Stage to California* (Topeka, Kans.: F. Root and W. Connelley, 1901), 142; *Overland Monthly* 2 (June 1869): 577; *Deer Lodge Weekly Independent,* May 15, 1869.

6. *Crofutt's New Overland Tourist, and Pacific Coast Guide* (Omaha, Neb.: Overland Publishing, 1880), 30.

7. *West Shore* 9 (November 1883): 274.

8. Harvey W. Scott, *History of the Oregon Country,* 6 vols. (Cambridge, Mass.: Riverside Press, 1924), IV, 249–250.

9. Scott, *History of the Oregon Country,* IV, 210.

10. John Mortimer Murphy, *Rambles in North-Western America from the Pacific Ocean to the Rocky Mountains* (London: Chapman and Hall, 1879), 194–195.

11. D. S. Tuttle, *Reminiscences of a Missionary Bishop* (New York: Thomas Whittaker, 1906), 242–243.

12. Deer Lodge *New Northwest,* March 12, 1880, 3.

13. As quoted in Betty M. Madsen and Brigham D. Madsen, *North to Montana! Jehus, Bullwhackers, and Mule Skinners on the Montana Trail* (Salt Lake City: University of Utah Press, 1980), 246–247.

14. *West Shore* 16 (May 3, 1890): 546.

15. *Bancroft's Guide for Travelers by Railway, Stage, and Steam Navigation in the Pacific States, July 1869* (San Francisco: H. H. Bancroft, 1869), 1.

16. Scott, *History of the Oregon Country,* IV, 249–250.

Monopoly Rules the Empire of the Columbia

1. John Mortimer Murphy, *Rambles in North-Western America from the Pacific Ocean to the Rocky Mountains* (London: Chapman and Hall, 1879), 152–154.

2. C. Aubrey Angelo, *Sketches of Travel in Oregon and Idaho* (Fairfield, Wash.: Ye Galleon Press, 1988 reprint of 1866 edition), 10.

3. Harvey W. Scott, *History of the Oregon Country,* 6 vols. (Cambridge, Mass.: Riverside Press, 1924), IV, 36; *Overland Monthly* 2 (April 1869): 378–386.

4. Scott, *History of the Oregon Country,* IV, 37–38.

5. *Oregon Weekly Statesman,* November 16, 1869.

6. J. H. Beadle, *The Undeveloped West; Or, Five Years in the Territories* (Philadelphia: National Publishing, 1873), 765.

7. Scott, *History of the Oregon Country,* IV, 74–75.

8. Scott, *History of the Oregon Country,* IV, 74–75.

9. Frederic Trautmann, ed. and trans., *Oregon East, Oregon West: Travels and Memoirs by Theodor Kirchhoff, 1863–1872* (Portland: Oregon Historical Society Press, 1987), 156–157.

10. P. W. Gillette, "A Brief History of the Oregon Steam

Wilhelm Hester photographed several tall-masted ships loading lumber at Port Blakely, Washington, in 1905. Courtesy San Francisco Maritime National Historical Park, F20.17887n1.

Navigation Company," *Oregon Historical Quarterly* 5 (June 1904): 131 (quotation); Throckmorton, *Oregon Argonauts*, 308, 309.

11. Portland *Morning Oregonian*, April 2, July 2 (quotation), 1879; June Crithfield, "The River Road to Ragtown That Opened the Palouse," *Bunchgrass Historian* 1 (Summer 1973): 1–7; *Lewiston Morning Tribune*, November 19, 1939.

12. David Newsom, *David Newsom, the Western Observer, 1805–1882* (Portland: Oregon Historical Society, 1972), 262; *An Illustrated History of North Idaho* (Chicago: Western Historical Publishing, 1903), 66.

13. Portland *Morning Oregonian*, May 18, 1880.

14. *West Shore* 8 (August 1882): 144–158; as quoted in Portland *Morning Oregonian*, September 13, 1880.

15. As quoted in *Weekly Missoulian*, April 27, 1883.

16. White Sulphur Springs *Rocky Mountain Husbandman*, September 6, 1883 (first quotation); Deer Lodge *New Northwest*, September 14, 1883 (second and third quotations).

17. Deer Lodge *New Northwest*, September 14, 1883.

18. White Sulphur Springs *Rocky Mountain Husbandman*, September 13, 1883.

19. Deer Lodge *New Northwest*, September 14, 1883; White Sulphur Springs *Rocky Mountain Husbandman*, September 13, 1883.

Winding down the Missouri

1. Paul F. Sharp, *Whoop-up Country: The Canadian-American West, 1865–1885* (Minneapolis: University of Minnesota Press, 1955), 157.

2. Virginia City *Montana Post,* June 13, 1867.

3. James Bradley, "Journal," *Contributions to the Historical Society of Montana* 8 (1917): 130–131.

4. Alton B. Oviatt, "Fort Benton, River Capital," in *A History of Montana*, 3 vols., ed. Merrill G. Burlingame and K. Ross Toole (New York: Lewis Historical Publishing, 1957), I, 140–141; James Bradley. "Journal," 130–131; William E. Lass, *A History of Steamboating on the Upper Missouri* (Lincoln: University of Nebraska Press, 1962), 53; Joel Overholser, *Fort Benton: World's Innermost Port* (Fort Benton: J. Overholser, 1987), 54.

5. Lass, *Steamboating on the Upper Missouri,* 53; Virginia City *Montana Post,* June 6, 1867.

6. Virginia City *Montana Post,* May 20, 1865.

7. Joseph Mills Hanson, *The Conquest of the Missouri: Being the Story of the Life and Exploits of Captain Grant Marsh* (New York: Murray Hill Books, 1946 reprint of 1909 edition), 217.

8. Hanson, *Conquest of the Missouri,* 303–304; Lass, *Steamboating on the Upper Missouri,* 123; James G. Swift, "Steamboating and Transshipment on the Missouri River," *Gone West* I (ca. 1980s): 10-ff.

9. Oviatt, "Fort Benton, River Capital," 149–150 (quotation); Sharp, *Whoop-up Country,* 162.

10. Overholser, *Fort Benton,* 93; Dan R. Conway, "The Famous 'Block P' Line," *Grass Range Review,* undated clipping in Montana Historical Society; Sharp, *Whoop-up Country,* 211.

11. Sharp, *Whoop-up Country,* 183, 185; Oviatt, "Fort Benton, River Capital," 151.

12. As quoted in Fort Benton *River Press,* November 5, 1884.

13. As quoted in Lass, *Steamboating on the Upper Missouri,* 58.

14. Hanson, *Conquest of the Missouri,* 129.

15. *The Union Pacific and Utah and Northern Through Rail Route to Montana* (Omaha: Daily Republican, 1880).

16. *The Union Pacific and Utah and Northern Through Rail Route to Montana.*

17. Conway, "The Famous 'Block P' Line."

18. Lass, *Steamboating on the Upper Missouri,* 153, 160, 163, 181. Block P was called the Benton Packet Company from 1904 to 1924.

19. As quoted in Betty M. Madsen and Brigham D. Madsen, *North to Montana! Jehus, Bullwhackers, and Mule Skinners on the Montana Trail* (Salt Lake City: University of Utah Press, 1980), 158.

Sail, Steam, and the Rise of Seattle

1. Charles Nordhoff, "The Columbia River and Puget Sound," in *Harper's New Monthly Magazine* 48 (February 1874), 338–348; *North Pacific Coast Resorts* (Saint Paul: Northern Pacific Railway, 1909), 35.

2. Samuel Bowles, *Across the Continent: A Summer's Journey to the Rocky Mountains, the Mormons, and the Pacific States* (Readex Microprint, 1966 reprint of 1865 edition), 205.

3. Gordon R. Newell, *Ships of the Inland Sea: The Story of Puget Sound Steamboats* (Portland: Binfords and Mort, 1960 edition), 10–11. This is an excellent source for Puget Sound maritime history.

4. Clarence B. Bagley, *History of Seattle from the Earliest Settlement to the Present Time,* 3 vols. (Chicago: S. J. Clarke, 1916), I, 649.

5. Charles Horetzky, *Canada on the Pacific* (Montreal: Dawson Brothers, 1874), 187–192.

6. Harvey W. Scott, *History of the Oregon Country,* 6 vols. (Cambridge, Mass.: Riverside Press, 1924), IV, 109.

7. Bagley, *History of Seattle,* I, 245.

8. C. H. Hanford, ed., *Seattle and Environs, 1852–1924,* 3 vols. (Chicago: Pioneer Historical Publishing, 1924), I, 183.

9. Julian Ralph, *Our Great West: A Study of the Present Conditions and Future Possibilities of the New Commonwealths and Capitals of the United States* (Freeport, N.Y.: Books for Libraries Press, 1970 reprint of 1893 edition), 298–99.

10. Ted Hinckley, "The Inside Passage: A Popular Gilded Age Tour," *Pacific Northwest Quarterly* 56 (April 1965): 67–74.

11. John Muir, *Travels in Alaska* (Boston: Houghton Mifflin, 1979 reprint of 1915 edition), 13.

12. As quoted in William R. Hunt, *North of 53°: The Wild Days of the Alaska-Yukon Mining Frontier, 1870–1914* (New York: Macmillan, 1974), 29–34.

13. Bagley, *History of Seattle,* I, 100 (first quotation); Ray Stannard Baker, "The Great Northwest," *Century Magazine* 65 (March 1903): 667 (second quotation); Robert D. Turner, *The Pacific Empresses: An Illustrated History of Canadian Pacific Railway's Empress Liners on the Pacific Ocean* (Victoria, B.C.: Sono Nis Press, 1981), 15; *West Shore* 3 (May 3, 1890): 546.

14. Scott, *History of the Oregon Country,* III, 111–113.

Symbols of an Era

1. As quoted in *Valley Irrigator,* December 21, 1972, clipping in the South Dakota Historical Society.

2. *Helena Weekly Herald,* July 14, 1887 (first quotation); Frank Root and William Elsey Connelley, *The Overland Stage*

to California (Topeka, Kans.: F. Root and W. Connelley, 1901), 438 (second quotation).

3. Virginia City *Montana Post,* May 4, 1867; Harvey W. Scott, *History of the Oregon Country,* 6 vols. (Cambridge, Mass.: Riverside Press, 1924), I, 242.

4. Robert Hereford, *Old Man River: The Memories of Captain Louis Rosché, Pioneer Steamboatman* (Caldwell, Idaho: Caxton Printers, 1943), 36; Portland *Sunday Oregonian,* October 25, 1896.

5. Oscar Osburn Winther, *The Transportation Frontier: Trans-Mississippi West, 1865–1890* (New York: Holt, Rinehart and Winston, 1964), 57; Agnes Wright Spring, *The Cheyenne and Black Hills Stage and Express Routes* (Glendale, Calif.: Arthur H. Clark, 1949), 87–88.

6. Spring, *The Cheyenne and Black Hills Stage and Express Routes,* 163.

7. Ernest Ingersoll, "Wheat Fields of the Columbia," *Harper's New Monthly Magazine* 68 (September 1884): 506, 507.

8. *Lemhi Herald,* June 9, 1910.

9. As quoted in *Helena Weekly Independent,* October 18, 1883.

10. Virginia City *Montana Post,* August 26, 1865; Walla Walla *Washington Statesman,* March 19, 1864.

11. D. S. Tuttle, *Reminiscences of a Missionary Bishop* (New

York: Thomas Whittaker, 1906), 152; Roscoe P. Conkling and Margaret B. Conkling, *The Butterfield Overland Mail, 1857–1869,* 3 vols. (Glendale, Calif.: Arthur H. Clark, 1947), I, 142.

12. Ralph Moody, *Stagecoach West* (New York: Thomas Y. Crowell, 1967), 51; Paul F. Sharp, *Whoop-up Country: The Canadian-American West, 1865–1885* (Minneapolis: University of Minnesota Press, 1955), 187; William Banning and George Hugh Banning, *Six Horses* (New York: Century, 1930), 400 (quotation).

13. J. V. Frederick, *Ben Holladay, the Stagecoach King: A Chapter in the Development of Transcontinental Transportation* (Lincoln: University of Nebraska Press, 1989 reprint of 1940 edition), 76 (first quotation); Spring, *The Cheyenne and Black Hills Stage and Express Routes,* 339.

14. James F. Rusling, *Across America; Or, The Great West and The Pacific Coast* (New York: Sheldon and Company, 1874), 42–43.

15. As quoted in Root and Connelley, *The Overland Stage to California,* 59.

16. Frederick, *Ben Holladay, the Stagecoach King,* 75.

17. Root and Connelley, *The Overland Stage to California,* 58, 61, 62.

18. Gordon R. Newell, *Ships of the Inland Sea: The Story of Puget Sound Steamboats* (Portland: Binfords and Mort, 1960 edition), 14.

19. *New York Times,* June 11, 1883; Portland *Morning Oregonian,* November 5, 1881.

20. Randall V. Mills, *Stern-Wheelers up Columbia: A Century of Steamboating in the Oregon Country* (Lincoln: University of Nebraska Press, 1977 reprint of 1947 edition), 156.

21. *Lewiston Morning Tribune,* December 13, 1942.

22. The original portage railroad between The Dalles and Celilo was used until the Oregon Railway and Navigation Company extended its tracks along the south bank of the Columbia River in 1882. The State of Oregon replaced the portage railway with a new one, which it opened June 3, 1905; the Oregon State Portage Railroad was a standard-gauge line that owned a couple of locomotives, a passenger car, and some boxcars. The new portage line probably was most useful in forcing the railroads to keep their grain rates lower than they might have been otherwise.

23. Mills, *Stern-Wheelers up Columbia,* 150.

24. *Lewiston Morning Tribune,* July 13, 1922, and December 30, 1928; Mills, *Stern-Wheelers up Columbia,* 83–84.

25. *Waterways Journal,* August 29, 1994, and January 2, 1995.

26. Miles C. Moore, November 18, 1889, in *Messages of the Governors of the Territory of Washington to the Legislative Assembly, 1854–1889,* ed. Charles M. Gates (Seattle: University of Washington Press, 1940), 278–279.

*N*ot all Northwest timber traveled aboard ship. This turn-of-the-century Benjamin Gifford photograph shows a cigar raft of logs on its way from the lower Columbia River to a sawmill in San Diego. Courtesy Oregon Historical Society, OrHi 79635, File 677.

A horse-drawn beer wagon pauses at the corner of Second and Washington streets in Portland in 1892. Courtesy Oregon Historical Society, CN 003770, 035P028.

Suggestions for Further Reading

The following bibliography seeks to guide readers to my sources and suggest opportunities for further study of a specific subject. Some sources are mentioned only in the Notes.

Introduction

Affleck, E. L. *Sternwheelers, Sandbars, and Switchbacks: A Chronicle of Steam Transportation in the British Columbia Waterways of the Columbia River System.* Vancouver, B.C.: Alexander Nichols Press, 1973.

Ainsworth, J. C. "Autobiographical Sketch." *Ninth Brand Book* (Los Angeles: Los Angeles Westerners, 1961): 117ff.

Ambrose, Stephen E. "'Immence Mountains to the West': Lewis and Clark Breach the Bitterroots." *Montana, the Magazine of Western History* 45 (Autumn/Winter 1995): 52–63.

Billington, David P. *The Tower and the Bridge: The New Art of Structural Engineering.* Princeton: Princeton University Press, 1985.

Boyd, Eva Jolene. *That Old Overland Stagecoaching.* Plano, Tex.: Wordware Publishing, 1991.

Briggs, Asa. *The Power of Steam: An Illustrated History of the World's Steam Age.* Chicago: University of Chicago Press, 1982.

Buerge, David M. "Stagecoaches to Trains, Just 100 Years Ago." *Columbia* 1 (Winter 1988): 20–29.

Burton, Richard F. *The City of the Saints, and Across the Rocky Mountains to California.* New York: Harper and Brothers, 1862.

Crandall, Lulu Donnell. "The 'Colonel Wright.'" *Washington Historical Quarterly* 7 (April 1916): 126–132.

Crithfield, June. *Of Yesterday and the River.* [Pullman, Wash.]: J. Crithfield, 1973.

Deatherage, C. P. *Steamboating on the Missouri River in the Sixties.* Fairfield, Wash.: Ye Galleon Press, 1971. Reprint of 1924 articles published in Kansas City.

Dietrich, William. *Northwest Passage: The Great Columbia River.* New York: Simon and Schuster, 1995.

Drago, Harry Sinclair. *The Steamboaters: From the Early Side-Wheelers to the Big Packets.* New York: Dodd, Mead, 1967.

Dunbar, Seymour. *A History of Travel in America.* 4 vols. Indianapolis: Bobbs-Merrill, 1915.

Faber, Jim. *Steamer's Wake: Voyaging down the Old Marine Highways of Puget Sound, British Columbia, and the Columbia River.* Seattle: Enetai Press, 1985.

Fishbaugh, Charles Preston. *From Paddle Wheels to Propellers in the Story of Steam Navigation on the Western Waters.* Indianapolis: Indiana Historical Society, 1970.

Flexner, James T. *Steamboats Come True: American Inventors in Action.* Boston: Little, Brown, 1978 reprint of 1944 edition.

Haites, Erik F., James Mak, and Gary M. Walton. *Western River Transportation: The Era of Early Internal Development, 1810–1860.* Baltimore: Johns Hopkins University Press, 1975.

Henry, John Frazier. *Early Maritime Artists of the Pacific Northwest Coast, 1741–1841.* Seattle: University of Washington Press, 1984.

Hunter, Louis C. *Steam Power: A History of Industrial Power in the United States, 1780–1930.* Charlottesville: University Press of Virginia, 1985.

Huntley, James L. *Ferry Boats in Idaho.* Caldwell, Idaho: Caxton Printers, 1979.

Jones, Nard. *Swift Flows the River.* Portland: Binfords and Mort, 1964 reprint of 1940 edition. A novel of the Columbia River.

Lang, William L., ed. *A Columbia River Reader.* Tacoma: Washington State Historical Society, 1992.

———. "Creating the Columbia: Historians and the Great River of the West, 1890–1935." *Oregon Historical Quarterly* 93 (Fall 1992): 234–261.

McCoy, Keith. *Melodic Whistles in the Columbia River Gorge.* White Salmon, Wash.: Pahto Publications, 1995.

MacGill, Caroline E., and others. *History of Transportation in the United States before 1860.* Edited by Balthasar Henry Meyer. Washington, D.C.: Carnegie Institution of Washington, 1917.

Moody, Ralph. *Stagecoach West.* New York: Thomas Y. Crowell, 1967.

Newell, Gordon, ed. *The W. H. McCurdy Marine History of the Pacific Northwest.* Seattle: Superior Publishing, 1966. Material since the Lewis and Dryden history.

Nottage, James H., and Jim Wilke. *Stagecoach! The Romantic Western Vehicle.* Los Angeles: Gene Autry Western Heritage Museum, 1990.

Oregon Historical Quarterly 93 (Fall 1992). Special issue on the Columbia River.

Oregon Historical Society Manuscript Collections: #2168, Fred Lockley Papers: Steamboat Accounts; #122, Oregon Steam Navigation Company; Leonard Hosford Coll., 34 volumes of detailed material on steamboats.

Palmer, Tim. *The Snake River: Window to the West.* Washington, D.C.: Island Press, 1991.

Payer, K. Jack. "Pacific Coastal Commerce in the American Period." *Journal of the West* 20 (July 1981): 11–20.

Petersen, William J. *Steamboating on the Upper Mississippi.* New York: Dover, 1995 reprint of 1968 edition.

Rushton, Gerald. *Echoes of the Whistle: An Illustrated History of the Union Steamship Company.* Vancouver, B.C.: Douglas and McIntyre, 1980.

Schwantes, Carlos A. "Promoting America's Canals: Popularizing the Hopes and Fears of the New American Nation." *Journal of American Culture* 1 (Winter 1978): 700–712.

Seelye, John. *Beautiful Machine: Rivers and the Republican Plan, 1755–1825.* New York: Oxford University Press, 1991.

Steamboat Days on the River. Portland: Oregon Historical Society, 1969.

Stratton, David. "Hell's Canyon: The Missing Link in Pacific Northwest Regionalism." *Idaho Yesterdays* 28 (Fall 1984): 3–9.

Taylor, George Rogers. *The Transportation Revolution, 1815–1860.* New York: Holt, Rinehart and Winston, 1951.

Timmen, Fritz. *Blow for the Landing: A Hundred Years of Steam Navigation on the Waters of the West.* Caldwell, Idaho: Caxton Printers, 1973.

Vance, James E., Jr. *Capturing the Horizon: The Historical Geography of Transportation since the Sixteenth Century.* Baltimore: Johns Hopkins University Press, 1990 reprint of 1986 edition.

Walker, Henry P. "Pre-Railroad Transportation in the Trans-Mississippi West: An Annotated Bibliography." *Arizona and the West* 18 (Spring 1976): 53–80.

Way, Frederick, Jr., comp. *Way's Packet Directory, 1848–1994.* Rev. ed. Athens: Ohio University Press, 1994.

White, Richard. *The Organic Machine: The Remaking of the Columbia River.* New York: Hill and Wang, 1995.

Winther, Oscar Osburn. *The Old Oregon Country: A History of Frontier Trade, Transportation, and Travel.* New York: Kraus Reprint, 1969 reprint of 1950 edition.

———. *The Transportation Frontier: Trans-Mississippi West, 1865–1890.* New York: Holt, Rinehart and Winston, 1964.

Wright, E. W., ed. *Lewis and Dryden's Marine History of the Pacific Northwest.* Portland: Lewis and Dryden Printing Company, 1895.

Soft Gold Defines a Distant Land

Ashley, William H. *British Establishments on the Columbia and the State of the Fur Trade.* Edited by Donald R. Johnson. Fairfield, Wash.: Ye Galleon Press, 1981 reprint of several reports originally published in the 1820s and 1830s.

Baldwin, Leland D. *The Keelboat Age on Western Waters.* Pittsburgh: University of Pittsburgh Press, 1941.

"The Beaver." *Washington Historical Quarterly* 16 (April 1925): 135–136.

Caruthers, J. Wade. "The Sea-borne Frontier on the Northwest Coast, 1778–1850." *Journal of the West* 10 (April 1971): 221–251.

Chittenden, Hiram Martin. *History of Early Steamboat Navigation on the Missouri River: Life and Adventures of Joseph La Barge.* 2 vols. New York: Francis P. Harper, 1903.

Delgado, James P. *The "Beaver": First Steamship on the West Coast.* Victoria, B.C.: Horsdal & Schubart, 1993.

den Otter, A. A. "Transportation and Transformation: The Hudson's Bay Company, 1857–1885." *Great Plains Quarterly* 3 (Summer 1983): 171–185.

Dohan, Mary Helen. *Mr. Roosevelt's Steamboat: The First Steamboat to Travel the Mississippi.* New York: Dodd, Mead, 1981.

Havighurst, Walter. "Steamboat to the Rockies." *American West* 7 (September 1970): 4–11.

Hewitt, Randall H. *Across the Plains and Over the Divide: A Mule Train Journey from East to West in 1862, and Incidents Connected Therewith.* New York: Argosy Antiquarian, 1964 reprints of 1906 edition.

Holbrook, Stewart. *The Columbia.* New York: Holt, Rinehart and Winston, 1956.

Hunter, Louis C. *Steamboats on the Western Rivers: An Economic and Technological History.* Cambridge: Harvard University Press, 1949.

Jackson, Donald. *Voyages of the Steamboat "Yellow Stone."* New York: Ticknor & Fields, 1985.

Lamb, W. Kaye. "The Advent of the *Beaver.*" *British Columbia Historical Quarterly* 2 (July 1938): 163–184.

Lang, William L. "Encounter on the Columbia: An Inner History of Trade and Its Consequences." *Columbia* 6 (Summer 1992): 4–9.

Larpenteur, Charles. *Forty Years a Fur Trader on the Upper Missouri: The Personal Narrative of Charles Larpenteur, 1833–1872.* Chicago: Lakeside Press, 1933.

Lass, William E. *A History of Steamboating on the Upper Missouri.* Lincoln: University of Nebraska Press, 1962.

Lyman, William Denison. *The Columbia River: Its History, Its Myths, Its Scenery, Its Commerce.* New York: G. P. Putnam's Sons, 1917.

Morgan, Murray. *The Columbia: Powerhouse of the West.* Seattle: Superior Publishing, 1949.

Neihardt, John G. *The River and I.* Lincoln: University of Nebraska Press, 1968 reprint of 1910 edition.

Overholser, Joel. *Fort Benton: World's Innermost Port.* Fort Benton: J. Overholser, 1987.

Parker, Samuel. *Journal of an Exploring Tour Beyond the Rocky Mountains.* Minneapolis: Ross and Haines, 1967 reprint of 1838 edition.

Porter, Joseph C. "Marvelous Figures, Astonished Travelers: The Montana Expedition of Maximilian, Prince of Wied." *Montana, the Magazine of Western History* 41 (Autumn 1991): 36–53.

Ravenswaay, Charles van. *Saint Louis: An Informal History of the City and Its People, 1764–1865.* Edited by Candace O'Connor. Saint Louis: Missouri Historical Society Press, 1991.

Ronda, James P. "River Worlds: The Sweep of Cultures on the Columbia." *Columbia* 5 (Fall 1991): 28–33.

Schultz, James Willard. *Floating on the Missouri.* Edited by Eugene Lee Silliman. Norman: University of Oklahoma Press, 1979.

Sunder, John E. *The Fur Trade on the Upper Missouri, 1840–1865.* Norman: University of Oklahoma Press, 1965.

Swagerty, William R. "A View from the Bottom Up: The Work Force of the American Fur Company on the Upper Missouri in the 1830s." *Montana, the Magazine of Western History* 43 (Winter 1993): 18–33.

Symons, Thomas William. *The Symons Report on the Upper Columbia River and the Great Plain of the Columbia.* Fairfield, Wash.: Ye Galleon Press, 1967 reprint of 1882 edition.

Thompson, Erwin N. *Fort Union Trading Post: Fur Trade Empire on the Upper Missouri.* Medora, N.D.: Theodore Roosevelt Nature and History Association, 1986.

Wade, Richard C. *The Urban Frontier: The Rise of Western Cities, 1790–1830.* Cambridge: Harvard University Press, 1959.

Wishart, David J. *The Fur Trade of the American West, 1807–1840: A Geographical Synthesis.* Lincoln: University of Nebraska Press, 1979.

The Way West by Land and Sea

Baydo, Gerald. "Overland from Missouri to Washington Territory in 1854." *Nebraska History* 52 (Spring 1971): 65–88.

Boag, Peter G. "Overlanders and the Snake River Region: A Case Study of Popular Landscape Perception in the Early West." *Pacific Northwest Quarterly* 84 (October 1993): 122–129.

Campbell, John F. "Marine Intelligence from the *Panama Star* and the *Star and Herald.*" *American Neptune* 20 (April 1960): 122, 124–129, 132, 133.

Clanin, Douglas E., ed. *California Gold Rush: Diary of Charles H. Harvey, February 12–November 12, 1852.* Indianapolis: Indiana Historical Society, 1983.

Conkling, Roscoe P., and Margaret B. Conkling. *The Butterfield Overland Mail, 1857–1869.* 3 vols. Glendale, Calif.: Arthur H. Clark, 1947.

Delgado, James P. *To California by Sea: A Maritime History of the California Gold Rush.* Columbia: University of South Carolina Press, 1990.

Gordon, Mary McDougall, ed. *Overland to California with the Pioneer Line: The Gold Rush Diary of Bernard J. Reid.* Urbana: University of Illinois Press, 1987.

Gregg, Josiah. *Commerce of the Prairies.* 2 vols. Philadelphia: Lippincott, 1962 reprint of 1844 edition.

Johnson, Overton, and William H. Winter. *Route Across the Rocky Mountains, with a Description of Oregon and California.* Lafayette, Ind.: John B. Semans, 1846.

Kemble, John Haskell. "Side-Wheelers Across the Pacific." *American Neptune* 2 (January 1942): 5–38, 243.

Knight, Donald G., and Eugene D. Wheeler. *Agony and Death on a Gold Rush Steamer: The Disastrous Sinking of the Side-Wheeler "Yankee Blade."* Ventura, Calif.: Pathfinder, 1990.

Lewis, Oscar. *Sea Routes to the Gold Fields: The Migration by Water to California in 1849–1852.* Sausalito, Calif.: Comstock Editions, 1987 reprint of 1949 edition.

Melder, F. E. "History of the Discoveries and Physical Development of the Coal Industry in the State of Washington." *Pacific Northwest Quarterly* 29 (1938): 151–165.

Monaghan, Jay. *Chile, Peru, and the California Gold Rush of 1849.* Berkeley: University of California Press, 1973.

Rydell, Raymond. *Cape Horn to the Pacific: The Rise and Decline of an Ocean Highway.* Berkeley: University of California Press, 1952.

Somerville, Duncan S. *The Aspinwall Empire.* Mystic, Conn.: Mystic Seaport Museum, 1983.

Taylor, Bayard. *Eldorado; Or, Adventures in the Path of Empire.* Lincoln: University of Nebraska Press, 1988 reprint of 1850 edition.

Weinstein, Robert A. "North from Panama, West to the Orient: The Pacific Mail Steamship Company, as Photographed by Carleton E. Watkins." *California Historical Quarterly* 57 (Spring 1978): 46–57.

Oregon Unbound, or the Formative Fifties

Abbot, Helen B. "Life on the Lower Columbia, 1853–66." *Oregon Historical Quarterly* 83 (Fall 1982): 248–287.

Bordwell, Constance. "Delay and Wreck of the *Peacock:* An Episode in the Wilkes Expedition." *Oregon Historical Quarterly* 92 (Summer 1991): 119–198.

Clark, Robert Carlton. *History of the Willamette Valley, Oregon.* Chicago: S. J. Clarke Publishing, 1927.

Corning, Howard McKinley. *Willamette Landings: Ghost Towns of the River.* Portland: Oregon Historical Society, 1947.

DeSmet, P. J. *Oregon Missions and Travels Over the Rocky Mountains in 1845–46.* New York: Edward Dunigan, 1847.

Edwards, G. Thomas. "The Oregon Trail in the Columbia Gorge, 1843–1855: The Final Ordeal." *Oregon Historical Quarterly* 97 (Summer 1996): 134–175.

Farquhar, Francis P., ed. *Up and Down California in 1860–1864; the Journal of William H. Brewer.* Berkeley: University of California Press, 1974 reprint of 1966 edition.

Gill, Frank B. "Oregon's First Railway: The Oregon Portage Railroad at the Cascades of the Columbia River." *Oregon Historical Quarterly* 25 (September 1924): 171–235.

Gillette, P. W. "A Brief History of the Oregon Steam Navigation Company." *Oregon Historical Quarterly* 5 (June 1904): 120–132.

Jackson, W. Turrentine. "Portland: Wells Fargo's Hub for the Pacific Northwest." *Oregon Historical Quarterly* 86 (Fall 1985): 229–267.

Johansen, Dorothy O. "The Oregon Steam Navigation Company: An Example of Capitalism on the Frontier." *Pacific Historical Review* 10 (June 1941): 179–188.

Knuth, Priscilla. *"Picturesque" Frontier: The Army's Fort Dalles.* 2d ed. Portland: Oregon Historical Society, 1987.

Layman, William D. "The Columbia before It Was Tamed: How a Raging River Was Opened to Steamboat Traffic." *Columbia* 1 (Winter 1988): 32–41.

Lockley, Fred. *History of the Columbia River Valley from The Dalles to the Sea.* 3 vols. Chicago: S. J. Clarke Publishing, 1928.

Lomax, Alfred L. *"Brother Jonathan:* Pioneer Steamship of the Pacific Coast." *Oregon Historical Quarterly* 60 (September 1959): 330–351.

———. "Commerce and Transportation in the Siuslaw and Willamette Valleys, 1850–91." *Oregon Historical Quarterly* 36 (September 1935): 217–246.

MacColl, E. Kimbark, and Harry H. Stein. "The Economic Power of Portland's Early Merchants, 1851–1861." *Oregon Historical Quarterly* 89 (Summer 1988): 116–156.

MacMullen, Jerry. *Paddle-Wheel Days in California.* Stanford: Stanford University Press, 1944.

Mills, Randall V. "A History of Transportation in the Pacific Northwest." *Oregon Historical Quarterly* 47 (September 1946): 281–312.

———. *Stern-Wheelers up Columbia: A Century of Steamboating in the Oregon Country.* Lincoln: University of Nebraska Press, 1977 reprint of 1947 edition.

Morison, Samuel E. "New England and the Opening of the Columbia River Salmon Trade, 1830." *Oregon Historical Quarterly* 28 (June 1927): 111–132.

Newsom, David. *David Newsom, the Western Observer, 1805–1882.* Portland: Oregon Historical Society, 1972.

Nordhoff, Charles. *Nordhoff's West Coast: California, Oregon and Hawaii.* London: KPI, 1987 combined reprint of *California: For Health, Pleasure and Residence* (1874) and *Northern California, Oregon and Hawaii* (1875).

O'Meara, James. "An Early Steamboating Era on the Willamette." *Oregon Historical Quarterly* 44 (June 1943): 140–146.

Palmer, Joel. *Journal of Travels over the Rocky Mountains.* Cincinnati: J. A. and U. P. James, 1847.

Perko, Richard. "A Forgotten Passage to Puget Sound: The Fort Steilacoom–Walla Walla Road." *Montana, the Magazine of Western History* 35 (Winter 1985): 38–47.

Poppleton, Irene Lincoln. "Oregon's First Monopoly—the O.S.N. Co." *Oregon Historical Quarterly* 9 (December 1908): 274–303.

Prosch, Thomas W. "Notes from a Government Document on Oregon Conditions in the Fifties." *Oregon Historical Quarterly* 8 (September 1907): 191–200.

Richards, Kent. D. "A Good, Serviceable Road: The Columbia River to Puget Sound Connection." *Columbia* 6 (Winter 1992/93): 6–11.

Robinson, Joan. "The Hard First Way across the Mountains." *Columbia* 2 (Summer 1988): 12–20. Naches Pass trail.

Scott, Harvey W. *History of the Oregon Country.* 6 vols. Cambridge, Mass.: The Riverside Press, 1924.

Smith, E. D. "Communication Pioneering in Oregon." *Oregon Historical Quarterly* 39 (December 1938): 352–371.

Stewart, Earle K. "Steamboats on the Columbia: The Pioneer Period." *Oregon Historical Quarterly* 51 (March 1950): 20–42.

Throckmorton, Arthur L. *Oregon Argonauts: Merchant Adventurers on the Western Frontier.* Portland: Oregon Historical Society, 1961.

Trautmann, Frederic, ed. and trans. *Oregon East, Oregon West: Travels and Memoirs by Theodor Kirchhoff, 1863–1872.* Portland: Oregon Historical Society Press, 1987.

Wilson, Richard. "Wait for a Pilot: The Charting of the Columbia River, 1775–1850." *Columbia* 6 (Fall 1992): 9–16.

Winther, Oscar Osburn. "California Stage Company in Oregon." *Oregon Historical Quarterly* 35 (June 1934): 130–138.

———. "Commercial Routes from 1792 to 1843 by Sea and Overland." *Oregon Historical Quarterly* 42 (September 1941): 230–246.

———. "Development of Transportation in Oregon, 1843–1849." *Oregon Historical Quarterly* 40 (December 1939): 315–326.

———. "Inland Transportation and Communication in Washington, 1844–1859." *Pacific Northwest Quarterly* 30 (October 1939): 371–386.

———. "The Place of Transportation in the Early History of the Pacific Northwest." *Pacific Historical Review* 11 (December 1942): 383–396.

———. "Roads and Transportation of Territorial Oregon." *Oregon Historical Quarterly* 41 (March 1940): 40–52.

———. *Via Western Express and Stagecoach: California's Transportation Links with the Nation, 1848–1869.* Lincoln: University of Nebraska Press, 1979 reprint of 1945 edition.

Winthrop, Theodore. *The Canoe and the Saddle: Adventures Among Northwestern Rivers and Forests. . . .* New York: J. W. Lovell, 1862.

The Pulse of a Continent

Alexander, Thomas G., and Leonard J. Arrington. "Camp in the Sagebrush: Camp Floyd, Utah, 1858–1861." *Utah Historical Quarterly* 34 (Winter 1966): 3–21.

Beadle, J. H. *The Undeveloped West; Or, Five Years in the Territories. . . .* Philadelphia: National Publishing, [1873].

Bloss, Roy A. *Pony Express: The Great Gamble.* Berkeley: Howell-North, 1959.

Bowles, Samuel. *Across the Continent: A Summer's Journey to the Rocky Mountains, the Mormons, and the Pacific States.* Readex Microprint, 1966 reprint of 1865 edition.

Carter, John Denton. "Before the Telegraph: The News Service of the San Francisco *Bulletin*, 1855–1861." *Pacific Historical Review* 11 (September 1942): 301–317.

Chandler, Robert J. "The California News-Telegraph Monopoly, 1860–1870." *Southern California Quarterly* 58 (Winter 1976): 459–484.

Coburn, Jesse L. *Letters of Gold: California Postal History through 1869.* Canton, Ohio: U.S. Philatelic Classics Society, 1984.

Gray, John S. "The Salt Lake Hockaday Mail, Part I." *Annals of Wyoming* 56 (Fall 1984): 12–19.

———. "The Salt Lake Hockaday Mail, Part II." *Annals of Wyoming* 57 (Spring 1985): 2–12.

Greeley, Horace. *An Overland Journey from New York to San Francisco, in the Summer of 1859.* Edited by Charles T. Duncan. New York: Alfred A. Knopf, 1969 reprint of 1860 edition.

Greene, A. C. *900 Miles on the Butterfield Trail.* Denton: University of North Texas Press, 1994.

Grossman, Peter Z. *American Express: The Unofficial History of the People Who Built the Great Financial Empire.* New York: Crown Publishers, 1987.

Hafen, Le Roy R. *The Overland Mail, 1849–1869: Promoter of Settlement, Precursor of Railroads.* Cleveland: Arthur H. Clark, 1926.

Hailey, John. *The History of Idaho.* Boise: Syms-York, 1910.

Hungerford, Edward. *Wells Fargo, Advancing the American Frontier.* New York: Random House, 1949.

Jackson, W. Turrentine. "A New Look at Wells Fargo, Stagecoaches, and the Pony Express." *California Historical Quarterly* 45 (December 1966): 291–324.

Klare, Normand E. *The Final Voyage of the "Central America," 1857.* Spokane, Wash.: Arthur H. Clark, 1992.

Loomis, Noel M. *Wells Fargo, an Illustrated History.* New York: Bramhall House, 1967.

Mackinnon, William P. "The Buchanan Spoils System and the Utah Expedition: Careers of W. M. F. Magraw and John M.

Hockaday." *Utah Historical Quarterly* 31 (Spring 1963): 127–150.

Majors, Alexander. *Seventy Years on the Frontier.* Minneapolis: Ross and Haines, 1965 reprint of 1893 edition.

Monahan, Doris. *Destination Denver City: The South Platte Trail.* Athens: Ohio University Press, 1985.

Ormsby, Waterman L. *The Butterfield Overland Mail.* Edited by Lyle H. Wright and Josephine M. Bynum. San Marino, Calif.: The Huntington Library, 1942.

Owens, Patricia Ann. "The Overland Mail in Wyoming." *Annals of Wyoming* 61 (Fall 1989): 13–19.

Reid, James D. *The Telegraph in America.* New York: Arno Press, 1974 reprint of 1879 edition.

Richardson, Albert D. *Beyond the Mississippi: From the Great River to the Great Ocean.* Hartford, Conn.: American Publishing, 1867.

Ridge, Martin. "Reflections on the Pony Express." *Montana, the Magazine of Western History* 46 (Autumn 1996): 2–13.

Settle, Raymond W. "The Pony Express: Heroic Effort—Tragic End." *Utah Historical Quarterly* 27 (April 1959): 102–126.

Settle, Raymond, and Mary Lund Settle. "Napoleon of the West." *Annals of Wyoming* 32 (April 1960): 4ff.

———. *Saddle and Spurs: Saga of the Pony Express.* Harrisburg, Pennsylvania: Stackpole, 1955.

———. *War Drums and Wagon Wheels: The Story of Russell, Majors and Waddell.* Lincoln: University of Nebraska Press, 1966.

Shumate, Albert. *The Notorious I. C. Woods of the Adams Express.* Glendale, Calif.: Arthur H. Clark, 1986.

Taylor, Morris F. *First Mail West: Stagecoach Lines on the Santa Fe Trail.* Albuquerque: University of New Mexico Press, 1971.

Thompson, Robert Luther. *Wiring a Continent: The History of the Telegraph Industry in the United States, 1832–1866.* Princeton: Princeton University Press, 1947.

Unrau, William E., ed. *Tending the Talking Wire: A Buck Soldier's View of Indian Country, 1863–1866.* Salt Lake City: University of Utah Press, 1979.

Rocky Mountain Gold Fever

Angelo, C. Aubrey. *Sketches of Travel in Oregon and Idaho.* Fairfield, Wash.: Ye Galleon Press, 1988 reprint of 1866 edition.

Athearn, Robert G. "The Civil War and Montana Gold." *Montana, the Magazine of Western History* 12 (Spring 1962): 62–73.

Bolino, August C. "The Role of Mining in the Economic Development of Idaho Territory." *Oregon Historical Quarterly* 59 (June 1958): 116–151.

Bright, Verne. "Blue Mountain Eldorados: Auburn, 1861." *Oregon Historical Quarterly* 62 (September 1961): 212–236.

Burcham, Ralph, ed. "Orofino Gold." *Idaho Yesterdays* 4 (Fall 1960): 2–5, 8–9.

Campbell, John L. *Six Months in the New Gold-Diggings: Placer Gold Mining in Idaho Territory in 1863.* Fairfield, Wash.: Ye Galleon Press, 1979 reprint of 1864 edition.

"Clearwater Gold Rush." *Idaho Yesterdays* 4 (Spring 1960): 12–15, 18–26.

Collins, John S. *Across the Plains in '64: Incidents of Early Days West of the Missouri River. . . .* Omaha: National Printing, 1904.

Elliott, T. C. "The Mullan Road: Its Local History and Significance." *Washington Historical Quarterly* 14 (July 1923): 206–209.

"Fabulous Florence." *Idaho Yesterdays* 6 (Summer 1962): 22–31.

Fisher, Vardis, and Opal Laurel Holmes. *Gold Rushes and Mining Camps of the Early American West.* Caldwell, Idaho: Caxton Printers, 1979.

Freeman, Otis W. "Early Wagon Roads in the Inland Empire." *Pacific Northwest Quarterly* 45 (October 1954): 125–130.

Frost, Robert. "Fraser River Gold Rush Adventures." *Washington Historical Quarterly* 22 (July 1931): 203–209.

"Gold in 1860." *Idaho Yesterdays* 3 (Fall 1959): 14–15, 18–21.

Goulder, William Armistead. *Reminiscences: Incidents in the Life of a Pioneer in Oregon and Idaho.* Moscow: University of Idaho Press, 1989 reprint of 1909 edition.

Hacking, Norman R. "Steamboat 'Round the Bend': American Steamers on the Fraser River in 1858." *British Columbia Historical Quarterly* 8 (1944): 255–280.

Howard, Addison. "Captain John Mullan." *Washington Historical Quarterly* 25 (July 1934): 185–202.

Jackson, W. Turrentine. *Wagon Roads West: A Study of Federal Road Surveys and Construction in the Trans-Mississippi West, 1846–1869.* Lincoln: University of Nebraska Press, 1979 reprint of 1964 edition.

———. "Banking, Mail, and Express Service in British North America: The Role of Wells, Fargo and Company on Vancouver Island and in British Columbia." *Pacific Northwest Quarterly* 76 (October 1985): 137–147.

Johanssen, Robert W. "A Political Picture of the Pacific Northwest in the Civil War." *Montana, the Magazine of Western History* 12 (Spring 1962): 38–48.

Leland, Alonzo. "The Salmon River Mines." *Idaho Yesterdays* 16 (Fall 1972): 30–31.

Martin, Charles W., ed. "Joseph Warren Arnold's Journal of His Trip to and from Montana, 1864–1866." *Nebraska History* 55 (Winter 1974): 463–552.

Miller, Cincinnatus H. "Old Baboon." *Idaho Yesterdays* 11 (Winter 1968): 2–8. Salmon River mines.

Mullan, John. *Miners and Travelers' Guide to Oregon, Washington, Idaho, Montana, Wyoming, and Colorado.* New York: William M. Franklin, 1865.

"News from the Nez Perce Mines." *Idaho Yesterdays* 3 (Winter 1959–1960): 18–29.

The Pierce Chronicle. Edited by J. Gary Williams and Ronald W. Stark. Moscow: Idaho Research Foundation, [ca. 1974].

Purple, Edwin Ruthven. *Perilous Passage: A Narrative of the Montana Gold Rush, 1862–1863.* Edited by Kenneth N. Owens. Helena: Montana Historical Society Press, 1995.

Reinhart, Herman Francis. *The Golden Frontier: The Recollections of Herman Francis Reinhart, 1851–1869.* Edited by Doyce B. Nunis, Jr. Austin: University of Texas Press, [1962].

"The Salmon River Mines." *Idaho Yesterdays* 6 (Spring 1962): 40–48.

Scott, Leslie M. "The Pioneer Stimulus of Gold." *Oregon Historical Quarterly* 18 (September 1917): 145–166.

Stuart, Granville. *Forty Years on the Frontier as seen in the Journals and Reminiscences of Granville Stuart, Gold-Miner, Trader, Merchant, Rancher and Politician.* 2 vols. Cleveland: Arthur H. Clark, 1925.

Trimble, William J. *The Mining Advance into the Inland Empire.* University of Wisconsin Bulletin No. 638. Madison: University of Wisconsin, 1914.

Walgamott, Charles S. *Six Decades Back.* Moscow: University of Idaho Press, 1990 reprint of 1936 edition.

"We're Off to the Mines." *Idaho Yesterdays* 5 (Summer 1961): 8–15, 18–20. Elk City, Pierce, and the Clearwater gold rush.

West, Elliott. "Five Idaho Mining Towns: A Computer Profile." *Pacific Northwest Quarterly* 73 (July 1982): 108–120.

Winther, Oscar O. "Early Commercial Importance of the Mullan Road." *Oregon Historical Quarterly* 46 (March 1945): 22–35.

Ho for Idaho! Steamboats to the Gold Country

Brazier, Helen H. "Missouri River Journey, 1866." *Montana, the Magazine of Western History* 3 (Summer 1953): 32–38.

Davison, Stanley R. "White Hopes of the Big Muddy." *Montana, the Magazine of Western History* 9 (April 1959): 2–15.

Gamble, John Mack. "Up River to Benton." *Montana, the Magazine of Western History* 6 (April 1956): 32–41.

Gilbert, Frank T. *Historic Sketches of Walla Walla, Whitman, Columbia and Garfield Counties, Washington Territory.* Portland: A. G. Walling, 1882.

Gillette, P. W. "A Brief History of the Oregon Steam Navigation Company." *Oregon Historical Quarterly* 5 (June 1904): 120–132.

Hanson, Joseph Mills. *The Conquest of the Missouri: Being the Story of the Life and Exploits of Captain Grant Marsh.* New York: Murray Hill Books, 1946 reprint of 1909 edition.

Johansen, Dorothy O. "Capitalism on the Far-Western Frontier: The Oregon Steam Navigation Company." Ph.D. dissertation, University of Washington, 1941.

Johnson, Dorothy M. "Slow Boat to Benton." *Montana, the Magazine of Western History* 11 (Winter 1961): 2–11.

Lyman, W. D. *Lyman's History of Old Walla Walla County.* 2 vols. Chicago: S. J. Clarke Publishing, 1918.

McKeown, Martha Ferguson. "Historic Umatilla House at The Dalles." *Oregon Historical Quarterly* 31 (March 1930): 37–41.

Miller, Henry. "Letters from the Upper Columbia." *Idaho Yesterdays* 4 (Winter: 1960–1961): 14–25. Transportation to Pierce gold rush.

Oviatt, Alton B. "Steamboat Traffic on the Upper Missouri River, 1859–1869." *Pacific Northwest Quarterly* 40 (April 1949): 93–105.

Parsons, John E. "Steamboats in the 'Idaho' Gold Rush." *Montana, the Magazine of Western History* 10 (Winter 1960): 51–61.

Petsche, Jerome E. *The Steamboat "Bertrand": History,*

*T*he age of the horse lived on in rodeos across the West, one of the most impressive spectacles being held annually in Pendleton, Oregon. The camera of W. S. Bowman captured a particularly dramatic moment at the Round-Up. Courtesy Oregon Historical Society, OrHi 48537 #1131-A.

BONNIE McCARROLL THROWN FROM "SILVER" PENDELTON, OREG. © W.S. BOWMAN

(DOUBLEPAY) PRINT

Excavation, and Architecture. Washington, D.C.: National Park Service, 1974.

Poppleton, Irene Lincoln. "Oregon's First Monopoly: The O.S.N. Co." *Oregon Historical Quarterly* 9 (December 1908): 274–304.

Raymer, Robert George. *Montana: The Land and the People.* Chicago: Lewis Publishing, 1930.

Senieur, Matilda. "Bismarck to Fort Benton by Steamboat in the Year 1869." *Montana, the Magazine of Western History* 2 (April 1952): 57–60.

Silliman, Lee. "'Up the Great River': Daniel Weston's Missouri Steamboat Diary." *Montana, the Magazine of Western History* 30 (July 1980): 32–51.

Simon-Smolinski, Carole. *Journal 1862: Timothy Nolan's 1862 Account of His Riverboat and Overland Journey to the Salmon River Mines, Washington Territory.* Clarkston, Wash.: Northwest Historical Consultants, 1983.

Stewart, Earle K. "Steamboats on the Columbia: The Pioneer Period." *Oregon Historical Quarterly* 51 (March 1950): 20–42.

———. "Transporting Livestock by Boat up the Columbia, 1861–1868." *Oregon Historical Quarterly* 50 (December 1949): 251–259.

Thompson, Erwin N. "Men and Events on Lower Snake River." *Idaho Yesterdays* 5 (Fall 1961): 10–15.

"Those Were the Days: When Sternwheel Steamers Came Clear to Idaho." *Idaho Yesterdays* 4 (Winter 1960–1961): 11–13.

Wood, Asa A. "Fort Benton's Part in the Development of the West." *Washington Historical Quarterly* 20 (July 1929): 213–22.

Via Shank's Mare and Stagecoach

Gamboa, Erasmo. "The Mexican Mule Pack System of Transportation in the Pacific Northwest and British Columbia." *Journal of the West* 29 (January 1990): 16–28.

———. "Mexican Mule Packers and Oregon's Second Regiment Mounted Volunteers, 1855–1856." *Oregon Historical Quarterly* 92 (Spring 1991): 41–59.

Gittins, H. Leigh. *Idaho's Gold Road.* Moscow: University Press of Idaho, 1976.

Goodwin, Victor O. "William C. (Hill) Beachey: Nevada-California-Idaho Stagecoach King." *Nevada Historical Society Quarterly* 10 (Spring 1967): 4–46.

Jones, Larry R. "Staging to the South Boise Mines." *Idaho Yesterdays* 29 (Summer 1985): 19–25.

Madsen, Betty M., and Brigham D. Madsen. *North to Montana: Jehus, Bullwhackers, and Mule Skinners on the Montana Trail.* Salt Lake City: University of Utah Press, 1980.

Madsen, Brigham D. "The Montana Trail: Salt Lake City–Corinne to Fort Benton." *Overland Journal* 13 (1995): 19–34.

Murray, Keith A. "Building a Wagon Road through the Northern Cascade Mountains." *Pacific Northwest Quarterly* 56 (April 1965): 49–56.

Oliphant, J. Orin. "Notes on Early Settlements and on Geographic Names of Eastern Washington." *Washington Historical Quarterly* 22 (July 1931): 172–202. Shipping points before railroads, post offices, etc.

Oviatt, Alton B. "Fort Benton, River Capital." In *A History of Montana.* 3 vols. Edited by Merrill G. Burlingame and K. Ross Toole. New York: Lewis Historical Publishing, [1957].

Rolle, Andrew, ed. *The Road to Virginia City: The Diary of James Knox Polk Miller.* Norman: University of Oklahoma Press, 1960.

Rusling, James F. *Across America; Or, The Great West and The Pacific Coast.* New York: Sheldon and Company, 1874.

Stansbury, Howard. "The Bannock Mountain Road." *Idaho Yesterdays* 8 (Spring 1964): 10–15.

Tuttle, D. S. *Reminiscences of a Missionary Bishop.* New York: Thomas Whittaker, 1906.

Watt, James W. "Experiences of a Packer in Washington Territory Mining Camps During the Sixties." *Washington Historical Quarterly* 20 (January 1929): 36–53.

Welch, Julia Conway. *The Magruder Murders: Coping with Violence on the Idaho Frontier.* Eagle Point, Oreg.: J. C. Welch, 1991.

Wells, Donald N. "Farmer Forgotten: Nez Perce Suppliers of the North Idaho Gold Rush Days." *Idaho Yesterdays* 2 (Summer 1958): 28–32.

Winther, Oscar O. "Inland Transportation and Communication in Washington, 1844–1859." *Pacific Northwest Quarterly* 30 (October 1939): 371–386.

———. "Pack Animals for Transportation in the Pacific Northwest." *Pacific Northwest Quarterly* 34 (April 1943): 131–146.

Long Hauls Overland: The Freighters

Brown, Jesse. "The Freighter in Early Days." *Annals of Wyoming* 19 (July 1947): 112–116.

Essin, Emmett M., III. "Mules, Packs, and Packtrains." *Southwestern Historical Quarterly* 74 (July 1970): 52–63.

Gamboa, Erasmo. "Supply Line to the New Frontier: The Mexican Mule Pack System of Transportation in the Pacific Northwest." *Columbia* 8 (Winter 1994/95): 21–28.

Hamilton, Ladd. *This Bloody Deed: The Magruder Incident.* Pullman: Washington State University Press, 1994. A retelling of the incident through a blend of fact and fiction.

Hewitt, Randall H. *Across the Plains and Over the Divide: A Mule Train Journey from East to West in 1862, and Incidents*

Connected Therewith. New York: Broadway Publishing,
[ca. 1906].

Hooker, William Francis. *The Bullwhacker: Adventures of a
Frontier Freighter.* Lincoln: University of Nebraska Press,
1988 reprint of 1924 edition.

Johnson, Dorothy M. "Flour Famine in Alder Gulch, 1864."
Montana, the Magazine of Western History 7 (Winter 1957):
18–27. When snow delayed freight wagons.

Lewis, William S. "The Camel Pack Trains in the Mining Camps
of the West." *Washington Historical Quarterly* 19 (October
1928): 271–284.

McElroy, Harold L. "Mercurial Military: A Study of the Central
Montana Frontier Army Policy." *Montana, the Magazine of
Western History* 4 (Autumn 1954): 9–23. Army transportation.

Madsen, Brigham D., and Betty M. Madsen. "The Diamond R
Rolls Out." *Montana, the Magazine of Western History* 21
(April 1971): 2–17. Freight from Salt Lake to Montana gold-
fields in 1869.

Munkres, Robert L. "Wagon Train Animals." *Annals of
Wyoming* 65 (Summer/Fall 1993): 15–27.

Murray, Henry T., and John A. Murray. "Montana Episodes—
Freighting in the Judith Basin, 1891–1902." *Montana, the
Magazine of Western History* 36 (Winter 1986): 60–65.

Sanders, Helen Fitzgerald. *A History of Montana.* 3 vols.
Chicago: Lewis Publishing, 1913.

Settle, Raymond W., and Mary Lund Settle. *Empire on Wheels.*
Stanford: Stanford University Press, 1949. The story of
Russell, Majors and Waddell.

Walker, Henry Pickering. *The Wagonmasters: High Plains
Freighting from the Earliest Days of the Santa Fe Trail to 1880.*
Norman: University of Oklahoma Press, 1966.

Watt, James W. "Experiences of a Packer in Washington Territory Mining Camps During the Sixties." *Washington Historical Quarterly* 19 (1928): 206–213, 285–293; 20 (1929): 36–53.

Winther, Oscar Osburn. "Pack Animals for Transportation
in the Pacific Northwest." *Pacific Northwest Quarterly* 34
(April 1943): 131–146.

Zontek, Ken. "Mules across the Mountains: Packing in Early
Idaho." *Idaho Yesterdays* 39 (Summer 1995): 2–10.

Contested Terrain

Chaney, Elijah. "A Visit to the Boise Basin, 1866." *Idaho
Yesterdays* 16 (Spring 1972): 26–27.

Doyle, Susan B. "Journeys to the Land of Gold: Emigrants on
the Bozeman Trail, 1863–1866." *Montana, the Magazine of
Western History* 41 (Autumn 1991): 54–67.

Edwards, G. Thomas. "Walla Walla: Gateway to the Northwest
Interior." *Montana, the Magazine of Western History* 40
(Summer 1990): 28–43.

Goodwin, Victor O. "William C. (Hill) Beachey: Nevada-
California-Idaho Stagecoach King." *Nevada Historical
Quarterly* 10 (Spring 1967): 4–46.

Gray, John S. "Blazing the Bridger and Bozeman Trails." *Annals
of Wyoming* 49 (Spring 1977): 23–51.

———. "The Northern Overland Pony Express." *Montana, the
Magazine of Western History* 16 (October 1966): 58–73. North
Dakota to Montana.

Harstad, Peter T. "The Lander Trail." *Idaho Yesterdays* 12 (Fall
1968): 14–28.

Hebard, Grace Raymond, and E. A. Brininstool. *The Bozeman
Trail: Historical Accounts of the Blazing of the Overland Routes
into the Northwest and the Fights with Red Cloud's Warriors.*
Lincoln: University of Nebraska Press, 1990 reprint of 1922
edition.

*In the Wake of the "Mary Moody": Historic Boat Tours on Lake
Pend Oreille.* Sandpoint: Idaho Panhandle National Forests,
[ca. 1990].

Jackson, W. Turrentine. "The Fisk Expeditions to the Montana
Gold Fields." *Pacific Northwest Quarterly* 33 (July 1942): 265–
282. Northern overland route, 1860s.

Johnson, Dorothy M. *The Bloody Bozeman: The Perilous Trail to
Montana's Gold.* Missoula: Mountain Press, 1983.

Lingenfelter, Richard E. *Steamboats on the Colorado River, 1852–
1916.* Tucson: University of Arizona Press, 1978.

McGregor, Alexander C. "The Economic Impact of the Mullan
Road on Walla Walla, 1860–1883." *Pacific Northwest Quarterly*
65 (July 1974): 118–129.

McIntosh, Clarence F. "The Chico and Red Bluff Route: Stage
Lines from Southern Idaho to the Sacramento Valley, 1865–
1867." *Idaho Yesterdays* 6 (Fall 1962): 12–15, 18–19.

Meyer, Bette E. "The Pend d'Oreille Routes to Montana, 1866–
1870." *Pacific Northwest Quarterly* 72 (April 1981): 76–83.

Myers, Alice V. "Wagon Roads West: The Sawyers Expedition of
1865–66." *Annals of Iowa* 3d ser. 23 (January 1942): 213–237.

Oviatt, Alton B. "Pacific Coast Competition for the Gold Camp
Trade of Montana." *Pacific Northwest Quarterly* 56 (October 1965): 168–176.

Ryan, Benjamin W. "The Bozeman Trail to Virginia City,
Montana, in 1864: A Diary." *Annals of Wyoming* 19
(July 1947): 77–104.

Smith, Sherry L. "The Bozeman: Trail to Death and Glory."
Annals of Wyoming 55 (Spring 1983): 32–48

"Steamboat down the Snake: The Early Story of the Stern-
wheeler *Shoshone.*" *Idaho Yesterdays* 5 (Winter 1961–1962): 22–
33.

Underhill, W. M. "The Northern Overland Route to Montana."
Washington Historical Quarterly 23 (July 1932): 177–195.
Minnesota to Montana for gold in 1860s.

Wells, Merle W. "The Creation of the Territory of Idaho." *Pacific Northwest Quarterly* 40 (April 1949): 106–123.

———, ed. "She Will Strike about There: Steamboating in Hell's Canyon." *Idaho Yesterdays* 1 (Summer 1957): 2–9.

Ben Holladay Builds a Stagecoach Empire

Frederick, J. V. *Ben Holladay, the Stagecoach King: A Chapter in the Development of Transcontinental Transportation.* Lincoln: University of Nebraska Press, 1989 reprint of 1940 edition.

Jackson, W. Turrentine. *Wells Fargo and Co. in Idaho Territory.* Boise: Idaho State Historical Society, 1984.

———. *Wells Fargo Stagecoaching in Montana Territory.* Helena: Montana Historical Society Press, 1979.

———. "Salt Lake City: Wells Fargo's Transportation Depot during the Stagecoach Era." *Utah Historical Quarterly* 53 (Winter 1985): 4–39.

Lucia, Ellis. *The Saga of Ben Holladay: Giant of the Old West.* New York: Hastings House, 1959.

Stewart, George R. "Travelers by 'Overland': Stagecoaching on the Central Route, 1859–1865." *American West* 5 (July 1968): 4–12.

Thompson, George A. *Throw down the Box! Treasure Tales from Gilmer and Salisbury, the Western Stagecoach King.* Salt Lake City: Dream Garden Press, 1989.

Stagecoaching Adapts to the Frontier West

Haines, Francis. "Horses and the American Frontier." *American West* 8 (March 1971): 10–15.

Meier, Gary, and Gloria Meier. *Knights of the Whip: Stagecoach Days in Oregon.* Bellevue, Wash.: Timeline Publishing, 1987.

Morris, Richard. "Horseshoe Economics: To Shoe or Not to Shoe, That Is the Issue." *Nevada Historical Society Quarterly* 30 (1987): 304–315.

Rosa, Joseph G. *They Called Him Wild Bill: The Life and Adventures of James Butler Hickok.* 2d ed. Norman: University of Oklahoma Press, 1974.

Travail by Stagecoach

Boyd, Mrs. Orsemus Bronson. *Cavalry Life in Tent and Field.* Lincoln: University of Nebraska Press, ca. 1982 reprint of 1894 edition.

Burgum, Edwin B. "The Concord Coach." *Colorado Magazine* 16 (September 1939): 173–180.

Dillon, Richard. *Wells Fargo Detective: A Biography of James B. Hume.* Reno: University of Nevada Press, 1986 reprint of 1969 edition.

Drago, Harry Sinclair. *Road Agents and Train Robbers: Half a Century of Western Banditry.* New York: Dodd, Mead, 1973.

DuBois, Fred T. *The Making of a State.* Edited by Louis J. Clements. Rexburg: Eastern Idaho Publishing, 1971.

Edwards, G. Thomas. *Sowing Good Seeds: The Northwest Suffrage Campaigns of Susan B. Anthony.* Portland: Oregon Historical Society Press, 1990. Includes several good descriptions of Anthony's travels by stagecoach across the Pacific Northwest.

Estes, George. *The Stagecoach.* Troutdale, Oreg.: G. Estes, 1925.

Hudman, Lloyd E. "Tourism in the American West." *Journal of the West* 33 (July 1994): 67–76. Includes a stagecoach phase.

Murphy, John Mortimer. *Rambles in North-Western America from the Pacific Ocean to the Rocky Mountains.* London: Chapman and Hall, 1879.

Nash, Wallis. *Oregon: There and Back in 1877.* Corvallis: Oregon State University Press, 1976 reprint of 1878 edition.

Richards, J. R. "Jaded Journey." *Montana, the Magazine of Western History* 4 (Summer 1954): 30–36. A stage ride in 1875.

Spring, Agnes Wright. *The Cheyenne and Black Hills Stage and Express Routes.* Glendale, Calif.: Arthur H. Clark, 1949.

Stewart, George R. "Travelers by 'Overland.'" *American West* 5 (July 1968): 4–12, 61.

Strahorn, Carrie Adell. *Fifteen Thousand Miles by Stage.* 2 vols. New York: Knickerbocker Press, 1911.

Taylor, Bayard. *Colorado: A Summer Trip.* Niwot: University Press of Colorado, 1989 reprint of 1867 edition.

West, Elliott. "Splendid Misery: Stagecoach Travel in the Far West." *American West* 18 (November/December 1981): 61–65.

Navigating on a Heavy Dew

Havighurst, Walter. "Steamboat to the Rockies." *American West* 7 (September 1970): 4–11, 61–62.

Lass, William E. "Missouri River Steamboating." *North Dakota History* 56 (Summer 1989): 3–15.

———. "Steamboating on the Missouri: Its Significance on the Northern Great Plains." *Journal of the West* 6 (January 1967): 53–67.

Mackintosh, Barry. "Lost and Found: One Missouri Steamboat." *American West* 13 (March/April 1976): 18–27. Archaeology of 1865 wreck.

Miles, Nelson A. *Personal Recollections and Observations of General Nelson A. Miles.* Lincoln: University of Nebraska Press, 1992 reprint of 1896 edition.

Wilson, Fred W. "The Lure of the River." *Oregon Historical Quarterly* 34 (1933): 1–18, 113–133.

Wright, Charles E., and Elizabeth W. Buehler. "James W. Troup: Captain on the Columbia." *Oregon History* 39 (Winter–Spring 1996): 22–26.

The Burdens of Time and Space

Bartky, Ian R. "The Adoption of Standard Time." *Technology and Culture* 30 (January 1989): 25–56.

Blake, Anson S. "Working for Wells Fargo—1860–1863: The Letters of Charles S. Blake." *California Historical Society Quarterly* 16 (June 1937): 172–181.

Chandler, Robert J. "The California News-Telegraph Monopoly, 1860–1870." *Southern California Quarterly* 58 (Winter 1976): 459–484.

Gilliss, Julia. *So Far from Home: An Army Bride on the Western Frontier, 1865–1869.* Edited by Priscilla Knuth. Portland: Oregon Historical Society Press, 1993.

Goulder, William Armistead. *Reminiscences: Incidents in the Life of a Pioneer in Oregon and Idaho.* Moscow: University of Idaho Press, 1989 reprint of 1909 edition.

Hines, Gustavus. *Oregon: Its History, Condition and Prospects.* New York: C. M. Saxton, 1859.

O'Malley, Michael. *Keeping Watch: A History of American Time.* New York: Penguin, 1990.

Rotter, Andrew J. "'Matilda for God's Sake Write': Women and Families on the Argonaut Mind." *California History* 57 (Summer 1979): 128–141.

Stephens, Charleen. "The Most Reliable Time: William Bond, the New England Railroads, and Time Awareness in 19th Century America." *Technology and Culture* 30 (January 1989): 1–23.

Landscapes of the Steamboat and Stagecoach Era

Boyd, Robert. "The Pacific Northwest Measles Epidemic of 1847–1848." *Oregon Historical Quarterly* 95 (Spring 1994): 6–47. Travel as link in spread of disease.

Dollar, Clyde D. "The High Plains Smallpox Epidemic of 1837–38." *Western Historical Quarterly* 8 (January 1977): 15–38.

Safford, Jeffrey J., ed. "Montana Episodes: From Horse to Machine." *Montana, the Magazine of Western History* 33 (Autumn 1983): 63–66.

Spence, Clark C. "The Livery Stable in the American West." *Montana, the Magazine of Western History* 36 (Spring 1986): 36–49.

Toedtemeier, Terry. "Oregon Photography: The First Fifty Years." *Oregon Historical Quarterly* 94 (Spring 1993): 36–76.

Overland to Promontory and Beyond

"The Ames Monument." *Annals of Wyoming* 2 (January 1925): 50–52.

Anderson, Bernice Gibbs. "The Gentile City of Corinne." *Utah Historical Quarterly* 9 (July–October 1941): 140–154.

Beal, Merrill D. "The Story of the Utah Northern Railroad, Part 1." *Idaho Yesterdays* 1 (Spring 1957): 3–10.

———. "The Story of the Utah Northern Railroad, Part 2." *Idaho Yesterdays* 1 (Summer 1957): 16–23.

Chisum, Emmett D. "Boom Towns on the Union Pacific: Laramie, Benton, and Bear River City." *Annals of Wyoming* 53 (Spring 1981): 2–13.

Cochran, John S. "Economic Importance of Early Transcontinental Railroads: Pacific Northwest." *Oregon Historical Quarterly* 71 (March 1970): 26–98.

Davison, Stanley R., and Rex C. Myers. "Terminus Town: Founding Dillon." *Montana, the Magazine of Western History* 30 (October 1980): 16–29.

Dieterich, H. R., Jr. "The Architecture of H. H. Richardson in Wyoming: A New Look at the Ames Monument." *Annals of Wyoming* 38 (April 1966): 49–53.

Galloway, John Debo. *The First Transcontinental Railroad.* New York: Dorset Press, 1989 reprint of 1950 edition.

George, Henry. "What the Railroad Will Bring Us." *American West* 4 (February 1967): 6–9, 66–69. Reprinted from the *Overland Monthly* of October 1868.

History and Business Directory of Cheyenne and Guide to the Mining Regions of the Rocky Mountains. New Haven: Yale University Library, 1975 reprint of 1868 edition compiled by E. H. Saltiel and Geo. Barnett.

Jackson, W. Turrentine. "Racing from Reno to Virginia City by Wells Fargo and Pacific Union Expresses." *Nevada Historical Society Quarterly* 20 (Summer 1977): 76–91.

Kraus, George. *High Road to Promontory.* Palo Alto, Calif.: American West, 1969.

Madsen, Brigham D. *Corinne: The Gentile Capital of Utah.* Salt Lake City: Utah State Historical Society, 1980.

Nicandri, David L. "John Mix Stanley: Paintings and Sketches of the Oregon Country and Its Inhabitants." *Oregon Historical Quarterly* 88 (Summer 1987): 149–173.

Ralph, Julian. *Our Great West: A Study of the Present Conditions and Future Possibilities of the New Commonwealths and Capitals of the United States.* Freeport, N.Y.: Books for Libraries Press, 1970 reprint of 1893 edition.

Rhodes-Jones, Carolyn. "An Evolving View of the Landscape: Trappers, Tourists, and the Great Shoshone Falls." *Idaho Yesterdays* 23 (Summer 1979): 19–27.

Riegel, Robert Edgar. *The Story of the Western Railroads: From 1852 through the Reign of the Giants.* Lincoln: University of Nebraska Press, 1964 reprint of 1926 edition.

Shearer, Frederick E., ed. *The Pacific Tourist: The 1884 Illustrated Trans-Continental Guide of Travel from the Atlantic to the Pacific Ocean.* New York: Bounty Books, 1970 reprint of *The Pacific Tourist: Adams and Bishop's Illustrated Trans-*

Continental Guide of Travel from the Atlantic to the Pacific Ocean, 1884.

Spence, Clark C. "The Boom of the Wood River Mines." *Idaho Yesterdays* 23 (Summer 1979): 3–12.

Stelter, Gilbert A. "The Birth of a Frontier Boom Town: Cheyenne in 1867." *Annals of Wyoming* 39 (April 1967): 4ff.

Stevenson, Robert Louis. *From Scotland to Silverado.* Edited by James D. Hart. Cambridge: The Belknap Press of Harvard University Press, 1966 reprint of Volume III of the Edinburgh Edition of Stevenson's work, 1895.

Stover, John F. *Iron Road to the West: American Railroads in the 1850s.* New York: Columbia University Press, 1978.

"Utah Northern Railroad." *Idaho Yesterdays* 22 (Spring 1978): 26–28. A description by Lorenzo Hill Hatch in 1874.

Utley, Robert M. "The Dash to Promontory." *Utah Historical Quarterly* 29 (April 1961): 98–117.

———, and Francis A. Ketterson, Jr. *Golden Spike National Historic Site.* Washington, D.C.: National Park Service, 1969.

Vance, James E., Jr. *The North American Railroad: Its Origin, Evolution, and Geography.* Baltimore: Johns Hopkins University Press, 1995.

Williams, John Hoyt. *A Great and Shining Road: The Epic Story of the Transcontinental Railroad.* New York: Times Books, 1988.

Monopoly Rules the Empire of the Columbia

Bailey, W. F. "The Story of the Oregon Railroad." *Pacific Monthly* 17 (May 1907): 449–561.

Boyd, William H. "The Holladay-Villard Transportation Empire in the Pacific Northwest, 1868–1893." *Pacific Historical Review* 15 (December 1946): 379–389.

Cleaver, J. D. "L. Samuel and the *West Shore:* Images of a Changing Pacific Northwest." *Oregon Historical Quarterly* 94 (Summer–Fall 1993): 166–224.

Cox, Thomas R. "Single Decks and Flat Bottoms: Building the West Coast's Lumber Fleet, 1850–1929." *Journal of the West* 20 (July 1981): 65–74.

Dana, Marshall N. "The Celilo Canal: Its Origin, Its Building and Meaning." *Oregon Historical Quarterly* 16 (June 1915): 108–124.

Elliott, T. C. "The Dalles-Celilo Portage: Its History and Influence." *Oregon Historical Quarterly* 16 (June 1915): 133–174.

Ganoe, John Tilson. "History of the Oregon and California Railroad." *Oregon Historical Quarterly* 25 (September 1924): 236–286.

Gill, Frank B., and Dorothy O. Johansen, eds. "A Chapter in the History of the Oregon Steam Navigation Company: The Steamship *Oregonian.*" *Oregon Historical Quarterly* 38 (September 1937): 300–322; (December 1937): 398–410; 39 (March 1938): 50–64.

Grinnell, George Bird. "Building the Northern Pacific." "Idaho Seaport." *Idaho Yesterdays* 16 (Winter 1972–1973): 10–13.

Johansen, Dorothy O., and Frank B. Gill. "A Chapter in the History of the Oregon Steam Navigation Company: The Ocean Steamship *Oregonian.*" *Oregon Historical Quarterly* 38 (March 1937): 1–43.

Kensel, W. Hudson. "Spokane: The First Decade." *Idaho Yesterdays* 15 (Spring 1971): 18–23.

Lomax, Alfred L. "*Brother Jonathan:* Pioneer Steamship of the Pacific Coast." *Oregon Historical Quarterly* 60 (September 1959): 330–351.

———. "Commerce and Transportation in the Siuslaw and Willamette Valleys." *Oregon Historical Quarterly* 36 (September 1935): 217–246.

Meinig, Donald W. "Wheat Sacks out to Sea: Early Export Trade from the Walla Walla Country." *Pacific Northwest Quarterly* 45 (January 1954): 13–18.

Mohr, Nicolaus. *Excursion Through America.* Chicago: Lakeside Press, 1973 reprint of 1884 edition. Contains a lengthy account of Villard's final spike ceremony in 1883.

Moore, Miles C. "A Pioneer Rail Road Builder: Dorsey S. Baker." *Oregon Historical Quarterly* 4 (September 1903): 195–201.

Oregon Business Directory and State Gazetteer. Compiled by John Mortimer Murphy. Portland: S. J. McCormick, 1873.

Thompson, Erwin N. "Men and Events on the Lower Snake River." *Idaho Yesterdays* 5 (Fall 1961): 10–15, 18–19.

Weatherford, Marion. "Fields of Amber Grain." In *The Western Shore: Oregon Country Essays Honoring the American Revolution.* Edited by Thomas Vaughan. Portland: Oregon Historical Society, [1976?].

Young, Frederick G. "Columbia River Improvement and the Pacific Northwest." *Oregon Historical Quarterly* 9 (March 1908): 79–94.

Winding down the Missouri

Anderson, John C. *Mackinaws down the Missouri: John C. Anderson's Journal of a Trip from Saint Louis, Mo., to Virginia City, Montana and Return, 1866.* Edited by Glen Barrett. Logan: Utah State University Press, 1973.

Bryan, Charles W., Jr. "Dr. Lamme and his Gallant Little *Yellowstone.*" *Montana, the Magazine of Western History* 15 (Summer 1965): 24–43.

Hammer, Kenneth M. "River and Rail Competition in the Upper-Missouri Basin." *Journal of the West* 17 (October 1978): 41–51.

Klassen, Henry C. "I. G. Baker and Company in Calgary, 1875–1884." *Montana, the Magazine of Western History* 35 (Summer 1985): 40–55.

Lass, William E. "Steamboats on the Yellowstone." *Montana, the Magazine of Western History* 35 (Autumn 1985): 26–41.

Leeson, M. A. *History of Montana, 1739–1885.* Chicago: Warner, Beers, 1885.

Lepley, John G. "'Old Reliable': The Steamboat *Benton* on the Upper Missouri." *Montana, the Magazine of Western History* 30 (July 1980): 42–51.

Malone, Michael P., and Richard B. Roeder. "Montana in 1876: Anxiety and Anticipation." *Montana, the Magazine of Western History* 25 (January 1975): 3–13. Towns and transportation in the U.S. centennial year.

Murray, Henry T., and John A. Murray. "Freighting in the Judith Basin, 1891–1902." *Montana, the Magazine of Western History* 36 (Winter 1986): 60–65.

Nolan, Edward W. "'Not without Labor and Expense': The Villard–Northern Pacific Last Spike Excursion, 1883." *Montana, the Magazine of Western History* 33 (Summer 1983): 2–11.

Seckinger, Katharine Villard, ed. "The Great Railroad Celebration: A Narrative by Francis Jackson Garrison." *Montana, the Magazine of Western History* 33 (Summer 1983): 12–23.

Sharp, Paul F. *Whoop-up Country: The Canadian-American West, 1865–1885.* Minneapolis: University of Minnesota Press, 1955.

West, Carroll Van. "Coulson and the Clark's Fork Bottom: The Economic Structure of a Pre-Railroad Community, 1874–1881." *Montana, the Magazine of Western History* 35 (Autumn 1985): 42–55.

Sail, Steam, and the Rise of Seattle

"Henry Yesler and the Founding of Seattle." *Pacific Northwest Quarterly* 42 (October 1951): 271–276.

Baker, Ray Stannard. "The Great Northwest." *Century Magazine* 65 (March 1903): 659–660.

Berton, Pierre. *Klondike Fever: The Life and Death of the Last Great Gold Rush.* New York: Alfred A. Knopf, 1982.

Bronson, William. "Rush to the Yukon." *American West* 12 (Spring 1965): 66–81. Photo essay on transportation.

Conant, Roger. *Mercer's Belles: The Journal of a Reporter.* Edited by Lenna A. Deutsch. Seattle: University of Washington Press, 1960.

Ducker, James H. "Gold Rushers North: A Census Study of the Yukon and Alaskan Gold Rushes, 1896–1900." *Pacific Northwest Quarterly* 85 (July 1994): 82–92.

Edwards, G. Thomas. "'Terminus Disease': The Clark P. Crandall Description of Puget Sound in 1871." *Pacific Northwest Quarterly* 70 (October 1979): 163–177.

Egan, Douglas. "Schooners 'n Steamers: Puget Sound Shipbuilding a Century Ago." *Columbia* 6 (Summer 1992): 10–12.

Ficken, Robert E. "Seattle's Ditch: The Corps of Engineers and the Lake Washington Ship Canal." *Pacific Northwest Quarterly* 77 (January 1986): 11–20.

Finger, John R. "The Seattle Spirit: 1851–1893." *Journal of the West* 3 (July 1974): 28–45. Transportation as aid to development.

Goetzmann, William H., and Kay Sloan. *Looking Far North: The Harriman Expedition to Alaska, 1899.* Princeton: Princeton University Press, 1982.

Hanford, C. H. "The Orphan Railroad and the Rams Horn Right of Way." *Washington Historical Quarterly* 14 (April 1923): 83–99.

Hinckley, Ted. "The Inside Passage: A Popular Gilded Age Tour." *Pacific Northwest Quarterly* 56 (April 1965): 67–74.

Ingersoll, Ernest. *Gold Fields of the Klondike and the Wonders of Alaska.* New York: W. W. Wilson, 1897.

Jonasson, Jonas A. "Portland and the Alaska Trade." *Pacific Northwest Quarterly* 30 (April 1939): 131–144.

McDougall, N. A. "Indomitable John: The Story of John Hart Scranton and His Puget Sound Steamers." *Pacific Northwest Quarterly* 45 (July 1954): 73–84.

Newell, Gordon, and Joe Williamson. *Pacific Coastal Liners.* Seattle: Superior Publishing, 1959.

Nichols, Jeannette Paddock. "Advertising and the Klondike." *Washington Historical Quarterly* 13 (January 1922): 20–26.

Reid, R. L. "The Whatcom Trails to the Fraser River Mines in 1858." *Washington Historical Quarterly* 18 (July 1927): 199–206; (October 1927): 271–276.

Weinstein, Robert A. *Tall Ships on Puget Sound: The Marine Photographs of Wilhelm Hester.* Seattle: University of Washington Press, 1978.

Symbols of an Era

"Address of Joseph N. Teal at Dedicatory Exercises on the Formal Opening of the Oregon City Locks and Canal at Oregon City, May 6, 1915." *Oregon Historical Quarterly* 16 (June 1915): 197–203.

Alcorn, Rowena L., and Gordon D. Alcorn. "Great Sternwheeler, *Bailey Gatzert.*" *Oregon Historical Quarterly* 63 (March 1962): 61–66.

Brown, Giles T. *Ships That Sail No More: Maritime Transportation from San Diego to Puget Sound, 1910–1940.* Lexington: University of Kentucky Press, 1966.

Campbell, Arthur H. "Charlie Clarno and the *John Day Queen.*" *Oregon Historical Quarterly* 88 (Winter 1987): 348–369.

Crawford, Lewis F. *The Medora-Deadwood Stage Line.* Bismarck, N.D.: Capitol Book, 1925.

Dana, Marshall N. "The Celilo Canal: Its Origin, Its Building and Meaning." *Oregon Historical Quarterly* 16 (June 1915): 108–124.

Doak, William E. "Pioneer Steamboating on the Kootenai River in Montana." *Montana, the Magazine of Western History* 2 (April 1952): 49–56.

Fugleberg, Paul. *Flathead Lake Steamboat Days.* Polson, Mont.: Treasure State Publishing, 1991.

Harden, Blaine. *A River Lost: The Life and Death of the Columbia.* New York: W. W. Norton, 1996.

Hess, Chester N. "Stagecoach Renaissance." *American West* 3 (Winter 1966): 30–33. Re-creation of early stagecoach.

Hult, Ruby El. *Steamboats in the Timber.* Caldwell, Idaho: Caxton Printers, 1952.

Jackson, W. Turrentine. "Wells Fargo: Symbol of the American West?" *Western Historical Quarterly* 3 (April 1972): 179–196.

Lamb, W. Kaye. *Empress to the Orient.* Vancouver, B.C.: Vancouver Maritime Museum Society, 1991.

Petersen, Keith C. *River of Life, Channel of Death: Fish and Dams on the Lower Snake.* Lewiston, Idaho: Confluence Press, 1995.

Reddick, SuAnn Murray. "From Dream to Demolition: The Yamhill Lock and Dam." *Oregon Historical Quarterly* 91 (Spring 1990): 43–80; (Summer 1990): 154–202.

Richardson, Warren. "History of First Frontier Days Celebrations." *Annals of Wyoming* 19 (January 1947): 39–41.

Sandvig, Earl. "Stage on the High Line." *Montana, the Magazine of Western History* 29 (October 1979): 67–70.

Scott, George W. "The Politics of Transportation: The Black Ball Line Becomes Washington State Ferries." *Columbia* 9 (Spring 1995): 13–19.

Simon-Smolinski, Carole. *Clearwater Steam, Steel, and Spirit.* Clarkston, Idaho: Northwest Historical Consultants, 1984.

Smalley, Eugene V. "The Great Coeur d'Alene Stampede of 1884." *Idaho Yesterdays* 11 (Fall 1967): 2–10.

Thorson, John E. *River of Promise, River of Peril: The Politics of Managing the Missouri River.* Lawrence: University Press of Kansas, 1994.

Turner, Robert D. *The Pacific Empresses: An Illustrated History of Canadian Pacific Railway's Empress Liners on the Pacific Ocean.* Victoria, B.C.: Sono Nis Press, 1981.

———. *The Pacific Princesses: An Illustrated History of Canadian Pacific Railway's Princess Fleet on the Northwest Coast.* Victoria, B.C.: Sono Nis Press, 1977.

White, Richard. *The Organic Machine: The Remaking of the Columbia River.* New York: Hill and Wang, 1995.

Willingham, William F. *Water Power in the "Wilderness": The History of Bonneville Lock and Dam.* Portland: Portland District, U.S. Army Corps of Engineers [ca. 1987].

———. "Engineering the Cascades Canal and Locks, 1876–1896." *Oregon Historical Quarterly* 88 (Fall 1987): 228–257.

Winther, Oscar O. "The Place of Transportation in the Early History of the Pacific Northwest." *Pacific Historical Review* 11 (December 1942): 383–396.

Capturing the new railway age on film: portrait of a conductor on the Rogue River Valley Railroad in Jacksonville. Courtesy Southern Oregon Historical Society, #11641.

Index

*P*eople riding a stagecoach along the rim of the Snake River canyon near Twin Falls, Idaho, in the early twentieth century. Courtesy Idaho State Historical Society, 73–221.1040.

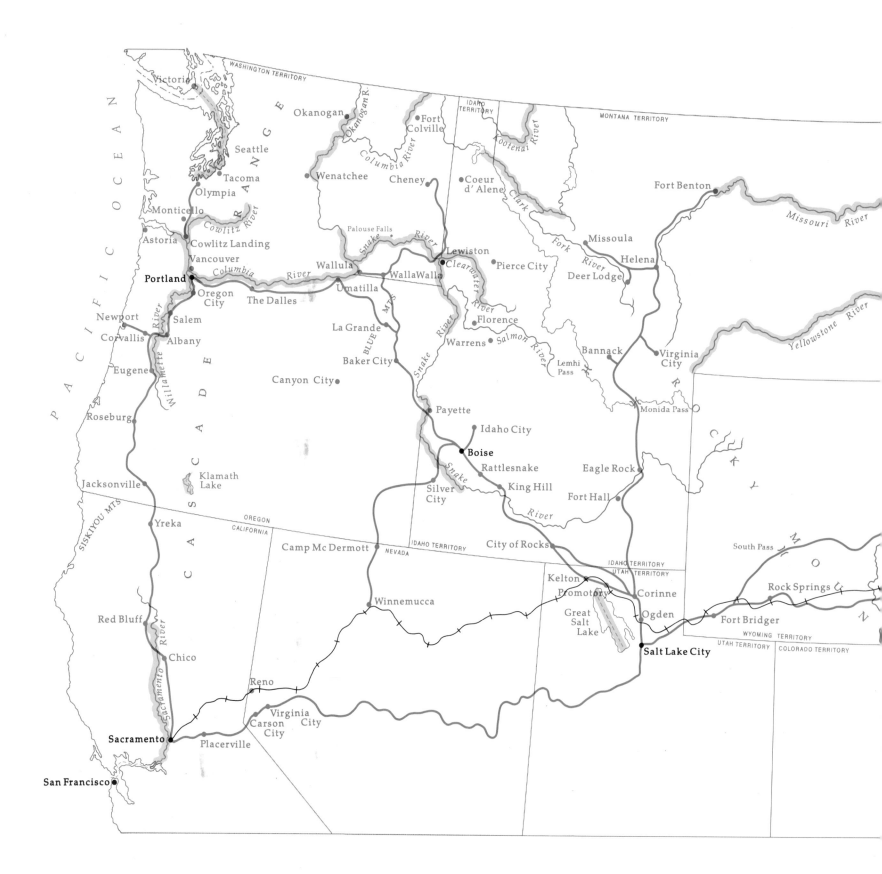